Ethics and Corporate Social Responsibility in the Meetings and Events Industry

The Wiley Event Management Series

Series Editor: Dr. Joe Goldblatt, CSEP

Ethics and Corporate Social Responsibility in the Meetings and Events Industry

**Elizabeth Henderson,
MBA, CMM, M.E. Des.**

**Mariela McIlwraith,
CMP, CMM, MBA**

FSC

WILEY

Henderson, Elizabeth Anne, 1967-
    Ethics and Corporate Social Responsibility in the Meetings and Events Industry / Elizabeth Anne Henderson, Mariela McIlwraith.
        pages   cm
    Includes index.
    ISBN 978-1-1180-7355-1 (cloth : acid-free paper)
        1. Business ethics.   2. Social responsibility of business.   3. Congresses and conventions.   4. Hospitality industry.   I. McIlwraith, Mariela, 1973–   II. Title.
    HF5387.H4546   2012
    174'.4—dc23
                                                                                        2012029609

CONTENTS

FOREWORD

By 2020, I want to live and work in Imagine, Nation.

But I'll settle for 2025, even 2030, if it means I can be part of an industry where Elizabeth Henderson's and Mariela McIlwraith's vision of a sustainable, socially responsible, ethical, relentlessly accountable meeting is so fully integrated in the day-to-day operating practices that every meeting and event professional takes for granted.

If you took a shortcut to Chapter 12 of this book and read about Imagine, Nation, right away, you might conclude that ethics, sustainability, and corporate responsibility were a kind of never-ending quest for meetings and events, the end point in a journey the industry can never really complete.

But if you read this book as intended—chapter by inspiring chapter, step by practical step—you'll see that that future is beginning right here, right now. All we need is the information to get started, the momentum to keep going, the tools and insight to translate our good intentions into measurable business results, and the ingenuity to mobilize the stakeholder and senior management buy-in that will follow the data. This spectacular piece of work—part textbook, part roadmap, part passionate call to action—brings all those elements together in a single, compelling package.

And none too soon. The last few years have not been easy for meetings and events, and the temptation in too many companies has been to treat sustainability as a passing fad, rather than a cornerstone for a more resilient industry. McIlwraith and Henderson build their analysis around the three traditional pillars of sustainability—the triple bottom line of people, planet, and profit—with a healthy dose of cultural awareness and a rigorous focus on business ethics. And through that lens, we see that a more proactive commitment to sustainability in all its dimensions could have prevented or mitigated many of the industry's biggest headaches in recent years: from the sharp pushback against incentive travel in response to the "AIG effect," to destinations' growing vulnerability to severe weather and other climate-related disruptions, to an overreliance on a fragile and decidedly unsustainable airline industry.

It isn't that meeting professionals haven't tried to embrace sustainability. It's hard to find a meeting planner or a supplier organization that doesn't claim some form of sustainable *bona fide*, and for the most part, they aren't deliberately greenwashing. They're members of a kindhearted profession, they want to make a difference, and they genuinely believe they're doing the right thing. Some of them are, and this book tells many of their stories.

But meetings and events is a young industry, sometimes described as a stepchild of hospitality and business travel, with a focus that is still largely tactical. There are practitioners still active in the industry who remember the days when their highest calling was to (literally) count the coffee cups before participants arrived on site, to make sure the host organization wasn't overcharged on beverages, and to cut the pastries in half to make the food last longer.

Today's meeting and event professionals operate from a vastly wider knowledge base, and they do so much more than count coffee cups. But it's still a stretch from meeting logistics and strategy to the world of carbon reductions, low-energy building design, sustainable supply chains, and an approach to business scenario planning that goes far beyond any conventional understanding of strategic meeting management. As a result, the lion's share of sustainable meeting activity takes place where it's most visible—to planners and suppliers, and to their clients and stakeholders—in the realm of recycling bins, reusable tableware, and social responsibility projects that are much more transactional than transformative. These initiatives matter in the moment, but they do little to reduce the industry's overall footprint, and virtually nothing to prepare us for the serious economic, environmental, and social challenges ahead.

Former U.S. President Dwight D. Eisenhower once said, "Whenever I run into a problem I can't solve, I always make it bigger. . . . If I make it big enough, I can begin to see the outlines of a solution."[1] That principle makes sense for sustainable, socially responsible meetings, but it runs headlong into a key cornerstone of meeting professionals' training and, often, their personal inclination: We all carry the deeply held conviction that if we can reduce a complex meeting assignment to a series of checklists and schedules, we'll get the job done against seemingly impossible odds.

Henderson and McIlwraith are not the first to try to express a strategic vision of sustainable meetings and events in a way that leads toward practical implementation. But ***Ethics and Corporate Social Responsibility in the Meetings and Events Industry*** might just be the first meetings industry textbook that synthesizes insights from environmental science, cultural anthropology, supply chain management, and MBA-level management theory, filters the resulting systems view through current industry standards and case studies, and concludes with a broad-ranging checklist that planners and suppliers can take away and begin applying. Right now. Today.

It's particularly timely and heartening that McIlwraith and Henderson recommend backcasting and scenario planning as key strategy tools for sustainable meeting and event professionals. As long as the industry's sustainability efforts are largely tactical, we'll never have a clear idea of what success really looks like or how to get there—and before long, impatience and disappointment will overwhelm the best of intentions. By crafting a clear, science-based understanding of what we mean by sustainability, then developing a series of scenarios to get from here to there, we'll find that we have a roadmap for the work ahead and a signpost to guide day-to-day decisions. Rather than insisting on a single, doctrinaire route to that conclusion, Henderson and McIlwraith lay out a set of decisions and trade-offs to help readers connect sustainability with their own organizational priorities and culture.

All of which brings us back to Imagine, Nation. There's something sad and frustrating in the realization that the single most hopeful moment in this book is a piece of fiction, but that's a shortcoming in our industry, not in the magnificent resource the authors have put in our hands. We have a long way to go before we can consider our industry sustainable, but if we want to create a different future, we have to be able to imagine it. Alongside a soaring vision, McIlwraith and Henderson have shown us the conceptual framework, the planning tools, and the practical innovations to make the hope a reality, step by painstaking step, in strategy and in execution.

Finally, we have a comprehensive roadmap for a truly sustainable meetings and events industry. So read this book. Read it cover to cover. Read it now. Then let's get on with it.

Mitchell Beer
President, The Conference Publishers
Founding chair, GMIC Sustainable Meetings Foundation
Ottawa, Canada

Note

1. Quoted in Amory B. Lovins and Rocky Mountain Institute, *Reinventing Fire: Bold Business Solutions for the New Energy Era* (White River Junction, VT: Chelsea Green Publishing Company, 2011).

SERIES EDITOR FOREWORD

Ethics and Corporate Social Responsibility

Between 2001 and 2012, the term *corporate* acquired a new and, to many, distasteful definition. The mention of the word *corporate* often reminds us of the collapse of such companies as Lehman Brothers, which triggered the global financial recession, or the earlier misdealings of Enron that led to the passage of the Sarbanes-Oxley legislation in the United States. Furthermore, who will ever forget the permanent loss of reputation by hundred-year-old accounting firm Arthur Andersen, the tarnished image of Exxon and British Petroleum due to their oil-spill catastrophes, and the tragic loss of 100 lives in the Station nightclub fire in Rhode Island? Indeed, the term *corporate* or *corporation* has taken on new and all too often negative meanings.

According to the *Merriam-Webster Dictionary*, the term *corporate* is defined as that which is formed into an association and endowed with the rights and laws of an individual. The term *corporate* was first used in 1512 as the Latin term *corporates*, and means that which is made into a body. It appears that in only 600 years that body is in need of attention. So, the question emerges: How do we repair and strengthen this body, the modern meetings and events industry, to ensure that future generations inherit a better and more sustainable industry?

The answer is provided most eloquently and comprehensively by Elizabeth Henderson and Mariela McIlwraith, who have diligently researched the new and emerging business field of study known as meeting and events corporate social responsibility and ethics. For **Ethics and Corporate Social Responsibility in the Meetings and Events Industry**, Henderson and McIlwraith have interviewed dozens of authorities throughout the world to provide you with not only the theory but also the current best practices to guide your decisions in the future.

Ethics and Corporate Social Responsibility in the Meetings and Events Industry includes numerous helpful checklists, tables, charts, references, and activities to assist the established and emerging meeting and event professional with the most difficult and challenging issues confronting them on a day-to-day basis. It is both practical and profound in that it provides members of the meetings and events community with a tool to ensure secure decisions and at the same time improve the world through meetings and events.

This book will greatly serve to reverse the recent trend with regard to the negative impression many corporate meetings and events create when publicized by the media. It demonstrates how every organization, both large and small, may practice corporate social responsibility and ethics to ensure that they are providing the best practice for their own body as well as greater society.

Scottish economist Adam Smith once remarked during the Scottish Enlightenment period of the eighteenth century, "Every business must first do good in order to do well."[1] Smith, whom many credit as the father of modern economics, understood that every organization has a greater responsibility than that of satisfying their owners' or shareholders' profit expectations. In fact, he understood, as do Henderson and McIlwraith, that the corpus that is post-modern society is more closely linked than ever before. Therefore, we need to revisit and remind ourselves of our unbreakable bonds and responsibilities to one another through the modern meetings and events industry.

Through the pages of **Ethics and Corporate Social Responsibility in the Meetings and Events Industry**, we now have a bright new beacon to ensure that we move forward with confidence and greater commitment to promoting positive and sustainable change for future generations to inherit. This may indeed be this book's greatest legacy, as through these pages, a better and nobler future may be unfolding for all.

Professor Joe Goldblatt, FRSA
Wiley Event Series Editor
Edinburgh, Scotland

Note

1. Cannan, E. (ed.), 1937, p. xxxix, Editor's Introduction, pp. xxxviii–xli to: Adam Smith, "An Inquiry into the Nature and Causes of the Wealth of Nations", NY.: Random House.

PREFACE

Ethics and Corporate Social Responsibility in the Meetings and Events Industry celebrates what has been already achieved in moving the meetings and events industry toward a more sustainable future, and pushes the boundaries of imagination to visualize what might be possible in the years to come. Existing information only becomes knowledge when it is learned and applied, and becomes important when it is shared and communicated with and to others. Sometimes we get mired in a web of familiar ideas, and this prevents us from finding a way forward. This book simultaneously leverages what we have and also pushes the thresholds of our knowledge and actions toward our vision of a sustainable future for the meetings and events industry. We hope that it will act in some ways as a compass, as shown on the cover, helping meeting and event professionals to find that way forward.

Ethics and Corporate Social Responsibility in the Meetings and Events Industry was written to act not only as a tool, but also as a capacity-builder for future sustainable leaders within our industry. We recognize that great tools cannot build without skilled practitioners.

The next few years will bring a wealth of new sustainability tools: new standards, new technologies, and, yes, even new books. These tools, as robust as they might be, will only help us in our journey toward sustainability if we have the motivation and will to use them. We hope the stories we've captured will instill this needed encouragement for us to become the master carpenters our industry needs to be sustainable.

On April 18, 2010, Adam Cohen wrote an opinion column in *The New York Times* called "Cassandra, the Ignored Prophet of Doom, Is a Woman for Our Times."[1] For those of you not familiar with classical mythology, Cassandra was a beautiful woman upon whom Apollo bestowed the gift of prophecy. But because she rejected his advances, Apollo also ensured that nobody would believe her prophecies. Dr. Seuss told a similar story in *The Lorax*. You know the one: "He was shortish. And oldish. And brownish. And mossy. And he spoke with a voice that was sharpish and bossy."[2] He warned the Once-ler not to chop down the trees, or do all of his other terrible deeds. Many sustainability practitioners would agree that this could be called The Age of Cassandra (or the Age of the Lorax), a time when those people speaking up for sustainability have been generally derided or dismissed as expensive opponents of profits. The meetings industry has not been an exception to this trend.

This is not to say that there have not been Cassandras or Loraxes among us, quietly or not-so-quietly telling the industry about change and then doing something about it. Corporate social responsibility (CSR) is, after all, a business "mega-trend," like globalization, according to "The Sustainability Imperative," an article in the *Harvard Business Review*.[3] **Ethics and Corporate Social Responsibility in the Meetings and Events Industry** is meant partially as a tribute to the meetings industry Cassandras and Loraxes we have known and admired, and whom we have tried to emulate. Many of them are interviewed or mentioned within these pages, while others have acted as forces of inspiration.

We also identified a need for a book that addressed not just the eminently worthy goal of environmentally friendly meetings and events, or what has come to be commonly known as *greener meetings*, but which also incorporated the bigger view of sustainability. This necessarily includes ethical business practices; the recognition that we are connected intimately to our communities, and vice versa; the importance of resource efficiencies to both the environment and to economic health of the industry; and the long-term goal of attempting to ensure that we leave our world just a little bit better for those who will follow.

We think sustainability is the defining issue of our times. It is both a great hope for the future and a constant challenge in the present. The meetings and events industry, even though an important driver of economic activity in the global economy, has been slow to act as a unified entity on many issues. This is, perhaps, because it is only just now being recognized as an industry in itself, and not simply a shadow industry, or as a subset of the hospitality industry. Now that it has gained recognition as an economic driver, it needs to take responsibility for its other effects on communities and the environment.

About This Book

In writing **Ethics and Corporate Social Responsibility in the Meetings and Events Industry**, we were given the opportunity to view our industry through the lens of sustainability; we've found excellent examples from around the world of meeting and event professionals utilizing events to conserve resources, create positive change through service, and act as catalysts for additional steps toward a sustainable future through education and motivation.

The chapters in the book provide guidance on achieving our vision:

An industry where meetings and events contribute positively to communities and cultures, and the business of meetings is conducted ethically; a future where meetings and events are realized within the regenerative capacity of the earth; where meetings and events are successful at achieving their objectives and provide better value to stakeholders than alternatives.

The following topics are addressed:

- **Chapter 1, Introduction to Corporate Social Responsibility and Ethics for Meetings and Events** defines the context of sustainability and introduces some common frameworks for assessing sustainability. This segues into the concept of corporate social responsibility (CSR) and the various ways of examining it and applying it. Finally, examples are given of how both sustainability and CSR are finding expression in the meetings and events industry.
- **Chapter 2, Business Ethics and the Meetings and Events Industry** provides a framework for addressing ethical dilemmas and examines some key ethical issues that meeting and event professionals might face during their careers. It identifies the types of rationalizations that might be used to justify unethical behavior and provides an analysis of repercussions that might occur.
- **Chapter 3, Strategies for Sustainable Meetings** uses a systems view to introduce a decision model to guide basic sustainability and CSR decisions in a meetings and events context. This includes recognizing that impacts of sustainability-related decisions affect

more than just you and your organization. Also provided is guidance on assessing service providers based on sustainable criteria.

- **Chapter 4, Social Responsibility and Culture** focuses on the ways that meetings and events can promote social responsibility through strategies, including community service. The MAUDE framework is introduced here, which helps industry professionals develop community service projects that are meaningful, aligned with organizational objectives, apply the organization's unique skills, are destination-specific, and are engaging.

- **Chapter 5, Meetings, Events, and Environmental Science** offers an overview of some of the environmental impacts generated by meetings and events, and their potential effects on the ecosystem. Most meeting and event professionals do not have core competencies in science, so this overview is paired with strategies that can be used to measure, reduce, eliminate, or mitigate the impact.

- **Chapter 6, Shared Value and Strategic Corporate Responsibility** outlines the business case for corporate social responsibility, including discussion of the different types of CSR (transactional, transitional, and transformational) as well as strategic CSR and the creation of shared value. The concept of cluster CSR, where several entities act together to increase the effectiveness of CSR applications, is also introduced.

- **Chapter 7, Communication, Marketing, and Public Relations** looks at issues related to how we promote events in a more sustainable way, how we communicate with stakeholders to promote sustainable behaviors, and how we can leverage CSR to create authentic experiences that generate goodwill. Also discussed are the issues of greenwashing and how to promote sustainable features of products and services.

- **Chapter 8, Sustainable Supply Chains for Meetings and Events** introduces key terminology and demonstrates how to map a sustainable supply chain—a core element of producing sustainable meetings and events. Seven steps to implement a sustainable supply chain in your organization are discussed, and examples are given of supplier codes of conduct that will help reinforce your expectations with partners and suppliers.

- **Chapter 9, Sustainability Measurement and Evaluation** identifies measurements that can be used within the context of sustainable meetings and events, and shows how to determine what should be measured based on the scale of the event. Measurement is an essential component of sustainable meetings and events, helping not only to prove actual performance but to track performance over time, and it is essential to the next step, reporting.

- **Chapter 10, Sustainability Reporting for Meetings and Events** introduces several reporting methodologies that can be used by meeting professionals. Reporting completes the cycle of sustainable events and allows you to share successes and challenges with key stakeholders. It also allows meeting professionals to integrate what they have learned into the next iteration of planning, to improve performance. Guidance is also offered on linking event objectives with broader organizational strategies and identifying and engaging key stakeholders.

- **Chapter 11, Risk Management and Legal Considerations** explains the key issues related to risk management and legal considerations as they relate to ethics and CSR. Included are ways that CSR and ethics can be a risk management tool. It also describes a risk management process for industry professionals to apply.

- **Chapter 12, Backcasting for a Sustainable Meetings and Events Industry** applies backcasting methodologies to help envision all of the steps needed to develop a sustainable future for our industry, and provides a vision for what we see as future benchmarks. A key chapter feature in this chapter is a list of 100 tweetable actions that will support the book's vision. Scenario planning is used as a call to action for the industry to become more flexible and creative in imagining its future within a rapidly changing world.

- **Glossary** This section includes key terms for corporate social responsibility ethics, and sustainability for meetings and events.

At the end of each chapter, you'll find a chapter review, a list of key terms, review questions, group activities, and, in many cases, additional resources or recommended readings to supplement the chapter.

Supplemental Offerings

A comprehensive online **Instructor's Manual** with **Test Bank** accompanies this book and is available to instructors to help them effectively manage their time and enhance student-learning opportunities.

The **Test Bank** has been specifically formatted for Respondus, an easy-to-use software program for creating and managing exams that can be printed to paper or published directly to Blackboard, WebCT, Desire2Learn, eCollege, ANGEL, and other eLearning systems. Instructors who adopt this book can download the **Test Bank** for free.

A password-protected Wiley Instructor Book Companion website devoted entirely to this book (www.wiley.com/college/henderson) provides access to the online **Instructor's Manual** and the text-specific teaching resources. The **Respondus Test Bank** as well as the **PowerPoint** lecture slides are also available on the website for download.

Note to the Readers

Readers of **Ethics and Corporate Social Responsibility in the Meetings and Events Industry** are leaders. They either are existing leaders in the industry or will become leaders by applying their knowledge and by standing up for environmental sustainability, economic prosperity, and social justice. The future lies on our side: Increasingly, people globally value sustainable concepts, and our emerging leaders, especially, are more aware of issues and are willing to address them.

We realize that one book cannot capture all of the ideas and real-life examples of what is already happening to make the industry more sustainable or what professionals are doing to conduct themselves ethically and to balance ethical dilemmas. We would like nothing better than to have many best practices outlined here to become obsolete as challenges are identified and sustainable solutions crafted. Many organizations have embraced sustainability, and we believe they should be celebrated as leaders, visionaries, and pioneers. We hope and expect that their numbers will multiply, and that they will increasingly look to collaborative and creative ways of anticipating and building our sustainable future.

The future starts here, and it starts with you.

Elizabeth Henderson, MBA, CMM, M.E.Des,
Calgary, AB, Canada
Mariela McIlwraith, CMP, CMM, MBA,
Vancouver, BC, Canada

Notes

1. Adam Cohen, "Cassandra, the Ignored Prophet of Doom, Is a Woman for Our Time," *The New York Times* (April 18, 2010). www.nytimes.com/2010/04/19/opinion/19mon4.html.
2. Dr. Seuss, *The Lorax* (New York: Random House, 1971).
3. David A. Lubin and Daniel C. Esty, "The Sustainability Imperative," *Harvard Business Review* (May 2010). hbr.org/2010/05/the-sustainability-imperative/ar/1.

ACKNOWLEDGMENTS

"KID, YOU'LL MOVE MOUNTAINS! So . . . be your name Buxbaum or Bixby or Bray or Mordecai Ali Van Allen O'Shea, you're off to Great Places! Today is your day! Your mountain is waiting. So . . . get on your way!"

—*Dr. Seuss, Oh, the Places You'll Go!*

This book was our mountain, and we are grateful to all those individuals who helped us on our way. Writing these acknowledgments is possibly the closest we'll get to giving an Academy Award acceptance speech, so, with that in mind, we'd like to thank . . .

The Inspirers

Three industry women have been a great influence on us: Terri Breining, Joan Eisenstodt, and Claire Smith. Their willingness to mentor, to support others, and to demonstrate business grace and ethical behavior, as well as their authentic kindness, are inspiring.

Mariela McIlwraith also thanks a few other inspirers—Peter Chapman, executive director of the Shareholder Association for Research and Education. He helped me to truly appreciate the business case for CSR, demonstrating conclusively, financially, legally, and ethically that environmental, social, and governance considerations enhance business performance. I also thank Mark Andrew, now regional vice-president for Fairmont Hotels and Resorts, and general manager of the Fairmont, Washington, DC, who took me under his wing in one of my first volunteer leadership roles. Over a shared breakfast of the world's greatest peanut butter and cheddar cheese omelet, I learned firsthand how to identify and implement strategic initiatives. I also thank Sunita Wiebe, PhD, faculty development director and academic director for general education at The Art Institute of Vancouver for all of her support with designing course materials to accompany this book, and for her inspiring work with learner-centered education.

Elizabeth Henderson would like to thank those around her who, through random acts of genius, humor, or sustainability, inspired her to write more than she thought she could (and more than she probably should have done). She also thanks the Cassandras among us. They have the courage to practice what they believe in and to evangelize those beliefs, and this will create a more sustainable world.

The Contributors

Many people allowed us to interview them or provided photos for this book. Several of them are quoted or featured in case studies, while others acted as *reality checkers*—those people who acted as sounding boards and who checked the relevance of the book's contents in different global regions. All of these thought leaders were instrumental for our book. We thank:

Kelly Bagnall, Dykema Gossett PLLC

Jose M. Barquin, Mexico Tourism Board

Victoria Bazan, Bazan Law

Mitchell Beer, The Conference Publishers

Jan Peter "JP" Bergkvist, SleepWell AB

Guy Bigwood, MCI

Lisa S. Bleakley, City of Virginia Beach

Jonathan Bradshaw, Meetology® Group

Theresa Breining, Breining Group LLC

Stephen G. Bushnell, Fireman's Fund Insurance Company

Eduardo Chaillo, Mexico Tourism Board

Chef Greg Christian, Greg Christian Consulting and the Organic School Project

Melanie Conn, Common Thread

Brian Dahl, PR1ME

Jill Doederlein, Lansing Community College

Jill Taub Drury, Drury Design Dynamics

Joan Eisenstodt, Eisenstodt Associates, LLC

Tahira Endean, Cantrav and Event Camp Vancouver

Michelle Evans, Aon Association Services, a Division of Affinity Insurance Services, Inc.

Steve Faulstick, The Portland Doubletree Lloyd Centre

Maaike Fleur, Global Reporting Initiative

Seth J. Fleischer, Aon Association Services, a Division of Affinity Insurance Services, Inc.

Elizabeth George, New Orleans CVB

Laura González, Society for Anthropology in Community Colleges / San Diego Miramar College

Bruce Harris, Retired Founder of Conferon (now Experient)

Mikey Hersom, ignition

Tyra W. Hilliard, PhD, JD, CMP, University of Alabama

Amber Hockin, Canadian Labour Congress

Joella Hopkins, Mumtaz Events

William R. Host, Roosevelt University

Yomtov Iskenazi, Ludicorp

Steen Jakobsen, Wonderful Copenhagen

Maggie Jensen, Securian Financial

Michelle Johnson, Creative Community Connections, llc (C3)

Keith Johnston, Planner Wire

Dr. David L. Jones, School of Hotel & Tourism Management, Hong Kong Polytechnic University

Meegan Jones, Greenshoot Pacific

Andre Kaldenhoff, Leipzig Congress Center

Tamara Kennedy-Hill, The Green Meeting Industry Council

Kevin Kirby, Hard Rock International

David Kliman, The Kliman Group

Jessica Koth, National Funeral Directors Association

Carol Krugman, MEd, CMP, CMM, Metropolitan State College of Denver

Justin Lam, Three Sixty Photography

Drew Leathem, MNP

Dr. Eyal Lebel, Vancouver Folk Music Festival

Lawrence Leonard, Convention Industry Council

Michael Luehrs, MCI

Heather McCarthy-Savoca, The Arrangers

Thomas McIlwraith, Douglas College

Shawna McKinley, MeetGreen

Fiona Pelham, Sustainable Events Ltd.

Jelena Milovic, International AIDS Society

Aaron Pickering, Fair Labor Association

Trish Richards, AVW TELAV

Roger Rickard, REvent LLC

Koleen Roach, Securian Financial

Paul Salinger, Oracle

Louise Schwartz, Recycling Alternative

Patti J. Shock, CPCE, University of Nevada Las Vegas

Martin Sirk, ICCA

Janet Sperstad, Madison Area Technical College

Robert Sumner, Sumner & Associates

Tim Sunderland, Sustainable Event Certification

Gene Takagi, NEO Law Group & Nonprofit Law Blog

Denise Taschereau, Fairware

Laura Tetzlaff, Laura Tetzlaff—Marketing & Business Development

Heidi Thorne, Promo With Purpose

Casey Vanden Heuvel, Squamish Lil'wat Cultural Centre

Sarah Vining, National Conference Center

Carl Wallace, Squamish Lil'wat Cultural Centre

Mike Wallace, The Global Reporting Initiative

Chef Steven Ward, DoubleTree Portland

Sunita Weibe, PhD, Art Institute of Vancouver

Heidi Welker, AVW TELAV

Jinny Wu, Vancouver Convention Centre

The Team

Though only two names appear as authors, we recognize that many others played important roles in the creation of this manuscript. First, our series editor, Professor Joe Goldblatt, who without flinching took on two novice authors and coached us through many a chapter (thank you!). We also thank Mary Cassells, Julie Kerr, Jenni Lee, and Anna Melhorn and all of the others at John Wiley & Sons who provided guidance, support, and trust. Jenni Lee in particular was our main point of contact, and we bombarded her with all the hundreds of itty-bitty details that are so important. Finally, this book wouldn't have been possible without a catalyst—Carol Krugman, our fairy godmother, who helped us get started with the initial introduction to Wiley—we are eternally grateful. Mitchell Beer was also a key supporter, answering millions of questions, reviewing many, many pages, and making sure we didn't use impact as a verb—but we might have slipped it in despite his best efforts at impacting us! Though we mentioned Joan Eisenstodt already once, we add her again to thank her for her incredible support in reviewing more than one chapter and giving us valued feedback. We also thank Teresa Christie at MPS Content Services, for getting us through the production stage, and Cheryl Ferguson, the person we never met but who managed to polish our words so beautifully.

The Supporters

We've both been greatly supported by our husbands (Charles and Tad), our parents, and our siblings.

Special thanks from Mariela to son Thomas for his song on perseverance, "You might find you can fly," and daughter Allie, whose art and words "I love you more than sky" worked wonders for encouragement.

We also thank those little carbon splurges in our lives. We believe in CSR, ethics, and imported Belgian chocolate.

A note from Mariela to Elizabeth: Thank you for being my partner in crime. Every Thing 1 needs a Thing 2, and I'm so glad we're each others'. It's always a pleasure working with you, and I'm glad we both believe that success is measured in laugh lines and bottom lines.

Well, Mariela, since you mentioned it. . . . We both know that collaboration grows capability exponentially. By collaborating with you, I feel I have become far more capable, and knowledge-able, and yes, even a bit more curious to see how this will all turn out in the long run. I raise another small carbon splurge in your honor—a glass of Okanagan red wine. Cheers!

Stone figures such as the one above are known as Inukshuks. They are found around the circumpolar world, and their traditional meanings include "Someone was here," or, "You are on the right path."[1] Like corporate social responsibility, an Inukshuk makes the best use of available materials.

Photo courtesy of Elizabeth Henderson

CHAPTER 1

Introduction to Corporate Social Responsibility and Ethics

"Great power involves great responsibility."

—U.S. President Franklin D. Roosevelt (1882–1945),
in his undelivered Jefferson Day address

Learning Objectives

After reading this chapter, you will be able to:

- Discuss different aspects and definitions of Corporate Social Responsibility (CSR), ethics, sustainability and sustainable development.
- Recognize four sustainability frameworks, including the Natural Step, the triple bottom line, the ecological footprint, and the sustainability hierarchy.
- Compare and contrast ideas about sustainability and corporate social responsibility.
- Recognize how sustainability and CSR are finding expression in certain parts of the meetings and events value chain.
- Identify various ways of looking at corporate social responsibility, including as philanthropy and as an expression of sustainability.
- Recognize the importance of ethical conduct for meeting and event professionals.
- Recognize differences in global perspectives on CSR, ethics, and sustainability.

Introduction

The meetings and events industry faces great challenges. It is not alone; the issues faced today reflect the economic, environmental, and social realities faced by all industries, governments, and individuals. Some of the greatest challenges relate to business ethics and **corporate social responsibility**—what we define as business practices that integrate social, economic and environmental concerns into decision-making and meet or exceed legal and ethical standards. These challenges include managing our environmental impact, withstanding scrutiny on spending, and ensuring that business practices are conducted in a fair and transparent manner.

During the last decade, there has been significant emphasis on financial aspects of meetings and events, including demonstrating return on investment and analyzing economic impact. During this time the industry has also made progress in becoming increasingly greener. Meetings and events have shown great potential in their ability to positively impact the communities in which they are held. These are not solitary objectives, to be addressed in isolation; only when an integrated approach is taken can the power of all three—economy, environment, and society—be leveraged and magnified. With this book, we will build on the industry's established success and strive to drive it forward to create multidimensional value for the industry, its stakeholders, and the global community.

We will introduce you to key terms, because it is important to speak the language of corporate social responsibility (CSR) and ethics in consistent terms to promote general understanding and communication. The book will then discuss ethics and how it relates to the industry in general, as well as give specific examples of problem areas to watch for; discuss how CSR, ethics, and sustainability relate to culture, and how they can vary within cultures; introduce readers to a systems view of integrating sustainability and CSR into your specific events; provide you with an introduction to environmental science, to better understand the pressing environmental issues impacting the industry and the global marketplace; show the relationship of marketing and communications to ethics and CSR and how to use it effectively; and discuss how to create a sustainable supply chain, how to measure, evaluate, and report on your activities, and how to use CSR and ethics as part of a risk management strategy.

This book will take you through concepts and tools to help you achieve your goals, and will discuss issues on both a micro (event-specific) and macro (global) level. We hope that by doing so, we will provide a greater understanding of social responsibility, sustainability, and ethics, as well as tools that students, meeting practitioners, and business at large can use to create value for their organizations and communities.

The key topics that will be covered in this book are shown in Figure 1.1. These are presented in a circular manner, indicating that they are part of a cycle of continual improvement for sustainability.

The Vision: A Sustainable Future for Meetings and Events

We begin this book with our vision for a sustainable future for the meetings and events industry, modeled on the concept of the triple bottom line, and address three facets that are presented in Figure 1.2.

Our vision is this: *An industry where meetings and events contribute positively to communities and cultures, and the business of meetings is conducted ethically; a future where meetings and events are realized within the regenerative capacity of the Earth; where meetings and events are successful at achieving their objectives and provide better value to stakeholders than alternatives.*

This book will provide insight into achieving this vision, and we will conclude with a summary roadmap of what is needed for us to achieve it.

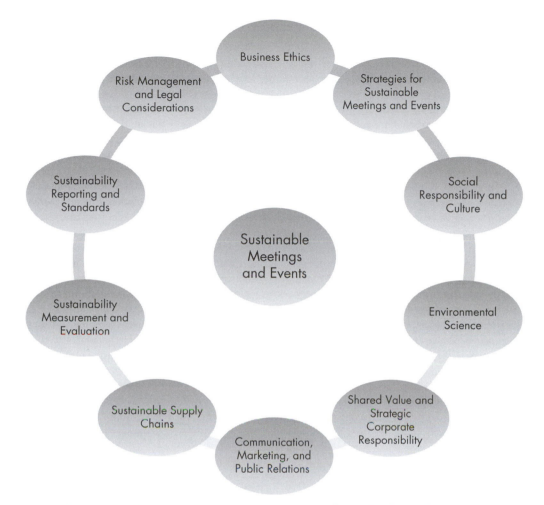

Figure 1.1   Elements of Sustainable Meetings and Events (McIlwraith-Henderson)

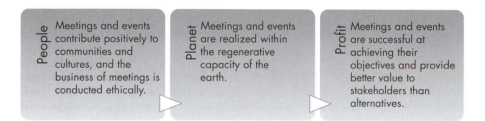

Figure 1.2   A Vision for a Sustainable Meetings and Events Industry (Henderson-McIlwraith)

Why CSR and Ethics in the Meetings and Events Industry?

The meetings and events industry has been trying hard to obtain recognition both at a **macro level** (the level of government and industry) and at the **micro level** (that fabled "seat at the table") within organizations themselves (see Figure 1.3). There has been some success in recent years to quantify the economic impact of meetings and events, specifically in Canada, Mexico, and the United States.[2] These studies have shown that the industry in the United States alone generates almost $1 trillion worth of direct, indirect, and induced benefits to the economy, through direct spending, the creation of jobs, and the generation of tax and local revenues.

At the beginning of the 2008–2010 global recession, meetings and events got a wake-up call with the so-called *AIG effect*. In September 2008, only a few days after American International Group (AIG) received an $85 billion bailout package, one of the firm's subsidiaries spent $443,000 on an incentive trip for select insurance agents at a five-star resort.[3] This created a furor in the press and in the general public, culminating in the implementation of regulations for companies that were recipients of bailout funds from the **Troubled Asset Relief Program (TARP)**. These regulations specified that all companies benefiting from public funds must develop companywide policies for meetings and events; in addition, meetings and events were categorized under "excessive or luxury expenditures."[4] This took the meetings and events industry largely by surprise. In reaction, several industry associations banded together to create the initiative "Meetings Mean Business" and its eponymous website.

Now that the industry has been getting recognized for its contributions to our economy, it is time to recognize that this confers an obligation to operate in an economically, environmentally, and socially responsible fashion (see Figure 1.4). Not only is there an implied responsibility but there is also an implied advantage; if the industry can operate responsibly and add value at many levels, it will be more likely to avoid crippling regulations in the future. According to ICCA CEO Martin Sirk, ". . . by articulating and promoting the CSR objectives and impacts of their events,

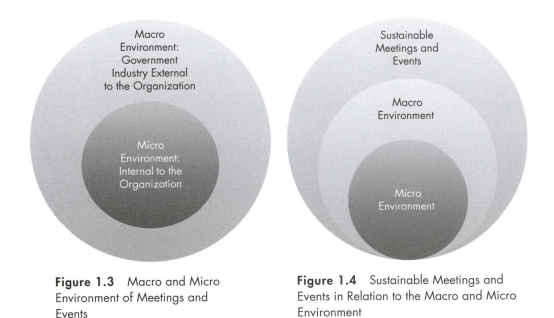

Figure 1.3 Macro and Micro Environment of Meetings and Events

Figure 1.4 Sustainable Meetings and Events in Relation to the Macro and Micro Environment

international associations can change the way they are perceived for the better, winning greater support from the destinations which host their congresses, improving their negotiating position vis-à-vis suppliers, and energising their various stakeholders."[5]

Corporate social responsibility and ethics will help move the industry from primarily a reactive role, responding to imposed legislation and regulation, to a proactive role, where the behavior of the industry helps to shape its own future.

The implementation of corporate social responsibility and ethics in meetings and events reflects global societal trends. For example, in late 2011, the Occupy Wall Street movement began to demonstrate in New York City against perceived social and economic inequality, high unemployment, and what was viewed as corporate greed and undue influence in economic affairs, with specific regard to the global economic crisis from 2008 to at least late 2011. This movement, the epicenter of which was in New York, spread to hundreds of North American and global cities, including Sydney, Auckland, Toronto, Vancouver, Tokyo, Paris, Madrid, Berlin, Buenos Aires, Sao Paulo, and London.[6] The slogan of protesters was, "We are the 99 percent," in reference to the 1 percent of people globally who are perceived to have economic control.[7]

Global Perspectives on CSR, Ethics, and Sustainability

Views on CSR, ethics, and sustainability are not universal. A study done by the Society for Human Resource Management in 2007 compared 10 CSR priorities in seven countries, and the results in some cases were strikingly different. As examples, donating and collecting money for natural disasters was a priority for 77 percent of U.S. respondents and 30 percent of respondents from Brazil. Conversely, 15 percent of U.S. respondents monitor global fair labor standards as compared to 73 percent of respondents from Brazil.[8]

Tamara Kennedy-Hill, the executive director of the Green Meeting Industry Council (GMIC) explained it this way in an e-mail in November 2011:

> How sustainability is valued in a particular region, country or within a country often influences the practice and adoption in meetings and events. There may be different environmental imperatives that influence the priorities in a world region; for example, in a desert region, water may be the priority for conservative practices which would impact the meeting sustainability goals; in another region with limited landfill (much of Europe) strong waste diversion practices, recycling and composting infrastructure and a culturally acceptable attitude toward less waste, less packaging and less "to go" may be the norm and make it easier for an event organizer. Regardless of the region, what is changing and starting to "universalize" the issues are international standards, global communities to share best practice, and governments seeing the value to support green infrastructure as a business value. Always, there will be nuances of cultural influences and regional priorities which may shape the sustainability goals and objectives of an event.

Although differences exist between world regions, increased cooperation and efforts to develop international standards related to sustainable events could help to reduce these differences. Kennedy-Hill adds:

> The growth of standards and certifications, with a focus on metrics, has shifted this to become more strategic and value added to both the event organizer as well as from the supplier (especially venues and accommodations which have a stronger ability to control the results and provide statistical

validation of change in behavior practices). Regions that are tying sustainability to economic devel-opment are more likely to have a proactive solution for event organizers seeking to plan sustainable meetings in their community.

Paul Salinger is the vice president of marketing for Oracle and 2011–2012 president of the Green Meeting Industry Council. Oracle holds more than 8,000 events per year around the world, and it has made sustainability a priority in the way that it manages its events. In respect to differences in approaches to sustainability in different world regions, Salinger commented in November 2011 that approaches to sustainable events as a part of event planning processes don't necessarily differ:

You still need to create an overall roadmap, objectives, key performance indicators and targets for measurement, just as in any event plan. Ideally sustainability is integrated into this. The reality depends on circumstances on the ground. Does the infrastructure of a particular locale support what you would like to accomplish—is there waste diversion methods in place to allow recycling or composting, for example? Many places are challenged with what is accepted practices now in other places.

He further adds that in places where so much is ingrained in the culture around sustainability, you can likely accomplish a higher degree of sustainable meetings than in places where infra-structure poses a challenge. He adds, "I think you have to work with cultural and local values as a starting point and see what is possible, then push for what may be beyond their capabilities and see if you can keep making continual improvements over time, especially if you can get any data at all and measure it year over year." He has observed particularly good practices in parts of Europe, noting that Denmark and all of Scandinavia have developed sustainable meeting protocols that incorporate some of the best practices for sustainability. He further comments:

The sense I get though is that there is more being done than we even know about, and what is really needed is for people to communicate more about what they are doing so that best practices and good ideas can be more broadly shared and then practiced. Within our Oracle global community we are already now seeing for the many small events that we do that have reported against our minimum guidelines that people are saving money just by doing simple things like reusing badges, eliminating bottled water, reusing signage, reducing printing. Basic things can make a big difference.

Salinger also provides recommendations for advancing sustainable events in a cross-cultural business relationship:

I'd say you have to step away from your preconceived notions and really understand the culture you are going to work in. What we hear is sometimes different than what is being said and vice-versa. Continual communication is vital to trying to understand what is possible and what to expect when working cross-culturally. Language can be a real barrier, but also just trying to set the right expectations can be a challenge. You probably need to spend more time researching what is possible to do and then spend even more time making sure that the communication is consistent and that the cultural hierarchies don't become a factor in making decisions and actually executing the plan. If you can at all afford to do an on-the-ground, face-to-face meeting with all of the stakeholders you will likely achieve more than if you just send a plan and hope for the best. Use visuals as much as possible to convey what you want to do to help overcome language barriers, both written and spo-ken. Don't try to do more than the local people are capable of doing. Let them see success in small steps and gain confidence in the process and then move on to bigger challenges.

What Is Sustainability?

Sustainability is a term that has multiple definitions. In simple terms, it can be defined as the capacity to endure, but the term has come to represent a more complex idea. The complexity usually includes ideas around environmental sustainability (the capacity for the ecosystem to endure with increasing use); economic sustainability (the ability for business to be successful and, in doing so, support the community around it), and social sustainability (the idea that communities and the people within them are affected by both economic and environmental factors as well as actions directed specifically at them in terms of labor and human rights). Intertwined with the concept of sustainability is also the idea of sustainable development. Implicit in this realization is that our view of sustainability is a systems view, where factors relate to each other as they are interconnected.

The most famous definition of **sustainable development** is that which stemmed from the **Brundtland Commission** after the 1992 Earth Summit in Rio de Janeiro: "Development that meets the needs of the present without compromising the ability of future generations to meet their own needs."[9] There are, however, issues with this definition, as authors Marshall and Toffel have pointed out; it is, for example, impossible to predict the needs of the future without knowing their abilities and technological capacities, and it would also seem morally necessary to do more than simply meet their needs.[10] The World Bank points out that there are even difficulties in identifying the needs of the present, and that even when we can identify needs, that they at times conflict with each other.[11]

Other concepts of sustainable development exist. For example, the Government of Canada frames sustainable development as "sustainable development is based on an ecologically efficient use of natural, social and economic resources and acknowledges the need to integrate environmental, economic and social factors in the making of all decisions by government."[12]

The Global Reporting Initiative (GRI) uses the Brundtland definition for sustainable development, and does not provide a direct definition for sustainability itself. It offers this instead: "The underlying question of sustainability reporting is how an organization contributes, or aims to contribute in the future, to improvement or deterioration of economic, environmental, and social conditions, developments and trend at the local, regional or global level."[13]

For our purposes, we will define sustainability as the sweet spot where concepts of environmental protection, economic prosperity, and social justice overlap. Out of this definition arise other concepts; for example, **eco-efficiency** is where environmental protection and economic efficiency overlap. **Fair trade** is the overlap between social justice and economic prosperity, and **environmental justice** is the overlap between environmental protection and social justice.[14]

Sustainability Frameworks

There are many frameworks that have been developed around the concept of sustainability. Here we will look at four frameworks: the **triple bottom line**, **the Natural Step**, the **ecological footprint**, and a **sustainability hierarchy**. These concepts will appear throughout this book, and we will conclude by using a methodology called *backcasting* from the Natural Step to envision and plan for a sustainable future for the meetings and events industry.

The Triple Bottom Line

The Polish poet Stanislaw Lec once asked, "Is it progress if a cannibal uses a fork?" John Elkington, who coined the term the *triple bottom line,* believes the answer is yes to this hopefully rhetorical question. The cannibals are organizations in capitalist economies, where the natural order of things is to devour your competition; the "fork" is a new way of doing business, which considers social and environmental factors as well as economic ones as a more sustainable way of doing business.[15] Elkington defines the triple bottom line itself as economic prosperity, environmental sustainability, and social justice, or what has become more popularly known as *people, planet, and profit* (see Figure 1.5). Only when all three aspects of business are considered can a sustainable solution be generated.

The triple bottom line has direct relevance for the meetings and events industry. Meetings and events involve people as direct attendees as well as other stakeholders in the community (people), they have an environmental impact (planet), and they create economic value (profit) for the organizations that implement them, the communities the events are held in, and the extended supply chain.

The Natural Step

The Natural Step is a nonprofit organization founded in Sweden in 1989 by Dr. Karl-Henrik Robèrt. The organization provides a framework that integrates environmental sustainability into business processes. Four processes lie at its core:

1. Realizing that existing business processes are not sustainable and recognizing the business case for sustainability
2. Understanding the underlying principles of sustainability (systems conditions)
3. Backcasting, using a sustainable visioning process
4. Identifying steps that will move organizations to more sustainable activities[16]

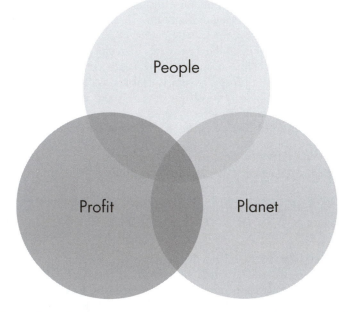

Figure 1.5 The Triple Bottom Line (Adapted from John Elkington)[17]

The four systems conditions referred to in step 2 are that "in the sustainable society, nature is not subject to systematically increasing:

1. Concentrations of substances extracted from the earth's crust;
2. Concentrations of substances produced by society; or
3. Degradation by physical means; and in that society
4. Human needs are met worldwide."[18]

This framework highlights primarily environmental, but also social, elements in a business context. The Natural Step framework has been adopted by the Green Meeting Industry Council (GMIC); this is an example of how a framework is being used currently in the meetings and events industry. The systems conditions embraced by the Natural Step have obvious repercussions within meetings and events; the industry relies on manufactured materials as well as energy taken from the Earth's crust to power transportation, heating, cooling, and the manufacture of materials.

The Ecological Footprint

Conceived in 1990 by Mathis Wackernagel and William Rees at the University of British Columbia, the footprint model compares the environmental impact of specific activities to the ability of the earth to support those actions.[19] It has been used on various scales, from the impact of an item to the impact of lifestyles in various countries. Earth Overshoot Day is a product of the ecological footprint model; it pinpoints the day of the year when the activities we demand from the earth—like clean air and water, and the production of food—has reached its "budget" for the year. In 2011, Earth Overshoot Day was calculated as September 27.[20]

The basis of the model is measuring the amount of water and land it takes to support various lifestyles. This has an impact not only on lifestyle but also on the ability of society to maintain itself economically, environmentally, and socially. Every meeting or event has a footprint that can be estimated, although in practice this might prove difficult.

Sustainability Hierarchy

Julian Marshall and Michael Toffel created another framework to view sustainability, called the *sustainability hierarchy*. Within this model, they identify four levels:

Level 1: Actions that endanger human survival

Level 2: Actions that reduce life expectancy or basic human health

Level 3: Actions that may increase the extinction of species or violate human rights

Level 4: Actions that reduce quality of life or that are inconsistent with value and beliefs[21]

This framework identifies levels of urgency, where levels 1 and 2 are considered more urgent than level 4. It allows for differences in the scope, meaning, and severity of different

An ecological footprint compares the impact of activities to the ability of the Earth to support them.
Photo courtesy of iStockphoto/CDH_Design

sustainable challenges. Within a specific meeting or event, it is most likely that levels 3 and 4 would come into play. Taking into consideration the cumulative impact of all activities within the meetings and events industry, levels 1 and 2 could also come into play; for example, massive carbon emissions from transportation of meeting and event attendees could contribute to climate change and air pollution, which could endanger human survival in the long term.

The Concept of CSR

Sustainability and corporate social responsibility are related, but do not mean exactly the same thing. Just like sustainability, there are different ways of looking at CSR as a concept for organizations. Many organizations call it by slightly different names, for example; these include social responsibility, business responsibility, corporate citizenship, social performance, or even as part of the health, safety, and environment (HSE) function. Intercontinental Hotel Group (IHG), Marriott, and Hilton call it corporate responsibility; the Global Business Travel Association calls it corporate social responsibility. Don't worry about what it is called; you should be able to recognize it for what it is based on what it is trying to do. What it tries to accomplish, generally speaking, is to create and implement activities that reduce the organization's environmental footprint; contribute to the bottom line (economic profit) through operational efficiencies and the creation of intangible benefits in the community, such as goodwill; and increase the positive footprint of the organization in the community.

For example, Foreign Affairs and International Trade Canada defines corporate social responsibility: "Corporate Social Responsibility (CSR) is defined as the way companies integrate social, environmental, and economic concerns into their values and operations in a transparent and accountable manner."[22] The World Business Council for Sustainable Development defines it in this way: "Corporate social responsibility is the commitment of business to contribute to sustainable economic development, working with employees, their families, the local community and society at large to improve their quality of life."[23]

There are typically four main reasons why organizations decide to implement a CSR program.[24] The first is that they perceive that they have a moral obligation to do so. "It is the right thing to do" is a statement that you can often see in CSR reports. The second is *sustainability*; this can refer to any of the three areas of people, planet, and profit, although it frequently refers to environmental sustainability and to the ability of CSR to help organizations build economic profits. Third, it can confer what is known as a **social license to operate** within the community. This is a kind of social capital built by organizations perceived to be good citizens. And finally, it enhances organizational reputation, which can impact not only the ability of an organization to be profitable but factors such as employee commitment and stakeholder relations.

As an example, here is a statement taken from the Intercontinental Hotel Group (IHG) 2011 Corporate Responsibility Report:

> *Corporate responsibility . . . is central to the way we do business. Acting responsibly creates value . . . while helping our hotels to manage costs, drive revenue and be prepared for the future. . . . Doing the right thing reinforces trust in our brands, builds competitive advantage and strengthens our corporate reputation.*[25]

A 2007 study looked at the CSR practices of the top 10 hotel companies in the world, including Marriott, Intercontinental, Hyatt, Starwood, Accor, and Hilton. It found that some hotels were highly focused on providing a balanced approach to social responsibility activities, including those in the areas of community, environment, marketplace, vision, and values in the workforce, while others lacked balance. Specific areas that seemed to be lacking were environmental, vision, and values.[26] This is somewhat surprising, given the almost exclusive focus on environmental initiatives in hospitality that are visible to the customer. For example, green hotel practices such as linen-and-towel reuse programs are common.

The most common practices identified in the study included philanthropic donations (80%); diversity policy for suppliers, business partners, and employees (60%); employee volunteer programs (50%); and having a socially responsible vision and/or mission statement (40%).[27]

CSR as Philanthropy

Inevitably when discussing CSR, the name of eminent economist Milton Friedman will arise. Friedman was famous for saying in a New York Times Magazine article in 1970 that the social responsibility of business is to increase profits. For him, governments and not-for-profits exist to provide a social safety net, not corporations.[28]

There is no arguing that a corporation must make money to survive, and that this benefits the shareholders and society at large; an organization that makes no money cannot survive, and cannot benefit anyone. But Friedman wrote his article in a very different political atmosphere. He wrote in the middle of the Cold War, and to him, the whole idea of CSR pitted the political ideologies of communism against capitalism. CSR was like the Cold War being fought at the level of corporate America. To Friedman, CSR meant only one thing—the giving of money to social organizations (what we would today call *philanthropy*); and to him, this subverted the power of the government and the capitalist ideology. The idea of CSR has evolved since then, as have our political battles. However, as we have already noted, the use of philanthropy in hospitality-related organizations is still common.

CSR as the Triple Bottom Line

CSR is often talked about as an expression of the triple bottom line, and it is here that we see an overlap with the concept of sustainability. This book uses the concept of the triple bottom line interchangeably with both ideas of sustainability and CSR. Earlier, we defined sustainability as "the sweet spot where concepts of environmental protection, economic prosperity, and social justice overlap." As you can easily see, this is an expression of the triple bottom line of people, planet, and profit.

CSR as Corporate Sustainability

Here is another overlap with the idea of sustainability, as defined by the Dow Jones Sustainability Index. "Corporate Sustainability is a business approach that creates long-term shareholder value by embracing opportunities and managing risks deriving from economic, environmental and social developments. Corporate sustainability leaders achieve long-term shareholder value by gearing their strategies and management to harness the market's potential for sustainability products and services while at the same time successfully reducing and avoiding sustainability costs and risks."[29] In this definition we see a definite focus on the idea of sustainability as something that creates business value for organizations and for investors. If we view the triple bottom line as a three-legged stool, this definition creates a platinum leg for the one labeled *profit*.

CSR in the Meetings and Events Industry

There has been increased recognition within the meetings and events industry of the importance of CSR, sustainability and ethics. The recently released Meeting and Business Events Competency Standards (MBECS) includes developing sustainability plans for meetings and events as a key skill under the category of strategic planning.[30] MBECS also lists exhibiting professional behavior (including ethical behavior) as a key skill under the category of professionalism. The Certified Meeting Professional International Standards (CMP-IS) have also recently been updated to reflect the MBECS, and, for the first time, have included developing a sustainability plan for meetings or events as a skill in the strategic planning domain.[31] The CMP-IS also recognizes local and cultural sensitivities and the demonstration of ethical behavior within the professionalism domain.[32]

Figure 1.6 shows the global and industry-specific drivers that are making CSR critical for meetings and events. From global issues, including consumer and economic trends, to industry drivers, including new standards and negative public perception of our industry, there is an increasing need for meeting and event professionals to demonstrate ethics and corporate responsibility. This will, in turn, lead to significant opportunities: from cost savings from greater efficiency, to increased trust and synergies with communities. We also have an opportunity to decrease our environmental footprint and increase the positive legacies of our meetings and events.

As you progress through the book, refer back to this framework. The final chapter contains a review of all the concepts covered and uses a technique called backcasting to describe a sustainable event in 2020, when the opportunities described in this framework have become simply the only way to do business in meetings and events.

Conventions, Conferences, and Congress Centers

What does corporate social responsibility mean to the meetings and events industry? Because of the variety of definitions and interpretations, we did a brief survey of publically available information on websites from selected suppliers globally to find out. Table 1.1 illustrates

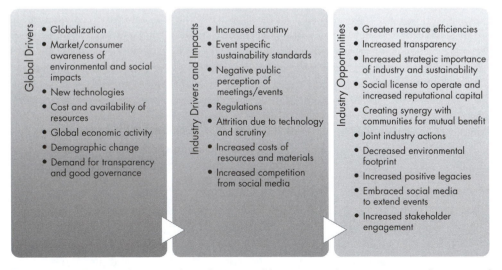

Figure 1.6 The Henderson-McIlwraith Sustainable Meetings/Events Conceptual Framework

Table 1.1   Marketing Focus of World Convention Centers on Social and Environmental Elements of Corporate Social Responsibility

Venue	Focus
Canada	
Vancouver Convention and Exhibition Centre	LEED Platinum facility; Mandate is to generate economic and community benefits; purpose is to provide sustainable experiences.
Edmonton (Shaw Convention Centre)	FRESH program recognizes environmental, social, and economic responsibility; focus is on environmentally sustainable events.
Calgary (TELUS Convention Centre)	Mission is economic development in an environmentally friendly facility.
Toronto (Metro Toronto Convention Centre)	The focus is on green events with some consideration for community support in the form of donations of time, money, and expertise.
United States	
Los Angeles Convention Center	The vision mentions both environmental and social sustainability.
San Francisco (Moscone Center)	The focus is on environmentally sustainable events; there is also some philanthropy as profits generated from recycling are donated to the community.
Pittsburgh (David L. Lawrence)	LEED Gold facility
Oregon Convention Center	LEED Silver facility
Australia	
Sydney Convention Centre	EcoWise program focuses on environmental sustainability; also supports the community through a food rescue program (ozHarvest).
Melbourne Convention Centre	Focus on green through building design; some focus on community through local purchasing.
Adelaide Convention Centre	The Centre has both environmental and social initiatives, including sponsorship of events, apprenticeships, and other capacity-building initiatives.

(continued)

Table 1.1 (*Continued*)

Venue	Focus
Europe	
Portugal (Estoril Conference Centre)	CSR statement recognizes social and environmental elements; innovative Green Fund and a focus on health and wellness.
Denmark (Bella Centre, Copenhagen)	CSR statement recognizes both social and environmental factors; social programs go beyond donations and sponsorship to hiring special needs people in the community; UN Global Compact signatory; also the Bybi initiative that links environmental, social, and economic prosperity through beekeeping. Has a Sustainability Code of Conduct.
United Kingdom (ExCel Centre, London)	Has a sustainability policy recognizing social responsibility and economic security, as well as environmental sustainability; works with community to promote sports and healthy eating.
Amsterdam RAI	Has a CSR policy and annual report. Policy has 7 theme areas including energy and climate; mobility; water; waste; employees; procurement; and social engagement.

the information available from world convention centers on both *sustainability* and *corporate social responsibility* as they relate to social and environmental factors. A focus on economic prosperity is assumed as a basic function of convention centers within their community.

It should be noted that this review is based on the marketing focus of these venues, and not a comprehensive review of their practices or of the practices available in their region. As an example, this marketing review does not factor in regional social programs (including government policies) and labor standards that may contribute to positive working conditions.

The information in Table 1.1 seems to indicate that many convention and congress centers view CSR primarily as a commitment to environmental sustainability, although there is geographic disparity; the Australian, European, and United Kingdom venues included in the table seem to have relatively broader concepts of CSR than their Canadian and U.S. counterparts. Alternatively, it could be argued that "green meetings" are simply top of mind, and the relatively broader concept of corporate social responsibility has yet to find broad support in the industry. Recent increasing trends that are placing a new focus on social responsibility may result in a shift toward a greater focus on this aspect of sustainability. A study conducted by BSR and GlobeScan indicates that human rights and workers' rights issues are becoming increasing priorities. Between 2009 and 2011, the priority for human rights increased from 56 to 65 percent, and workers' rights from 56 to 61 percent. Climate change experienced a slight decline from 66 to 63 percent.[33]

Some convention and congress centers do have CSR policies and/or statements. Table 1.2 provides some examples.

Table 1.2   Selected Global Convention Center CSR Statements

Center	Statement/Policy/Vision
Los Angeles Convention Center	To inspire a "Beyond Excellence" culture that establishes the Los Angeles Convention Center as the only venue of choice for our customers, the only employer of choice for our employees, and the most enduring symbol of environmental sustainability and social responsibility for our community and future generations.[34]
Moscone Center, San Francisco	The intent of sustainable programs is to promote and support operational and business practices which lessen adverse environmental impact, benefit the local community and make economic sense.[35]
Oregon Convention Center	The Oregon Convention Center believes that service to the community carries rewards beyond the obvious and tangible. Providing environmental stewardship, meaningful opportunities for local businesses, and quality jobs to individuals helps to build a rich and supportive community . . ..[36]
Adelaide Convention Centre, Australia	We act in the best interest of our clients, the community, and the environment. We take responsibility for our actions, knowing they are fair and honest and will stand up to any scrutiny.[37]
Estoril Conference Centre, Portugal	Corporate social responsibility is a leading trend in business policy commitment . . . It's about making better business, taking responsibility for one's actions and making a difference for future generations; in other words, it's another approach to being sustainable.[38]
ExCel Centre London	We will implement practices that promote economic security, social and environmental responsibility and will continuously seek to improve performance in these areas.[39]
Amsterdam RAI	We have translated our CSR ambitions into a concrete and practical CSR policy, which is divided into three specific policy areas: "Within the RAI," "Around the RAI," and "The RAI in society."[40]

The Vancouver Convention Centre's living roof is the largest in Canada and the largest nonindustrial green roof in North America. It is landscaped with more than 400,000 indigenous plants and grasses from 25 different species of the Pacific Northwest. The facility's sophisticated black water treatment plant collects and cleans water from washrooms for use in the living roof irrigation system in the summer. The living roof also acts as an insulator, reducing heat gains in the summer and heat losses in the winter.
Photograph Courtesy Vancouver Convention Centre

There is some indication that the scope of an organization's CSR activities is dependent on its size. A 2009 report commissioned by Business Events Australia, Tourism Australia found that large and/or international organizations in the business events sector are better equipped and have more resources to undertake CSR initiatives.[41] For a discussion on how small and medium-sized enterprises can mitigate this disadvantage, see the discussion on cluster CSR in the chapter on shared value and strategic CSR.

Industry Associations, CSR, and Ethics

There are a large number of industry associations in the meetings and events sector. Several of them offer resources to the community to help implement CSR, and some have CSR policies of their own. Table 1.3 summarizes a select number of these.

The existence of these task forces, policies, and resources indicates that CSR and ethics are issues of some importance to the sector.

Table 1.3 CSR and Meetings/Event Industry Professional Associations

Association	CSR Resources or Policy	Ethics Resources or Policy
Professional Convention Management Association (PCMA)	Has a CSR task force with a triple bottom line focus. Three areas under this task force include 1. Network for the Needy, transactional events held at their annual conference; 2. Green and Sustainable Meetings; and 3. Ethics and Responsible Business.[42]	The "PCMA Code of Ethics" includes sections on an ethics check, warning signs, and values. The focus of the code is on professional conduct.
International Congress and Convention Association (ICCA)	ICCA's CSR policy seeks to influence three areas: 1. The policies, activities, and impact of the association itself; 2. Member's policies, activities, and impacts; and 3. Global advocacy in partnership with other industry organizations.[43]	ICCA has integrated a section on "Running ICCA as an ethical association" directly into its strategic plan.
Meeting Professionals International (MPI)	Offers a CSR portal with case studies of its own events and other CSR tools and resources for its members.[44] Has partnered with LEEDS Metropolitan University on a three-year study of CSR.	MPI's "Principles of Professionalism" is focused on professional conduct and includes a section on diversity.
American Society of Association Executives (ASAE)	Created Global Principles for Socially Responsible Associations and Nonprofits, aligned with the United Nations Global Compact.[45]	The "ASAE Standards of Conduct" was updated in August 2011. Core standards are adapted for Association Professionals/Executives, Consultants and Industry Partners. Greatest focus is on professional conduct, with some references to social and environmental responsibility.

(continued)

Association	CSR Resources or Policy	Ethics Resources or Policy
Green Meeting Industry Council (GMIC)	The reason for the GMIC's existence is to inspire sustainability within the meetings and events sector. The focus is undeniably on environmental sustainability, but with recognition that social and economic sustainability are also important.	GMIC has both an "Individual Member Code of Conduct" that focuses on business, social, and environmental practices and a "Partner Code of Conduct" that has detailed social and environmental requirements that extend to the partner's supply chains.
Site Global	Organization offers resources on CSR and incentive travel, and an award for the most impactful effort toward CSR as part of an incentive program.	The "Site Code of Ethics" is prominently placed on their website. It includes both a creed and code of ethics. The policy focuses on professional conduct. The creed includes social responsibility aspects.
International Special Events Society (ISES)	They include a section on green meetings and resources in their website's "Learn" page. It includes links to outside organizations.	Website includes their "ISES Principles of Professional Conduct and Ethics." The policy focuses on professional conduct.

What Are Ethics, and Why Do They Matter?

In his perfectly titled article *Defining "Business Ethics": Like Nailing Jello to a Wall,* Phillip V. Lewis synthesizes business ethics definitions from an extensive review of textbooks, articles, and surveys to produce the following definition: "'Business ethics' is rules, standards, codes, or principles which provide guidelines for morally right behavior and truthfulness in specific situations."[46] A second definition is provided by our own series editor, Joe Goldblatt: ". . . Ethics are the principles of conduct governing individuals or groups. These principles are based on the business culture that is accepted at the time of the action. Although ethics are personal decisions, they are guided by group behavior and group acceptance."[47] What is valuable to see from both of these definitions is that neither explicitly states what is right or wrong. Instead, these definitions provide the context in which ethics lives: they are part of business culture and include principles that are shaped by society.

Warren Buffett once told his son, "It takes 20 years to build a reputation and five minutes to ruin it. If you think about that, you'll do things differently."[48] This holds true for meeting and event professionals, and damage to an individual or an organization's reputation can be disastrous in an industry where human relationships are critical for success. When actions are viewed as unethical or questionable, there can be significant repercussions, including the loss of business or employment. It can be important to remember that actions and perceptions are different; although one person may see their action as being ethical, from a different angle or perspective, much like seeing an image refracted or reflected in water. Things can appear to be crooked.

Safeguarding a professional reputation involves conducting business in a manner that not only meets *personal ethical standards* but also reflects accepted business norms and the *perceptions of outside observers*, including past, present, and future clients, employers, and partners. Consider this situation: You are a meeting planner and you are invited to participate in

A boat appears crooked when reflected in the water.
Photo courtesy of Elizabeth Henderson

a **familiarization trip** in a destination where you currently have no plans to hold a meeting. If you accept the invitation, you run the risk of damaging your reputation. Disclosing your lack of business opportunity potential to the suppliers that are have invited you to participate will demonstrate to them your professional ethics. Disclosure is important, but not sufficient to safeguard your reputation. If, for example, the organizers of the familiarization trip do not retract the invitation after you disclose your business potential and you accept the invitation, you could still run the risk of being perceived by other event participants and sponsors as having acted unethically.

Meeting and event professionals will almost inevitably face ethical dilemmas at some point in their careers that can be difficult to navigate. The types of ethical dilemmas can arise from a variety of interactions. These can include interaction between:

- Planners and suppliers: such as in the cases of fair negotiation practices, acceptance or offering of bribes, or abuse of offers such as familiarization trips.
- Employers and employees: examples in this area include safe, respectful, inclusive, and fair labor practices.
- Event attendees: examples include inappropriate behavior, interpersonal conflicts, theft, and privacy violations.
- Events and communities or the environment: meetings and events can also have a negative impact on the environment, through pollution, carbon emissions, waste creation, and consumption of resources.

Having a process for addressing these situations is critical for being able to make decisions efficiently about ethical dilemmas. Resources available to meeting and event professionals include these two:

1. *Organization specific code of conduct or ethics policy*: Many organizations will have specific codes of conduct that can help navigate ethical decisions. This should be the first point of reference for meeting and event professionals when seeking clarity on issues such as gift giving and acceptance policies, personal use of company resources including hotel or mileage "points" earned on company business, and human resources policies. These codes may also provide guidance on organizational priorities that can help a meeting or event professional choose between options, such as a more environmentally responsible or a more socially responsible supplier.
2. *Professional associations' codes of conduct:* Table 1.3 provides a list of professional codes of conduct that apply to associations within the meetings and events industry. In the absence of an organization specific code of conduct or ethics policy, these can help to provide guidance on expected behaviors within the industry. They can also be a practical tool for helping to develop or update an organization's code of conduct or ethics policy. (Please see Chapter 8 on Sustainable Supply Chains and Chapter 7 on Communications, Marketing, and Public Relations for more information on Codes of Conduct.)

For organizations working to foster an ethical culture, creating a code of conduct or ethics policy is an important step. Information on how to do this is provided in Chapter 2, Business Ethics and Meeting and Events. It is also important to ensure that the organization lives and breathes these values, and that they don't get confined to a policy manual that collects dust on a shelf. Five practical steps help promote the use of ethics policies in an organization:

1. Align human resource practices, from hiring to performance evaluations, with the ethics policy.
2. Incorporate ethics training into new employee orientation and ongoing professional development for team members.
3. Reference the policy in staff meetings, and use it as a reference for addressing business issues.
4. Convene an ethics committee to regularly review and update the ethics policy.
5. Apply the policy at all levels of the organization. An effective ethics policy will apply to all levels of an organization, including senior leadership and front line staff.

Applied CSR and Ethics

Moving from the theoretical to the applied aspects of corporate social responsibility and ethics leads to three areas where meetings and events can implement these concepts. As shown in Figure 1.7, they can act as conservers, creators, and catalysts.

Meetings and Events as Conservers

This book will address many ways that meetings and events can help conserve resources, including energy management, reduction in the use of materials, and efficient use of financial resources. (For more information on conservation of resources, please see Chapter 3 on Strategies for Sustainable Meetings and Events and Chapter 9 on Measurement.) Although sustainability and "green meetings" are sometimes viewed as a new trend for the meetings and events industry, conservation is not a new concept. In 1908, Gifford Pinchot, a forester for the USDA who later went on to become the first chief of the U.S. Forest Service, discusses conservation in the USDA's Farmer's Bulletin. His words, "Not only must we meet our own needs from this property, but we must see to it that our children come in for their fair share of it; so that after a while, the happiness we have had here may be carried on by them."[49] This quote seems to be a precursor to the previously mentioned definition of sustainability from the Brundtland Commission. Regardless of whether or not conservation is a new trend or an established practice, meetings and events can and should practice conservation methods in respect to consumption of energy

Figure 1.7   Meetings and Events as Conservers, Creators, and Catalysts (McIlwraith-Henderson)

and materials. Not only will the impact be felt from an environmental perspective, but purchasing and using less is an excellent method of conserving financial resources.

Meetings and Events as Creators

Meetings and events can also serve as creators: that is to say, they can help create a positive change in communities and the environment. A **carbon footprint** (similar in concept to the ecological footprint term previously discussed in this chapter) is used to measure the depth of the negative impact on the environment through the creation of carbon emissions. (For more information on carbon footprints, please see Chapter 5 on Meetings, Events, and Environmental Science.) There is an opportunity that extends beyond the idea of a negative imprint, the idea of leaving an embossed relief on the communities where meetings and events are held and on the natural environment. Consider how you might create a positive legacy from your event. The goal then changes from designing events to be carbon *neutral* to planning the event to be carbon *positive*. This concept is not limited to carbon emissions but also encompasses leaving a positive legacy on communities through service to society and economic impact. (For more information on community service programs and legacy, please see Chapter 4 on Social Responsibility and Culture and Chapter 6 on Shared Value and Strategic CSR.)

Meetings and Events as Catalysts

Meetings and events present an exceptional opportunity to change behaviors through education and motivation. Through our meetings and events, we have the opportunity to inspire participants to incorporate sustainable practices in their business operations and daily lives. Aspects of meetings and events that can help promote this type of *sustained sustainable behavior* include:

- Education on sustainable best practices within an industry at an educational conference
- Encouragement of participants to continue to practice and report sustainable actions through social media (For more information on reporting, please see Chapter 10.)
- Replacing participant gifts and materials with ones that encourage a sustainable behavior, such as replacing bottled water with a reusable container and water stations
- Recognition and awards of best in class sustainable practices
- Facilitating a network effect by building in mechanisms for meeting and event participants to communicate their sustainable actions and education to their connections

Case Study: Oracle OpenWorld

Conscientious application of CSR, ethics, and sustainability can result in events that promote all three of these aspects. As shown in Table 1.4, an excellent case example is Oracle's OpenWorld, an event that had more than 46,000 attendees in 2011. According to Vice President of Marketing Paul Salinger, Oracle's sustainability initiatives have saved the company more than $1.5 million over the past four years. He adds, "If you look at sustainability as a lens to see the entire conference through, and integrate it throughout the entire conference, then you do save money and build brand value . . ."[50]

Table 1.4   Oracle OpenWorld as Conservers, Creators, and Catalysts[51]

Oracle OpenWorld as Conservers	Oracle OpenWorld as Creators	Oracle OpenWorld as Catalysts
Among their many environmental achievements, Oracle OpenWorld's paper reduction strategies have saved the equivalent of 1,373 trees. Using recycled content paper when printing and eliminating bottled water has conserved more than 800,000 gallons of water since 2008.	Oracle arranged local community service projects including tree planting in the neighborhoods around the convention center and two days of ocean-related volunteer work with the Golden Gate National Parks Conservancy.	Oracle encourages sustainable behavior through the awarding of its Eco-Enterprise Innovation Awards at OpenWorld. The award recognizes customers and/or partners for their achievements in using Oracle products to create sustainability solutions for their businesses.

The Numbers behind the Narrative

This chapter has focused significantly on many intangible considerations. We would like to therefore conclude this chapter with a few additional statistics that demonstrate the importance of sustainability, CSR, and ethics from a business perspective within the meetings and events industry:

- *MPI FutureWatch 2010*: 64 percent of meeting planners report that CSR will be addressed in 2010. This includes 73.1 percent of corporate planners, 48.4 percent of association planners, 76 percent of EMEA planners and 63 percent of U.S. planners.[52]
- *IMEX 2011 Global Insights*: 42 percent of respondents are fully committed to CSR; 26 percent are currently developing policies to fulfill this brief. Nevertheless, over 25 percent responded that, while they understood the importance of CSR, they had yet to introduce policies that embrace and support local communities and charitable causes.[53]
- *IMEX 2008 Survey*: 80 percent of international buyers have taken environmental issues into account in their work and 79 percent would deliberately avoid destinations/venues known to have a poor environmental record.[54]

These numbers indicate that the incorporation of CSR, ethics, and sustainability are not just "the right thing to do" socially and environmentally. They are also important business considerations for meeting and event professionals.

Chapter Review

Sustainability has many definitions, and means different things to different people and organizations. Sustainability tends to be viewed as being the same thing as sustainable development. The most famous definition of sustainable development was created through the efforts of the Brundtland Commission. We define it in this book as the sweet spot where the concepts of environmental protection, economic prosperity, and social justice overlap. There are many sustainability frameworks, including the triple bottom line, the Natural Step, the ecological footprint, and the sustainability hierarchy models.

CSR and sustainability are not the same but are complementary concepts. Like sustainability, there are many different definitions. Four reasons to implement CSR include moral obligation ("it's the right thing to do"), sustainability, social license to operate in the communities organizations do business in, and enhancement of reputation.

There are many examples of CSR being implemented within the meetings and events value chain, although some geographic disparity exists. Industry associations have recognized CSR as an important issue, and are addressing it through policy, task forces, and the provision of resources to their members.

Review Questions

1. What are four sustainability frameworks?
2. What is the Natural Step?
3. What is an ecological footprint?
4. What are the four levels in the sustainability hierarchy?
5. Why can it be difficult to define sustainability and sustainable development?
6. What is CSR trying to achieve?
7. How do the concepts of meetings and events as conservers, creators, and catalysts relate to CSR and ethics?

Activities

1. Compare and contrast the four sustainability frameworks as presented in this chapter. What do you see as being important?
2. Choose an organization within the meetings and events industry and analyze its CSR activities. What is the focus of the organization's activities? Can you identify opportunities for improvement?

Key Terms

- corporate social responsibiity
- macro level
- micro level
- Troubled Asset Relief Program (TARP)
- sustainability
- sustainable development
- Brundtland Commission
- eco-efficiency
- Fair trade

- environmental justice
- triple bottom line
- the Natural Step
- ecological footprint
- sustainability hierarchy
- license to operate
- familiarization trip
- carbon footprint

Resources

Related to the Resources listed below, please visit the Book Companion Site (located at www.wiley.com/college/henderson) for a complete list of websites. Additional referential websites related to this chapter's content can also be found on the BCS.

Green Meeting Industry Council
>This association offers resources and case studies on its website.

International Congress and Convention Association (ICCA) CSR Report
>This report supports the association's CSR policy.

Meeting Professionals International (MPI) CSR Portal
>This site offers case studies, a measurement tool, and other CSR resources.

American Society of Association Executives Social Responsibility Portal
>This portal has research and tools for CSR in associations.

Notes

1. Inukshuk Gallery, "What Is an Inukshuk?" Accessed December 5, 2011, from www .inukshukgallery.com/inukshuk.html.
2. Pricewaterhouse Coopers, "The Economic Significance of Meetings to the U.S. Economy," Study Findings at a Glance. Accessed November 10, 2011, from meetingsmeanbusiness.com/.
3. Mark Lewis, "The AIG Effect," *Forbes* (February 16, 2010). Accessed November 10, 2011, from www.forbes.com/2010/02/16/aig-business-travel-leadership-meetings-10-corporate-conferences.html.
4. Corporate Meetings and Incentives, "Financial Companies Learn New Treasury Rules for Meetings" (June 15, 2009). Accessed November 10, 2011, from meetingsnet.com/corporatemeetingsincentives/news/0615-treasury-rules-troubled-asset-relief/.
5. Martin Sirk, "CSR and Its Relationship with International Association Congresses & Conventions," *ICCA Intelligence* (May 2008). Accessed November 24, 2011, from www .iccaworld.com/nlps/story.cfm?nlpage=192.
6. Wikipedia.org, "List of Occupy movement protest locations." Retrieved November 26, 2011, from en.wikipedia.org/wiki/List_of_Occupy_movement_protest_locations.
7. "We Are the 99 Percent." Retrieved November 26, 2011, from wearethe99percent.tumblr .com/.
8. Society for Human Resource Management (2007), *Workplace Visions: Exploring the Future of Work—Social Responsibility and HR Strategy.* Accessed November 24, 2011, from www .shrm.org/Research/FutureWorkplaceTrends/Documents/SocialResponWV.pdf.
9. The Brundtland Commission, "Our Common Future." Retrieved January 27, 2012, from www.un-documents.net/ocf-02.htm.
10. Julian Marshall and Michael W. Toffel, "Framing the Elusive Concept of Sustainability: A Sustainability Hierarchy," *Environmental Science and Technology*, 39 (3) (2005).

11. The World Bank Group. "What is Sustainable Development?" Retrieved January 31, 2012, from www.worldbank.org/depweb/english/sd.html.
12. Department of Justice Canada, "Federal Sustainable Development Act s.c. 2008, c 33." Retrieved January 31, 2012, from laws-lois.justice.gc.ca/eng/acts/F-8.6/page-1.html#h-5.
13. Global Reporting Initiative, "G3 Guidelines," version 3.0, p. 11. www.globalreporting.org/reporting/latest-guidelines/g3-guidelines/Pages/default.aspx.
14. Marshall and Toffel.
15. Ronald Jeurissen, "Book Review: Cannibals With Forks: The Triple Bottom Line of Twentieth-Century Business," *The Journal of Business Ethics*, 23 (2) (January 2000): 229.
16. Brian Nattrass and Mary Altomare, *The Natural Step for Business: Wealth, Ecology and the Evolutionary Corporation* (Gabriola Island, BC: New Society Publishers, 2006).
17. Adapted from John Elkington, *Cannibals with Forks: The Triple Bottom Line of 21st Century Business* (Gabriola Island, BC: New Society Publishers, 1998).
18. Nattrass and Altomare, Op. cit., p. 23.
19. The Global Footprint Network, "Footprint Basics—Overview." Accessed November 3, 2011, from www.footprintnetwork.org/en/index.php/GFN/page/footprint_basics_overview/.
20. The Global Footprint Network, "Earth Overshoot Day, Sept 27, 2011" (Sept. 26, 2011). Accessed November 3, 2011, from www.footprintnetwork.org/en/index.php/GFN/blog/today_is_earth_overshoot_day.
21. Marshall and Toffel.
22. Foreign Affairs and International Trade Canada, *Corporate Social Responsibility*. Retrieved January 31, 2012, from www.international.gc.ca/trade-agreements-accords-commerciaux/ds/csr.aspx?view=d.
23. Richard Holme and Phil Watts, The World Business Council for Sustainable Development (2000), "Corporate Social Responsibility: Making Good Business Sense." Retrieved January 31, 2012, from www.wbcsd.org/web/publications/csr2000.pdf.
24. Michael Porter and Mark Kramer, "Strategy and Society: The Link Between Competitive Advantage and Corporate Social Responsibility," *Harvard Business Review* (December 2006).
25. Intercontinental Hotel Group, *Corporate Responsibility Report* (2011). Accessed November 9, 2011, from www.ihgplc.com/files/pdf/2010_cr_report.pdf.
26. Judy L. Holcomb, Randall S. Upchurch, and Fevzi Okumus, "Corporate Social Responsibility: What Are Top Hotel Companies Doing?" *International Journal of Contemporary Hospitality Management,* 19 (6) (2007).
27. Ibid.
28. Milton Friedman "A Friedman doctrine—The Social Responsibility of Business Is to Increase Its Profits" *The New York Times Magazine*, September 13, 1970.
29. Dow Jones Sustainability Indexes, "Corporate Sustainability." Retrieved November 8, 2011, from www.sustainability-index.com/07_htmle/sustainability/corpsustainability.html.
30. Canadian Tourism Human Resource Council, *Meeting and Business Event Competency Standards.* Ottawa, Ontario, 2011.
31. Convention Industry Council, *CMP International Standards*, 2011.
32. Ibid.
33. BSR and GlobeScan, *State of Sustainable Business Poll 2011* (November 2, 2011), Accessed November 24, 2011, from www.bsr.org/reports/BSR_Globescan_State_of_Sustainable_Business_Poll_2011_Report_Final.pdf.
34. Los Angeles Convention Center. Vision Statement. Retrieved January 27, 2012, from www.lacclink.com/About_Us.aspx
35. Moscone Center, "Sustainability." Accessed November 10, 2011, from www.moscone.com/community/sustain.html.

36. Oregon Convention Center, *2009 Annual Report*. Accessed November 10, 2011, from findit .oregoncc.org/Annual%20Report/occ_annualreport.pdf.

37. Adelaide Convention Centre, "Corporate Responsibility." Accessed November 10, 2011, from www.adelaidecc.com.au/about-us/corporate-social-responsibility/corporate-social-responsibility.

38. Estoril Conference Centre, "Social Responsibility." Accessed November 10, 2011, from www.estorilcc.com/en/services/social-responsibility.aspx.

39. ExCel Centre London, "Sustainability Policy." Accessed November 10, 2011, from www .excel-london.co.uk/exhibitionorganisers/planningyourevent/recyclingandgreencredentials.

40. Amsterdam RAI, "Sustainability Report 2010." Accessed November 11, 2011, from www.rai .nl/RAI%20Afbeeldingen/Corporarate%20Sustainability%20Report%202010.pdf.

41. Business Events Australia, *National Corporate Social Responsibility (CSR) Audit* (February 2009).

42. Professional Convention Management Association, Accessed November 11, 2011, from www.pcma.org/about/governance/committees-and-task-forces/headquarter-volunteer-opportunities.htm.

43. International Congress and Convention Association, "ICCA CSR Policy." Accessed November 11, 2011, from www.iccaworld.com/abouticca/csrpolicy.cfm.

44. Meeting Professionals International, "Corporate Social Responsibility." Accessed November 11, 2011, from www.mpiweb.org/Portal/CSR.

45. American Society of Association Executives. "Global Principles for Socially Responsible Associations and Nonprofits." Accessed November 11, 2011, from www.asaecenter.org/ Forms/SocialResponsibilityPrinciples/index.cfm.

46. Phillip V. Lewis, "Defining Business Ethics: Like Nailing Jello to a Wall," *Journal of Business Ethics*, 4 (5) (1985): 377–383.

47. Joe Goldblatt, *Special Events: A New Generation and the Next Frontier* (Hoboken, NJ: John Wiley & Sons, 2011), p. 410.

48. Janet Lowe, *Warren Buffet Speaks: Wit and Wisdom from the World's Greatest Investor* (Hoboken, NJ: John Wiley & Sons, 2007), p. 27.

49. Gifford Pinchot, "The Conservation of Natural Resources," *USDA Farmer's Bulletin* 327 (1908), Accessed November 24, 2011, from hdl.handle.net/10113/3336.

50. Greg Oates, "Sustainability: The Next Big Thing," *Prevue Online* (September 1, 2011). Accessed November 24, 2011, from: www.prevueonline.net/blog/themes/food-drink/ sustainability-the-next-big-thing-2.

51. Information for this table was sourced from: Oracle, "Green at Oracle OpenWorld: Oracle Event Sustainability." Accessed November 24, 2011, from www.oracle.com/ openworld/get-started/at-event/green/index.html.

52. American Express and Meeting Professionals International, *FutureWatch 2010: A Comparative Outlook on the Global Business of Meetings and Events.* p. 10. www.rigsbee .com/2010-FutureWatch.pdf.

53. IMEX, Press Release: "Confidence Replaces Caution for the Year Ahead, Reveals Latest IMEX Global Insights Report" (November 29, 2010). Accessed November 24, 2011, from www.imex-frankfurt.com/press.php?action=showstory&newsid=241.

54. IMEX, "Meetings Planners Demonstrate 'Green' Leadership—IMEX Poll Reveals Growing MICE Sector 'Responsibility'" (September 2008). Accessed November 24, 2011, from www .imexamerica.com/documents/September2008GlobalWarmingandBusinessTourism.pdf.

Business ethics often involves finding clarity. This chapter will look at ways that meeting and event professionals can find this clarity, often balancing competing values.
Photo courtesy of Elizabeth Henderson

CHAPTER 2

Business Ethics and the Meetings and Events Industry

"Management is doing things right; leadership is doing the right things."
—*Peter Drucker, economist, management guru, author (1909–2005)*

Learning Objectives

After reading this chapter, you will be able to:

- Identify the business ethics issues faced by industry professionals.
- Describe the rationalizations applied in attempts to excuse actions taken.
- Identify the challenges of competing values and learn how to apply a framework for addressing these challenges.
- Describe the key elements required to develop and implement a code of conduct.

The Importance of Business Ethics

Meeting and event professionals are often faced with **ethical dilemmas** and need tools to understand how to address them. Companies and associations can benefit from having clearly established ethics policies to guide employees and members. These policies can help organizations to protect their reputations and can provide guidance to team members in making ethical decisions that align with the organization's objectives.

Ethical Dilemmas in the Meetings and Events Industry

The meetings and events industry ethical dilemmas can be grouped broadly into planner/supplier relationship issues, employer/employee relationship issues, attendee issues, and the impact that meetings and events have on society and the environment.

The Planner/Supplier Relationship

The planner/supplier relationship is particularly vulnerable to ethical abuses. The unethical practices of planners accepting undisclosed commissions, or incentives, including **familiarization trips** (events where a destination will host prospective clients as a way of introducing them to their destination), with no intention of booking business can be further complicated by the pressures on sales managers to identify potential customers and secure bookings that make them willing to look the other way when they suspect unethical conduct by a planner. In addition, there may be pressure on planners and suppliers to collude in unethical pricing strategies to circumvent spending restrictions. For example, if a planner has restrictions about purchasing food and beverage, a venue may offer a package rate for the meeting space that includes the restricted items. Planners and suppliers participating in these activities may face repercussions both personally and for their organizations, including lost future business or employment challenges. A final challenge arises when uneven negotiation skills and/or contracting knowledge between a planner and supplier results in one taking unfair advantage of the other. Consider a novice event planner being asked to sign a much more stringent agreement than is usually offered by a more experienced sales manager.

The Employer/Employee Relationship

In respect to the employer/employee relationship, the 24/7 nature of the meetings and events industry can prove to be challenging in supporting a healthy life balance for employees. Interpersonal ethics issues, including harassment and bullying, can lead to loss of productivity and staff retention and recruitment challenges.

Employee theft, ranging from office supplies to intellectual property, is also a concern in the industry. Consider the conflict that arises when highly mobile sales managers take client lists to their new employers. Employers can provide some protection to themselves through noncompete clauses in employment agreements.

Attendee Issues

Examples of unethical behavior by meeting and event attendees include failure to pay admission fees and abuses of corporate travel policies. With the increasing use of technology and the ability to track attendees at events, meeting and event organizers must also consider potential privacy violations.

A further example is what is referred to as **suitcasing** or **outboarding**. Many events that include an exhibit component are including policies against this practice, defined as "the solicitation of business by non-exhibitors and non-sponsors at or around the convention center or by exhibitors or sponsors in non-designated areas."[1]

Impact of the Industry on Society and the Environment

As was previously discussed in Chapter 1, meetings and events have the potential to have a significant negative impact on society and the environment. Often, meeting and event professionals face situations where they need to choose between competing financial, social, and environmental priorities and can benefit from having established guidelines for addressing these types of situations.

Categories of Ethical Dilemmas

From a more general business ethics perspective, the list of categories of ethical dilemmas shown in Table 2.1 was developed in Brigham Young University's Marriott School of Business magazine, *Exchange*, and elaborated on by Marianne Jennings.[2] Examples of these categories of ethical dilemmas faced in the meetings and events industry are also provided in Table 2.1.

Table 2.1 Categories of Ethical Dilemmas

Category	Example from the Meetings and Events Industry
Taking things that don't belong to you	A planner accepts "hotel points" for group business booked for personal use that should be remitted to the client or organization according to corporate policy.
Saying things you know are not true	Misrepresentation during negotiations: A sales professional might state or imply that a competitor's product or services are inferior in order to secure a contract. Alternatively, an event planner might misrepresent a competitor's bid to a potential supplier to receive a lower bid.
Giving or allowing false impressions	A meeting planner might misrepresent his or her decision-making responsibilities or the amount of business that he or she conducts in order to receive incentives from a supplier.
Buying influence or engaging in conflicts of interest	An organization offers or accepts undisclosed commissions.
Hiding or divulging information	Client lists from a previous employer are provided to a new or prospective employer.
Taking unfair advantage	A planner requests complimentary nights at a hotel for personal use while negotiating with a sales manager.
Committing acts of personal decadence	A planner accepts invitations for familiarization trips with no reasonable expectation of booking future business.
Perpetrating interpersonal abuse	Employees or managers demean or harass colleagues, front-line staff, or suppliers.
Permitting organizational abuse	Workers are treated unfairly, with practices such as requiring excessive hours without reasonable compensation.
Violating rules	A supplier solicits business at a tradeshow without purchasing a booth.

(continued)

Table 2.1 (*Continued*)

Category	Example from the Meetings and Events Industry
Condoning unethical actions	Someone in the organization fails to report unethical behavior by a colleague, client, or supplier.
Balancing ethical dilemmas	An organization must decide whether to hold an association meeting in an area with high potential for attendance and new membership but with a history in the region of human rights violations.

Categories are from JENNINGS. *Business,* 9E. © 2012 South-Western, a part of Cengage Learning, Inc. Reproduced by permission. www.cengage.com/permissions. Examples are provided by this author.

Possible Consequences of Unethical Actions

In the cases in Table 2.1, there can be negative consequences for meeting and event professionals that participate in unethical behaviors. These include, but are not limited to, damage to your reputation and damage to your bottom line. There might also be legal and liability implications, and this will be discussed in Chapter 11.

Damage to Your Reputation

According to Theresa Breining, managing director of Breining Group LLC, former chairwoman of the board of Meeting Professionals International, and an inductee to the Convention Industry Council's Hall of Leaders, "The major repercussion (assuming the actions aren't illegal, just unethical) is a stain on the reputation of the individual and/or company. And, in an industry where relationships are so important, it can impact one's ability to find a job or secure clients."

Unethical behavior can also damage your organization's reputation. This can lead to lost business opportunities and difficulties in attracting and retaining top talent.

Damage to Your Bottom Line

Bruce Harris, retired founder of Conferon, Inc. (now Experient) and inductee to the Convention Industry Council's Hall of Leaders, demonstrates that applying strong business ethics is an important negotiation tool. He describes the following scenario:

> *Ethics and Negotiation Skills: A meeting planner is negotiating with a hotel and the sales manager tells the planner that the hotel will beat any competitor's rate. The meeting planner would be required to divulge confidential bid information in order to obtain this rate. According to Harris, not only would it be unethical for the planner to divulge this information, it removes the incentive for the hotel to offer their most competitive offer. In other words, the hotel only needs to beat the competitor's bid by 10 percent—even though they might have offered a better package to the planner. If planners find themselves in this situation, Harris recommends advising the sales manager that all bid information is kept confidential. Just as the planner would not reveal the quote provided by the sales manager to a competitor, they will not divulge the competitor's quote to the sales manager.*

Table 2.2 Rationalizations for Avoiding Ethical Dilemmas and Industry Examples

Rationalization	Examples
"Everybody else does it."	Failing to disclose commissions
"If we don't do it, someone else will."	Creating "packages" that include items not approved by the client's official budget policy, but requested by the planner as a condition for securing a contract
"That's the way it has always been done."	Distributing registration lists with potential personal information to vendors and other delegates without consent
"We'll wait until the lawyers tell us it's wrong."	Disregarding negative environmental impacts of meetings and events
"It doesn't really hurt anyone."	Individuals attending meetings or events without paying registration or admission fees
"The system is unfair."	Absenteeism as a response to unpaid overtime
"If you think this is bad—you should have seen…"	Theft of "minor items" such as office suppliers, as compared to theft of "major items" such as audiovisual equipment
"I was just following orders."	Underrepresenting or overrepresenting quarterly forecasts
"It's a gray area."	Accepting hotel or airline points offered to a meeting planner by a supplier in exchange for booking a group if there is no official policy

Rationalizations for Avoiding Ethical Dilemmas

Marianne Jennings identifies a list of frequently used **rationalizations** for avoiding facing ethical dilemmas[3] that are summarized in Table 2.2, along with industry-specific examples. *It is important to note that these rationalizations do not mitigate the impact of the actions, nor do they protect individuals or organizations from potential liability or penalties.* As will be discussed in greater detail in a subsequent chapter on legal requirements, there is increasing legislation (such as the **Sarbanes-Oxley Act** of 2002 in the United States) that requires ethical and transparent behavior from organizations.

Business Ethics and Competing Values

Perhaps the greatest challenge that can face meeting and event professionals is not in choosing between "right" and "wrong" actions but, as described by Joseph Badaracco Jr., in his article "The Discipline of Building Character," in choosing between "right" and "right" actions.[4] An example of such a conflict within the meetings and events industry follows.

Competing Values: Inclusivity and Environmental Impact Conflict

Your organization is planning a meeting and a segment of the audience has limited economic resources. Participation from this segment will greatly enhance the outcomes of the meeting. You have also prioritized minimizing your environmental impact.

You have identified two potential locations for your meeting. The first location is more affordable and would allow you to set affordable registration fees and hotel room rates, but the venue has a poor environmental record. The second location has an excellent environmental record but would be cost prohibitive for some attendees.

Your choice is to compromise either the affordability and inclusivity of your event or its environmental impact.

Finding balance can be difficult for meeting and event professionals when competing values are present. The photo shows an Event Camp Vancouver 2011 participant balancing inside circus rings.
Photo courtesy of Elizabeth Henderson

A Framework for Approaching Ethical Dilemmas with Competing Values

When choosing between competing **values**, the following steps are recommended. See Table 2.3 for the steps applied to the competing value example from above.

1. *Identify the competing values and available alternatives.* When considering available alternatives, be creative. Are there less obvious options available to you that will allow you to achieve your goals?
2. *Identify the consequences of each alternative for all stakeholders.* This might include yourself, your meeting or event, work group dynamics, your organization, sponsors, the environment, and the community. Recognize that some actions might have irreversible consequences. Consider the impact to your reputation or to that of your meeting, event, or organization if the decision was public.
3. *Ensure that legal obligations are being met.* At a minimum, be aware of any legal obligations that exist and ensure that they are met. If the decision involves an ethical conflict with a legal or contractual requirement, seek legal advice before proceeding.
4. *Mitigate negative aspects and/or maximize positive aspects.* Mitigating negative aspects of a decision may involve training, public relations, or remediation work. Maximizing positive benefits will help to ensure that the cost of the action will result in a higher return.
5. *Select a course of action and enlist support for your decision.* Once you have reviewed the alternatives and decided on a course of action, recognize that there may be other interpretations of the ethics of the situation that may be very persuasive.[5] Consider possibilities for influencing others to adopt your position, and gain support from potential allies.

Table 2.3   Application of Framework to Inclusivity versus Environmental Conflict

Step	Application
Identify the competing values and available alternatives.	At conflict are the ability to be affordable and therefore inclusive, and environmental impact.
	Obvious alternatives are to choose the more affordable venue or the more environmentally-friendly venue.
	Creative alternatives include negotiating a tiered rate structure with the environmentally-friendly option, or to influence the more affordable venue to incorporate more environmental practices.
Identify the consequences of each alternative for all stakeholders.	Selecting the environmentally-friendly option will likely reduce overall attendance and the lack of diversity will impact the quality of the program.
	Selecting the affordable option will have a negative environmental impact.
Ensure that legal obligations are being met.	The host organization may have policies that require the selection of "green venues." If this is the case, speak with the key decision makers to request an exemption from this policy should you choose the more affordable option.
Mitigate negative aspects and/or maximize positive aspects.	If selecting the green venue, explore the feasibility of offering a reduced-rate room block for specific delegates, or introducing a scholarship program. Develop a communication plan to ensure that delegates are using the environmental programs.
	If selecting the affordable venue, implement environmental practices that are under your direct control, such as through menu choices or reduced paper usage. Ensure that the marketing plan effectively targets a diverse audience.
Select a course of action and enlist support for your decision.	In choosing either venue, enlist the support of the client, or of your supervisor and colleagues. Be prepared to address their concerns. Explain how your decision will meet the meeting or event's overall objectives.

Cross-Cultural Differences and Ethics

Culture plays a significant role in shaping ethical values. Individuals are influenced not only by their national culture but also by other forms of culture, including religion, ethnic background, generation, and **organizational culture**. These forms of culture, and their impact on ethics and corporate responsibility, will be covered in greater depth in a subsequent chapter.

In approaching ethical dilemmas or developing a code of ethics for an organization, it is important to keep in mind the influence of culture on stakeholders, including staff members, meeting and event attendees, and the public. Organizers of international meetings and events need to be sensitive to potential cultural differences between stakeholders that may result in conflicts in ethical perspectives.

Culture and Ethics: Bribery versus Business Process

Many organizations, including many governments, have policies against accepting or offering gifts due to concerns about perceived or actual bribery and corruption. Gift giving, however, is not universally equated with potential bribery; conversely, it can be viewed as an important business process. As an example, in Japan, gift giving is an important element of developing business relationships.[6] In developing a code of ethics, organizations should consider the cultural lens through which actions and behaviors are viewed. Hospitality industry leader David Kliman, president of the Kliman Group and former chair of Meeting Professionals International (MPI), has also served as a delegate on the White House Conference on Travel and Tourism. Kliman specializes in market trends and advises that "when it comes to the Chinese or Japanese tradition in business of gift exchanging, it is impossible to do business in those countries absent that, and a regulated company that has restrictions on gift giving needs to have an exception and a written policy regarding how to do business in those countries."

Developing and Implementing a Code of Conduct

A **code of conduct** provides direction to individuals within an organization about expected behaviors and communicates these expectations to the broader community. It is not sufficient to expect that everyone will act according to an organization's standards if they are not clearly stated. As Bruce Harris explains, "Since everyone has a different basis or foundation for their values and ethics, it is crucial that you start by setting a standard within your organization that everyone can refer to. In essence, every organization has to have a defined culture, and its values are the foundation of its culture."

A code of conduct is equally applicable to volunteer groups formed to organize a meeting or event as it is to a company or organization. The key to the successful implementation of a code of conduct is to reference it regularly and communicate it widely within an organization to ensure adoption. Furthermore, "While having a code of ethics is important—they are worthless unless there are consequences if they aren't followed. Every company should have the courage to enforce what it believes," says Harris.

Some initiatives will help to embed the code of conduct into the organizational culture:

- *Include the code of conduct as part of orientation programs.* Example: Include scenario discussions about frequently encountered ethical issues, such as the acceptance of gifts or familiarization trips, as part of new team member training.
- *Use the code of conduct to develop performance metrics for staff evaluations.* Example: Incorporate specific questions about ethics and following the code of conduct in performance evaluations. Include specific consequences for failing to follow the code of conduct.
- *Refer to the code of conduct during staff discussions of business issues.* Example: When determining gifts that will be given to clients, discuss what would be appropriate and consistent with the internal code of conduct and those of the gift recipients.

- *Review the code of conduct annually*. Example: Establish an ethics committee for your organization that is assigned to review the code regularly. This committee may also act as peer advisors on ethics matters.
- Provide quarterly ethics training, and include ethics as a component in education programs. Example: Include ethics as a topic for corporate retreats, or conference sessions on ethics in events.

Joan Eisenstodt, chief strategist of Eisenstodt Associates, LLC, and inductee to the Convention Industry Council's Hall of Leaders, is a consultant, facilitator, and trainer who speaks regularly at association events on the subject of ethics in the meetings industry and helps organizations make their codes of ethics more specific to meetings departments. Eisenstodt notes that many companies ensure there is an ethics assessment yearly. This is done with virtual training and then an electronic assessment. In most cases, discussions of ethics policies and principles, company values, and practices are not held on a regular basis outside of these annual assessments. In fact, many ethics policies are buried in employee manuals and not seen after one is first hired, if then. Eisenstodt recommends the following safeguards that can be implemented to ensure that ethics guidelines are applied:

- Make ethics and the discussion thereof part of weekly or monthly staff meetings.
- Allow people to submit, anonymously if desired, ethical dilemmas they face and discuss these dilemmas in staff or other meetings.
- From the top down and the bottom up, provide role models who will demonstrate ethical behavior. Use their actions as examples for others.
- Provide quarterly ethics training. For industry associations, ensure ethics is a built-in component of all education.
- Provide clear ethics guidelines—including Frequently Asked Questions (FAQs)—for everyone. Review these guidelines regularly.

A Supplier Code of Conduct

In addition to implementing their own code of conduct, meeting and event professionals should consider the codes of conduct of organizations in their supply chain. As will be further discussed in Chapter 11 on risk management and legal considerations and in Chapter 8 on supply chains, the actions of organizations from which we purchase products or services can have a direct impact on the success and reputation of an event. Reviewing a potential supplier's code of conduct is helpful for identifying potential risks and for ensuring that suppliers conform with the standards set by the event organizers. In addition to reviewing codes of conduct, meeting and event professionals should monitor their implementation by the suppliers to ensure that they follow their own code. An example of a code of conduct provided by the Fair Labor Association is provided in Chapter 7.

The Global Business Standards (GBS) Codex and Ethical Principles

The GBS Codex[7] formulated by Lynn Paine, Rohit Deshpandé, Joshua D. Margolis, and Kim Eric Bettcher is a collection of widely endorsed conduct guidelines developed from a review of codes from international organizations, some of the world's largest companies and legal and regulatory requirements. It provides an excellent starting point for the development of a code of conduct or a review of an existing code. The GBS Codex is formulated from eight ethical principles that are listed in Table 2.4.

Table 2.4 GBS Codex Principles*

Principle	Key Concepts / Meetings and Events Example
Fiduciary	Diligently carry out the financial interests of the company and its investors; disclose and/or refrain from conflicts of interest; abstain from the use of company resources for personal gain.
	Example: Do not select venues or destinations in exchange for personal benefits, including hotel points.
Property	Respect property and ownership rights, protect assets, and refrain from theft.
	Example: Refrain from all forms of stealing, including office materials, intellectual property in supplier bids, and speaker materials.
Reliability	Honor all voluntary commitments, agreements, and promises regardless of whether they are legally enforceable.
	Example: Fulfill your commitments in a thorough and timely manner.
Transparency	Conduct business openly and truthfully, and without deception.
	Example: Disclose commissions received.
Dignity	Respect and protect the dignity, health, safety, privacy, and human rights of others; abstain from the use of force and coercion; and support association, expression, learning, and development.
	Example: Ensure that workers are treated fairly and have safe working conditions.
Fairness	Conduct business in a manner that treats all parties, including investors, clients, employees, and suppliers/partners fairly and equitably.
	Example: Have open and transparent selection processes for hiring and supplier selection.
Citizenship	Obey laws and regulations; support sustainability and do not condone bribery or abuses; avoid improper political involvement and contribute to the community.
	Example: Develop a legacy project to contribute to the community where you are holding your events.
Responsiveness	Engage with parties who have justifiable claims about the company's activities and address their concerns respectfully, with good faith and in a timely manner; collaborate with community groups to promote sustainability and eliminate corruption.
	Example: Address community concerns related to environmental and noise pollution related to your events.

*Adapted from Paine, Deshpandé, Margolis, & Bettcher, 2005.

Table 2.5   Code of Conduct Issue Areas

Business Operations	Environmental Issues	Social Issues
• Gift exchanges • Familiarization trips • Upgrades, points, and meals • Supplier selection, contract negotiations and commissions • Intellectual property • Conduct while representing the organization	• Business practices • Issue prioritization in vendor selection	• Site selection and related labor, human rights, and human resources issues • Community service

Codes of Conduct for Meeting and Event Professionals

Organizations in this industry should consider addressing a variety of issues that are specific to our industry as part of their code of conduct. As shown in Table 2.5, the first area addresses business operation issues; particularly those that reflect business conduct by professionals. The second and third areas establish the organization's position on environmental and social issues.

Business Operation Issues

■ Gift Exchanges

Gift exchanges are a normal part of conducting business in this industry, and might be as minor as trinkets given away at a tradeshow booth to more elaborate gifts. Each organization should establish a policy to determine what is acceptable for gifts between suppliers and clients. The policy should include specific monetary limits for gifts (e.g., $25 or $50). This should also address what should be done if a gift exceeds this value: For example, should it be returned to the supplier or shared within the organization? The policy should also state when gifts may be exchanged. For example, they may be permitted as a thank-you gift at the conclusion of an event, but not during contract negotiations. Exceptions for business norms in different cultural settings should also be addressed, particularly for organizations that plan global meetings and events.

■ Familiarization Trips

Familiarization trips (often referred to as *fam trips*) are events where a destination will host prospective clients as a way of introducing them to their destination. These are typically co-hosted by local businesses and are offered at little or no cost to the prospective client. This section should address the circumstances under which an invitation should be extended or accepted for a familiarization trip. From a supplier's perspective, as familiarization trips are generally hosted by various partners, to invite an unqualified planner to participate would be a disservice to other contributing partners. Suppliers should be cautious to not confuse quantity of clients over quality of clients. From a planner's perspective, an invitation to a familiarization trip must be accepted only with a reasonable expectation that the destination will be considered for future substantial business opportunities for the hosts.

■ Upgrades, Points, and Meals

Your code of conduct should outline expectations for the acceptance and use of upgrades, hotel and airline points, and meals from suppliers. Some organizations may permit a traveler to keep points for flights and hotel nights for personal use while others may expect these to be remitted to the organization for future business travel. The policy related to points may also distinguish between points earned by a traveler and those earned for booking group business. Most organizations will expect group-booking points to be used for future travel by the organization and not for personal use. The code of conduct should also address when meals and upgrades (hotels and flights) may be accepted.

■ Supplier Selection, Contract Negotiations, and Commissions

It is important to clearly articulate your contract negotiation policies (including areas such as not disclosing confidential bid information from competitors) regarding transparency in selecting suppliers to ensure that your organization protects its professional reputation. According to David Kliman, "If a commission is being earned, it must be transparent to all parties and the commission must be legal. Nothing should be under the table."

■ Intellectual Property

Establishing conduct expectations regarding the use of intellectual property, including agreement to not use confidential information received in proposals, sets a strong internal standard. It also signals to suppliers and partners that they can be confident in sending you information and can assist in increasing the level of quality of bids that you receive.

■ Behavior While Representing the Organization

The code of conduct may also outline acceptable business behavior, particularly when representing the organization at social events. It may also cover acceptable uses of social media.

Bribery and Major Sporting Events

Some major events have had scandals related to real or perceived issues of bribery in the bid process. The 2002 Olympics held in Salt Lake City came under close scrutiny after allegations of bribery of International Olympic Committee Officials were made. Although the

Photo courtesy of iStockphoto/Nick Baker

organizers were eventually acquitted of charges,[8] the allegations were damaging to the reputation of the event and the event organizers. Allegations of this kind have also been made about other major events, including bids for the 2018 and 2022 FIFA World Cup.[9]

Environmental Issues

■ Business Practices

Your code of conduct is an excellent opportunity to outline expectations related to environmental best practices. This may include items such as requirements for the use of sustainable materials and carbon offset policies related to travel.

■ Issue Prioritization in Vendor Selection

It can be a challenge for meeting and event professionals to decide between two different environmental choices. A code of conduct can provide clarity by outlining priorities. For example, third-party certification might be ranked highest, or your organization might place higher importance on other aspects such as waste minimization. Throughout this book we will be providing examples of trade-offs in decisions related to CSR and sustainability. These can be difficult to manage in the absence of a clear code of conduct. We will also be discussing new event standards that are being released that will help provide guidance for meeting and event professionals in making more sustainable choices for their programs. More information about this will be provided in Chapter 9 on measurement.

Social Issues

■ Supplier Selection and Related Labor, Human Rights, and Human Resource Issues

Your supplier selection policies have the potential to help influence ethical behavior. In addressing this in your code of conduct, consider areas such as fair treatment and wages for workers, fair trade product use, the use of child labor, and crossing of picket lines. Supply chain issues present reputation risks for an organization and should be taken into consideration. This will be discussed in greater detail in Chapters 8 and 11.

■ Community Service

Meetings and events have the potential to have a positive impact on communities. Your code of conduct can help strengthen this by including a mandate for community service, including permitted volunteerism by team members or as part of your meeting or event program. The MAUDE framework introduced in Chapter 4 provides guidance on developing community service projects that will be of high value to communities and the event organizers.

In the Absence of a Code of Conduct

Ethics Resources

If your organization does not have a code of conduct to help guide decision making, many other resources are available. According to Joan Eisenstodt, these include the Ethics Resource Center and the Society of Human Resource Professionals.

Many industry associations and professional designations will also have codes of conduct for their members that may serve as a starting point for developing your own code of conduct. Eisenstodt notes that industry codes are designed to be "aspirational," setting broader goals than what may be required by a specific corporate policy. As such, organizations should consider making their codes more specific, measurable, and enforceable and less open to interpretation in order to be effectively utilized in a corporate setting. Sample industry codes of conduct include:

- Convention Industry Council: Certified Meeting Professional (CMP) Program Ethics Statement and Disciplinary Policy
- Meeting Professionals International: Principles of Professionalism
- Professional Convention Management Association: Principles of Professional and Ethical Conduct
- Green Meeting Industry Council: Individual Member Code of Conduct and Partner Code of Conduct

Other Decision-Making Tools

Sometimes you do not have an external reference point, such as a code of conduct or industry standards, to refer to when making a decision about an ethical issue. In these cases, ask yourself some questions:

- Are my actions legal?
- Are my actions truthful?
- Would I be comfortable if my decision were made public in an industry magazine or on Twitter?
- Would I be proud of a family member or co-worker for making this decision? Would they be proud of me?

Ethics and Business Strategy

Organizations run the risk of losing credibility if their actions do not align with their stated mission, vision, and values. Consider the impact on an environmental organization if its meetings and events do not implement sustainable practices.

Many meeting and event planners have codes of conduct or ethical guidelines that address the business operations issues outlined in the previous section. As professionals progress in both strategic and logistical competence, as shown in Figure 2.1, they will both expand the breadth of the areas covered in their codes and guidelines and further integrate them into their decision-making process. An organization that fully integrates social and environmental issues into its business strategy will take this even further by ensuring that these codes and guidelines are applied, reviewed, and systematically incorporated into operations to advance the organization. These integrated meeting and event leaders value ethics as a core competency.

Increasing CSR and Ethics Competency ↑

High CSR/Ethics Focus	**High Integrated Focus**
• Management supports business ethics and CSR. • Management is competent in addressing "green meetings" issues. • Code of conduct for social and environmental issues is applied. • Organizational strategy and sustainability are not yet linked.	• Business strategy, ethics, and CSR are core competencies, with support from all levels of the organization. • Code of conduct covers a broad range of social, environmental, and business issues and is integrated in human resources practices; it is also used extensively for decision making. • Ethics and CSR are leveraged to help achieve organizational objectives.
Low CSR/Ethics and Strategy Focus	**High Strategy Focus**
• Organization may have a code of conduct or ethics policy. • Code of conduct may have little application in day-to-day operations.	• Highly strategic organization. • Code of conduct covers a limited range of social and environmental issues but extensively covers business issues and is integrated in human resource practices. It is used extensively for decision making. • Organizational strategy and sustainability are not yet linked.

Increasing Strategic Competency →

Figure 2.1   Integrated Sustainable Event Management (Ethics)

Ethics and the Law

Although it is natural to assume that actions and behaviors that are legal would also be ethical and hopefully lead to sustainable business practices, there are times when these come into conflict. Chapter 11 addresses how to manage this conflict and ways for meeting and event professionals to protect their legal interests.

Photo Courtesy of iStockphoto/ericsphotography

Chapter Review

Addressing ethical dilemmas can be one of the most difficult challenges faced by professionals. This chapter reviewed many of the ethical dilemmas frequently facing meeting and event professionals, including planner/supplier relationship issues, employer/employee relationship issues, attendee issues, and impact on society and the environment. Categories of ethical dilemmas, and rationalizations used to avoid them, were also explored. A framework for addressing ethical dilemmas with competing values was presented. It is important to recognize the role of culture in shaping ethical perspectives, and this will be presented in greater detail in a subsequent chapter. Finally, recommendations for developing or reviewing a code of conduct using the GBS Codex were presented, along with recommendations for embedding it into an organization's way of conducting business.

Review Questions

For each of the following scenarios:

1. Identify the category of ethical dilemmas being faced (from Table 2.1).
2. Identify potential rationalizations that might be factors (from Table 2.2).
3. Identify applicable GBS Codex principles (from Table 2.4).
4. Formulate a recommendation.

Example:

Dilemma	Category/Categories	Potential Rationalization	Relevant Principles
Accepting and/or offering gifts (including hotel points), entertainment, or trips with no likely future business	• Taking things that don't belong to you • Committing personal decadence	• Everybody else does it. • That's the way it's always been done. • It doesn't really hurt anyone.	• Fiduciary • Property

Recommendation: (Supplier-side) Develop and enforce corporate policies about offering gifts and qualifying prospective planners to be invited on familiarization trips. (Planner-side) Develop and enforce corporate policies about receiving gifts and participation on familiarization trips.

Scenario 1:
> You are a hotel sales manager and you are asked by a third-party meeting planner to include a commission without informing the client.

Scenario 2:
> You are a caterer and you were contracted three months earlier to supply a wild salmon buffet for an event at a set price. Since the time of the contract, wild salmon prices have tripled and you will lose money on the event if you meet the terms of the agreement. You have been advised that farmed salmon is available at a significantly lower price and switching would likely be unnoticed by the client.

Group Exercise: Scenario Discussion #1

You are a meeting planner and are interested in including pre- and post-conference tours with your event. You are not familiar with the local area or attractions, and request a bid from a local destination management company (DMC) to plan and manage these events for you. The DMC sends you a detailed proposal, including several options for pre- and post-events that perfectly meet your needs. In reading the proposal, you realize that you could use this information to book directly with the attractions and tour companies, and therefore avoid paying commissions to the DMC. This would allow you to offer the tours at a more affordable rate to your price-sensitive attendees.

Questions:
1. Apply the framework for approaching ethical dilemmas with competing values to the example above.
2. What are the potential positive and negative implications for the planner if he or she books directly with the attractions and tour companies?
3. If you were an attraction approached by a planner in this situation, how would you respond? How would your actions affect future business with the DMC or the planner?
4. As a DMC, what could you do to protect your intellectual property?

Projects

1. Develop a Code of Conduct:
   a. Develop a code of conduct for a sustainable meeting and event management company. Include specific guidelines related to business operations, as well as environmental and social issues.
   b. Make recommendations for embedding the practices into your organization. Include specific references to performance evaluations and review of the guidelines.

2. Develop a Suitcasing and Outboarding Policy: Develop a policy to prevent suitcasing and outboarding for a convention to be held in your own city. Include information on what constitutes suitcasing and outboarding and opportunities for legitimate participation in the event.

Note: Resources for this project may be available at the website for the International Association of Exhibitions and Events. Please visit the Book Companion Site (located at www.wiley.com/college/henderson) for a complete list of referential websites related to this chapter's content.

Key Terms

- ethical dilemmas
- familiarization trips
- suitcasing
- outboarding
- rationalizations
- Sarbanes-Oxley Act
- values
- culture
- organizational culture
- code of conduct

Notes

1. USGBC, "Greenbuild International Conference and Expo: USGBC Suitcasing and Outboarding Policy." Accessed December 3, 2011, from 2010.greenbuildexpo.org/Files/2010SuitcasingandOutboarding.pdf.
2. M. M. Jennings, *Business: Its Legal, Ethical and Global Environment, 9th ed.* (Cincinnati, OH: Cengage Learning, 2012).
3. Ibid.
4. J. L. Badaracco Jr., "The Discipline of Building Character," *Harvard Business Review* (March–April 1998): 115–124.
5. Ibid.
6. R. Bailes, "Facilitating Payments: Culturally Acceptable or Unacceptably Corrupt?" *Business Ethics: A European Review*, 15 (3) (2006): 293–298.
7. L. Paine, R. Deshpandé, J. D. Margolis, and K. E. Bettcher, "Up to Code: Does Your Company's Conduct Meet World-Class Standards?" *Harvard Business Review* (December 2005): 122–133.

8. Lex Hemphill, "OLYMPICS; Acquittals End Bid Scandal That Dogged Winter Games," *The New York Times* (December 3, 2003). Accessed December 3, 2011, from www.nytimes.com/2003/12/06/sports/olympics-acquittals-end-bid-scandal-that-dogged-winter-games.html?ref=davidrjohnson.

9. Press Association, "Fifa World Cup bidding process not 'fit for purpose', says Lord Coe," *The Guardian* (June 5, 2011). Accessed December 3, 2011, from www.guardian.co.uk/football/2011/jun/05/fifa-world-cup-lord-coe.

Springboard to Sustainability.
Photograph courtesy of iStockphoto/Hulton Archive

CHAPTER 3

Strategies for Sustainable Meetings

"I'm not running for sainthood. I just happen to think that in life we need to be a little like the farmer, who puts back into the soil what he takes out."

—*Paul Newman, American actor, entrepreneur, humanitarian (1925–2008)*

Learning Objectives

After reading this chapter, you will be able to:

- Use a simple decision model to guide basic sustainable meetings and events decisions by applying a meetings ecosystem approach.

- Follow the decision model to see where your primary triple bottom line issues of people, planet, and profit might arise along the path and what issues you should be aware of when making decisions specific to your meeting/event.

- Assess food and beverage for meetings/events based on the carbon footprint resulting from where it is from, how it is moved, what it is, and how it was produced.

- Assess service providers based on their policies, training, and programs as they relate to environmental sustainability and social impacts.

- Recognize the impact that you and your decisions about sustainability have on you, your organization, and both local and global communities.

- Relate the concepts presented in this chapter to more detailed information in other chapters specifically relating to environmental sustainability, ethics, measurement, reporting, and sustainable sourcing.

Introduction

This chapter complements but does not repeat what other books and resources on green meetings will tell you, including *The Complete Guide to Greener Meetings and Events* in the Wiley Event Series. It offers a **systems view** (the process of understanding how elements of the whole relate to each other) of sustainable meetings to help guide you on your journey to make better sustainable decisions. Think of a meeting or event as being an **ecosystem**, a web of decisions made up of separate parts that interact to form the whole. We will use a **decision model**, or a framework that presents information about sustainability decisions, to assist you in making relevant decisions for your unique meeting/event, to illuminate sustainable pathways for a simple meetings and events ecosystem. There are many different **decision points**, or points in time when a specific course of action needs to be decided on through evaluating alternatives, including balancing minimum acceptable levels for each of people, planet and profit dimensions, and choosing a solution. This model is intended to help meeting professionals make better informed, and more strategic, sustainability decisions. We will also explore specific subsystems important to environmentally sustainable meetings and events including food and beverage and hotel services.

Linkages

Meeting and event professionals, like any other kind of professionals, sometimes behave in a fashion similar to the blind men in a famous Indian fable, who are asked to describe an elephant.

How would you describe an elephant if you could not see it?
Courtesy iStockphoto/Harry Kolenbrander

Each of the men touches a different part of the animal; one touches his tusk and declares that the elephant is like a pipe; a second touches the elephant's leg and is convinced that the elephant is like a pillar; a third encounters the tail and believes that the elephant is like a rope. The moral of the story is, of course, that we usually make our decisions based on what we know. Learning a systems view of a relatively simple event structure will help you understand its subsystems more completely, and be able to understand how they relate to the whole. A systems approach will also encourage meeting and event professionals to ask relevant questions about sustainability while providing guidance as to what the sustainable solutions could be. We will be using a systems approach in many of the chapters in this book, including our final chapter where we apply backcasting and scenario planning for identifying sustainability-related strategies.

The Meeting and Event Ecosystem

Although each meeting or event is different based on organizational objectives, audience, and purpose, meetings and events also display some remarkable similarities. This makes it possible to use a simplified model of a meeting/event ecosystem to illustrate sustainable systems thinking. The ecosystem model we have created uses the basic elements of meetings and events as sustainability decision points, where the meeting professional must consider various options that affect overall event sustainability, including social, environmental, and economic sustainability—or people, planet, and profit.

The use of a systems approach has its roots in two economic theories, both with implications for sustainability. The first is **cradle-to-cradle design**, which is a holistic framework considering economics, environment, and social systems. The point of cradle-to-cradle design is to create a system that works efficiently and is waste-free. This goes beyond the traditional linear economy, which works on a "make-take-dispose" system, where liability stops at the point of sale.[1] The second is **circular economy**, which advocates a closed-loop approach that mimics natural systems, where the waste generated is then reused in the system. The circular economy has five principles[2]:

1. *Waste is food.* Eliminate waste that cannot be reused.
2. *Diversity is strength.* Diverse systems are more robust and more resilient in crises.
3. *Energy should come from renewable sources.* This mimics natural systems.
4. *Prices must tell the truth.* People use prices as cues for value, so prices must reflect the real cost of an activity or product.
5. *Thinking in systems is key.* Understanding how things influence each other within a whole is important to make sustainable decisions.

According to Walter Stahel, whose writings in the 1970s and beyond helped define not only cradle-to-cradle design and the circular economy, but also the concept of sustainability, these type of closed-loop systems create a functional economy: "The economic objective of the functional economy is to create the highest possible use value for the longest possible time while consuming as few material resources and energy as possible."[3]

The ecosystem approach that we use here advocates a system that is similarly holistic, taking into account not only environmental issues but social and economic systems. The purpose of using an ecosystem approach is to help meeting professionals make better sustainable decisions. Here is a five-step model[4] to making better decisions as suggested by Harvard Business School:

1. Create context to make good decisions possible.
2. Frame the issue to better understand what we are trying to decide.
3. Generate alternatives.
4. Evaluate the feasibility, risk, and sustainable implications of each choice.
5. Choose the best alternative.

Used in conjunction with the ecosystem approach we have created, this decision model creates a springboard to better sustainability decisions, by creating the context for making sustainable decisions specifically for meetings and events, and framing the sustainability issues. Meeting and event professionals are then in a good position to generate alternatives, evaluate their options, and choose the best sustainable alternative. The ecosystem approach focuses on steps 1 and 2 of the decision model.

As you use the model, keep in mind that making decisions will involve **trade-offs**, or situations where being able to take advantage of one quality or aspect in relation to goods and services means not being able to take advantage of another. Even simple decisions can involve trade-offs, and meetings and events can be of various levels of complexity. Sustainability itself is not an absolute condition; technology improves, world events occur, science illuminates the natural world more precisely, and people change behavior. In response, sustainability standards, expectations, and imperatives change, too. Any decision has an element of uncertainty to it; personal beliefs and organizational priorities will also influence the sustainability decisions made by meeting and event professionals. The interplay of a number of factors, including cost, risk, meeting goals and objectives, and imperfect knowledge will all help to determine the choices made. More information on decision making with trade-offs is included in chapter 2, Business Ethics.

The decision model we have created reflects some of the components of more rigorous mathematical and analytical models used in economics and other sciences, such as decision trees and influence diagrams. However, it is much simpler and is created specifically for sustainable meetings and events. For each section of the ecosystem, we will look at the original decision to be made—the why, where, how, what, and who aspects—and then outline the sustainability issues that are brought into play. For these issues, we then ask specific questions about its environmental, economic, and community impacts. Sustainable decisions are then presented, but keep in mind that these are outcomes that disregard the complexity of event decisions, as already outlined. They are simply presented as sustainable outcomes to strive for, noted as "all other things being equal."

The Why of the Meeting Ecosystem

Meetings and events exist in the context of an organization. The organization, or its goals and objectives, drive the need for a meeting or event. This is the **why dimension**. In fact, the first question in a sustainable meeting and event decision model is probably, "Does the meeting/event

Figure 3.1   Sustainability Impacts of the Hamlet Decision (the Why Dimension)

help us accomplish our goals?" If there is no reason to have a meeting or event and it takes place anyhow, then we will have wasted not only time but also other resources; we will have generated carbon and waste; and we may have contributed to social problems along the supply chain. We have dubbed this **the Hamlet decision**, after the famous soliloquy in Shakespeare's *Hamlet*: "To be, or not to be, that is the question."

Note from Figure 3.1 that if the decision is made to go ahead and invest resources to further organizational goals, there are social, environmental, and economic consequences in terms of a waste stream, expenses, and human impacts. These impacts can be either positive or negative, depending on how they are managed and whether they can be mitigated (see Chapter 5 for a discussion of *externalities*).

If there is no reason to have a meeting, don't.
Photo courtesy of Elizabeth Henderson

The Where of the Event Ecosystem

Not all meeting or event professionals need to decide where the event will be held. Sometimes destinations themselves host large meetings or events, such as large sporting events, festivals, political rallies, or cultural showcases. But for many meetings and events, such as those hosted by corporations or associations, choosing a destination is a key decision point, and one that sparks many sustainability-related decisions that revolve around environmental sustainability, including energy use, waste production and management, economic sustainability, and social equity. As shown in Figure 3.2, this is the **where dimension** of the ecosystem model.

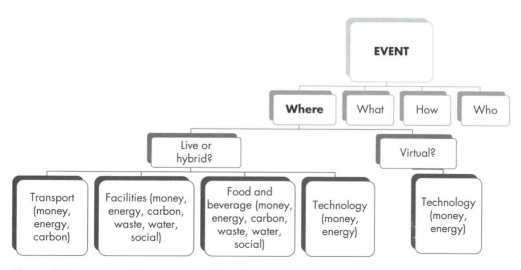

Figure 3.2 Sustainability Impacts of the Where Decision

Geographic Context Matters: Maintaining water quantity and quality is important in a national park. Bow Lake, Banff National Park, Alberta, Canada.
Photo courtesy of Elizabeth Henderson

Geographic Context Matters: Quantity of water may be a controlling factor in a desert.
Photo courtesy of Elizabeth Henderson

The first "where" decision is not perhaps the first one that comes to mind: meeting and event professionals should consider the virtual landscape as well as a geographic one. This decision is, therefore, first of all, whether the meeting/event will be exclusively face-to-face, exclusively virtual, or a hybrid with both face-to-face and virtual elements.

As you can see in Figure 3.2, making the "where" decision has several sustainability decisions embedded in it. If the decision is made to have a purely face-to-face meeting or a hybrid meeting, this triggers decisions about transportation of both goods and people, facilities that will be used such as hotels or meeting venues, any food or beverages that will be offered, and the use of technology. We will look at these more closely when we discuss the "what" decisions later in this chapter.

Issues to consider (the context) and questions to be asked (the framework) when making the "where" decisions are suggested in Tables 3.1 and 3.2.

When considering the *where* decision, we observe that:

- *How far* people and materials travel matters.
- Destination *infrastructure* matters.
- The *geographic context* matters.
- The *cost of alternatives* matters.
- *How people are treated* legally and customarily matters.

Table 3.1   Examples of Destination-Related Sustainability Issues

Planet	Profit	People
• Energy used to transport people and goods • Carbon emissions from transport • Recycling and waste handling systems • Ecology/geographic context (i.e., desert, national park)	• Cost of transporting people and goods • Relative cost of hotels and venues compared with alternatives • Economic benefit to host community	• Human rights • Labor rights • Local goods and services

Table 3.2   Decision Model for Destination-Related Sustainability Outcomes

	Questions	Optimal Decision Outcomes
Planet	• Where will the majority of participants, including staff, travel from? • How much energy will it take to get people from their original city to the ultimate destination, including taxis, public transit, train, or air? • What is the carbon equivalent of its use and combustion? • What systems are in place in the various destinations to handle waste streams and recycling? • How much energy will be needed to transport goods or other service providers? • How much carbon will be generated to move goods and services to the destination? • What is the **geographic context**, or specific environmental issues at the destination, such as shortages of water?	If all other things are equal: • Choose a destination close to the majority of participants. • Reduce the amount of energy expended on transportation. • Reduce the amount of carbon generated both through distance traveled and through use of low-carbon alternatives such as public transit. • Choose a destination with well-developed waste and recycling systems. • Choose a destination that does not have endemic issues in specific environmental areas.
Profit	• What are the relative costs between different destinations? • What are the relative costs of facilities, such as hotels or meetings venues, compared between possible destinations?	If all other things are equal: • Choose the destination that offers best value for money and allows you to meet your sustainability objectives.
People	• Does the destination have any human rights issues, such as discrimination on the basis of sex, religion, or place of origin? • Does the destination have ongoing issues or a record of poor labor rights, including lack of a minimum wage, suppressing strikes or unions, or forced or child labor?	If all other things are equal: • Choose destinations that have good human rights records. • Choose destinations that uphold labor laws and do not use underpaid, forced, or child labor.

Low carbon transportation in China.
Photo courtesy of Elizabeth Henderson

In tables 3.2 and 3.4, we recommend choosing the more sustainable alternative if all other things are equal. In many cases, organizations may also have minimum requirements related to people, planet or profit that will also influence the decision. If the decision is made to use technology, either as a stand-alone or as part of a hybrid meeting solution, questions about both the ability of the technology to meet your needs and its environmental pedigree need to be answered. (More information on hybrid meetings is provided in Chapter 11.)

Should I use a technological solution? Sustainability issues related to using technology for virtual or hybrid meetings/events are suggested in Tables 3.3 (context) and 3.4 (framework).

Table 3.3   Examples of Sustainability Issues for Using a Technological Component

Planet	Profit	People
• Change in travel and transportation • Energy use of technology	• Cost of technology • Change in number of people the event can reach • Risk of meeting/event interruption	• Access for people with disabilities • Access for people with limited financial resources • Access for those in geographically remote areas

Table 3.4   Decision Model for Integration of Technology into Destination Decisions

	Questions	Optimal Decision Outcomes
Planet	• Will the use of technology decrease travel for people and goods? • Will technology reduce the use of energy and the creation of carbon?	If all other things are equal: • Use technology if it decreases the use of resources and still meets the objectives of the meeting/event.
Profit	• How much does it cost? • How effective is it in comparison to how much it costs? • Will it increase or decrease the number of people in our target audience who can attend? • Will it mitigate any risks that would otherwise impact revenues, such as a travel interruption due to weather, war, or terrorism?	If all other things are equal: • Choose technology that offers the best value for money, based on your sustainability objectives. • Use technology if it increases the reach of your event into your target audience. • Use technology if it mitigates risks, such as when the event is business-critical.

(continued)

	Questions	Optimal Decision Outcomes
People	• Will use of technology increase access for people with disabilities, in remote areas, or without sufficient financial ability to attend in person? • How effective is the technology in meeting your goals? • Is the technology reliable?	If all other things are equal: • Use a technological solution if it provides better access for the target audience who may be disabled, geographically remote, or without the financial ability to attend. • Use technology that helps you meet your goals most effectively.

The "What" of the Event Ecosystem: Materials

In the decision model, the **what dimension** refers to the materials needed for your meeting/event. As we saw previously, certain decisions are triggered by earlier decisions, in this case, where (live, virtual, or hybrid) the meeting or event will take place. This could include anything from audiovisual equipment, décor, and staging to nametags, raw materials for building facilities, and food and beverage. Obviously, the specific materials used will vary for each meeting/event, and will depend on type of event (e.g., a sporting event, a sales launch, a conference, or a political summit), size of event, and even the location of the meeting/event. Figure 3.3 shows only some of the possibilities.

As you can see from Figure 3.3, the "what" decision also creates sustainability decision points that affect outcomes. Each of these areas creates the need to make a sustainability decision (a sustainability decision point). The nature of the decision will rest with the specific item. Possible models for sustainability decision points are those in new sustainable event standards, such as the relevant areas of APEX (possibly communications, audiovisual, on-site office, food and beverage, exhibits) or selected core indicators from one or more of the Global Reporting Initiative event organizers sector supplement categories of economic, environmental, labor and decent work, human rights, society, product responsibility, legacy, and sourcing.

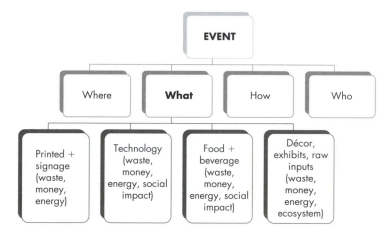

Figure 3.3   Sustainability Impacts of the What Decision

There is a set of questions particularly important to ask about materials, based on the following observations:

- Where it is *from* matters.
- How it is *moved* matters.
- What it *is* matters.
- How it was *procured* matters.
- The *waste* it generates matters.

The context and framework for sustainability decision points related to materials are shown in Tables 3.5 (context) and 3.6 (framework).

Table 3.5 Examples of Sustainability Issues for Materials

Planet	Profit	People
• Energy used to produce or transport materials/services • Carbon footprint of energy and resource use • Waste generated/ability to recycle materials • Sustainably produced/renewable materials • Compostable materials • Donations	• Cost of materials or services • Economic benefit to host community • Cost avoidance (decide not to purchase) • Cost savings (purchase only what is needed)	• Ability to source in the local community • Fair trade or other sustainable sourcing • Ability to receive donations • Development of capabilities and capacity to provide products

Table 3.6 Decision Model for Procurement of Materials

	Questions	Optimal Decision Outcomes
Planet	• How is it produced? • How much energy is consumed during production and transport? • How much waste is produced through its production, use, and disposal? • How much of the material can be reused, recycled, or donated?	If all other things are equal: • Choose goods that have a lower energy footprint. Use eco-labels to help if needed. • Choose goods that are transported with a lower carbon footprint, smaller distances, or by less carbon-intensive methods. • Choose goods that do not generate waste or have a low waste footprint. • Choose materials that are recyclable, can be composted, or have an end-of-life use in the community and can be donated.

(continued)

	Questions	**Optimal Decision Outcomes**
Profit	• How much does it cost? • Do I need to purchase it, or is it only "nice to have"? • Are there substitutes or more sustainable alternatives that will cost less? • What steps can I take to reduce the total amount purchased?	If all other things are equal: • Choose the material that offers the best value for money and enables you to meet your sustainability objectives. • Do not buy materials that are not directly related to the objectives of your meeting/event. This also positively impacts your waste stream. • Reduce total amount procured when possible.
People	• Is it available locally? • Can it be sourced from fair trade or other environmentally or socially supportive vendors? • Does the supply chain meet environmental and social minimums, such as being manufactured with good human rights and labor practices? • What products relating to the meeting/event would the community be interested in receiving?	If all other things are equal: • Choose local products if they are also low energy and low waste but don't automatically assume that local is more sustainable. • Choose products that are manufactured in locations that support human rights and labor rights. • Donate goods/services to the community that meet a specific need.

In Depth: Food and Beverage Industry

There is probably no better way to illustrate that where it is from matters, how it is moved matters, what it is matters, how it was procured matters, and the waste it generates matters than by looking closely at sustainable choices for food and beverages. Table 3.7 offers some general sustainability issues around food and beverages in environmental, economic, and community subgroups.

Carbon Footprints of Food

One of the ways to assess the sustainability of food is by looking at its carbon footprint relative to other available options. Although we will explore more relative to carbon and carbon footprints in

The Vancouver Convention Centre proudly operates a scratch kitchen using primarily fresh, local, and seasonal ingredients—from freshly caught seafood to produce from nearby farms, and pastries baked from scratch. This commitment to promoting and using locally grown products means less energy consumption for transporting products to the facility.
Photograph courtesy of the Vancouver Convention Centre

Table 3.7 Examples of Sustainability Issues for Food and Beverage

Planet	Profit	People
• Resource choice • Resource use • Where it is produced • Waste produced • Energy used to produce, process, and transport • Method of production	• Cost savings • Market availability • Market price • Cash flow	• Health and safety • Labor standards • Local sourcing • Cultural importance of food source • Sustainable sourcing

Table 3.8 Salmon—Where It Is from and How It Is Produced Matters

Food	Source	Carbon Equivalent (CO2e)[5]
Salmon	Farmed	1203 g
	Wild, far away	991 g
	Wild, regional	75 g

Chapter 5, for now it is sufficient to recognize that the energy used to create, transport, and dispose of things can be expressed in grams of carbon dioxide equivalents, or CO_2e. This is the measure that we will be using in the next series of tables so we can compare the environmental impact of different items more easily. In this series of tables, you will be able to see the differences in carbon footprints caused by where things are from, what they are, and how they are produced.

Where it is from and how it is produced matters. Pretend that you are a meeting professional planning a menu for a specific function related to your meeting/event. You are trying to plan a sustainable meeting, and you want the menu to reflect good sustainable choices. Take a look at Table 3.8. What this illustrates is different kinds of salmon, all of which are available to the chef at your hotel or meeting venue.

As you can see from Table 3.8, farmed salmon has the highest carbon footprint, at 1203 grams, as opposed to wild regional salmon, at 75 grams.[6] This reflects several components involved in the harvesting of this seafood, probably including processed food for farmed salmon, energy used by harvesting ships for wild salmon, and transport for wild salmon harvested far away. Note that meeting and event professionals choosing wild regional salmon may have other factors to consider other than its lower carbon footprint; it would not be a good choice, for example, if it were endangered or scarce in that area. Sustainable choices are about balance and trade-offs, given the information available.

What it is matters. You've decided on wild regional salmon for the dinner, but now you need to choose a lunch menu protein item for the same event. The chef has offered several choices, including beef, chicken, turkey, pork, lamb, and a tofu dish for vegetarians. Take a look at Table 3.9 to see how these protein items stack up.

As you can see in Table 3.9, the kind of protein matters in terms of the carbon footprint it generates. For example, beef and lamb have relatively high carbon footprints; this is because they are ruminants and emit methane. Cows and sheep may also be less efficient at turning their food (like grass and grain) into meat than chicken or pigs.

Table 3.9 What It Is Matters

Protein (4 oz/113 gram portions)	Type	Carbon Equivalent (CO2e)[7]
Beef	Prime rib, roasted	4838 g
	Tenderloin, grilled	7641 g
Poultry	Chicken breast, grilled	401 g
	Turkey, roasted	613 g
Lamb	Chops, roasted	2034 g
Pork	Chops, grilled	753 g
Tofu	Grilled	1110 g

Table 3.10 How It Is Grown Matters

Vegetable (4 oz/113 gram portions)	How it is Grown	Carbon Equivalent (CO2e)
Mixed root vegetables[8]	Local hothouse	767 g
	Local and seasonal	95 g
Tomatoes[9]	Local, seasonal, organic	45 g
	On the vine, hothouse, cherry, nonseasonal	5650 g
Carrots[10]	Local, in season	28 g
	Baby carrots, shipped	113 g

How it is grown matters. So, you've chosen a protein for your lunch, finally settling on roast turkey and grilled tofu for the vegetarians. Now you need to choose vegetables to go with it. You ask the chef for local options, because you have heard that local is the best sustainable choice. Refer to Table 3.10 to see how local vegetables rate.

As you can easily see in Table 3.10, procuring vegetables that are local and in-season has a far lower carbon footprint than vegetables that are also grown locally but in an energy-intensive hothouse, or those that have been shipped from elsewhere. You end up choosing mixed-root vegetables that are in season to go with your roast turkey. Note, however, that not all greenhouses are created equal and some may be using alternative energy sources that are low in carbon emissions. For example, a carbon offset project funded by Offsetters.ca made it possible for a greenhouse facility in British Columbia, Canada, to convert to a biomass boiler for its heat requirements, reducing annual operating emissions by 7,500 tCO2e relative to the natural gas baseline.[11]

Locally grown peppers at the Bearspaw Farmers Market, Calgary, Canada.
Photo courtesy of Elizabeth Henderson

Case Study: Sustainable Seafood

Sustainable seafood provides another opportunity to demonstrate that where it is from, how it is moved, how it was produced, and what it is matters.

What It Is

Check that the fish or seafood is able to withstand the fishing pressure without endangering the species. Consider if the lifecycle makes it more vulnerable and if it exists in abundance. Many species are considered endangered in certain parts of the world; what is sustainable in one area might not be considered so in another. For

Freshly caught seafood, Venice, Italy Fish Market.
Photo courtesy of Elizabeth Henderson

example, using information available from the Monterey Bay Aquarium, compare and contrast seafood that is considered a "Best Choice" in each region; a small sample is in Table 3.11.

Notice that the only fish recommended consistently in this example in all areas are halibut, char, and Dungeness crab. This reflects sustainability decisions made by Monterey Bay Aquarium.[12] Sustainable seafood choices change over time. The information above should be verified for a particular event, season, and location. Resources are provided at the end of the chapter.

The "How" Dimension of the Event Ecosystem: Services

The **how dimension** of the decision model refers to service providers within the meeting/event ecosystem. Services procured by each meeting/event will of course be different due to more or less complexity, where the event is, what materials have been procured, the objectives, and the type of meeting/event. Some common services might include audiovisual technologists, hotels, meeting/event venues (unless you are building venues for a major event, at which point they would likely be classified as materials), caterers, or decorators, as can be seen in Figure 3.4.

As Figure 3.4 shows, services have both their own set of **sustainability decision points** relating to the people within them and the materials they use and procure. While we will explore procurement of materials and services in more detail in Chapter 8 on sustainable sourcing, this decision model will familiarize you with the issues that need to be balanced in procuring materials and services. Emerging event standards, including the Global Reporting Initiative (GRI) event organizer sector supplement and ISO 20121 for sustainable event management (both discussed in more detail in Chapter 10), can help guide the identification of issues, including standard disclosures on governance and management approach, and indicators in the labor practices and decent work, human rights, and society sections.

How It Is Produced

Harvesting: Some methods are not selective, meaning that other species (including some that may be endangered) might be inadvertently caught. Increasing awareness of dolphins and sea turtles as *bycatch,* the term for the nontarget species, has led to innovations in fishing methods. Watch for dolphin-friendly symbols on tuna as an example.

Aquaculture: Also known as farmed seafood, aquaculture can be a sustainable seafood source, provided it is managed to restrict discharge of waste, disease, and parasite transfer and escapes.

As well, plant-based feed ensures that more seafood is created than used in production. New developments in closed-containment farming are improving aquaculture sustainability.

Environmental impact: Some fishing methods, including dredging, are damaging to the sea floor. As well, consider if the species is high on the food chain. Removal of top predators can disrupt other species.

A more in-depth analysis of sustainable seafood issues can be found on the Ocean Wise website.

Table 3.11   Best Choice Seafood by Region (Subject to change)

Region	Selected "Best Choice" Seafood
U.S. West Coast[13]	Pacific halibut, Arctic char, Dungeness crab, BC spot prawns, BC/ Alaskan sablefish, spiny lobster (California or Mexico), white seabass
U.S. Northeast[14]	Pacific halibut, Arctic char, stone or Dungeness crab, mackerel
U.S. Southeast[15]	Arctic char, Pacific halibut, stone or Dungeness crab, mackerel, freshwater prawn, wreckfish
U.S. Central[16]	Arctic char, Pacific halibut, stone or Dungeness crab, mackerel, perch, whitefish

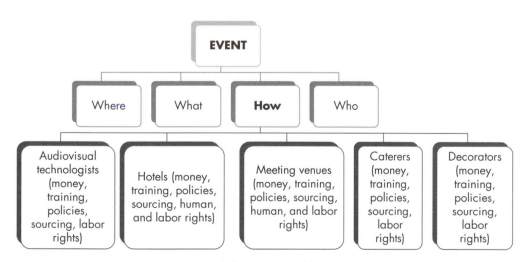

Figure 3.4   Sustainability Impacts of the How Decision

Based once again on observation, the most important qualities of sustainable services, including facilities, are as follows:

- Who *works there* matters.
- How they *implement* sustainability policies matters.
- How they *train* people matters.
- How they *treat* people matters.
- How they *source materials* matters.

See Tables 3.12 and 3.13.

Table 3.12 Examples of Sustainability Issues for Services

Planet	Profit	People
• Sustainable procurement (purchasing) • Environmental policies • Environmental programs • Certification • Standards	• Cost of services • Cost avoidance • Cost savings	• Sustainability training • Diversity • Labor rights • Human rights • Management support

Table 3.13 Decision Model for Services

	Questions	Optimal Decision Outcomes
Planet	• Does the service provider have environmental or sustainability policies? • Are they enforced? • Does the service provider have environmental certification or eco-labeling, or do they use accepted standards? • Is there a sustainable procurement policy in place and is it followed?	If all other things are equal: • Choose service providers who have environmental or sustainability policies, and enforce them. • Choose providers who have certifications, eco-labels or who have achieved industry sustainability standards.
Profit	• How much does the service cost? • Is it needed to meet the goals of the meeting/event? • What are the alternatives?	If all other things are equal: • Choose the service that offers the best value for money and enables you to meet your sustainability objectives.

(continued)

	Questions	Optimal Decision Outcomes
People	• How does the service provider train their staff? How often? • Is it part of the hiring and on-boarding process for new employees? • Does the service provider have a good record of human rights? • Does the service provider have a good record of labor rights? • Is their workforce diverse?	If all other things are equal: • Choose service providers that train their staff regularly on environmental and sustainability aspects of their work. • Choose providers who practice diversity in hiring practices. • Choose service providers who have good labor and human rights records.

In-Depth: The Portland Doubletree Hotel

The Doubletree Hotel in Portland, Oregon, has many sustainability accolades, including being the first property in Oregon to achieve Green Seal certification. It is also Energy Star certified. Steve Faulstick, the area general manager for the Westmont Hospitality Group, which owns the hotel, believes that people are the key to sustainability:

> *To us, it is the most important part. Culture is more than a buzzword for us, it's the foundation for how we run our business. We thrive on a culture of respect, dignity and character. We know that by 'treating our people right' that will convey to our customers and our supply chain.*
>
> *Over the years the team has challenged us to serve our community, and that has taken form by serving meals twice a month at the Ronald McDonald House, serving holiday meals to our local fire departments, volunteering to clean our park, partnering with a homeless shelter to provide food, and an endless amount of support and service to organizations like the American Cancer Society, Susan G. Komen, Leukemia and Lymphoma Society, and many others. Another clear example is through our award winning food systems program. The team has worked very hard to source locally, supporting our local community and helping small business owners like farmers, cheese artisans, brewers, fisherman, and ranchers. The team isn't forced to do business this way, it's common sense and they get it. The team has selected the hotel four times as one of the 100 Best Workplaces in Oregon. I believe our focus on the 'people' part is the primary reason.*

The hotel does not have a sustainability policy (it does have an environmental purchasing policy) per se. However, Faulstick said, "We do not use what you might call a mainstream policy, yet. We've integrated sustainability as our core business value, not just a novelty or niche." He said, "We've pointed people to Andrew Savitz's quote in the *Triple Bottom Line*, which states, 'a sustainable corporation is one that creates profit for it's shareholders, while protecting the environment, and improving the lives of those with whom it interacts.' That is the compass we use for everything we do." The website for the Portland Doubletree also offers a sustainability pledge:

• Lead by example, sharing our successes and failures with our community and industry partners.

- Hold every decision to the standard of our triple bottom line: benefiting the community, providing the best workplace for our employees, and enhancing our guest experience.
- We look to grow our business responsibly, by tracking the progress of our efforts and by continuously seeking areas for improvement.
- And, above all, to maintain transparency in all of these efforts.[17]

Faulstick again emphasizes that sustainability relies on people:

We start with recruitment of new employees. All of our jobs are green jobs, and we point people to looking at who we are even before they apply. It is then emphasized through the interview process, orientation, in day one training . . . and then throughout their daily jobs. We have a defined Green Team, although we consider our entire staff part of that team. It is an all-inclusive process that teaches the staff what sustainability is (and is not), and allows them to create and improve their own areas of expertise based on those principles.

To ensure that sustainability remains top of mind, the Doubletree implements a training program. "We have several methods in which we do this. We've utilized the Natural Step for many of our key leaders, which has provided us all with a framework for what we are doing. I work to educate and challenge my department heads on running a responsible business, and allow them to drive that within their disciplines. We have a focus on the triple bottom line, which provides clarity for all of our decisions in the hotel."

Ensuring that the hotel has a sustainable supply chain is also a key consideration. Faulstick emphasizes both this and the practical application of trade-offs. "Using the triple bottom line lens, our decision makers are able to discern the most sustainable products to bring into the hotel, which aren't necessarily the greenest, and certainly not the cheapest. Very seldom does a product fit all three definitions, but it gives them a guideline in which to choose products or services 'guilt free.' For us, it's all about idea sharing, creativity, and research. Without the defining triple bottom line lens, they can all be futile efforts."

Chef Steven Ward of the Doubletree Hotel, Portland, Oregon, with locally caught salmon.
Photo courtesy of M. McIlwraith

From a food and beverage perspective, executive Chef Steven Ward at the Portland Doubletree Hotel has made significant strides in sourcing sustainable products. An excellent example is how the hotel purchases wild salmon. Working with the Columbia River Inter-Tribal Fish Commission (CRITFC), Chef Ward and his team identified a Yakama Indian Nation fisherman who was able to provide enough Columbia River wild salmon to meet their annual needs. The purchase allows the hotel to buy directly from the fisherman, avoiding intermediaries and therefore reducing costs. It also provides the Doubletree with a high-quality product with a lower carbon footprint. Chef Ward comments that they needed to look at the return on investment of making a large single purchase of this nature: fortunately, the hotel's management was able to see the long-term financial savings, even though it meant higher up-front costs.

Chef Ward comments, "Meeting planners can change the industry if they demand for it to be sustainable." His recommendations for planners include:

1. Provide chefs with flexibility to use sustainable products that are available at the time of the event, rather than trying to determine the menu far in advance, when it will be difficult to predict the most sustainable options.
2. Communicate your priorities and budget restrictions. This will allow the chef to identify the most suitable menu to suit your needs. In some cases, there will be trade-offs, such as locally sourced or organic produce: by identifying your priorities for one over the other, the chef is better equipped to make recommendations.

The "Who" Dimension of the Event Ecosystem

We have left the who dimension for last, not because it is unimportant but because it is the thread that weaves the ecosystem together. It is people who make decisions about the where, what, and how dimensions, and this creates the sustainability ecosystem for your meeting/event. The decisions that meeting and event professionals make about sustainability have an effect on not only you, your organization, and its stakeholders, but have a broader impact in the world, both locally and globally, on environmental sustainability, economic prosperity, and social justice. Sustainability still comes down to human decisions and actions. It is a personal decision with global repercussions. Many people may think that their actions, decisions, or meeting/event is too small to make a difference; it is, however, the **cumulative impact** (something that may be relatively insignificant on its own that has increasing, incremental importance over time) of many small decisions that have a powerful effect on sustainable outcomes.

When assessing the who dimension as shown in figure 3.5, it is important to consider that:

- It matters if it uses *too many resources.*
- It matters if *people and communities* are negatively impacted.
- It matters how *you implement sustainability* through policies, training, standards, measurement, and reporting.
- It *still matters* if it doesn't directly affect you or your organization.

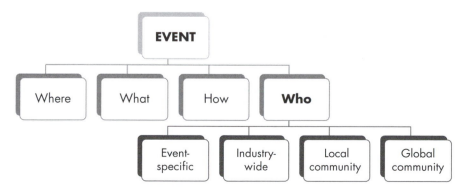

Figure 3.5   Sustainability Impacts of the Who Dimension

Five-Step Decision Model

In the first part of this chapter, we introduced you to a five-step model for making decisions:

1. Create context to make good decisions possible.
2. Frame the issue to better understand what we are trying to decide.
3. Generate alternatives.
4. Evaluate the feasibility, risk, and sustainable implications of each choice.
5. Choose the best alternative.

Throughout this chapter, we have tried to complete the first two steps, by setting the context of sustainability issues and giving you a framework for assessing these issues. The next three steps are up to meeting and event professionals to generate alternatives, evaluate options, and choose the best option in the specific context of their meeting/event.

An Aid to Decision Making: Sustainable Event Standards

It matters if it uses too many resources. New event sustainability standards are emerging to help make those decisions, measure their impact, and report on them to stakeholders (there is more detailed information in the chapters of this book on ethics, social sustainability, measurement, and reporting). For environmentally sustainable meetings, the APEX/ASTM green meeting standards provide quantitative baselines on progressively more rigorous levels for meeting professionals to strive for in collaboration with their suppliers. The Global Reporting Initiative (GRI) event organizers supplement does not offer specific numerical baselines, but it does specify areas of environmental impact to measure and report.

It matters if people or communities are negatively affected. The social side of sustainability, which is explored in more detail in chapter 4 on social responsibility and culture and in Chapter 6 on shared value and strategic corporate social responsibility, is also explicitly included in the GRI event organizers sector supplement. The supplement has core indicators for meeting and event professionals in areas such as recruitment and training; nondiscrimination, freedom of association, and collective bargaining; child and forced labor; local engagement projects, impact assessments and other legacy projects; impact of initiatives on inclusion and accessibility; and health, wellness, and safety of stakeholders, as well as stakeholder satisfaction.

It matters how you implement sustainability through policies, training, standards, measurement, and reporting. To assist with areas that will define your policies and management approach, both the GRI event organizer sector supplement and the ISO 20121 (British Standard 8901's next evolution) give direction on policies, training, measurement, and reporting.

It still matters even if it doesn't directly affect you or your organization. Sustainable event standards also look at indirect impacts of activities, in the environmental, economic, and social realms. Stakeholder identification and engagement are key concepts in the GRI event organizer sector supplement and in ISO 20121, as is the impact of meeting/event activities on the environment (including greenhouse gases, waste, and other environmental impacts), and the development and impact of infrastructure and services for public benefit.

Chapter Review

In this chapter, we introduced a systems view to guide meeting/event professionals to make better sustainability decisions. Using an ecosystem approach, we presented a decision model to frame sustainability decisions. The *why* dimension helps you to determine if you need an event. The *where* dimension offers decision points based on both technology (live, virtual, or hybrid) and geography (destination). The *what* dimension considers the materials needed for meetings/ events and sets the context based on where it is from, how it is moved, what it is, how it was procured, and how much waste it generates, with specific reference to food and beverage and sustainable seafood.

The *how* dimension looks at sustainability decisions related to services, and outlines the context based on who works there, how they implement sustainability policies and programs, how they train and treat people, and how they source materials. The *who* dimension is the thread that ties it together. Your decisions as meeting and event professionals matter; they matter not only to you, but also to your organization, its stakeholders, and to both local and global communities.

Review Questions

1. What is meant by a systems view?
2. Define cradle-to-cradle and the circular economy.
3. What is a decision point?
4. What is meant by the term decision model?
5. What are five steps to making better decisions?
6. What is a trade-off? Give an example.
7. What are the two different decisions to be made in the *where* dimension?
8. When considering materials, what are the five observations that matter to how sustainable the product is?
9. When considering services, what are the five observations that matter to how sustainable the service is?
10. When considering the *who* dimension, what are four considerations that impact sustainability?

Projects

1. Using a carbon calculator available through online research, create a low carbon menu for an event.
2. Find an example of an organization's meeting. Assume that you are now the lead planner for this event. Using the decision model from this chapter, assess the why, where, what, and how dimensions to create a short report assessing at least two destinations, and make a recommendation as to where you will situate the meeting and your rationale for doing so. Include environmental, economic, and social arguments.

Key Terms

- systems view
- ecosystem
- decision model
- decision points
- cradle-to-cradle design
- circular economy
- trade-offs
- why dimension

- the Hamlet decision
- where dimension
- geographic context
- what dimension
- how dimension
- sustainability decision points
- cumulative impact

Resources

Related to the Resources listed below, please visit the Book Companion Site (located at www.wiley.com/college/henderson) for a complete list of websites. Additional referential websites related to this chapter's content can also be found on the BCS.

Marine Stewardship Council
The MSC, based in the United Kingdom, is the world's leading certification and eco-labeling program for sustainable seafood.

Ocean Wise
A Vancouver Aquarium conservation program created to educate and empower consumers about the issues surrounding sustainable seafood. Look for the Ocean Wise logo on local restaurant menus.

Seafood Watch
The Monterey Bay Aquarium program that tracks sustainable seafood issues. They offer a pocket guide and great online resources.

The Meat Eaters Guide to Climate Change + Health
This guide provides a lifecycle assessment of meat, aimed at reducing our impact on climate and improving health.

Eat Low Carbon Calculator
This tool is from the Bon Appétit Management Company, which has a mission to educate consumers about how food choices impact the environment, local economies, and health.

Global Reporting Initiative
This organization is network-based and provides a framework for sustainability reporting used by many global corporations and other organizations. It has developed an event-sector supplement that was released in January, 2012.

ISO 20121 event sustainability management system
The International Organization for Standardization (ISO) has been developing a standard, based on British Standard 8901, for international use.

APEX/ASTM standards for environmentally sustainable meetings
>   These organizations have been working to create "green meetings" standards.

Recommended Books

Sam Goldblatt, *The Complete Guide to Greener Meetings and Events* (Hoboken, NJ: John Wiley & Sons, 2011).

Meegan Jones, *Sustainable Event Management: A Practical Guide* (London: EarthScan, 2010).

Notes

1. Walter Stahel, "The Functional Economy: Cultural and Organizational Change," in Deanne J. Richards, ed., *The Industrial Green Game: Implications for Environmental Design and Management* (Washington, DC: The National Academic Press, 1997).

2. Joss Bleriot, (2010) *The Circular Model's Founding Principles.* Accessed October 13, 2011, from www.ellenmacarthurfoundation.org/about/circular-economy/part-ii-the-circular-models-founding-principles

3. Stahel.

4. Harvard Business School Publishing, *Decision Making: 5 Steps to Better Results* (Boston: Harvard Business School Press, 2006).

5. Bon Appetit Management Company, "Eat Low Carbon Calculator." Accessed October 7, 2011, from www.eatlowcarbon.org/Carbon-Calculator.html.

6. Ibid.

7. Ibid.

8. Ibid.

9. Mike Berners-Lee, *How Bad Are Bananas? The Carbon Footprint of Everything* (Greystone Books, D&M Publishers Inc. Vancouver/Toronto/Berkeley, 2011); 99.

10. Ibid., 47.

11. Offsetters, Sunselect Produce Limited (Aldergrove) Accessed December 5, 2011 from; offsetters.ca/offset-projects/by-country/sunselect-produce-limited-aldergrove

12. Monterey Bay Aquarium Seafood Watch, *Developing Sustainable Seafood Recommendations.* (2008). Accessed October 7, 2011, from www.montereybayaquarium.org/cr/cr_seafoodwatch/content/media/MBA_SeafoodWatch_RecommendationProcess.pdf.

13. Monterey Bay Aquarium Seafood Watch. "West Coast Regional Guide." Accessed October 8, 2011, from www.montereybayaquarium.org/cr/SeafoodWatch/web/sfw_regional.aspx?region_id=1.

14. Monterey Bay Aquarium Seafood Watch, "Northeast Regional Guide." Accessed October 8, 2011, from www.montereybayaquarium.org/cr/SeafoodWatch/web/sfw_regional.aspx?region_id=2.

15. Monterey Bay Aquarium Seafood Watch, "Southeast Regional Guide." Accessed October 8, 2011, from www.montereybayaquarium.org/cr/SeafoodWatch/web/sfw_regional.aspx?region_id=5.

16. Monterey Bay Aquarium Seafood Watch, "Central U.S. Guide." Accessed October 8, 2011, from www.montereybayaquarium.org/cr/SeafoodWatch/web/sfw_regional.aspx?region_id=6.

17. Doubletree Hotel Portland, "Sustainability Pledge," Accessed October 12, 2011, from doubletreegreen.com/.

The Freiheit (Freedom) mural on the side of the Marriott Hotel in Leipzig, Germany, depicts significant local cultural events, including the role of the citizens of Leipzig in bringing down the Berlin Wall.
Photo courtesy of Elizabeth Henderson

CHAPTER 4

Social Responsibility and Culture

"Service to others is the rent you pay for your room here on earth."
—*Muhammad Ali, American boxer (1942–Present)*

Learning Objectives

After reading this chapter, you will be able to:

- Recognize the three areas of social responsibility for meetings and events: participants, workers, and communities.

- Identify issues related to socially responsible labor practices for meetings and events.

- Understand the MAUDE framework for selecting CSR projects.

- Identify tools for faith-based considerations for meetings and events.

- Understand the types of dietary restrictions that may influence participation in meetings and events.

- Learn how to incorporate authentic cultural experiences into programs.

Overview of Social Responsibility and Culture

Meetings and events can have a positive impact on participants, workers, and communities (see Figure 4.1). Social responsibility for participants can be demonstrated through the incorporation of health and wellness considerations, and through accommodating and welcoming diversity. Social responsibility for workers can be demonstrated by supporting fair labor practices. Finally, social responsibility for communities can be demonstrated by incorporating local cultural traditions or participating in a community service project.

Culture and Sustainability

Jon Hawkes, author of *The Fourth Pillar of Sustainability: Culture's Essential Role in Public Planning*, states, "Cultural vitality is as essential to a healthy and sustainable society as social equity, environmental responsibility and economic viability."[1] Further support of culture being an integral part of sustainability is provided by Dr. Sacha Kagan, research associate at the Leuphana University, Leueneburg, and founding coordinator of Cultura21 International. In an interview for LabforCulture, Kagan discusses his concept of the cultural dimension of sustainability and adds that in addition to climate change, other dimensions of sustainability include global justice, biodiversity, water, peace, cultural diversity, and other important issues.[2] Meetings and events have an excellent opportunity to celebrate cultures by incorporating arts and local perspectives into programs, as well as acting as a way of sustaining cultures through festivals or events that act as both a celebration and education.

Defining Culture

To provide clarity and context for the following sections, we will begin by providing a definition for **culture**. Although many definitions of culture exist, we will be relying on the United Nations Educational, Scientific and Cultural Organization's definition. UNESCO states, ". . .[C]ulture should be regarded as the set of distinctive spiritual, material, intellectual and emotional features of society or a social group, . . . [I]t encompasses, in addition to art and literature, lifestyles, ways of living together, value systems, traditions and beliefs."[3]

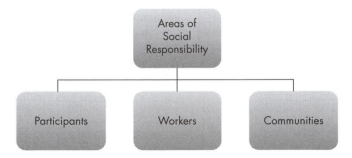

Figure 4.1 Areas of Social Responsibility for Meetings and Events

Incorporating Cultural Experiences into Meetings and Events

Meeting and event planners who plan to incorporate cultural experiences into their programs should consider a few aspects:

1. Is the experience authentic, or does it promote negative and inaccurate stereotypes?
2. How will participants respond to the experience, and is advance education needed?

■ Authentic Experiences

There are many ways that meeting and event professionals can incorporate aspects of local cultures into their programs. Some of these involve performances from local artists, musicians, or dancers and the inclusion of traditional local foods. Events may also include a welcome from a cultural leader, such as an indigenous elder.

In developing experiences such as these, a significant challenge can be in determining what is truly authentic and what might be promoting negative or inaccurate stereotypes. Within the meeting and event industry context, the challenge is in identifying what is an authentic experience for participants. According to sociologist Kevin Scott Gotham, "Authenticity is a notoriously labyrinthine concept that can refer to a variety of idealized representations of culture, identity and place."[4] Although identifying what is truly authentic might be difficult and subjective, four general guidelines can help to narrow the field. Here are the recommendations for ensuring that the experiences are authentic and not based on outdated stereotypes:

1. Identify partners with recommendations from authorities in the local culture. Some destinations will have cultural resource centers that may provide a good starting point for this research.
2. If the strongest cultural partners that you identify have not been involved in the meetings and events industry in the past but have an interest in doing so, consider working with these cultural leaders to help build services for your event and future events in the area.
3. Be open to including traditional as well as evolving expressions of local culture, such as performances by emerging artists.
4. Be attentive to the risk of hiring suppliers that exploit workers, including indigenous peoples, and ensure the use of fair labor practices and wages.

■ Focus: Squamish Lil'wat Cultural Centre (SLCC)

The Squamish Lil'wat Cultural Centre (SLCC) is located in Whistler, British Columbia. It opened in 2008 as a collaboration between the Squamish and Lil'wat Nations, two First Nations with a historic precedence of shared lands and interests in land stewardship. The SLCC functions as both a museum and a venue for meetings and events.

Carl Wallace is the sales and events coordinator at the SLCC and a member of the Lil'wat Nation. According to Wallace, "Many of today's conference and meeting goers have experienced first-class venues. Few, however, have come across authentic cultural experiences combined with our world-class award-winning facility. Our event clients are looking for a great venue that's both interesting and highly functional. We're successful in attracting conference and event clients because we offer a beautiful building that is well designed for events and also offers a special First Nations cultural experience that adds meaningfulness to the event. We offer ways to blend authentic presentations of local culture through artifacts, song, art, and people in a way that differentiates their experience here from any other."

Table 4.1   SLCC Stakeholder Benefits

Squamish and Lil'wat Nations	Whistler Community	Tourists and Event Participants
• A gathering place with opportunities to share knowledge • Employment, market, and training opportunities	• A first-class tourist attraction • Venue for meetings and events	• Information • Experiences related to the local cultures

As shown in Table 4.1, the SLCC benefits multiple stakeholders.

In addition to the benefits to stakeholders, the SLCC can be seen to exemplify a triple bottom line (people, planet, and profit) approach. An example of the "people" focus that the SLCC is actively involved in is education about local cultures. The SLCC supports weaving programs that are helping to bring back traditional blanket, basket, and other weaving practices by identifying remaining master weavers and providing a venue for them to pass on their considerable knowledge to a new generation. The weavers in the program are creating both contemporary and traditional designs, exemplifying the evolving expressions of the art forms. From a "planet" perspective, the SLCC is a LEED® gold certified building. Environmental considerations were incorporated into the design of the building, respecting the land stewardship values of both nations. From a "profit" perspective, the SLCC creates employment opportunities and generates revenues for both nations. As well, the gift shop offers First Nations artists a place to sell original artwork and jewelry.

Supporting organizations and venues, such as the SLCC, that are actively working to promote cultural education is an excellent way for meeting and event professionals to incorporate authentic cultural experiences into their programs.

■ Participant Reactions and Education

When meetings and events bring different cultures together, there is an opportunity to educate about other cultures, but there is also a possibility that participants' reactions might not always be favorable to specific aspects of the program. For example, participants might be apprehensive about trying traditional foods, and there is a risk of offending local hosts if participants react negatively. Laura González is a food anthropologist and assistant professor of Anthropology at San Diego Miramar College. She is the college's faculty sustainability coordinator and the advisor for the Food and Culture Club, a student club whose mission is to explore the world's cultures through cuisine. She recommends providing education in advance to participants, outlining the foods that will be served as well as their cultural significance. She also suggests offering other food items, such as a vegetarian option, when possible.

Labor Practices

Labor practices are an important consideration related to social responsibility for the meetings and events industry. When selecting destinations or venues, meeting and event planners should consider these issues:

- Protection against forced labor and the exploitation of vulnerable groups, including children and migrant workers
- Fair treatment of workers, including reasonable working hours and fair wages

- Provision of safe working conditions, including proper training, protective equipment, and avoidance of hazardous chemicals
- The right to form and join trade unions, and the right to collective bargaining

When evaluating proposals, if poor labor practices are discovered, planners have an opportunity to use their buyers' influence to effect change. Expressing concern about labor practices and linking this to buying decisions can be a strong motivator for suppliers to change their practices. As part of site inspections, planners can also meet with personnel or union representatives to understand the working conditions.

The term **precarious employment** refers to jobs "with a short time horizon, or for which the risk of job loss is high."[5] According to Gerry Rodgers, director of the Institute for International Labor Studies at the International Labour Organization, job insecurity in precarious employment can be measured on four dimensions: certainty of continuing work, worker control, protection of workers, and economic vulnerability. Meeting and event planners should be attentive to precarious employment issues and whether actions related to environmental initiatives might negatively affect workers. For example, a hotel that offers delegates an opportunity to decline housekeeping service at check-in in exchange for a reduced room rate has the potential to result in last-minute cancellations of shifts for housekeepers. As an alternative, asking the same question at the time that reservations are made would allow for better forecasting and fewer last-minute shift cancellations.

Social Responsibility and Meeting and Event Participants

Meeting and event professionals design the environment in which participants will be living during their program. These environments can be designed to be socially responsible for participants by promoting health and wellness and accommodating diversity.

Health and Wellness

Meeting and event professionals can demonstrate care and concern for participants by incorporating health and wellness considerations into their programs. Some examples include:

- Adequate facilities and time for exercise (with accommodations for various abilities)
- Activities to promote mental and physical relaxation
- Healthy food options to aid on-site performance
- Good air quality in the event venues (this may also include a scent-free policy)

According to Jonathan Bradshaw, founder of the Meetology® Group, incorporating health and wellness is beneficial for meeting organizers in that it enhances participants' performance in programs. He adds, "A large proportion of the scientific research that we share with the meetings industry relates to mental and physical wellness, and we expect that this will only become more relevant to meeting organizers in the future. Attendees are the heart of any meeting and their performance directly affects the ROI of the event; anything organizers can do to help maximize this can only be a good thing."

Religious Festivals and Holy Days

Meeting and event professionals need to consider many aspects in selecting dates for an event, including competing programs and availability of key performers. In addition, an important consideration is whether the proposed date occurs during a religious festival or holy day. Failure to consider this can have a negative impact on the availability of attendees, performers, speakers, and staff members. As well, it can reflect poorly on the host organization for failing to consider the needs of stakeholders. Fortunately, many excellent resources exist to help meeting and event professionals avoid this issue, including several online interfaith calendars. Please see the end of chapter resources for more information.

Dietary Requirements

In selecting menus for events, meeting and event professionals should keep in mind various forms of dietary requirements. This not only demonstrates concern and respect for participants' health and beliefs, it helps to ensure that more people will be able to fully participate in events.

Types of requirements include faith-based, medically-based, and values-based. Some of the more common requirements are listed next. Although this is not an exhaustive list of all dietary requirements, it is intended to provide an overview of some of the more frequent ones and to raise awareness of the importance of the issue in menu selection. Meeting and event planners may also want to consider incorporating healthy menus and portion sizes as a best practice for improving participants' ability to fully engage in programs, and for waste reduction (see Chapters 3 and 8 for more information on food and waste reduction).

■ Faith-Based Dietary Requirements

Faith-based dietary requirements include year-round requirements and those that are specific to holy days or festivals. For example, many faiths have periods of fasting, or abstinence, such as the practice by many Christians to abstain from meat during Lent and on Fridays, or fasting during Ramadan by Muslims. According to ethnobiologist Victor B. Meyer-Rochow, most religions have food restrictions. He adds, "An ecological or medical background is apparent for many, including some that are seen as religious or spiritual in origin."[6] There are many types of faith-based diets and requirements. Two examples of these are kosher dietary laws, which have biblical origins and are derived from the Torah, and halal dietary laws, which are derived from the Quran. Both kosher and halal regulations include specifications on hygiene practices and minimization of animal suffering in slaughtering practices:

- *Kosher:* Jewish dietary laws are known as Kashrut and include two main aspects: permissible foods and food preparation. Forbidden foods include swine (pork) and shellfish. Food preparation laws include the separation of meat and dairy products and slaughtering practices that minimize animal suffering. The U.S. market for kosher foods is predicted to be $13 billion by 2013.[7] The eco-kosher movement "combines traditional Jewish dietary laws with new concerns about industrial agriculture, global warming and fair treatment of workers."[8]
- *Halal:* Halal food is prepared according to Islamic dietary laws. These laws govern permissible foods, prohibited foods, and food preparation, including slaughtering practices that minimize animal suffering. Prohibited foods include swine and alcohol. According to Agriculture and Agri-Food Canada, the global market for halal foods is estimated at $580 billion a year and, as of 2006, there are 1.6 billion Muslims in over 112 countries, including 1,061 million in Asia, 443 million in Africa, 51 million in Europe, and 9 million in North America.[9]

■ Medically Based Dietary Requirements

Brian Dahl is both a trained chef and senior project manager at PR1ME Strategies, a Vancouver-based full-service meeting, incentive, and event management company. He regularly collaborates with chefs in hotels and venues in menu development that is geared toward the medical requirements of his delegates—notably, celiac-friendly and diabetic-friendly menus.

Dahl said, "Whether it is the menu for breakfast, morning or afternoon breaks, lunch or dinner, the consideration of the medical conditions of the delegates is paramount." According to Dahl, "This will entail not only sourcing and substituting gluten-free items, for example, but also ensuring that for diabetics, the time periods between meals and breaks are medically manageable. I often develop custom break menus that are gluten-free, high-protein, and low-carbohydrate. In addition, many, if not all, of the desserts and sweet items are developed using natural sugar-free products."

Examples of medically based dietary requirements include:

- Gluten-free: Celiac disease is one of the most common chronic health disorders in western countries. It affects 3 million Americans.[10] People with celiac disease have an intolerance to gluten that is found in wheat, rye, triticale, and barley.
- Lactose-free: Lactose intolerance is the inability or insufficient ability to digest lactose, a sugar found in milk and milk products. According to the National Institutes of Health, the prevalence of lactose intolerance in the United States cannot be estimated based on available data.[11]
- Diabetic-friendly: Diabetes affects 8.3 percent of the U.S. population.[12] Diabetics need to monitor their consumption of foods that affect blood glucose levels, including sugar and high-fat foods. Event planners should ensure that food is available at regular intervals.
- Allergy-friendly: Six and a half million Americans (or 2.3 percent of the general population) are allergic to seafood, and more than 3 million people in the United States report being allergic to peanuts, tree nuts, or both. Event planners should be conscious of potentially life-threatening allergies and identify at-risk participants through registration forms and coordination with food service providers.

■ Values-Based Dietary Requirements

Values-based dietary requirements include various forms of vegetarian diets that restrict the consumption of animal-based foods. Although many vegetarians follow their diet due to their ethical concerns related to animal cruelty, others do so for faith-based reasons (e.g., many paths of Hinduism), for health reasons (e.g., to reduce cholesterol), or for environmental reasons (e.g., to reduce the carbon footprint of their meals).

- Lacto-ovo vegetarians consume dairy foods, eggs, and plant-based foods.
- Ovo-vegetarians consume eggs and plant-based foods.
- Vegans (also known as strict vegetarians) do not consume any animal-based foods, including meat, dairy, eggs, or animal-based byproducts.

Another aspect of values-based food consumption is a focus on social sustainability—in particular, growing awareness about **fair trade products**. The Fair Trade Federation defines fair trade as "an economic partnership based on dialogue, transparency, and respect."[13] Features of fair trade include a focus on poverty alleviation by providing fair wages to producers, and protection against exploitative child labor. The interest and support for fair trade products is significant.

THE NATIONAL CONFERENCE CENTER®

The Science of Food for Thought: Enhancing Meetings Through Food

Meeting planners everywhere are always looking for the answer to this question: how can I help my attendees gain and retain the most from their meeting experience? One might answer that question by looking into the meals and break stations served. The center of all brain focus at meetings comes down to: what are my attendees consuming and what is the timing of those meals?

Neuroscience research such as how food affects the brain can be very helpful. Research by Andrea Sullivan, M.A., of BrainStrength Systems has proven functional foods and timing both serve as a factor for productive meetings. Her research demonstrates that in basic brain chemistry, "Neurotransmitters are required for memory, cognition, learning, attention and action.

NCC's Executive Chef Craig Mason
Corporate & Incentive Travel magazine,
August 2011

"The main thing that impacts whether the brain is stimulated or relaxed is based on the balance between carbohydrates and proteins."

Specific foods are a key component of these powerful chemicals in the brain, along with timing."

At The National Conference Center, we have taken a closer look at the meals and snacks we serve in terms of creating meeting alertness and engagement. Our Executive Chef Craig Mason now offers a solution of brain-friendly foods which he coined as The National Conference Center's Food for Thought program.

What does Chef Mason have to say about morning and afternoon snacks?

There is a significant difference between past items on our break stations and what snacks we're currently invested in serving. Previous break stations served chips, cookies, gummy bears and pastries. Chef Mason describes it as the ultimate sugar rush, "Guests experience an overload of sugar and suffer from a mental crash in their afternoon meetings." Present break stations by Mason favor an array of fresh fruits, nuts, boiled eggs, energy bars and the occasional gummy bears. The same correlation between food and mind alertness also lies within Andrea Sullivan's research. As an organizational psychologist, she was able to drill down food choices enhance mood, learning and

performance.

Her research has lead to several findings for improved performance in the meetings industry. "Breakfast should consist of a complex carbohydrate and a protein," Sullivan states, "A whole-grain bagel helps to sustain energy along with a hard-boiled egg which contains Choline, a chemical building block to learning." She suggests avoiding simple carbohydrates such as white bread, white rice and pastries which increase sugar levels and then crash, making sustaining alertness difficult.

Top Brain Meeting Snacks

H2O
Granola
Energy Bars
Nuts
Blueberries
Yogurt
Mangos
Bananas
Spinach
Broccoli
Whole Grain Breads
Hard-Boiled Eggs
Peanut Butter
Dark Chocolate

To read the full white paper, visit www.conferencecenter.com

The National Conference Center in Washington, D.C., offers brain-friendly menus.
Document courtesy of Sarah N. Vining, National Conference Center

According to the United Kingdom's Fairtrade Foundation, 2008 worldwide fair trade sales totaled $4.12 billion.[14] Meeting and event planners interested in including fair trade products, such as coffee, should consider speaking with food service providers well in advance. If the provider does not currently serve fair trade products, it might be required to pay a premium to purchase the product from a new supplier (see Chapter 8 for more information on fair trade).

Social Responsibility and Communities

Meetings and events can have both a positive and a negative impact on communities. Among the positive aspects, meetings and events can create employment and provide educational and cultural experiences. Meetings and events can also help advance social issues, particularly when coordinated efforts leverage the industry's economic influence. As an example, the National Football League relocated the 1993 Super Bowl from Arizona when the state wouldn't recognize Martin Luther King Day. This played an important role in a change in this policy, making it possible for the 1996 Super Bowl to be held in Arizona.[15] Many destinations are leveraging their inclusive policies, including legalized same-sex marriage, to attract a larger percentage of the significant lesbian, gay, bisexual, and transgender (LGBT) market. "Based on tourism industry data from the U.S. Department of Commerce and CMI sample demographics, the annual economic impact of LGBT travelers is approximately $64.5 billion in the U.S. alone."[16]

If not properly managed, events can also result in negative aspects such as waste generation, environmental degradation, and supporting unfair labor practices. One alarming issue is the connection between meetings and events and human trafficking. A report by a leading counter-human trafficking organization found that human trafficking to meet a short-term increase in the demand for prostitution at the 2006 Germany FIFA World Cup was avoided through effective prevention measures, but found that a correlation between the Athens Olympics, where prevention efforts were poor, and a 95 percent increase in human trafficking victims could not be discounted.[17]

Selecting Community Service Projects: The MAUDE Framework

Meetings and events have the potential to positively influence communities in which they hold their events through direct economic impact, engaging community members, and through **community service**—the act of volunteering or donating to community groups, including charitable organizations.

As shown in Figure 4.2, the MAUDE framework for socially responsible events is a tool for identifying and developing projects that are *meaningful, are aligned, apply unique skills, are destination specific, and are engaging*—key considerations for high-impact, authentic initiatives.

Meeting Professionals International's 2010 World Education Congress held in Vancouver, Canada, included a community service project that helped restore a stream habitat for wild salmon.
Photo courtesy of M. McIlwraith

| Meaningful | Aligned | Unique skills | Destination specific | Engaging |

Figure 4.2 MAUDE Framework for Socially Responsible Events

- *Meaningful:* Is the project effective at achieving the community service and legacy objectives? Are there alternatives, such as cash donations, or a different event, that would be more effective for achieving the same objective? Ultimately, participants who get involved in a community service project want to know that their efforts are actually making a positive impact and that this impact is sustainable in the long-term.
- *Aligned:* An often-overlooked aspect of designing community service projects is to align them with your organizational objectives. Although many great projects are held that don't incorporate this aspect, by doing so, you are able to help to advance your overall mission. Two ways of doing this are to address a social issue that may have a negative impact on your business, such as cleaning up a park near your venue. You can also consider ways of participating in an action that supports your organization's mission. For example, if you are designing a community service project for an academic association you could support a project with a local school.
- *Unique skills:* Does the project utilize your organization's unique skills, abilities, or resources? For example, a marketing firm donating volunteer time to a charitable organization to develop a marketing plan for an event is more valuable than the same amount of time donated for staffing the registration desk because it leverages the marketing firm's expertise to help make the event more successful.
- *Destination specific:* Is the project meaningful for your event destination and can the project be sustained after the event concludes? Environmental issues will have different degrees of impact depending on the location. If your event is being held in an oceanside community, you might select a project that involves a benefit to a marine habitat.
- *Engaging:* Will the project help engage your meeting or event participants? Is there a theme or issue that is important to your stakeholders that would increase their interest in participating, and increase the potential support (such as sponsorship) for your project? Many factors may influence this, including corporate culture, demographics, and whether there has been a significant event or disaster that mobilizes people's interest in volunteerism.

Designing for Engagement

The final aspect in the MAUDE framework is *engaging*—but finding a program that does this can be elusive. The Volunteer Functions Inventory (VFI), developed by E. Gil Clary and Mark Snyder, identifies six motivations for volunteering.[18] These are presented in Table 4.2, with examples of

Table 4.2   The Volunteer Functions Inventory Applied to Community Service Projects

Function	Community Service Project Design Element
Values	Including humanitarian aspects
Understanding	Including educational aspects about the project or community, and allowing volunteers to practice their skills
Enhancement	Providing opportunities for personal growth, and recognizing contributions
Career	Providing opportunities for career skills building, as well as potential letters of reference for volunteers
Social	Incorporating networking and social aspects
Protective	Provide a supportive environment and mechanisms for volunteers to reduce negative feelings, such as guilt or to escape personal problems

how they can apply to community service projects. Designing community service projects in such a way that they appeal to multiple motivators will help engage a larger percentage of your audience in the program. Note that one individual might have several motivations.

MAUDE Framework Supplier Focus: Hard Rock International

An example of an industry supplier whose social initiatives follow the MAUDE framework is Hard Rock International (see Table 4.3). It is a for-profit company that leverages its unique connections, strong brand loyalty, and global reach to make a meaningful impact on charitable organizations around the world. According to Kevin Kirby, senior director of worldwide sales, Hard Rock International was founded with guiding principles that strongly support philanthropic efforts. "Those were created long before CSR was a buzzword. These were the beliefs of our founders back in 1971 in London." He adds, "We happen to be in 52 countries around the world and we have an opportunity to touch a lot of people and to have an impact on lives."

Forty years ago, the late John Lennon dared to "Imagine" a world free from hunger, poverty, and at peace forever, with the release of his album's title track. Decades later, his legacy thrives as his wife, artist and musician Yoko Ono Lennon, joins Hard Rock International and WhyHunger again for IMAGINE THERE'S NO HUNGER, a global campaign to combat childhood hunger and poverty around the world. Dedicated to the brand's "All is One" core value, proceeds from Hard Rock's campaign will directly benefit WhyHunger, a leader in building the global movement to end hunger and poverty, and its grassroots partners around the globe in hopes of finding long-term solutions through sustainable agriculture. *Photo courtesy of Hard Rock International*

Table 4.3 MAUDE Framework and Hard Rock International

Meaningful	As of October 2011, Signature Series sales have raised over $11 million.[19] Hard Rock's Signature Series t-shirt line was started as a way for musicians and artists to raise funds for charities of their choosing. Artists donate an original piece of artwork that is reproduced for a limited number of shirts and sold worldwide.
Aligned	Hard Rock International was established with a guiding service philosophy of "Love all, serve all" and works with charitable organizations that align with their mottos that are displayed prominently in their venues: TAKE TIME TO BE KIND (humanitarian), SAVE THE PLANET (environmental), and ALL IS ONE (entertainment industry). A list of the humanitarian organizations that Hard Rock partners with can be found on its website.
Unique Skills	Hard Rock International leverages its connections with musicians and artists, worldwide venues, and marketing abilities to raise both funds and awareness for breast cancer research through its annual Pinktober® concerts, events, and sales of apparel and accessories. During the month of October, its website provides breast cancer awareness information, and their hotels have special promotions to raise further funds for the cause.

(continued)

Table 4.3 (*Continued*)

Destination Specific	Hard Rock International is in an excellent position to mobilize its global presence to address destination-specific concerns. As an example, in 2006 it partnered with Music Rising, a campaign that was launched by The Edge, Bob Ezrin, and Henry Juszkiewicz to rescue the musical culture of the Central Gulf region of the United States by replacing the musical instruments lost or destroyed by Hurricane Katrina. Hard Rock's philanthropic team is also prepared to act quickly and effectively to respond to other natural disasters. Within 30 minutes of the 2011 earthquake in Japan, plans were under way for a benefit t-shirt to raise funds for the American Red Cross's efforts. In addition to the efforts coordinated through its international headquarters, individual cafes also support local projects and charitable organizations.
Engaging	The success of Hard Rock International's philanthropic efforts can be attributed in great part to the success it has had in engaging artists, team members, and patrons. As an example, following the earthquake in Haiti, Hard Rock was approached by Haitian artists including Wyclef Jean to raise funds for disaster relief. Frontline staff, notably servers, were instrumental in asking patrons to contribute to the cause, with small actions such as rounding their check to the nearest dollar. Several benefit concerts were held in Hard Rock Cafe venues.

Community Service at Securian Financial, an Interview with Koleen Roach

Koleen Roach is the director of meetings and conference management at Securian Financial in St. Paul, Minnesota. She was honored in 2009 with the Society of Incentive Travel Executives (SITE) Crystal award in recognition of the philanthropic elements of Securian's corporate business and incentive meetings.

What motivates you to incorporate community service into your events?

Community is one of our fundamental corporate values. The culture of our company is community service-oriented, and it starts at the top. Our chairman and CEO, Bob Senkler, requested that philanthropy be included in our recognition trip to Africa in 2009. We've incorporated some form of philanthropy into most of our meetings ever since. My department organizes more than 80 recognition and business meetings every year.

How has community service affected your business internally (such as team morale and engagement) and externally (client relationships and public relations)?

Community service is an integral part of Securian's culture. We encourage our associates to volunteer in a wide variety of community programs every year, and the Securian Foundation gives more than $1 million to local nonprofits annually. The annual United Way campaign at Securian has become a companywide celebration of community and the spirit of volunteerism. In addition to encouraging all associates to pledge to the United Way, every department and business unit hosts unique, fun fundraising events. Securian is not the largest employer in the Twin Cities, but we are one of the top contributors to the United Way. All of these activities create a very strong sense of community among our associates and contribute to the high ratings they give Securian when asked how they feel about the company. We've won several "Best Employer" awards based on workforce polls.

What recommendations do you have for meeting professionals interested in community service projects?

The hotel where your event is held or your destination management company (DMC) may have existing relationships with local charitable organizations that you can draw upon to include an element of corporate social responsibility (CSR) in your event. You also can do your own research on the web to look for and find ways to do something for your host community that is an especially good fit for your group. It is important, though, to ensure that you are partnering with a charity that will use your group's contributions appropriately. The National Council of Nonprofits is one of many organizations that can help you determine the effectiveness of a charity.

Can you describe some of the projects that you have been involved in?

One especially gratifying experience was a recognition trip for our top-performing financial advisors to South Africa and Zambia in 2009. On my site inspection trip the year before I learned about an orphanage and school for children whose parents died of AIDS. One woman started the Ebenezer Trust School and Orphanage in Livingstone, Zambia, and continued to run it mostly by herself, but with a lot of support from the local community. She was providing a safe environment and schooling for dozens of children, but the program was woefully underfunded. We chose her program as the beneficiary of the philanthropic element of our trip.

Our approach was twofold. Instead of room gifts for our guests, we left school supplies in their rooms every night while they were in South Africa. They eventually packed them into backpacks and hand-delivered to the children. It was a very moving scene and strongly affected all of us who participated. Many of those advisors still have relationships with Ebenezer Trust. We also donated the money we would have spent on room gifts in Zambia—about $25,000—directly to the Ebenezer Trust.

The next year, we held our biannual national sales conference in San Diego and developed our Bears, Bikes 'n Buds program for the advisors and their families who attended. They could choose from a Build-a-Bear event that benefited a local children's hospital; a Build-a-Bike program to assemble bikes for children in the local Boys and Girls Clubs; or volunteer for an afternoon to help cultivate and plant the "buds" in a community garden in a distressed neighborhood. We provided our guests with gardening equipment that they left behind for the local gardeners.

Some of the events we organize are business meetings. In those cases, we offer less complex philanthropic opportunities. I often work through an organization called GlobalGiving, which represents hundreds of charities. We give our guests gift cards from GlobalGiving so they can go to the site and donate the value of the card to the charities of their choice. I should point out that we don't raise our meeting budgets to accommodate philanthropy. We spend some of the money otherwise earmarked for room gifts on the items they end up giving away. We have received no complaints and many commendations about this approach to funding philanthropy at our events.

Securian Financial's CEO, chairman, Bob Senkler, inflating soccer balls at the Ebenezer School.
Photo courtesy of Securian Financial Group, Inc.

How do you select your projects?

The project we select depends on the size of the group and the nature of the meeting. The Bears, Bikes 'n Buds program worked well in San Diego because we were hosting hundreds of guests, many of whom brought their families along. Something simpler like the charitable gift cards works better for business meetings.

We have introduced the MAUDE framework for community service projects for events. How would your programs, in retrospect, fit into this model?

Meaningful: When planning a recognition event or business meeting, it's important to know your group, understand why they are attending the event, and tailor the philanthropy to that specific gathering. But regardless of the reason your company brought them together, it says a lot about your corporate culture when you use the money you would have spent on room gifts to provide your guests with an opportunity to give back to the community that is hosting them. The impact it has on your company's relationships with your guests is phenomenal. It makes them proud to be associated with your company. It's the right thing to do on many levels.

Aligned: Our philanthropic activities align with our goal to serve the financial security needs of others.

Unique skills: It makes sense for a group of builders to volunteer with the local chapter of Habitat for Humanity for an afternoon or for medical practitioners help out at a free clinic. When those connections aren't as obvious, you can opt for something less specialized, such as our Bears Bikes 'n Buds program in San Diego.

Destination specific: Depending on the group and the nature of the gathering, we make an effort to identify local needs and offer our guests the opportunity to help meet those needs during their brief visit.

Engaging: Our recognition events are very important to our relationships with the financial advisors who market our products. They are careful about choosing the financial providers they represent and we are careful about choosing the people who represent us. The majority of our advisors are engaged in their own communities: They do a lot of charitable work and volunteer many hours through nonprofit organizations, their places of worship, local schools or local government. When we sponsor philanthropic activities at our meetings and events, we show them that our values align with theirs. We want to make them feel good about representing us. And we want to give them experiences that create memories that last a lifetime.

Examples of Integration of Local Culture or Social Considerations into Conferences and Events

◼ Canadian Labour Congress Pacific Winter School

The Canadian Labour Congress holds an annual winter school that offers a series of week-long courses in January and February of each year. The CLC has a strong commitment to social and environmental responsibility, and they demonstrate this in a number of ways in their event planning. In developing their program, they have paid close attention to social issues that could be a barrier to participation, such as access to child care and travel costs. According to CLC Pacific Regional Director Amber Hockin, CLC has introduced these measures:

- Free child care services with an early childhood educator are provided for delegates with children.
- Travel subsidies are provided for those traveling greater distances.

- A scent-free environment is provided for those suffering from allergies, asthma, and other health conditions.
- Alcohol-free social events and a nightly Alcoholics Anonymous meeting are included.
- Coach service with pickup service from various locations reduces the event's carbon footprint.
- The school is always held in a unionized facility.
- Social and environmental considerations are integrated into their purchasing practices by selecting more sustainable and union-made products.

National Funeral Directors Association

The National Funeral Directors Association (NFDA) held its 2010 International Convention and Expo October 10–13, 2010, in New Orleans, Louisiana, and drew nearly 6,000 total attendees. The NFDA Convention is an excellent example of incorporating local traditions in a way that extends the education of the conference, celebrates local culture and heritage, and improves the event's environmental impact.

An important part of its annual convention is to hold a service of remembrance. This is an important community service for the convention attendees to celebrate the lives and mourn the loss of loved ones, friends, and colleagues who died in the previous year. The NFDA integrated local culture into this service by embracing the unique funeral traditions of New Orleans and including a horse-drawn hearse, a horse-drawn carriage, and a jazz band. In keeping with tradition, at the end of the service, all in attendance formed a "second line" and paraded down Convention Center Boulevard.

2010 NFDA Convention, Service of Remembrance, New Orleans.
Photo courtesy of National Funeral Directors Association

NFDA also incorporated the New Orleans tradition of the Mardi Gras Parade for its president-elect party. At the appointed hour, convention attendees gathered at one of their official convention hotels. From there, led by a marching band and an authentic Mardi Gras parade float, attendees made their way to Generations Hall for the event. Shuttles transported guests back to the hotel later in the evening. This practice not only introduced cultural elements into the program, it also reduced their carbon footprint by reducing the amount of shuttles that were required.

■ Society for Anthropology in Community Colleges (SACC)

Laura González is a food anthropologist and assistant professor of anthropology at San Diego Miramar College, her view is that "every purchasing decision is an opportunity, including supporting local food and ethical businesses." One of the ways that they are incorporating social and environmental considerations into the planning process is by supporting small businesses that source ingredients from local farms. As two examples, they arranged for on-site gourmet food trucks for lunch breaks. SACC arranged for MIHO Gastrotuck, a small business that uses fresh, local ingredients to be on-site during the conference to provide "farm to street" food. This allowed the conference to offer affordable, local food options to delegates. They also purchased popsicles from Viva Pops, a small, woman-owned business that also sources ingredients from local farms. They held their banquet at the San Diego Zoo and Safari Park, where they are able to offer sustainably sourced meat and fish entrees.

■ Timberland

Michelle Johnson is the chief gathering officer for C3 Communications, an independent meeting planning company based in Hampton, New Hampshire. She was previously the senior manager of global meetings for the Timberland Company, and she recounts her experience with integrating social responsibility into the Timberland annual sales meeting. The community service program they did was destination specific:

In December 2006 we held the Timberland Company annual sales meeting to showcase their next selling season's line of fall shoes. This year a conscious choice was made to hold the meeting in New Orleans, LA. The hope was we could find a way to offer assistance and give back to the community. It was just over a year since the devastating destruction of hurricane Katrina and the leadership agreed that visiting NOLA was a perfect match for Timberland in the partnership of commerce and justice that the company holds at the heart of its community.

It was a beautiful day to see over 300 people working in groups along the Oretha Castle Haley Boulevard, in an effort to bring life back into the community. You could see them up and down the street, working to restore nature and gardens to the sidewalks, rebuild local restaurants, paint murals along the columns that line the entrance and gut homes that were left to be condemned, never to be returned to. It was a long, hard day of service, but so rewarding for all who had a part in it. As the day began, someone asked why we were not going to the 9th ward. They wanted to see the part of town that had been hit so hard by the levee damages. In an effort to give them the experience, we scrambled to find buses and local folks that would be able to talk them through the route and give them a firsthand narration of what transpired.

We left the boulevard to board buses for those that wanted to go. Needless to say, there was not a soul left behind. All five buses were loaded and we drove through the streets of the lower 9th ward, witnessing what unbelievable sadness stood before them. Homes that had been moved two to three blocks from where they once laid. Cars that were overturned and sitting in a neighbor's living room. So much to absorb and hearts that wanted to understand how it could have happened. As we got off the buses and walked through the streets it was quiet and solemn as we tried to digest the overwhelming pictures that will be forever in our minds.

There was a man who worked on the sales team who went into the local shelter to talk to the keeper and see how things were going. In their conversation he asked him what he needed for the families and people in the area. The man simply said shoes. It was without hesitation he took his boots off and gave them to the man. The man said thank you very much and the sales rep turned around and walked towards the bus. As people were boarding the bus they asked him where his shoes were? He said simply, the shelter said they needed shoes, so I gave up mine. At that moment every person who was on the trip, got off the buses, took their shoes off and gave them to the shelter. There was not a word spoken or question as to why. . . . it was just done.

The drive back to the hotel was very quiet, and I know personally it was a time of reflection for me trying to imagine a better life for those people, someday, somehow. As we got off the bus at the hotel, word had gotten back to them about what had happened, and people were there to greet us with thank yous and hugs. The staff of the hotel was there clapping us off the bus, thanking us for what we did. One of the bellmen came up to an attendee and thanked him for their actions. He lived there once and being his community, hoped to return there someday.

The message of hope is a strong one and one I hope to have you be inspired by in this story. You have a chance to make a difference in even the smallest of acts you can offer in every event you do. Don't ever forget that! It's not always a village—it sometimes just needs YOU!

Concluding Thoughts

This chapter has discussed issues that have moral, legal, and ethical aspects. Professor Joe Goldblatt provides distinctions between each of these:[20]

- *Morals* are personal decisions that have personal consequences for right or wrong behavior.
- *Ethics* are the principles of conduct governing individuals or groups.
- *Laws* are enacted by groups, and punishment is imposed by peers (juries) or judges.

Meeting and event professionals might find themselves in situations where determining the correct course of action may be difficult, particularly where there is inconsistency between these areas. Laws and local customs vary around the world, and even across state borders within a country: such as the case with marriage-equality laws or immigration laws in the United States, making these issues even more complex.

Chapter Review

In this chapter, we introduced how meetings and events can incorporate socially responsible practices for participants, workers, and communities. We examined ways of incorporating authentic cultural experiences for meetings and events.

Using the MAUDE framework, we provided methodology for designing community service projects that are *meaningful*, and sustainable in the long-term, *aligned* with organizational objectives, apply the organization's *unique skills*, address a *destination-specific* issue, and are *engaging*.

Review Questions

1. What are the three areas of social responsibility for meetings and events? Provide examples of ways that meetings and events can demonstrate social responsibility in each of these areas.
2. Using the interfaith calendar resources provided at the end of this chapter, identify dates that should have been avoided by an international academic association annual meeting during your current month.
3. Provide three examples of incorporating health and wellness considerations into your event program.

Group Exercises

1. Using the MAUDE framework, design a community service project for an event that will be held in your destination for each of the organizations listed below. You may find it helpful to start with the unique skills of the organization.
   a. A pharmaceutical company sales representative meeting
   b. A technology company training event for clients
   c. A corporate retreat for a financial organization

Key Terms

- culture
- precarious employment
- community service
- fair trade products
- precarious employment

Resources

Related to the Resources listed below, please visit the Book Companion Site (located at www.wiley.com/college/henderson) for a complete list of websites. Additional referential websites related to this chapter's content can also be found on the BCS.

BBC Interfaith calendar

This site provides information on religious festivals and holy days by faith or by date, and includes a description for each of the festivals and days.

Interfaith Calendar

This site provides information on primary sacred times for world religions. On the site you are able to search by date or by faith to view calendars. Primary holy days of a tradition are bolded.

The GMIC Guide to Socially Responsible Projects for Events

This guide provides resources and tools for integrating socially responsible community actions into event management processes.

Recommended Books

Joe Goldblatt, *Special Events: A New Generation and the Next Frontier* (Hoboken, NJ: John Wiley & Sons, 2011).
Sam Goldblatt, *Greener Meetings and Events* (Hoboken, NJ: John Wiley & Sons, 2011).

Notes

1. Jon Hawkes, "The Fourth Pillar of Sustainability: Culture's Essential Role in Public Planning." www.fourthpillar.biz/about/fourth-pillar/.
2. LabforCulture.org, "A Researcher's View: Sacha Kagan." www.labforculture.org/en/home/contents/climate-change-artists-respond/a-researcher-s-view-sacha-kagan.

3. UNESCO, "UNESCO Universal Declaration on Cultural Diversity," www.unesco.org/education/imld_2002/unversal_decla.shtml#2.

4. Kevin Fox Gotham, *Authentic New Orleans: Tourism, Culture, and Race in the Big Easy* (New York: NYU Press: 2007).

5. Gerry Rodgers, "Precarious Work in Western Europe: The State of the Debate," in Gerry and Janine Rodgers, ed., *Precarious Jobs in Labour Market Regulation: The Growth of Atypical Employment in Western Europe* (Brussels: International Institute for Labour Studies, Free University of Brussels,1989).

6. Victor B. Meyer-Rochow, "Food Taboos: Their Origins and Purposes," *Journal of Ethnobiology and Ethnomedicine* (2009). www.ethnobiomed.com/content/5/1/18.

7. Agriculture and Agri-Food Canada, "United States Kosher Food Market Brief" (August, 2010). www.ats.agr.gc.ca/amr/4975-eng.htm.

8. Alan Cooperman, "Eco-Kosher Movement Aims to Heed Tradition, Conscience," *Washington Post* (July 7, 2007). www.washingtonpost.com/wp-dyn/content/article/2007/07/06/AR2007070602092.html.

9. Agriculture and Agri-Food Canada, "Global Halal Food Market Brief" (June 2008) www.ats.agr.gc.ca/afr/4491-eng.htm.

10. Jefferson Adams, *Celiac Disease Statistics.* www.celiac.com/articles/1164/1/Celiac-Disease-Statistics/Page1.html.

11. NIH Consensus Development Conference, *Lactose Intolerance and Health.* consensus.nih.gov/2010/lactosestatement.htm#q1.

12. U.S. Department of Heath and Human Services, "National Diabetes Statistics" (2011), diabetes.niddk.nih.gov/DM/PUBS/statistics/.

13. Fair Trade Federation, www.fairtradefederation.org/ht/d/sp/i/2733/pid/2733.

14. Fair Trade Federation, www.fairtradefederation.org/ht/d/sp/i/197/pid/197.

15. Richard Sandomir, "Super Bowl: A Condition of the Game," *New York Times* (January 21, 1996). www.nytimes.com/1996/01/21/sports/super-bowl-a-condition-of-the-game.html?scp=1&sq=martin+luther+king+superbowl&st=nyt.

16. Community Marketing Inc. *CMI's 12th Annual Gay & Lesbian Tourism Study,* San Francisco, CA. www.communitymarketinginc.com/.../LGBT-TourismAbstract-DMAI.pdf.

17. The Future Group, *Report Finds Human Trafficking Risk at 2010 Olympics* (November 1, 2007). www.thefuturegroup.org/id50.html

18. E. Gil Clary and Mark Snyder, "The Motivations to Volunteer: Theoretical and Practical Considerations," *Current Directions in Psychological Science* 8 (5) (October 1999).

19. See: Hard Rock Cafe, "Philanthropy: Signature Series." www.hardrock.com/philanthropy/signature-series.aspx.

20. Joe Goldblatt, *Special Events: A New Generation and the Next Frontier* (Hoboken, NJ: John Wiley & Sons, 2011).

Photo courtesy of iStockphoto/Jim Hughes

CHAPTER 5

Meetings, Events, and Environmental Science

"The beginning of knowledge is the discovery of something we do not understand."

—*Frank Hebert*

Learning Objectives

After reading this chapter, you will be able to:

- Define and be prepared to use key terms significant to sustainable events, including carbon footprint, externality, event miles, carbon offsets, and carbon dioxide equivalent.

- Recognize the inherent connection between the health of the economy, the management and mitigation of energy use and other environmental factors, and the success of events in the short to long term.

- Describe strategies you can implement as a meeting professional to manage the environmental impact of events.

- Recognize strategies you can implement as a meeting professional to mitigate the impact of events on the environment, your budget, and the communities you do business in.

- Learn accepted carbon footprint methodology that will assist you in measuring, reporting, and managing your events' environmental footprint.

Introduction

The natural world environment is an increasingly important consideration when planning and executing meetings and events. The term **green meetings** has become well known in professional meeting planning circles over the past few years. This refers to planning and executing meetings in an environmentally friendly manner. More recently, the term **greener meetings** has been proposed by Sam Goldblatt, and is a term that recognizes that meetings and events always have a degree of negative impact on the environment, but that we can take actions to mitigate this impact.[1] Green meeting standards are being developed through a coalition amongst the Convention Industry Council's (CIC) APEX (Accepted Practices Exchange) initiative, the United States Environmental Protection Agency, and ASTM, a U.S.-based standard-making organization. As of April 2012, eight of nine standards have been completed and the ninth is in draft form. Another standard that measures sustainability on a broader scale (environment, economy, and community) is British Standard 8901 (BS 8901) for sustainable event management that is now being used as the model for a new standard: ISO 20121. All of these standards are discussed in greater detail in Chapters 9 and 10 on measurement and reporting.

Malcolm Gladwell, in his bestseller *The Tipping Point*,[2] makes the case that ideas start small and then spread like viruses; that practices and ideas are contagious. The idea of environmentally sustainable meetings reached a tipping point not too long ago. The next step is now to integrate this existing knowledge with an understanding of economic and social issues. This chapter will explore key terms related to the linkages between the environment and the economy, introduce the connection between energy, economy, and events and suggest ways to reduce and mitigate the resulting environmental impact.

Linkages

Some students or teachers might be surprised at the inclusion of a chapter on environmental science in a book on CSR and ethics in the meetings and events industry. But the linkages are clear and direct. Meeting and events have an environmental footprint; however, we tend to think of the visible impacts, such as waste, and forget about those that aren't as readily visible, such as energy and carbon. Just because we can't see it doesn't mean it isn't happening. This is called the **ostrich effect**—dealing with potentially risky situations by pretending they don't exist.[3] The use of energy and the generation of carbon, in the form of nonrenewable fuels and climate change, affect society as a whole. The ethical implications of this are also clear; as we reduce available resources and change climate, we change not only familiar landscapes but familiar ways of doing—whole cultures—and possibly contribute to bigger global problems around scarce resources, human rights, social and environmental justice, disparate income distributions, and environmental degradation. At an organizational level, increasing the effectiveness of your meeting/event through wise environmental management affects economic success and intangibles such as organizational reputation. You might be right in thinking that your meeting or event has only a small impact; taken as a whole, the industry has a massive impact. By working at the "micro-meetings" level, individual meeting and event professionals can make a difference.

Key Terms

This section will introduce key sustainability terms. They are important to know, as detailed sustainable event reporting will refer to many of them. The intent is not to give a detailed science lesson but to give a basic background to empower event professionals to be successful in their quest for sustainable events.

Carbon

Carbon is a building block of life and a byproduct of modern society. Carbon is found in coal, diamonds, rocks, and all life. It has become a significant word in both business and governmental circles because of its role in climate change. The public awareness of the role of carbon in climate change has instigated this high level of discussion, which has, in turn, created a shift in global and domestic policy initiatives related to carbon. The United Nations declares, "Climate change is one of the greatest challenges of our time,"[4] although countries have not been able to agree on terms that would lead to emission reductions that would help mitigate its impact.

Countries such as Denmark and Norway have already set emission reduction targets. The governments of Denmark, France, and the United Kingdom[5] are also requiring that large companies report not just financial but also environmental and social factors in their standard reporting. This government activity will filter down to business; in fact, the insurance industry in the United States has already begun to require its members to report the possible impact of climate change on their books.[6] Because meetings and events are such powerful and widespread business communications tools, carbon strategies will begin to filter down to this level, too.

Some of the terms that meeting professionals will need to be aware of in relation to carbon include *carbon footprints, carbon dioxide equivalent (CO$_2$e), event miles,* and *offsets.* In order to understand these terms, a brief lesson in carbon and the carbon cycle is needed.

Carbon and the Carbon Cycle

We are all made of carbon. There is no life that has been observed to date that is not carbon-based. Carbon is circulated on earth by four major processes:[7]

1. *Between plants and the atmosphere:* Plants absorb carbon dioxide (CO$_2$) during photosynthesis and emit it back during respiration.
2. *Between the oceans and the atmosphere:* Oceans store carbon absorbed from the atmosphere, where it is used by marine organisms to breathe, which returns some of it to the atmosphere. Circulation between plants and oceans and the atmosphere is cyclical; that is, both processes absorb and emit carbon.
3. *The burning of fossil fuels, such as oil, gas, and coal:* This is not a cyclical process; it emits carbon to the atmosphere but does not absorb any.
4. *Changing land use:* Such as for agriculture, urban development, deforestation, or reforestation. This process can both absorb carbon, as through reforestation, and emit carbon, as when forests are cut down for agriculture.

So, if carbon is so common, why is it a big concern?

Earth is a closed system to matter but not to energy, which comes from the sun. That is, all of the building blocks for whatever we have, had, or will have in the future, for cars, airplanes, convention centers, marketing materials, computers, or hotels, is from a nonrenewable source: the Earth. It doesn't grow, nor does it get any large amounts of matter from elsewhere in the solar system. Matter cannot be created or destroyed (for any budding meeting professional physicists, this is the first law of thermodynamics[8] and the principle of the conservation of matter).

But wait a second. What about renewable resources, like trees and grass and other vegetation? Although it might appear like it, the matter used to create these renewable resources is not new. It is being recycled through the system through the process of photosynthesis, where energy from the sun provides the input that changes the form the matter takes. In fact, photosynthesis is the only process on earth that does this.

As already mentioned, burning fossil fuels is not cyclical, like the exchange that happens between plants and the atmosphere and between the ocean and the atmosphere. It is unidirectional; that is, the energy is burned and rises into the atmosphere as carbon dioxide. The fossil fuel is gone, replaced by gases, including greenhouse gases, which, unfortunately, are contributing to climate change.

A **greenhouse gas**[9] is one that reduces the loss of heat into space by helping to retain heat in the atmosphere, also called the *greenhouse effect*. There are several greenhouse gases, but the most important are water vapor and carbon dioxide (CO_2). They don't block incoming radiation from the sun, which are short waves, but are resistant to long-wave radiation reemitted by the Earth, thus acting in the same way a greenhouse does. The earth is slowly getting warmer, most probably due to the burning of fossil fuels.

Fossil fuels are the Achilles' heel of the meeting industry; cheap travel, driven by cheap oil, has made the current industry model both possible and profitable. Travel is the number one contributor to the carbon emitted by a meeting or event. Regulation of carbon at the governmental and industry level could have a dramatic effect on how face-to-face meetings and events are planned in the future. Climate change is why carbon has become such an important word in government and business, and it is why meeting industry professionals should understand how meetings and events can contribute to both the problem and the solution.

Travel is the number one contributor to the carbon footprint of a meeting or event.
Photo courtesy of Elizabeth Henderson

Carbon Footprint

A **carbon footprint** is the total amount of emissions caused by an individual or organization as measured in tons of carbon dioxide. Why do we measure this in carbon dioxide? The air we breathe is made up of approximately 78 percent nitrogen, 20.9 percent oxygen, and about 0.9 percent argon. If our atmosphere was made up of only these gases, we would have no life at all and no atmosphere as we know it. The small remainder, about 0.03 percent, is made up primarily of carbon dioxide. It is because carbon dioxide is a greenhouse gas and reflects heat back to earth that our planet has any life at all. It is the very small amount of carbon dioxide in the atmosphere that should make us cautious of the amounts that we add to it through the burning of fossil fuels; even a relatively small amount can change the atmospheric percentage dramatically and cause the heat on our planet to rise. This is why, even though there are other greenhouse gases, we measure our footprint in carbon dioxide equivalent (CO_2e). You can think of this like a foreign exchange rate; currently, the United States dollar is considered the standard reserve currency globally and is held at $1. Other currencies are measured in relation to it. Carbon dioxide is the standard reserve currency of greenhouse gases.

A meeting or event participant using a bullet train in Kyoto, Japan, is an example of a scope 3 emission.
Photo courtesy of iStockPhoto/Imre Cikajlo

When we are asked to measure the carbon footprint of an event, we would need to take into consideration many factors. Factors are typically organized into scopes 1, 2, and 3, following a hierarchy developed by the Greenhouse Gas Protocol, shown in Table 5.1. **Scope 1 factors** are direct emissions that your organization controls, such as company cars or power plants. Most meetings/events will have few, if any, scope 1 emissions. **Scope 2 factors** are indirect factors, such as electricity and heat that your organization uses but does not control. Offsite meetings will have few, if any, scope 2 emissions. **Scope 3 factors** are again indirect, and this is where the majority of offsite meeting and event emissions will lie. This category includes the use of taxis, emissions created by contractors (such as convention centers) and outsourcing, the use of products, waste disposal, and water consumption.

Table 5.1 Greenhouse Gas Protocol Hierarchy

Scope 1	• Company-owned cars
	• Company-owned power plants
Scope 2	• Electricity (consumed in an organization-owned building)
	• Heat (consumed in an organization-owned building)
Scope 3	• Employee and delegate travel to event site
	• On-site transportation (taxis, buses)
	• Contractor/exhibitor travel
	• Use of products (badges, ribbons, food and beverage)
	• Production of purchased materials (books, badges, ribbons, etc.)
	• Shipping (to venues)
	• Waste disposal (at contracted venues)
	• Water and energy consumption (from contracted venues)

Environment and Economy

The environment and the economy are inextricably linked: the health of our natural environment depends on businesses and industries acting responsibly, and businesses and industries depend on natural resources, including water, clean air, and energy sources to operate.

The term *capital* has several meanings. First, there is financial capital, or money, which can buy what is known as "real" capital, the means of production. An example of this is the manufacturing equipment used to make ribbons and registration bags. Hotels, airplanes, and convention centers are also the means of producing services (room nights, travel, and meeting space). Human capital (association managers, event professionals, suppliers) is the set of skills and abilities that the workforce brings to the system, helping real capital in producing a good or service. Knowledge capital—specialized understanding of how to do something—is part of human capital, as it represents the unique know-how produced by an experienced workforce and leads to competitive advantage in the marketplace. Social capital is the value to an organization of its social networks, tied to the concept of goodwill, an intangible but powerful benefit to an organization.

Natural capital is defined by the Organization for Economic Cooperation and Development (OECD) as follows: "*Natural capital are natural assets in their role of providing natural resource inputs and environmental services for economic production.*"[10] The 1999 book *Natural Capital* by Paul Hawken, Amory Lovins, and L. Hunter Lovins expands on this concept, describing "the birth of a new kind of industrialism," where valuation of the system goes far beyond economics.[11] Natural capital can include renewable resources, such as trees, crops, sunlight, or wildlife; it can also include nonrenewable resources such as oil, gas, or minerals; or ecosystem services, such as clean water and clean air. The point is that, unlike financial or real capital, natural capital is not given a value on an organizational financial statement such as a balance sheet; it is viewed as an externality.

An **externality** is a third-party effect rising from the consumption of goods and services, but for which no compensation is paid. Natural capital is viewed as such an externality. There is no value placed by the manufacturer of a good or service on clean air, clean water, or the opportunity cost of using a nonrenewable resource now rather than in the future. The producer (manufacturer, hotel, airline, city) is often interested only in maximizing profits, and therefore takes into account only its own private costs and benefits. In addition, the producer may be said to have a fiduciary duty to maximize profits on behalf of the company shareholders, although of course risk to reputation, brand, and assets through its activities must also be considered. In fact, increasing regulation and research on the impact of environmental, social, and governance matters on financial performance and increasing awareness on the part of shareholders is transforming the expectations of companies to be more responsible.[12] Natural capital is not viewed as a cost to the organization; rather, it refers to social and environmental costs of production that are borne by everyone in society.

An externality can be both positive and negative in nature. An externality is considered positive when the benefit to society is greater than the private benefit to the organization. It is considered negative when the private individual or organization does not have to pay the full cost of their decision; they pass some of those costs on to society. An example of a positive environmental externality related to our industry could be the expansion of a rapid transit system in preparation for a mega-event, such as the Olympics. Local residents would benefit from this expansion for many years, but the investment would have come from funding not generally available to the community for this expansion. A negative externality related to our event would be damage to a

Table 5.2   Potential Positive and Negative Externalities of Meetings and Events

Negative Externality	Positive Externality
Pollution	Idea generation
Litter	Sense of community
Waste	Morale enhancer
Noise pollution	Education
Generation of CO_2 or CO_2e	Creation of personal networks
Water reduction	Collaboration/alliances
Air pollution	Common understanding/agreements

park from an outdoor festival. Table 5.2 illustrates further examples of the potential positive and negative externalities a meeting or event may produce.

As illustrated by Table 5.2, meetings and events have both positive and negative externalities. Many of the negative externalities are related to the environment; the choices we make as meeting and event professionals are intricately linked not only to our organization but also to society and the environment in general. The design of a meeting or event should take into account the deliberate increase of positive externalities, and the minimization of the negative externalities. Research has shown that reducing negative externalities that your organization is directly responsible for often has a more direct relationship with increased economic performance than amplifying positive externalities, possibly because positive externalities can be difficult to quantify.[14]

The Green Balloon Experiment

In order to conceptualize the amount of carbon dioxide equivalent emitted by common event-related actions, think of it in terms of the number of green balloons it would fill. To fully inflate a party balloon (about 1 cubic foot of volume), you need about 10 grams of **carbon dioxide**

Case Study: ABC Conference

The ABC Company is holding a three-day conference for 1,000 people. The conference includes lunch daily, and an exhibition with approximately 200 exhibitors. Each day, the planner orders lunch for 1,200 people at a cost of $35 each, of which only 900 are consumed. Each exhibitor leaves behind an average of 20 pounds of garbage.[13] The uneaten meals are thrown out, as is the garbage left by the exhibitors. The organization is charged the full amount for the lunches, which is $42,000, and then they are charged for two garbage pulls at $250 each, for a total of $500. Total cost to the organization is $42,500. The cost of wasted inputs is the difference between the meals ordered but not consumed, or $10,500, plus the cost of the garbage pulls ($500), for a total of $11,000.

Elizabeth Henderson and Mariela McIlwraith demonstrate the amount of carbon dioxide it takes to fill one green balloon.

Photo Courtesy of M. McIlwraith and E. Henderson

equivalent (CO_2e). To help to provide some perspective for the carbon footprint of some typical meeting and event activities:

- *A night in an average hotel = 2,650 balloons.* This is for a hotel with some "green" credentials, estimated as producing about 24 kilograms, or 53 pounds of CO_2e.[15]
- *An air flight from Vancouver to Rome, return = 300,000 balloons.* This flight would produce just over three tons of CO_2e, per person, economy class.[16]
- *A mega event, like The World Cup = 280 billion balloons.* The 2010 World Cup is estimated to have generated about 2.8 million tons of CO_2e, including all of the air travel and accommodation of teams and fans.[17] This is the same volume of about *3,181,818 Olympic-sized swimming pools.* This would cover a country the size of Sweden ten times!

Measuring the Carbon Footprint of an Event

In order to measure the actual carbon footprint of an event, you will need to follow a system. This ensures that you will measure all events in the same way.

A method suggested by the Greenhouse Gas Protocol Initiative is:[18]

1. Define the methodology
2. Specify the scope and boundaries of the measurement
3. Collect data
4. Verify the results (third party)
5. Report

Remember that each carbon footprint for each meeting will be unique, based on a variety of factors, including the destination, venue, type of energy used in the venue, distance traveled, and products used.

■ Defining the Methodology

The first step is to define your methodology, or what you are going to do and how it will be done. For a meeting or event, this might include:

1. Defining the scope and boundaries of the meeting/event
2. If you will use a previously defined methodology, such as the Greenhouse Gas Protocol
3. How you will measure your emissions, using what data and what conversion factors
4. How the data will be collected, and by whom
5. How the results will be verified, and by whom
6. How the results will be reported

It is important for stakeholders, such as shareholders, members, employees, or members of the community that the methodology is relevant to your event and to your business or industry sector, that it is complete, that it will remain consistent between events, that the process is transparent and accurate, and that the conversion figures are estimated in a conservative manner.

■ Specifying the Scope

This step defines the size of the project. The scope might be set as the entire event or a small portion of the event. For example, it might be the ABC Company sales conference, or it might be the exhibition at the ABC Company sales conference. In this step, be very specific. Four questions need to be answered:

1. What event are we measuring?
2. Which parts of the event are included? (i.e., exhibits, staff travel, delegate travel, on-site transportation, meals, housing, venue, off-site events)
3. What specific activities are we going to measure? (i.e., energy use, waste generation, water consumption)
4. Who is responsible for collecting the data?

■ Collecting the Data

Collecting the data might seem like the simplest step, but it can take a lot of work to do so. Here are eight ways you can collect data:

1. Facility energy bills, prorated for your group if the facility cannot provide exact figures. Make sure you ask what kind of fuel is being used to heat and light the facility, as this will decide what conversion factors you use to convert to carbon dioxide equivalent.
2. Facility water bills, prorated for your group.
3. Waste in pounds/kilograms, based on waste removal bills.
4. Staff travel miles, to and from the event. Make sure you collect the method of travel (i.e., car, train, bus, plane).
5. Delegate travel miles, to and from the event. You can collect this on the registration form, on-site, or estimate this based on the registration list.
6. On-site shuttle transportation, miles/kilometers driven and type of fuel used, using information provided by the transportation company and the distance the shuttle bus travels daily. Use odometer readings or take the distance of the shuttle route and multiply it by the number of times the shuttle drives this route. Alternatively and possibly easier, collect the amount of fuel used by each vehicle during your event as provided by the shuttle company.
7. The percentage of local food versus the percentage of food shipped from elsewhere. Estimate the amount of miles/kilometers that the nonlocal food traveled (see Chapter 3).
8. Recycled materials in pounds/kilograms based on removal estimates.

■ Verifying the Results

If the initial data collection and conversion into carbon dioxide equivalent have been done in-house, it might make sense to have the figures verified externally by a third-party auditor.

■ Reporting the Results

You may choose not to report the results to your stakeholders, but in the interests of a transparent process, it is a good idea to do so. This is particularly true internally, and it may serve to emphasize the strategic importance of the events function within your organization. This might take the form of an event-specific case study, be inserted into an annual report, or be an internal memo.

■ Conversion Factors

There are conversion factors for various inputs, shown in Table 5.3. These factors take the initial fuel or product and convert them into carbon dioxide equivalent (CO_2e). The initial fuel is often recorded in kilowatt-hours (kWh) or in liters/quarts. For example, 1000 kWh of gas = 0.185 × 1000 = 185 kilograms of carbon dioxide.

Table 5.3 Common Conversion Factors (Source: DEFRA)[19]

Usage	Input	Country or Type of Use	Unit	Conversion Factor
Air	Jet Fuel	Domestic	Kg CO_2e per passenger km	0.19518
		Short haul international, economy class		0.10928
		Short haul international, business class		0.16392
		Long haul international, economy class		0.09635
		Long haul international, business class		0.27941
		Long haul international, first class		0.38540
Road	Petrol/Gas	Small car	Kg CO_2e per liter	0.2049/km and 0.32427/mile
		Medium car		0.24978/km and 0.40199/mile
		Large car		0.35228/km and 0.56694/mile
		Taxi	Kg CO_2e per passenger km	0.18038/km
Electricity	Various, based on national 2008 averages	Australia	Kg CO_2e per kilowatt-hour	1.01893
		Africa		0.71269
		Canada		0.22521
		Denmark		0.36205
		China		0.88062
		European Union		0.40700

(continued)

Usage Electricity, continued	Input	Country or Type of Use	Unit	Conversion Factor
		Germany		0.48890
		Latin America		0.21952
		Middle East		0.78106
		Netherlands		0.44629
		Norway		0.00734
		Philippines		0.51791
		Russian Federation		0.36871
		United States		0.62747

Calculating Emissions from Air Travel

I am traveling from Calgary, Alberta, Canada to Denver, Colorado, USA. This is considered a short-haul international flight. I am flying economy class. The total miles traveled (usually available on your itinerary document) are 922 miles, or 1485 kilometers. To convert this to kilograms of CO_2e, I would do this:

$$\text{Distance traveled} \times \text{Conversion factor} = \text{kg } CO_2e$$
$$1485 \text{ km} \times 0.10928 = 162.2 \text{ } CO_2e$$

To do this for a meeting, collect the travel distance from all participants as well as the mode of travel, and do the above calculation.

Case Study: Intercontinental Hotel Group and Marriott International

Intercontinental Hotel Group, as part of its strategic corporate responsibility strategy, has measured its carbon footprint on a per-occupied room basis. It used the Best Foot Forward methodology.[20] The analysis showed that 51 percent of its emissions were scope 1 and 2 emissions, and the remaining 49 percent were scope 3 emissions. Total estimated emissions annually were 9 million tons. The best hotel averaged 22 kilograms of CO_2e per occupied room; the average was 59 kilograms per occupied room, or 0.059 metric tons.

Marriott Hotels calculates that its carbon footprint is 0.031 metric ton per occupied guest room, for a total footprint of 3 million metric tons of carbon dioxide annually.[21] The methodology that Marriott followed to calculate its footprint included measuring the electricity and gas consumption in guest rooms and public spaces at almost 1000 hotels worldwide, as well as at its headquarter offices. They used the Greenhouse Gas Protocol,[22] and it was third-part verified by ICF International.

A meeting or event participant using public transit counts toward the calculation of event miles. The Portland, Oregon, MAX light rail system connects the airport with conference venues, including the Portland Doubletree Hotel that is featured in the sustainable meetings chapter of this book.
Photo courtesy of iStockphoto/Ryan J. Lane

Event Miles

The concept of **event miles** is relatively new. It is possible that the first time it was used was by Tim Sanders, one of the founders of Yahoo!, at a conference hosted by Meeting Professionals International in 2008. Event miles are one way of tracking the impact of a meeting or event on the environment. The intent is to track the distance traveled by all elements of your meeting or event.

Event Mile/Event Kilometre Measurements

- Staff travel
- Delegate travel
- Speaker travel
- Exhibitor travel
- Contractor travel
- Supplier travel
- Shipping miles
- Entertainments miles
- Audiovisual miles
- Food and beverage miles

Not only will this measurement assist in measuring the carbon footprint of the event, it is also a possible way of helping to decide what destination to select based on both environmental and economic factors. Destinations farther away from the majority of sources will likely cost more in terms of travel, and will create more emissions to get there.

ABC Company

Seattle-based ABC Company is trying to decide between holding the annual sales meeting in Orlando or in Denver. Of the 1,000 expected meeting attendees, 80 percent are based in Seattle and the other 20 percent are elsewhere in the United States. All travel is expected by short haul economy class flights.

Option 1: Denver

	Travel Miles	Costs
Attendee travel from Seattle	1021 miles × 800 people = 816,800 miles	$250 (Average ticket) × 800 = $200,000
Attendee travel (other)	Average 1250 miles × 200 people = 250,000 miles	$350 (average ticket) × 200 = $70,000
Denver Totals	**1,066,800 miles = 1,716,848 km**	**$270,000**
		Carbon
		1,716,848 × 0.10928 = 187,617.15 kg CO$_2$e (187.6 tons CO$_2$e)

Option 2: Orlando

	Travel Miles	Costs
Attendee travel from Seattle	2553 miles × 800 = 2,042,400	$350 (average ticket) × 800 = $280,000
Attendee travel (other)	2553 × 200 = 510,600	$250 (average ticket) × 200 = $50,000
Orlando Totals	**2,553,000 miles = 4,108,655 km**	**$330,000**
		Carbon
		4,108,655 km × 0.10928 = 448,993.82 kg CO_2e (448 tons CO_2e)

Carbon Offsets

As carbon offsets have become more common over the last few years, their use in conjunction with meetings and events has also become a strategy to reduce their carbon footprints. A **carbon offset** is a conceptual financial tool used to help individuals and organizations mitigate the impact of their activities on the environment. The theory is that since climate change is a global problem, and since air pollution and emissions are not geographically based (today you may be breathing air that was on the opposite side of the world last week), a reduction in emissions elsewhere will have a balancing effect on the emissions you are creating over here. The intention is to create a balancing effect overall. There has been some controversy over offsets for various reasons, with some critics, such as Carbon Trade Watch[23] likening them to the sale of indulgences by the Catholic Church in the Middle Ages—a strategy designed to buy your way out of carbon emissions without trying to reduce them first. An offset, while not perfect, and not a better choice than reducing emissions, is still a valid strategy for reducing emissions on a global basis. Offsets can also play an important role in mitigating carbon emissions that cannot be eliminated through reduction strategies.

Choosing an offset can be complicated, because there are so many different types on the market. Many organizations offer offsets using vehicles such as planting trees (sequestration of carbon) or renewable energy such as wind or solar power (see Table 5.6 for a more complete list and description of renewable energy source and examples of how they are being used in the meetings and events industry). Projects are based all over the world, both in developed and developing countries. Choosing an offset means that the meeting and event professional should have a basic knowledge of important offset terms (see Table 5.4).

Offsets can be good strategies for reducing the overall footprint of a meeting or event. There are considerations the planner must take into account as seen in Table 5.5.

A wind turbine generating alternative energy is barely visible on the side of a mountain.
Photo courtesy of Thomas McIlwraith

Table 5.4   Definitions of Terms

Term	Definition
Additionality	Ensuring the project is new and not something that would have happened anyhow during the normal course of business operations
Renewable energy certificates	Usually for wind or solar power generation, also called "green tags"
Sequestration	The storage of carbon in a geological formation or living matter, such as a tree
Registration	Designation of offset projects if they meet certain criteria
Gold Standard	An independent best practice benchmark for carbon offsets
Retiring credits	When an offset is removed so it cannot be counted twice
Banking credits	Saving an offset benefit to apply against a future project instead of applying it to a current one

Table 5.5   Carbon Offset Factors to Consider

Positive Factors	They are relatively easy to find and procure.
	They are better than doing nothing.
	There are organizations that can help with verification, such as the Gold Standard.
	They do help the creation and operation of beneficial projects.
	They have helped to raise awareness of the need to address emissions and their impacts.
Negative Factors	Additionality is important in selecting a credible offset, but is hard to verify.
	There is a lack of regulation in many areas of offsets, such as sequestration and reforestation projects.
	They cost organizations to buy them.
	They tend to make people feel better about emissions without actually trying to reduce them.
	They are being used as marketing tools for organizations claiming to be "carbon neutral" (*greenwashing*—see Chapter 7).
Other Factors	They are one tool to consider using, along with others.
	Depending on the type of offset, they may not produce an immediate benefit.
	Not always certain of administrative charges.
	Not always certain of precise weight-for-weight calculations of offsets; formulas differ between providers.
	They don't take into account the social or "shadow" cost of carbon.[24]

Changing Your Energy Appetite

In his book *The End of Energy Obesity,* author Peter Tertzakian uses the analogy of an energy appetite.[25] As meeting and event professionals, we know food, and can apply this knowledge to an understanding of carbon consumption. So, think of carbon this way. Teens eat junk food. As

Marriott International

Marriott Hotels calculates that its carbon footprint is 0.031 metric ton per occupied guest room, for a total footprint of 3 million metric tons of carbon dioxide annually.[26] The hotel chain has taken steps to reduce that footprint, detailed in its environmental plan, *Spirit to Preserve*. To help offset the remainder of its carbon footprint, Marriott International has committed to help protect the Juma Rainforest Preserve in Brazil. Guests are given the opportunity to add $10.00 to their bill to offset their stay.

you mature, the wrong diet leads to health problems. You might need less quantity of food, but of a higher nutritional quality. The same is true for meetings and events; as the industry matures, it needs to move out of energy adolescence to prevent "energy obesity." You need to consume just enough energy for your meeting or event to be successful and meet its objectives, but not so much that it is wasteful. An energy menu for a meeting or event might therefore include these items:

- Decrease the use of junk energy (such as for materials and services really not needed).
- Increase the use of renewable energy.
- Go "low carb and low cal" (low carbon and less energy).

The goal is to use energy intelligently and to make the attendees' experience—and lives—better.

Renewable Energy Sources

Renewable energy is called *renewable* because the sources it uses to create energy replenish themselves very quickly. For example, renewable energy includes solar, wind, water, biomass, and geothermal heat. Just because energy is renewable does not mean it is environmentally sustainable, however. For example, large-scale hydroelectric dams use renewable sources (water) but contribute to large-scale destruction of habitat, flooding, and sometimes community relocation.[27] Renewable energy may also be intermittent, meaning that the sun doesn't always shine, and the wind doesn't always blow. Fossil fuels and nuclear energy are not considered renewable, as oil, gas, and uranium take millions of years to form in the earth and do not quickly replenish themselves. Table 5.6 provides an overview of several types of renewable energy sources.

Carbon Philanthropy

Hugo Kimber of the Carbon Consultancy in the United Kingdom coined the phrase *carbon philanthropy* for how he and his company approach the management of their carbon footprint, and suggest that others may find this approach beneficial as well. **Carbon philanthropy** is a sustainable, long-term approach to carbon management and reduction that analyzes the costs and benefits of various operational strategies to reduce both carbon emissions and costs. Supporting this strategy are investment strategies that encourage emission reductions in the community. This might mean supporting projects that employees are engaged with, that support organizational core values, organizational mission and vision, or its marketplace.[28] In Chapter 4 on social responsibility and culture, we introduced the MAUDE framework. One of the elements of this framework

Table 5.6 Renewable Energy Sources and Meetings and Events Industry Examples

Type of Energy	Overview	Issues to Consider
Solar energy	**Solar energy** is derived from the sun. It is collected through solar panels (also called photovoltaic cells or panels) and converted into electricity. Some event venues, including the Hyatt Regency New Brunswick in New Jersey, have installed solar panels on their rooftops.[29]	Solar is an intermittent form of energy, and so needs to be evened out. Photovoltaic cells are currently only 12% to 15% efficient in their conversion of sunlight to electricity.[30]
Wind power	**Wind power** is the result of transforming energy from wind into a usable form. Examples include using wind in sails to propel ships, or converting wind energy into electricity using wind turbines. Wind farms are a large collection of wind turbines that produce electricity for a utility grid. Sofitel Hotels announced in 2008 that it had become the world's first wind-powered hotel chain in the United States after purchasing wind energy for all nine of its U.S. locations.[31]	Wind is intermittent. Turbines are loud.
Hydropower	**Hydropower** converts energy from falling water, such as at a dam, into electricity using turbines or generators. According to the Worldwatch Institute, global use of hydropower increased by more than 5% between 2009 and 2010 to about 16.1% of global electricity consumption.[32] Bullfrog Power, a Canadian green energy provider, sources its power from wind and hydro facilities that have been certified as low impact by Environment Canada's EcoLogo™ program. Several Canadian hotels, including the Atlantica Hotel in Halifax and the Hyatt Regency in both Calgary and Vancouver, use Bullfrog Power.[33]	Large-scale hydro can destroy habitat and force communities to relocate. However, because water can be stored behind the dam and released as needed, it overcomes the problem of being intermittent and provides a constant source of energy.[34]
Geothermal energy	**Geothermal energy** is thermal energy stored within the earth itself. It can be used to heat and cool buildings using geothermal heat pumps, The Kirkland Hotel in Kingston, New York, is a restored 17th century boarding house that uses geothermal energy.[35] Geothermal energy can also be used to naturally heat pools, such as the hot springs pools at the Harrison Hot Springs Resort in British Columbia, Canada.[36]	Geothermal energy access depends on the geothermal gradient of Earth where the building is located. However, once it is accessed, the energy is both constant and nonpolluting.[37]

(continued)

Type of Energy	Overview	Issues to Consider
Biomass, biofuels, and biogas	Energy can also be derived from biological matter: 1. **Biomass:** According to the Biomass Energy Centre in the United Kingdom, biomass is "biological material derived from living, or recently living organisms." In the context of biomass for energy, this is often used to mean plant-based material, but can equally apply to both animal and vegetable derived material."[38] The Matfen Hall hotel, golf, and spa in the UK's Tyne Valley has installed a biomass boiler that will provide all its heating requirements using wood chips from the sustainably managed woodland on the surrounding estate.[39] 2. **Biofuels:** According to the Clean Energy Institute, biofuel is "Fuel produced from renewable biomass material, commonly used as an alternative, cleaner fuel source."[40] Examples of biofuels include biobutanol, biodiesel, bioethanol, biogas, and vegetable oil.[41] The Fairmont St. Andrews in Scotland has a program that "converts used cooking oil from the hotels kitchens into biodiesel through an on-site process that can be used to fuel the hotel's shuttle bus and the grounds machinery."[42] 3. **Biogas** is derived from the breakdown of organic material without the presence of oxygen and can be a substitute for natural gas. It consists primarily of methane and carbon dioxide, and is considered a relatively clean fuel.[43] Taj Hotels' Jai Mahal Palace in Jaipur, Rajasthan, in India has a biogas plant that is fed by kitchen and garden waste.[44] Several Taj Hotels are zero-discharge operations and a few have anaerobic digesters to tap biogas from kitchen wastes.[45]	Planting crops to supply energy from biomass can divert food crops from human consumption[46] and can serve to create monocultures more susceptible to disease.
Tidal power	**Tidal power** is a type of hydropower that converts energy from tides into usable forms. The largest facility in the world is based in La Rance, France, and it attracts approximately 70,000 visitors per year.[47]	In order to capture energy effectively, the tidal range must be at least 5 meters between high and low tides. Only about 40 sites in the world have this tidal range.[48]

U.S. Green Building Council (USGBC) Greenbuild

The USGBC 2008 event, Greenbuild, took place in Boston, Massachusetts. First, the organizers of Greenbuild worked with the Leonardo Academy to quantify and reduce the amount of emissions related to the event. Then, Greenbuild partnered with Enterprise Community Partners "to bring home the benefits of green building to low-income families."[49] Enterprise has a Green Communities Offset Fund that Greenbuild then used to offset the remaining emission from the event. It worked by introducing an equivalent amount of emissions reductions in low-income housing. Benefits include not only emissions reduction but also cost savings through lower energy bills and health benefits to low-income families.

The mission of Enterprise Community Partners is ". . . we create opportunities for low-and-moderate income people through fit, affordable housing and a diverse, thriving community."[50] Compare this with the USGBC mission: "to transform the way buildings are designed, built, and operated, enabling an environmentally responsible and socially responsible, healthy and prosperous environment that improves quality of life."[51] The mission of both organizations is being upheld by partnering in this philanthropic offset project, which we will explore more in Chapter 6.

is being destination specific, which links to the carbon philanthropy approach of encouraging emission reductions in the community.

This approach seems to be particularly relevant to the meetings and events industry. The focus on return on investment as part of a cost-benefit analysis is something that most meeting professionals are familiar with, and carbon philanthropy is less numbers-focused than carbon offsets and more people-focused instead. This approach also takes full advantage of the powerful communication potential of meetings and events by allowing the organization to support a project that supports its own mission, vision, and marketplace.

Peak Oil

The concept of **peak oil** revolves around the fact that oil and other fossil fuels are nonrenewable resources. Peak oil production is thought by many to have already happened; certainly in the United States peak production was reached in 1970.[52] However, consumption of oil has continued to increase worldwide. This has implications for meetings and events, specifically in the price of oil. We may not think about it, but oil and oil products make the meetings industry run—think transportation, heating/cooling, buildings, or food fertilizers and transport. If the price of oil increases, the cost of events also rises. Being aware of what we consume and conserve is a simple business proposition in this context.

The linkages between meetings and events and environmental science are simple and direct. The industry creates externalities that affect everyone else globally. It is our responsibility to be aware of these, manage them, reduce them, and report them to our stakeholders in a spirit of transparency, responsibility, and good business management.

Chapter Review

In this chapter, you were introduced to key terms that are being used more often in relations to meetings and events, such as carbon footprint, carbon offsets, and event miles. We also introduced terms that are not in general use in the meetings industry but are common to other disciplines and industries, such as externalities, peak oil scope 1, 2, and 3 emissions and the carbon cycle.

The connection of meetings and events to corporate social responsibility and ethics is clear and direct. The ostrich effect—ignoring the problem—is not an effective management technique. Acknowledging the industry's use of resources and the resulting impact on the environment, communities, and the economy will help the industry measure and manage its impact to create positive outcomes. Translating methods that are used in other industries and sectors contribute to the validity and comparability of the measurement, increasing both accuracy and profile. Leading organizations in the sector, such as Marriott hotels, are implementing practices into their operations.

Review Questions

1. What are some of the different kinds of capital to consider in a business context?
2. What is meant by the term *externality*? What are some of the positive and negative externalities in a meetings context?
3. Why is carbon a leading business concern?
4. What scope are most meetings-related emissions likely to be? What are some of these?
5. What is meant by event miles? What are some items to consider when measuring event miles?
6. What methodology would you use to measure the carbon footprint of an event?
7. What is a carbon offset? What are some of the factors to consider when implementing an offset?
8. What are the linkages between environmental science and meetings, and why are they important?

Group Activities

1. Create a carbon philanthropy strategy for a conference you are participating in, or for a hypothetical conference or organization. Give your reasons why you approached it this way, with reference to your organization's mission, vision, core objectives, and the mission, vision, and core purpose of the organization you partner with.
2. Find an event to use as a case study—either one that is in the planning process or one that has occurred and for which information is available. Using records of attendance, calculate the approximate air miles traveled by participants and calculate the carbon equivalent.
3. This project can be divided into two parts: a proposal and a demonstration. Create a proposal for a science experiment that illustrates an issue related to sustainable events. This should be a very basic experiment, using safe household items only. As an alternative, find an online science experiment on YouTube that relates to a sustainable event issue.

Please visit the Book Companion Site (located at www.wiley.com/college/henderson) for a list of additional websites where videos can be found.

The proposal will include:

○ List of materials
○ Brief description of the experiment
○ Description of the sustainable event issue in the experiment

Students will perform the science experiment for the class. The primary goal of the assignment is to clearly communicate an understanding of the sustainability issue presented in the experiment.

Sample proposal:

Name: Pat Smith

Title: The Carbon Footprint of Events

Materials:

○ 1 cup vinegar
○ 5 tablespoons of baking soda
○ 1 empty pop bottle
○ 1 balloon

Experiment description:

○ Vinegar is place inside the empty bottle.
○ Baking soda is placed inside the balloon.
○ Balloon is attached to the bottle and inverted, releasing the baking soda into the bottle.
○ Vinegar and baking soda react, creating carbon dioxide and filling the balloon.

Sustainable event issue: Events create a significant amount of carbon dioxide, particularly from travel-related carbon emissions. Increased levels of carbon dioxide "trap" more heat from the sun, resulting in climate change and global warming.

Key Terms

- green meetings
- greener meetings
- ostrich effect
- greenhouse gas
- carbon footprints
- scope 1, 2, and 3 factors
- natural capital
- externality
- carbon dioxide equivalent
- event miles
- carbon offset
- additionality
- renewable energy certificates
- sequestration

- Gold Standard
- retiring credits
- banking credits
- solar energy
- wind power
- hydropower
- geothermal energy
- biomass
- biofuels
- biogas
- tidal power
- carbon philanthropy
- peak oil

Resources

Related to the Resources listed below, please visit the Book Companion Site (located at www.wiley.com/college/henderson) for a complete list of websites. Additional referential websites related to this chapter's content can also be found on the BCS.

Department for Environment Food and Rural Affairs (DEFRA)

This site, maintained by the government of the United Kingdom, gives information and guidance on current energy conversion factors. It offers a Small Business User Guide for small and medium enterprises (SMEs) to provide assistance in measuring and reporting energy use.

The Carbon Trust

The Carbon Trust is a United Kingdom–based not-for-profit organization with a mission to accelerate the move to a low-carbon economy. On its site can be found footprint calculators and emissions factors (from DEFRA).

The Gold Standard

The Gold Standard is a not-for-profit operating in Switzerland that operates certification for high-quality carbon offset credits. It is recognized under the Clean Development Mechanism of the Kyoto Protocol.

David Suzuki Foundation

David Suzuki is a well-known and respected Canadian environmental scientist. His foundation website maintains resources on both carbon offsets and on strategies for sustainable events.

The Carbon Consultancy

The Carbon Consultancy is a for-profit organization based in the United Kingdom. However, it offers resources on its website on carbon offsets, carbon philanthropy, and other topics.

Pollution Probe

Pollution Probe is a not-for-profit organization in Canada seeking to define environmental probems, promote understanding through education, and seek practical solutions. Its Primer on the Technologies of Renewable Energy is an excellent resource.

Notes

1. Sam Goldblatt, *Greener Meetings and Events* (Hoboken, NJ: John Wiley & Sons, Inc., 2011).
2. Malcolm Gladwell, *The Tipping Point: How Little Things Can Make A Big Difference* (New York: Little, Brown and Company, 2000).
3. Dan Galai and Orly Sade, "The 'Ostrich Effect' and the Relationship between the Liquidity and the Yields of Financial Assets," *Journal of Business* 79 (5), 2006.
4. United Nations Environment Program (UNEP), "Climate Change." Retrieved February 5, 2012 from www.unep.org/climatechange/Introduction.aspx.
5. Corporate Sustainability Reporting: National Guidance. Retrieved from http://www.reportingcsr.org/national_guidance-p-19.html.

6. The National Association of Insurance Commissioners, as reported in the *Wall Street Journal* (March 18, 2009). online.wsj.com/article/SB123733370641063551.html.

7. NASA Earth Observatory. The Carbon Cycle. Retrieved from http://earthobservatory.nasa .gov/Features/CarbonCycle/?src=eoa-features

8. en.wikipedia.org/wiki/First_law_of_thermodynamics.

9. www.thefreedictionary.com/Greenhouse+gases.

10. Organisation for Economic Co-Operation and Development. *Natural Capital* Glossary of Statistical Terms. Accessed February 5, 2012 from: stats.oecd.org/glossary/detail.asp?ID=1730.

11. Paul Hawken, Amory Lovins, and L. Hunter Lovins, *Natural Capitalism: Creating the Next Industrial Revolution* (New York: Little, Brown and Company, 1999).

12. Resources on responsible investment can be found at www.share.ca.

13. The Green Meeting Industry Council estimates that the average meeting produces 20 pounds of waste per person, per day.

14. L. Lankowski, "Differential Economic Impacts of Corporate Responsibility Issues," *Business and Society*, 8 (2) (2009).

15. Mike Berners-Lee, *How Bad Are Bananas? The Carbon Footprint of Everything* (Vancouver, BC: Greystone Books, 2011).

16. Ibid.

17. Ibid.

18. The Carbon Trust. *Carbon Footprinting: An Introduction for Organizations* (2007, August). www.carbondecisions.ie/resources/footprint_for_organisations.pdf.

19. 2011 Guidelines to DEFRA/DECC's GHG Conversion Factors for Company Reporting, Accessed from http://archive.defra.gov.uk/environment/business/reporting/pdf/110707-guidelines-ghg-conversion-factors.pdf.

20. Best Foot Forward is a private company that uses an ecological footprint method rather than the greenhouse gas accounting methodology used by the Greenhouse Gas Protocol. Ecological footprinting not only takes into account greenhouse gas emissions but is a broad measure of resource use. www.bestfootforward.com.

21. www.marriott.com/green-brazilian-rainforest.mi.

22. The Greenhouse Gas Protocol is a widely accepted accounting methodology for measuring and reporting greenhouse gas emissions www.ghgprotocol.org.

23. The Carbon Neutral Myth: Offset Indulgences for Your Climate Sins carbontradewatch .org/pubs/carbon_neutral_myth.pdf.

24. The social or "shadow" cost of carbon is the cost to society of the environmental damage caused by emitting one ton of carbon (or carbon dioxide equivalent) into the atmosphere. The cost to society might include damage from more severe storms (i.e., Hurricane Katrina), rising ocean levels, changing weather patterns, or the loss or change of formerly profitable industries (i.e., automotives).

25. Peter Tertzakian, *The End of Energy Obesity: Breaking Today's Energy Addiction for a Prosperous and Secure Tomorrow* (Hoboken, NJ: John Wiley and Sons, 2009).

26. www.marriott.com/green-brazilian-rainforest.mi.

27. Pollution Probe, "Primer on the Technologies of Renewable Energy" (2003). www .pollutionprobe.org.

28. H. Kimber, *Carbon Philanthropy: Supporting a New Approach to Carbon Management and Reduction* (2008, August). www.thecarbonconsultancy.co.uk/pdfs/Carbon-Philanthropy.pdf.

29. Hyatt Friday Photo: Hyatt Regency New Brunswick Switches to Solar Power, Friday, Sept. 17, 2010, Accessed February 5, 2012 from: blog.hyatt.com/hyattblog/2010/08/hyatt-friday-photo-hyatt-regency-new-brunswick-switches-to-solar-power/2010/09/hyatt_friday_photo.html.

30. Pollution Probe.

31. Staff writers, "Sofitel Hotels Become First Wind Powered Hotel Chain in the US, *Energy Tech*." Accessed February 5, 2012, from: www.energy-daily.com/reports/Sofitel_Hotels_Become_First_Wind_Powered_Hotel_Chain_In_The_US_999.html.

32. Worldwatch Institute, *Use and Capacity of Global Hydropower Increases* Accessed February 5, 2012 from: www.worldwatch.org/node/9527.

33. "The bullfrogpowered Green Directory." Accessed February 5, 2012, from www.bullfrogpower.com/powered/directory.cfm?starts_with=&company_search=&city_search=&keyword_search=&postal_code_search=&category_select=Hospitality&green_index_category_id_select=-1&region_select=-1&submit=Search.

34. Pollution Probe.

35. Kingston Happenings. *Creativity with a Purpose: A Green Corridor Vision for Kingston.* July 5, 2011, Accessed February 5, 2012, from: www.kingstonnycalendar.org/2011/07/05/creativity-with-a-purpose-a-green-corridor-vision-for-kingston/.

36. James Glave, "Harrison Hot Springs Resort a Green Getaway in BC. Enjoy the Decadence Guilt-Free," *Canadian Tourism Commission Media Centre* (October 21, 2010). Accessed February 5, 2012, from: mediacentre.canada.travel/content/travel_story_ideas/harrison_green_getaway

37. Pollution Probe.

38. Biomass Energy Centre, *"What Is BIOMASS?"* Accessed February 5, 2012, from: www.biomassenergycentre.org.uk/portal/page?_pageid=76,15049&_dad=portal.

39. Janet Harmer, "Biomass Boiler at Matfen Hall Hotel Provides CO_2 and Financial Savings," *Caterer and Hotel Keeper* (October 10, 2011). Accessed February 5, 2012, from www.caterersearch.com/Articles/10/10/2011/340632/biomass-boiler-at-matfen-hall-hotel-provides-co$_2$-and-financial-savings.htm.

40. Clean Energy Ideas, *Biofuel Definition*, Accessed February 7, 2012 from www.clean-energy-ideas.com/energy_definitions/definition_of_biofuel.html.

41. Ibid.

42. Fairmont Hotels and Resorts, "Eco-Innovations Signature Projects." Accessed February 5, 2012, from: www.fairmont.com/EN_FA/AboutFairmont/environment/ProgramsandInitiatives/EcoInnovationsSignatureProjectsEnvironment.htm.

43. Pollution Probe.

44. Claire Baker, "A Welcome Sign: Hotels Adopt Reuse and Recycling," *Waste Management World*. Accessed February 7, 2012, from www.waste-management-world.com/index/display/article-display/271254/articles/waste-management-world/volume-7/issue-7/features/a-welcome-sign-hotels-adopt-reuse-and-recycling.html.

45. Indian Hotels Company Limited, *Beyond the Numbers: Indian Hotels Company Limited, 8th Corporate Sustainability Report 2010–2011*, p. 31. Accessed February 8, 2012, from: www.tajhotels.com/About-Taj/Company-Information/8th-Corporate-Sustainability-Report.pdf.

46. Pollution Probe.

47. Wyre Tidal Energy. "La Rance Barrage." Accessed February 5, 2012, from: www.wyretidalenergy.com/tidal-barrage/la-rance-barrage.

48. Pollution Probe.

49. Press Release: "Enterprise, U.S. Green Building Council Partner to create Carbon Offsets to Fund Green Homes for Low-Income Families," November 24, 2008.

50. www.enterprisecommunity.org/about.

51. www.usgbc.org/DisplayPage.aspx?CMSPageID=124.

52. Hirsch, Robert L., Roger Bezdek and Robert Wendling (2005). Peaking of World Oil Production: Impacts, Mitigation and Risk Management, February 2005. Retrieved from http://www.netl.doe.gov/publications/others/pdf/Oil_Peaking_NETL.pdf.

Working together helps all participants reach their goals.
Photo courtesy of iStockphoto/Vernon Wiley

CHAPTER 6

Shared Value and Strategic Corporate Responsibility

"Companies have to be socially responsible or the shareholders pay eventually."
—*Warren Shaw, US former CEO of Chancellor LGT*
Asset Management (1950–Present)

Learning Outcomes

After reading this chapter, you will be able to:

- Articulate the business case for corporate social responsibility.
- Recognize the difference between transactional and transformational community-based CSR.
- Discuss the idea of strategic CSR and the creation of shared value in a meetings and events situation.
- Consider if cluster CSR might work for your organization or community.
- Apply a framework for identifying CSR initiatives for your meeting or event.
- Recognize the benefits of authentic CSR from both an internal efficiency perspective and an external outreach perspective.

Introduction

CSR is often dismissed as being too expensive or as not making business sense. We challenge that premise in this chapter by assessing both tangible and intangible benefits of CSR on organizations and those specifically related to the event function. Time-bound meetings and events have other challenges in implementing CSR in a meaningful way. This chapter introduces the concepts of both transactional and transformational CSR.

Strategic corporate social responsibility—or strategic CSR—is an idea that links organizational strategy and objectives with the needs of the community for the benefit of both. The intended result is the creation of shared value between organizational skills and capacity and the needs of the community over the long term. A possible extension of this concept directly into the infrastructure of an industry is that of cluster CSR, which has the potential to allow small-to-medium-sized organizations in the meetings and events industry to participate in CSR in a meaningful way.

Linkages

Sustainability has become an important driver for meetings and events. Many people are familiar with what has become known as "green" or "greener" meetings. Sustainable meetings and events take this concept one step further, through the integration of community and environmental factors.

Meeting professionals may think that they have very little impact on organizational strategy, and that therefore the idea of strategic CSR in meetings and events is too remote for them to consider implementing. The idea of strategic CSR in meetings and events is, however, not to create strategy but to implement it in a way that benefits stakeholders—including employees, shareholders, members, or suppliers—as well as the community in which the organization does business. In fact, it goes beyond just benefit to *mutual* benefit. The basis of the concept is that of shared value. Meetings and events have long been about sharing value, making the implementation of strategic CSR principles within them a natural fit.

The Business Case for CSR

The biggest concern typically heard about implementing CSR initiatives is that it does not make financial sense. Fortunately, that is becoming an easier myth to dispel as more research is done into CSR in general. CSR is arguably a multidimensional and effective management tool, not a cost center.[1] Both tangible (financial and/or measureable) and intangible (reputational or contingent benefit) benefits accrue from a good CSR program. Business issues that CSR can help to address include:

- Operational inefficiency
- Poor stakeholder relations
- Negative publicity
- Loss of business
- Poor employee morale
- Risk mitigation
- Decision-making ability
- Poor reputation

An interesting perspective is to think of CSR as a tool with two levers. The first lever is the "positive CSR" lever; this lever controls many of the morally, socially, and environmentally positive actions of the organization. The second lever is not "negative CSR" but, rather, avoiding the harm that might come from not implementing CSR.[2] Although it takes a long time to build the effects accruing from positive CSR, it may take only days to destroy unless the organization has built up so much positive social capital it can mitigate potential damage. We quoted Warren Buffett, the American business magnate, in Chapter 1 and repeat it here: "It takes 20 years to build a reputation and five minutes to ruin it. If you think about that, you'll do things differently."[3]

Table 6.1 categorizes these issues along with potential benefits from an integrated CSR program in a meetings context.

Table 6.1 Tangible and Intangible Impacts of CSR

Issue	Benefit
Operational inefficiency	A focus on environmental improvement reduces operational inefficiencies through streamlined use of resources, such as less paper use, fewer shipping miles, or less materials brought on site, which reduces waste and recycling streams. Green meetings programs address many operational inefficiencies in terms of purchasing, resources, waste, and energy. APEX/ASTM green meetings standards directly target operational inefficiencies in the areas of destination, venues, accommodations, office activities, communication, audiovisual, transportation, food and beverages, and exhibitions.
Poor stakeholder relations	A focus on supporting the community improves trust and strengthens relationships within the supply and value chains. Relationship management is a core competency of many meeting professionals. Benefits of working with value chains include cost-effectiveness and buy-in, saving event professionals time and money. ISO 20121 and British Standard 8901 help event professionals identify and communicate more effectively with stakeholders.
Negative publicity	A comprehensive CSR program that has successfully built trust and enhanced brand and reputation in the community will help counteract negative publicity. For example, if the industry as a whole had a good reputation for CSR in the community, the AIG effect might have been toned down or negated entirely (for more on the AIG effect, see Chapter 1).
Loss of business	Customers and stakeholders are increasingly looking for organizations that demonstrate a link to their own values; not having a CSR policy gives the competition a competitive advantage. For example, if an organization is shopping for a supplier, all other things being equal, they may use CSR as a tiebreaker.
Poor employee morale	Employees increasingly want to work for organizations that share their values.[4] A CSR program that involves its employees in their initiatives can enhance retention and improve morale.
Risk mitigation	CSR helps build brand, organizational, and even industry reputation. By having a policy and program in place, it is less likely that the industry or organization will face regulation and can help mitigate poor public opinion.
Decision-making ability	Having a CSR policy helps guide actions of employees, volunteers, speakers, consultants, and suppliers. By providing guidance, it assists decision-making ability in a variety of situations.
Communicate values	CSR policy and programs not only state organizational values but also put them in motion. Events are perfect communication vehicles for CSR expressions.

Event professionals should make a case for CSR that fits their specific situation and organization. To articulate a business case, the first place to start is with a CSR policy for events.

Focus: Human Resources Benefits of Corporate Social Responsibility

Table 6.1 discusses the benefits of CSR for improving employee morale. Other human resource benefits exist as well. In a report for Industry Canada, consultant Coro Strandberg comments, "Employees prefer to work for organizations aligned with their values; thus, incorporating CSR into the employee brand can enhance recruitment and retention, particularly in tight labor markets."[5]

Attendees participate in a teambuilding session after building bikes for kids.
Photo courtesy of Tamara Kennedy-Hill, Green Meeting Industry Council, 2011 Conference

Through meetings and events, there is the potential to benefit organizations by creating engaging team-building activities that have a focus on CSR. Chapter 4 introduced the MAUDE framework—a tool for identifying these types of opportunities.

Mikey Hersom, president of experiential marketing company *ignition*, comments that sustainability is something that unites the company. The company regularly keeps sustainability top of mind by ingraining it into its office operations with recycling programs, energy reduction tactics, and offset purchases. It then reinforces the commitment through contests and fun, lighthearted reminders. As he notes, "It is definitely a morale booster, it's a huge uniter." Not only that, but Hersom notes that while *ignition* directly affects its 75 team members through its sustainability education initiatives, this extends further when those team members share their knowledge with their own network of family and friends.

Transactional versus Transformational CSR

Within community engagement aspects of CSR ("people"), it is possible to classify different initiatives as being transactional, transitional, or transformational.[6] Bowen, Newenham-Kahindi, and Herremans characterize these three levels as follows: transactional can be viewed as "giving back," transitional can be viewed as "building bridges," and transformational can be viewed as "changing society."[7] The different levels may be thought of as being part of a spectrum, from basic to more complex; the spectrum is not a reflection of the value of the initiative itself. **Transactional CSR** in the community may be thought of as the most basic strategy; this would include actions such as donating money to a charity, donating time (volunteering) to a not-for-profit in the community (e.g., volunteering at a food bank or painting a community center). It is transactional type of efforts that are most often seen at meetings and events, where people come together for a short period of time, and donate time, money, or even limited expertise to help out community organizations in the destination where the meeting or event is taking place. Communication with the community takes place one-way in this scenario, where benefits flow from the donating organization to the intended recipient organization and the service/final benefit is then communicated back to interested parties. As already mentioned, this type of program can be classified as "giving back."[8] Just because this is called *transactional* does not mean that it is not important; these kinds of projects provide something of real value for the community, and give a sense of contributing to the host community, as well as the opportunity to network with others, to the volunteer participants.

Transformational CSR, in contrast to transactional CSR, is a two-way street. Communications, benefits, and learning within the program accrue to both participants in the exchange, and both are involved in decision making and solutions. "Transformational engagement is distinctive because (1) organizations may achieve outcomes that were unattainable without the engagement of the community and (2) the community takes a supported leadership role in framing problems and managing solutions."[9] This kind of a program is far more than just "giving back," creating marketing opportunities or a case study to put into a corporate responsibility report. It creates authentic value for each participant that would not have otherwise existed. An example of transformational CSR would be a sustainable development exchange program conducted by a university. In this example, student participants interact and engage with a community and together work on a sustainable development project. The community benefits from the resources work done, and the students and university benefit from the opportunity for applied learning. Importantly, in this case, the community is actively involved in the creation, development, and implementation of the sustainable development project. Transformational CSR leads us to a discussion of a similar concept, that of strategic CSR and the creation of shared value.

Transitional CSR has elements of both transactional and transformational CSR: it includes more interaction than transactional CSR, but is not as collaborative as transformational CSR. Some community service projects implemented in meetings and events would fall into this category. In these examples, the primary beneficiaries are the community groups, with the event participants gaining some benefits, such as awareness about an issue.

Fiona Pelham decorating a wall. A community service project at a conference gathered volunteers to paint a community space for disadvantaged youth.
Photo courtesy of Elizabeth Henderson

Strategic CSR and the Creation of Shared Value

Strategic CSR

We have talked about the general concept of CSR and its relationship to the triple bottom line of people, planet, and profit. The idea of **strategic CSR**, pioneered by Michael Porter and Mark Kramer of Harvard Business School, takes this idea up a level, to the interaction between your organization and society at large. To apply the concept of strategic CSR, they recommend asking two questions. First, how does your organization affect society? And second, how does society affect your organization? It is in the process of answering these questions and finding the intersection between them that the organization determines where its notion of strategic CSR lies.[10]

Let's discuss the example of a hotel. Our hotel is located in the downtown of a large city where the cost of living is high. This hotel has difficulty in finding qualified staff willing to work in its housekeeping department because of long commute times and the high cost of transportation to the areas of the city where workers can afford to live. Our hotel affects society through the provision of jobs. Society is likewise affecting the hotel, because they have a lack of skilled workers. The intersection between the hotel and society is therefore a skilled workforce. The hotel might therefore choose to take actions that create shared value such as, for example, providing transportation from the outlying regions to the hotel on a daily basis at no cost to employees. It might also begin a program to help employees save wages or invest to ensure prosperity into the long term. Or perhaps the hotel decides to invest in a program that trains disadvantaged inner-city youth to perform duties needed at the hotel, which provides a long-term advantage to both the city and to the hotel.

All organizations have areas where they can create shared value in the community. Meeting and event professionals should look to their organizational goals and objectives as well as the core competencies of their organizations to help determine how this can be most effectively expressed in a meeting or event situation. The limited-time aspect of meetings and events can be obstacles to imagining how this shared value can be creatively and effectively expressed within its structure. The intent of strategic CSR is to use the core competencies and capacity of an organization to create shared value with communities; it is supposed to be a unique reflection of that intersection. It is therefore difficult to recommend a specific strategy for an organization within a meeting or event, but Table 6.2 is an example.

Table 6.2 Example of Creating Shared Value through Events

Organization	Core Competency	Issue	Community Need	Intersection
A film production company	Film production	Not enough skilled technical labor	Education for youth, permanent employment	Hosting a student open house event and behind-the-scenes tour of the film set. Students get interested in film production and gain some skills; organization gets a skilled workforce; community gains a skilled workforce, employment, and a tax base.

Shared Value

The idea of **shared value**, also pioneered by Michael Porter and Mark Kramer of Harvard Business School, proposes a new approach to value creation by businesses, where short-term profit is no longer the goal. Instead, the goal is long-term creation of value, which helps to ensure long-term profitability, customer satisfaction, and a positive contribution to broader social issues. Shared value is viewed not as corporate responsibility or sustainability, but as a way to achieve economic profitability over the long term. Shared value can be created through rethinking products and markets, and by redefining the value chain by looking specifically at elements such as the use of energy, logistics, resources, procurement, and distribution.[11]

Shared value is essentially a new business model. How, then, can it be applied to the world of meetings and events? A start might be asking two questions:

1. Is our event or meeting good for our customers/attendees?
2. Is our meeting or event good for society?

For example, the first question in the framework of an educational conference might consider product-specific factors such as educational quality, the protection of intellectual property rights of presenters, and the health and safety of attendees. All of those elements contribute to the meeting being good for customers and attendees.

Moving a level up, factors we might consider when assessing if our product (meeting/event) is good for society include our expenditure of energy, our consumption of resources, and how and where we procure goods and services. In the context of our educational conference, for example, we might ask ourselves how we can influence the procurement of quality education, since quality education helps our meeting be good for our customers/attendees. The answer might include providing scholarships or other educational opportunities for potential speakers/educators, to ensure their availability in the marketplace.

We could also redesign our logistics and distribution models to use fewer resources. For example, location matters for a number of reasons. Let's take our example of an educational conference. First, shipping is expensive, and it uses other resources such as energy and time; shipping lots of goods and transporting high numbers of people add to costs and energy use. The rising cost of energy means that maybe a regional model for meetings is a more effective use of resources and has the capability of adding value to society. A regional model allows event organizers to create long-term local relationships with their value chain suppliers. This, in turn, helps create two things: First, it helps create capacity and skills in the local community to support the event. Second, it supports the economic health of the local area in the longer term, as businesses can hire more people and pay better wages more consistently, leading to spin-off effects and greater general prosperity.[12]

We are not suggesting that the only meeting and event model is a regional one. We are, however, using this as an example to demonstrate the concept of shared value.

Social Return on Investment

Calculating a monetary value for social impact, or your social return on investment (SROI), is difficult, but there are methodologies to help you do this. As one group that has defined a process for measuring SROI states, "What gets measured gets valued."[13] Organizations also tend to use "social" as shorthand for the triple bottom line of social, environmental, and economic impact[14] or, as referred to by The Carleton Centre for Community Innovation, "blended value," which they define as "the notion that all organizations create value that consists of economic, social, and environmental value."[15]

Although SROI seeks to quantify social impact in monetary terms, it is ultimately about a broader concept of value than simply a financial one. A definition of SROI is "a framework for measuring and accounting for this much broader concept of value; it seeks to reduce inequality and environmental degradation and improve well-being by incorporating social, environmental and economic costs and benefits."[16]

There are four key elements to the process of quantifying SROI as defined by a group including the London Business School:[17]

1. **Inputs** are the resources that go into the project and that are a cost to the organization.
2. **Outputs** are the direct results of the program.
3. **Outcomes** are defined as the change that occurs in the long term as a result of the outputs.
4. **Impact** is the outcome minus what would have happened anyhow. This is similar to the concept of additionality discussed in relation to carbon offsets in Chapter 5.

One such methodology, developed by The Office of the Third Sector of the Scottish Government in conjunction with various stakeholder groups, defines a six-stage process to identify, measure, and evaluate social return on investment. The model proposed by The Guide to Social Return on Investment includes six steps:[18]

1. Establish the scope of the project and key stakeholders.
2. Map outcomes to show relationships.
3. Evidence the outcomes through search for data and evaluation of that data.
4. Establish impact. During this stage, you should discard what would have happened anyhow. Again, this is similar to the concept of additionality when considering carbon offsets as we discuss in Chapter 5; the Guide defines the concept as "deadweight" when used in this context.
5. Calculate a numerical value for SROI. This stage uses the concepts of net present value (NPV) and sometimes the simpler model of financial payback period. These concepts are discussed later in this chapter.
6. Report.

Calculating the SROI of meetings and events is a new way of looking at the value that the industry can bring to communities. It ties in with the idea of "legacy" introduced by new standards such as the Global Reporting Initiative's Event Organizer Sector Supplement (GRI EOSS) in Chapter 10.

Shared Value and Meetings Industry
Return on Investment

The concept of shared or blended value can also be integrated into traditional return on investment methodologies for meetings and events. The Phillips ROI Methodology considers seven data types related to the return on investment for a meeting or event.[19] Table 6.3 shows the seven data types from the Phillips ROI Methodology and relates these to applications for blended value.

Table 6.3   Blended Value and Meetings Industry Return on Investment

Data Type	Application
Inputs and Indicators	This section measures meeting basics, such as the number of attendees, costs, and efficiencies. Tracking increased efficiencies from environmental initiatives can be incorporated in this area to demonstrate their financial benefits. This relates to the "conservers" aspect of meetings and events as introduced in Chapter 1.
Reaction and Perceived Value	In this section, meeting and event professionals are able to track participant reaction to the program. Aspects such as their perceived value of community service projects can be measured in this area.
Learning and Confidence	Aspects to measure in this section include what participants learned during the program. It can integrate sustainability, ethics, and corporate responsibility education components of the program content.
Application and Implementation	This section looks at how participants apply what they learned during the program, and is an excellent opportunity to gauge what was introduced in Chapter 1 as the "catalyst" aspect of meetings and events, and how they inspire future action.
Impact and Consequences	This relates to the "creators" aspect of meetings and events as introduced in Chapter 1. Aspects to consider in this section include business benefits from the application of sustainability, ethics, and corporate responsibility education components of the program content.
Return on Investment	Integrating the SROI methodology described in the previous section enhances the overall value of the return on investment of a meeting or event. By incorporating social value, it strengthens the case for meetings by demonstrating a broader concept of value.
Intangibles	The ROI methodology also captures as an important aspect intangible benefits, and this can integrate the nonmonetary value of elements, including community service conducted by meeting and event participants.

Case Study: ICCA Green Traffic Project

In 2011, the International Congress and Convention Association (ICCA) held its meeting in Leipzig, Germany. Chief Executive Martin Sirk explains how ICCA integrated social and environmental responsibility into its original bid, and the results it saw at the Leipzig Congress.

Amongst the 11 standard criteria for evaluating bids for the Congress, one is called "Green/CSR." Destinations are asked to showcase either initiatives that they wish to introduce into the Congress to enhance the program or delegate experience, to highlight local environmental challenges that can be addressed by holding the Congress in their destination (e.g., need to raise awareness), or to highlight local strengths in this area (e.g., existing sustainability programs that go beyond the local norm).

The bid document received from Leipzig highlighted the very strong regulatory framework and pro-green activism in Germany and its meetings industry, the measures the venue (Congress Centre Leipzig) takes that go beyond the norm, and suggested one offsite trip to a green industrial facility. The intention to initiate moves to make use of public transport to reduce bus transfers and overall carbon impact was also raised. So, the Green Traffic Project was part of a broader theme within its successful bid.

The Green Traffic Project evolved to serve nine objectives:

1. Reduce carbon impact of the Congress on the destination.
2. Reduce costs of the local host committee budget.
3. Improve long-term collaboration between the venue, CVB, and local city-owned transport company.
4. Raise local awareness (corporate/public/political) of the importance of the meetings and trade fair industry to the city.
5. Change perceptions of former East German cities and especially Leipzig with former West German conference buyers (e.g., there are generalized perceptions of lower friendliness and efficiency).
6. Create a grassroots sense of welcome amongst delegates.
7. Create an experiential case study for the delegates, rather than talking about this type of project in the congress education sessions.
8. Design a new business model for transport that can be replicated for other major events, and in doing so differentiate Leipzig from rival destinations.
9. Engage and motivate young people working in the Congress Centre Leipzig, the wider Messe (the tradeshow arm of the venue), and the transport company to build an understanding of the key elements that build the capacity to deliver team objectives. Deliver a bottom-up solution, not a top-down plan, so the volunteers take ownership and really learn valuable lessons.

To bring the Green Traffic Project to Life, students, interns, and trainees were given the responsibility to design the project; it was not a top-down mandate. The team created solutions that benefited delegates while still serving the Leipzig citizens; for example, the tram timetable changed to match event delegate flows. The team also provided welcome signs and green footprints that led from each hotel to the nearest tram station. Each hotel hosted a table where volunteers gave out city maps and tram timetables. Volunteers were briefed to be proactive and engaging with delegates. Student volunteers on the trams, easily identifiable by bright green jackets marked with the conference and sponsor logos, gave away apples to delegates, as a symbolic and simple way to start conversations with people from all over the world.

The project evolved through the participation of four different companies: (1) Congress Centre Leipzig; (2) Fairgourmet Leipzig (Congress Centre catering company); (3) Fairnet GmbH (Congress Centre management company); and (4) Leipziger Verkehrsbetriebe GmbH (public transportation company). To begin, there was a joint meeting of all the organization's human resource departments to create the concept of having students/apprentices involved both during and after working hours. To follow was a kick-off meeting/workshop to introduce ICCA and to talk about the project goals. Students were an integral part of the meetings. The first task in the workshop was to set up teams and assign responsibility, ensuring that the teams were both cross-disciplinary and cross-organizational. The students then worked out details, such as tram schedules, maps, a video trailer that played on the tram detailing ICCA activities from the previous day of the conference, announcements in both German and English, and back-up plans, should the tram lines be obstructed. The students also worked out a catering menu for both tram riders and the student teams riding the trams. Students were responsible for arranging press conferences and for briefing their organizations and conference hotels.

The municipality also had to be involved in the project, as this allowed students to paint green footprints in the streets, directing attendees to the trams from the hotels. The final step in the project preconference was to create a detailed project management plan, including time schedules, human resource management, quality control, risk management, a sponsorship concept, and a public relations strategy for the Leipzig public to let them know what was happening.

ICCA raised sponsorship from an international meetings industry media group, whose logo was placed on the bright green jackets worn by volunteers on the tram. As well as covering most of the costs of the jackets, this sponsor made a €3000 donation to the local Leipzig Children's Hospital, our Congress charity recipient. This provided the foundation of our major CSR charity project: this hospital doesn't just serve the local market but also does tremendous outreach work to developing countries.

The Green Traffic project was one of the key newsworthy stories fed out to meetings industry media by ICCA. It also became a big story on social media throughout Congress. Leipzig convened a major news conference on the Congress in the week prior, attended by ICCA CEO Martin Sirk; the story that gained most attention was the Green Traffic project. This, in effect, enabled CCL/Leipzig Messe to communicate its broader message of how critical the venue is to the local economy to a wide audience of decision influencers. Members of the national press were also involved, enabling Leipzig to showcase itself to a wide audience.

This project is an outstanding example of strategic CSR at work in the meetings and events industry. ICCA's social responsibility policy has the goals of influencing the activities and impact of ICCA members around the world as well as the activities and impact of the association itself. The Green Traffic project accomplished both of these goals and created value for the community where it held its event.

(continued)

(continued)

It had these outcomes shown in Table 6.4.

Table 6.4 Outcomes of the ICCA Green Traffic Project

People	Planet	Profit
• Engaged and motivated young people in Leipzig • An experiential case study that can be duplicated in other events • Created a sense of welcome and community among delegates • Created a sense of community among Leipzig agencies • Built capacity in the community for future projects	Reduced carbon emissions from fewer shuttles and taxis	• Saved money for congress organizers (fewer shuttles) and for delegates (fewer taxis) • Allowed Leipzig to position itself as an innovative destination • Increased collaboration between CVB, the destination, and local suppliers • Raised local awareness of the convention industry impact on local economy

Implementing CSR in Meetings and Events

The reality is that most conferences and events take place within a very specific period of time, from a few hours to a few days. Occasionally, events extend for a few weeks (e.g., the Olympics) or even a few months (e.g., the Cultural Olympiad). Meeting and event professionals, therefore, need to take this timing into account when choosing how to implement a CSR program within their product, as this will help determine their scope.

Many large organizations within the meetings and events industry have existing CSR programs. Some, of course, do not; also, many organizations that hold meetings or events cannot be said to be within the meetings and events industry. They are simply organizations that hold events, and they may belong to any number of other industry sectors, such as pharmaceutical, automotive, manufacturing, technology, or service industries. So how can social responsibility initiatives be most effectively implemented through an event strategy?

Here are four possibilities to consider:

1. You can look at your own organization's CSR strategy and align the goals and objectives of your event CSR with those overarching goals. This strategy leverages the power of the larger program, and expresses it within the meeting and event. Meetings

and events are expressions of organizational philosophy and are how people perceive your organization; ensuring that CSR objectives are met in this way is a powerful statement.

2. If your organization does not have a social responsibility strategy or if you are not able to effectively express it in the meeting or event, you can consider participating in a program available through the venue or the destination. This is hopefully a program that benefits the local community and that operates continuously with the support of the venue and/or destination.

3. You can create a transactional activity, where the people who attend your meeting or event can donate time or money to a cause. This activity does not need to be tied to a larger CSR strategy.

4. You can create a long-term transformational CSR strategy within your event portfolio, which finds expression during events but which operates on a continuing basis with partners in the community. Use of the MAUDE framework to develop this opportunity will help you create such a long-term, transformational program.

Meetings and Events Industry: International Bee Projects

Meeting and event professionals are responding to a need to support bee populations. Why are bees so important? "Bees are responsible for pollinating plants that provide much of our food. In North America it is believed that 30% of food for human consumption originates from plants pollinated by bees." In the United States alone, insect-pollinated crops were worth $20 billion at 2000 prices.[20] Other initiatives to help protect bees by meeting and event industry professionals include installations of beehives in hotels and convention centers. These include the Lancaster London,[21] the Vancouver Convention Centre,[22] and the Intercontinental Boston.[23]

Case Study: Slovenia Convention Bureau: To Bee or Not to Bee

Slovenia is a small country in central Europe, bordering Italy on the west, Austria on the north, Hungary on the east, and Croatia on the south. It has a great diversity of geography, from the Alps to the Mediterranean, and Slovenians believe that it is this natural diversity that brings meetings and events to their country. The Slovenian Convention Bureau has therefore created a socially responsible campaign that they encourage all meeting and event professionals to participate in.[24]

The idea behind the program is this: "The BeBee campaign focuses on protecting bees that symbolize the diversity of natural resources and unspoiled nature in Slovenia.

Bees reveal the level of environmental protection and symbolize the Slovenian vision of preserving nature. Furthermore, bees relate to the Slovenian uniqueness, seeing that Slovenia is the only European country that has protected its indigenous species, the Carniolan bee."[25] The Slovenian CVB is encouraging all meeting and event professionals to adopt a bee colony to help preserve the environmental heritage of Slovenia. In this way, the CVB is creating shared value: it is offering meeting and event professionals an opportunity of "giving back" while helping the country preserve the environmental heritage that attracts more meeting and event business.

Four beehives are located on the Vancouver Convention Centre's living roof, each housing up to 60,000 European honeybees. Apart from keeping the roof's plants flourishing, the bees produce a wildflower honey used in the facility's scratch kitchen and for client gifts. *Photo courtesy of the Vancouver Convention Centre*

Cluster CSR

The idea of creating shared value is potentially very powerful for the meetings and events industry, especially when considering the idea of clusters. Cluster thinking recognizes that the success of all organizations is affected by the success of those around it, and that productivity and innovation can stem from working together.[26] **Cluster CSR** is the banding together of organizations to benefit their businesses and address issues important to the market and to society. Simon Zadek introduces a similar concept—what he views as the final stage of the path to corporate social responsibility. In Zadek's **civil stage**, "Companies promote collective action to address society's concerns."[27]

The meetings and events industry as a whole has a significant opportunity to create value for both the industry and society. Working collaboratively to address issues common to the meetings and events industry globally—such as environmental and economic impact, human rights, an educated workforce, or carbon mitigation—brings greater impacts overall and a greater recognition of the industry as an agent for positive change. Behaviors and tools are created by and for the cluster, not independently by all the organizations within it, significantly benefiting the ability of small and medium-sized enterprises to implement CSR.[28]

The cluster CSR approach would seem to offer opportunities for both convention and visitor bureaus and for large organizations and their value chains. For convention and visitor bureaus, creating policies, tools, and resources for the community standardizes expectations within their membership and allows more efficient marketing and implementation. For large organizations, such as hotel chains, convention centers, or large trade fairs such as IMEX (a large meetings and events industry tradeshow), it helps bring their value chains into line with their own efforts. This makes it easier to achieve certifications such as APEX or ISO 20121, and to report using

Global Reporting Initiative (GRI) guidelines (as discussed in other chapters). It also provides more opportunity to engage in transformational or strategic CSR and create shared value with the community.

We believe that it has potential to create transformational change. This is exemplified by the Copenhagen Sustainable Meetings Protocol.

The Copenhagen Sustainable Meetings Protocol

In December 2009, Copenhagen hosted the United Nations Conference of Parties (COP 15), a high-profile international meeting discussing climate change and the international response to it. Over a two-week period, more than 33,000 delegates participated, representing 192 countries. In addition, the event was covered by 6,000 international journalists. Organizers wanted to ensure that this event carefully controlled its own environmental impact. In the process of doing so, they created what became known as the **Copenhagen Sustainable Meetings Protocol** (CSMP). The intention of creating the protocol was not only to serve this event but also to serve as a model for cities and events all over the world.[29]

The CSMP was a collaborative effort between these agencies:

- The Royal Danish Ministry of Foreign Affairs
- Bella Center A/S
- Visit Denmark
- Wonderful Copenhagen Convention & Visitors Bureau
- The City of Copenhagen
- MCI Copenhagen
- Novo Nordisk A/S

The CSMP takes the three international standards, APEX/ASTM green meetings standards (logistics), British Standard 8901 (management process), and the GRI G3 guidelines (reporting) and integrates them into a unified model. Only British Standard 8901 existed at the time; APEX was in development and the GRI event organizers' sector supplement was yet to be built, so organizers relied on existing G3 guidelines. As such, it is not an additional process, but the overlay that binds the use of the three standards together.

The CSMP made the business case for sustainable events by making the arguments that sustainable meetings provide the following:

- Cost savings
- A social license to operate
- Staff motivation
- A healthy workforce
- An enhanced reputation
- A more inclusive event

A canal in Copenhagen.
Photo courtesy of Elizabeth Henderson

The Copenhagen Sustainable Meetings Protocol is not a CSR policy as such. What it does is create an integrated way of working toward sustainable meetings and events, while taking into account positive social effects for both local and global society through diversity and inclusivity. Organizers viewed a sustainable event as acting as a multiplier by providing "a model environment within which people can discuss and live the values and visions of the brands sustainable commitment."[30] It creates policy and tools that can be used by many different entities, and through bringing together a community in a united sustainability front in Copenhagen during the event, worked as a cluster CSR approach.

A Framework for Strategic CSR Initiatives for Meetings and Events

The concept of aligning business, environmental, and social objectives is very appealing, though not always easy to implement. There are several challenges:

- Identifying actions that provide positive returns on multiple dimensions (economic, environmental, and social)
- Balancing the potentially competing interests (such as environmental vs. social, as might be the case in selecting between organic or locally grown produce)
- Gaining support (including financial) for benefits that will only be realized in the long term (such as energy cost savings)

To help address these challenges, we are introducing a framework for the identification, implementation, and extension of strategic CSR initiatives (see Figure 6.1).

■ Step 1: Identification

The first step in developing a strategic CSR initiative is to identify how your business or event depends on environmental, social, or cultural resources. As examples:

- Will your event attract more participants if it is held in a destination with a rich cultural history or natural environment?
- Will your food costs be higher if local seafood populations decline?
- Will your venue be able to operate if there is a lack of affordable transportation, child care, medical services, or other social infrastructure for your workforce?

Issue Identification	Design and Implementation	Extension and Legacy
• Do you depend on environmental, social or cultural resources for your success? • What issues are motivating for your stakeholders or aligned with your organizational mission?	• How can you design the initiative to maximize the benefits and engagement? • Are there possible partners that could make your initiative more effective?	• What elements can you introduce to extend the impact of your program? • Can cluster CSR be a tool to create a more effective legacy?

Figure 6.1 A Strategic CSR Framework

- Will increased efficiency in the areas of energy use, waste management, water consumption, or other resource use improve your financial bottom line?
- Will your brand capture higher market share by being a recognized leader in sustainability and ethics?

As a second stage, identify issues that are particularly meaningful or motivating for your stakeholders. In Chapter 4, we introduced the MAUDE framework: this builds on engaging aspect of the MAUDE framework.

- Will the networking at your event be improved through the inclusion of a community service project?
- Would your workforce be motivated by participating in initiatives related to a particular charitable cause?

Once you've answered these questions, you'll begin to identify the points of intersection between your organization or event's business interests and those of society or the environment. In considering this triple bottom line approach, it is valuable to consider that not all initiatives will neatly lie in the convergence of all three interests, and that there may be ways of improving your business context through a focus on either environmental or social issues. Although the intersection of all three can be viewed as **sustainable** (see Figure 6.2), the intersection of business and social interests can be viewed as **equitable**, and the intersection of business and environmental interests can be viewed as **viable**. These areas follow concepts originally presented in the Brundtland Commission report, *Our Common Future*, and have been extensively reproduced elsewhere.[31] These issues identified through this process will form the basis for the development of your CSR initiatives.

ignition developed the Aquarius Spring! Bus Tour as a way of capturing preferred water brand status by demonstrating sustainable community action and participation. The tour visited 10 priority markets, participated in 69 local events, and created mass news media interest. By partnering with 12 of the country's top water conservation NGOs to organize volunteer watershed cleanup events, over 1 million consumers became aware of the brand's work to help remove 37 tons of trash. The bus itself was modified to run on used cooking grease and had two solar panels on the roof that powered every piece of AC equipment used at the events. The interior of the bus was constructed from recycled steel and aluminum materials, all decals were made from 50 percent recycled PVC with soy-based inks, and the paint on the bus was zero VOC. *ignition* was recognized with awards for "Best Activation of a Cause" and "Best Green Campaign" at the Ex Awards—the preeminent award for event marketing, judged by industry peers. *Photo courtesy of Mikey Hersom*, ignition

Step 2: Design and Implementation

Having identified the strategic issues for your organization and event, you can now begin to design your authentic CSR initiatives. The types of initiatives that meeting and event professionals can implement fall into two broad categories:

1. *Internal business process improvements:* These initiatives are generally focused on improved efficiency, such as reduced energy consumption over the long term from an investment in more energy-efficient equipment. They are more likely to emphasize reducing an organization's or event's negative impact on society or the environment.

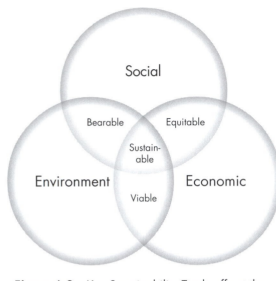

Figure 6.2 Key Sustainability Trade-offs at the Intersection of the Triple Bottom Line. *Adapted from Barbier, 1987.*

2. *External outreach programs:* These initiatives focus on creating positive impacts on society or the environment, such as through a community service projects.

Table 6.5 gives examples of internal business process improvements and external outreach programs for both environmental and social issues related to the meetings and events industry.

Long-Term Benefits versus Short-Term Investment

As mentioned at the beginning of this section, a significant challenge can be securing the initial funding for a CSR initiative that will only see the financial benefit in the long term. For example, Hilton Worldwide's LightStay program saved the company $74 million in energy costs in 2010.[33]

In financial terms, it may be useful to determine the **net present value (NPV)** of a CSR initiative. Net present value accounts for all of an initiative's future cash flows, less the costs of the initiative, all converted to today's value. This is more effective than the more commonly used **payback period** approach, which looks at how long it will take to generate sufficient funds from an initiative to recover the investment. While the payback period is appealing in that it can be simply calculated, it does not account for all future cash flows, nor does it adjust for the time value of money (a dollar today is worth more than a dollar tomorrow because of its earning potential).

Optimizing Benefits, Engagement, and Effectiveness

Meeting and event professionals should consider how to design their CSR initiatives in a manner that maximizes the intended benefits and engagement of stakeholders and leverages the skills and resources of partners to make initiatives more effective.

Table 6.5 Authentic and Strategic CSR Initiative Examples

	Business Process Improvement Example	External Outreach Program Example
Environmental and Business Issue: Deforestation is having a negative impact on tourism and the destination's reputation.	Reduce the amount of paper used for event marketing: saves costs and helps slow deforestation for paper production.	Organize a tree-planting activity: helps restore the forest and generate goodwill for the organization.
Social and Business Issue: Increased health risks from poor diets are affecting event attendance.	Reduce the amount of "junk food" served in your events: saves costs and reduces health risks.	Establish a community organic vegetable garden: promotes healthy food choices and creates a positive legacy in the community from your event.

To maximize the benefits and increase engagement, consider some of the following initiatives:

- Ensure that volunteers have appropriate training and resources to fulfill their commitments.
- Work with experienced team-building companies to design projects that engage and motivate.

From a partner perspective, consider whether your suppliers, clients, or other stakeholders have unique skills, resources, or abilities that can help you to achieve your goals more effectively than you could on your own. Examples could include:

- A hotel's engineering staff may be able to provide training and supervision for a community service project that involves construction work.
- A marketing firm client may be able to support a fundraiser by helping to promote the event.

Focus: Ludicorp's ¡MANOS A LA OBRA!

Ludicorp is a human development company that offers creative solutions in human resources, marketing, communication, and social responsibility. Its services include team building, leadership, and strategic planning programs in Mexico.

Ludicorp's creative director, Yomtov Iskenazi, comments that one of its services, ¡MANOS A LA OBRA!, brings together team building with social responsibility. Ludicorp's programs are designed to be collaborative with community groups, creating meaningful shared experiences that are mutually beneficial. The community group receives support, and the event participants achieve a sense of accomplishment, team building, and leadership skills.

■ Step 3: Extension and Legacy

Too often, community service is viewed as a standalone project, one where event participants make a short-term commitment that injects benefits to the community but that are not sustained, rendering the outcome less valuable. For example, after a garden is built, it needs to be tended for the plants to grow.

Meeting professionals should ask two valuable questions in designing community service initiatives:

1. What elements can you introduce to extend the impact of your program?
2. Can cluster CSR be a tool to create a more effective legacy?

Extending the impact could include elements such as incorporating an educational component to inspire a behavior change in participants that will cause a ripple effect: ongoing.

An example of an event that looked at extending the impact and cluster CSR is a project done by the Site Chicago Chapter at the 2010 Annual Meeting in Costa Rica. Keith Johnston, the publisher and chief writer of *Planner Wire* attended

A community service project by Ludicorp's ¡MANOS A LA OBRA! at an elementary school, Benitos Juarez, Puerto Vallarta, 2010.
Photo courtesy of Yomtov Iskenazi

the program and recounts how it introduced a postevent fundraising element and enlisted cluster support from suppliers in Costa Rica:

> *I was just in Costa Rica with Site Chicago for our annual meeting (I am on the board as the communications director). An amazing country, democratic and safe (about as safe as New York or Cleveland) with natural beauty and a firm commitment to the environment, Costa Rica provides very well for its people but, like all nations, there are shortcomings.*
>
> *Case in point is Cen Cinai in Cartagena. A school, well, actually a day care center, I am a guy so they are one and the same for me. A place where average Costa Ricans send their kids to be cared for when they go to work at the resorts, restaurants, and the sugarcane fields. A safe place staffed by wonderful, loving providers who make sure that the kids are not only cared for and safe, but receive an education as well. In short, an amazing place to spend your time if you are a kid. Until the fire. Late last year, when no one was there (thankfully), the building burned, fast. Now . . . there is no school.*
>
> *What there is, is a group of dedicated professionals who so desperately want to provide for "their" kids and they are doing a pretty good job. In the lot next to the school, they have a concrete slab that has a roof where the kids are coming daily. That is OK in the dry season, but the rainy season is right around the corner. When that happens, they will not have any walls to keep out the water, and water there will be.*
>
> *Site Chicago went to the school to provide some toys, not many, a few suitcases full, but badly needed. Toys were one of the things that went up in smoke. It was supposed to go [like this:] Go to meeting, go help for a few hours, go home.*
>
> *How it is supposed to go and reality are two different things, as every meeting professional knows. Make a plan, watch it go out the window, and then tweak the program on the fly.*
>
> *What happened to our group should happen to every group. We were not just seeing something, we were becoming a part of it.*
>
> *It started with the people. All of the parents were there with their children, they knew we were coming and made a point to come and thank us, a gesture that was not lost in the din of yelling kids. The hotel had sent balloons and cookies for the event so that everyone would have a common point. It worked like a charm; after being there for only five minutes we were chatting and talking. Two cultures, two languages connected by nothing more than the sound of children laughing and sharing their, and our, experience.*
>
> *Then we broke out the toys and we saw why children are special, they get it, they get that life is life and you should have a good time no matter what. I honestly don't think the children cared why we were there. They were just happy that we were there.*
>
> *The children jumped in with both feet, playing and being kids. The biggest hit we brought were items from IKEA. Crawl-though tubes and pop-up tents and stuffed animals. The adults were laughing and smiling and treating us like we belonged, not like we were "the Americans or outsiders," and the kids were including us like we were members of the family. These items, that cost us a small amount of money, provided so much joy and happiness. Silly, but true. Here is where things began to change . . . how you become part of something, an active participant and not just a fly on the wall.*
>
> *The folks from the Paradisus Resort were saying, "We can send people to paint, we can even provide the paint," then, "We may have some furniture," and then it was our turn, our turn to do more.*
>
> *We started asking the important questions: is the building structurally sound (yes), what else do they need (a roof) and how much does it cost (8K). This is when we said, "Eight thousand dollars! That's not a lot, we can do something."*
>
> *This is the moment that we decided to come back to the States and actually do something more than dropping off some trinkets and hanging out for a couple of hours. We are going to raise the $8000 that the school needs to rebuild the roof. If they raise the money before we can, then*

we will give them the money for school supplies. The point is, we are now in it, we are a part of it. We are not casual observers sitting on the sidelines watching CNN and saying, "look at those poor people, someone should do something." We are now the something.

Cluster CSR and Destination Management Companies

Destination management companies (DMCs) can act as cluster CSR facilitators by coordinating multiple groups to help address a community need. Heather McCarthy-Savoca is the director of sales and marketing for the Arrangers, a Colorado-based DMC and event-planning company. The Arrangers has been increasingly involved in producing community service projects for its clients, and it has observed an increase in interest in this type of work following the economic downturn in 2008. From a

Site Chicago changed lives at Cen Cinai day care, Cartagena, Costa Rica.
Photo courtesy of Keith Johnson

strategic CSR perspective, McCarthy-Savoca works with organizations to identify the right organization for them to support by understanding what the organization's stakeholders are passionate about, or if there is a specific theme for the event that can align with a community need.

The Arrangers has also established relationships with community service organizations, including the Boys and Girls Club and Ronald McDonald House. It is able to coordinate multiple programs coming to Colorado to provide sustained support to these community groups. Coordinating multiple programs also allows it to leverage economies of scale: for example, the Arrangers buys tricycle building kits in bulk, and can use its buying power to stretch the budget further and have a greater impact.

Chapter Review

Transactional CSR is what we most often see in meetings and events; it is the donation of time, money, or goods. Transformational CSR is used to create long-term conversations and value within communities. It is a concept similar to the one of strategic CSR, which is finding the intersection between the abilities and capacities or your organization and the needs of society for the benefit of both. The creation of shared value takes this concept one step further. The concept of cluster CSR may be the next step for small and medium enterprises in order to effectively implement CSR and create value. An example of cluster CSR is perhaps the Copenhagen Sustainable Meetings Protocol.

Review Questions

1. What is the business case for CSR?
2. What is the difference between transactional and transformational CSR?
3. What are four reasons organizations implement CSR activities?
4. Define strategic CSR and the concept of shared value.
5. What is meant by cluster CSR?

Activities

1. Working in a small group, pick an organization and create a possible strategic CSR activity it could implement in an event to create shared value.
2. Working in a small group, identify a community you could work with to create a cluster CSR program. If the community is interested, work with it to create a workable plan.
3. With reference to the Copenhagen Sustainable Meetings Protocol, which activities did each of the three international standards (APEX/ASTM, British Standard 8901, and GRI) govern within the event and event reporting?

Key Terms

- transactional CSR
- transformational CSR
- transitional CSR
- inputs
- outputs
- outcomes
- impact
- strategic CSR
- shared value

- cluster CSR
- civil stage
- Copenhagen Sustainable Meetings Protocol
- sustainable
- equitable
- bearable
- viable
- net present value (NPV)
- payback period

Resources

Related to the resource listed below, please visit the Book Companion Site (located at www.wiley.com/college/henderson) for a complete list of websites. Additional referential websites related to this chapter's content can also be found on the BCS.

Copenhagen Sustainable Events Protocol

The document, as well as its sister publication, the COP 15 United Nations Climate Conference, Copenhagen, Event Sustainability Report, can be accessed at the Copenhagen Sustainable Meetings Protocol website.

Notes

1. Gupta, Sanjeev and Nidhi Sharma. "CSR—A Business Opportunity," *The Indian Journal of Industrial Relations* 44 (3) (January 2009).
2. Dylan Minor and John Morgan, "CSR as Reputation Insurance: Primum Non Nocere," *California Management Review* 53 (3) (Spring 2011).
3. Janet Loew, *Warren Buffett Speaks: Wit and Wisdom from the World's Greatest Investor* (Hoboken, NJ: John Wiley & Sons, 2007), p. 27.
4. Coro Strandberg, *The Business Case for Sustainability, Strandberg Consulting* (2009). Retrieved December 5, 2011, from www.corostrandberg.com/pdfs/Business_Case_for_Sustainability_21.pdf.
5. Coro Strandberg, *The Role of Human Resource Management in Corporate Social Responsibility: Issue Brief and Roadmap Report for Industry Canada* (May 2009). corostrandberg.com/.../files/CSR_and_HR_Management1.pdf.

6. Francis Bowen, Aloysius Newenham-Kahini, and Irene Herremans. "When Suits Meet Roots: The Antecedents and Consequences of Community Engagement Strategy," *The Journal of Business Ethics* (2010).

7. Ibid., p. 305.

8. Ibid., p. 305.

9. Ibid., p. 306

10. Michael Porter and Mark Kramer, "Strategy and Society: The Link Between Competitive Advantage and Corporate Social Responsibility," *Harvard Business Review* (December 2006).

11. Michael Porter and Mark Kramer, "Creating Shared Value," *Harvard Business Review*, 89 (1,2) (2011).

12. Ibid.

13. London Business School, NEF, and Small Business Service (2004), "Measuring Social Impact: The Foundation of Social Return on Investment." Retrieved February 10, 2012, from sroi.london.edu/.

14. Cabinet Office, Office of the Third Sector, "A Guide to Social Return on Investment" (April 2009). Retrieved February 10, 2012, from www.socialevaluator.eu/ip/uploads/tblDownload/SROI%20Guide.pdf.

15. The Carleton Centre for Community Innovation (2008), "Social Return on Investment." Retrieved February 10, 2012, from www3.carleton.ca/cedtap/stories/sroi.pdf.

16. Cabinet Office, Office of the Third Sector.

17. London Business School.

18. Cabinet Office, Office of the Third Sector.

19. Jack J. Phillips, Theresa M. Breining, Patricia Pulliam Phillips, *Return on Investment in Meetings and Events*, (Oxford) Elsevier, 2008: p. xviii.

20. Bumblebee.org, "The Economic Importance of Bumblebees." Accessed November 22, 2011, from www.bumblebee.org/economic.htm.

21. Lancaster London, *Bee Blog*. Accessed November 22, 2011, from www.lancasterlondon.com/sections/beeblog.php.

22. The Vancouver Convention Centre, "Sustainable Meetings and Events." Accessed November 22, 2011, from www.vancouverconventioncentre.com/thefacilities/environment/.

23. Intercontinental Boston, "Intercontinental Boston Abuzz with First Honey Harvest from Own Rooftop Apiary of 40,000 Bees." Accessed November 22, 2011, from www.intercontinentalboston.com/images/pdf/intercontinental-boston-first-honey-harvest.pdf.

24. Slovenian Convention Bureau, "BeBee: Slovenia, Destination to Preserve." Accessed November 9, 2011, from www.bebee.slovenia-green-meetings.si/bebee/.

25. Ibid.

26. Porter and Kramer.

27. Simon Zadek, "The Path to Corporate Responsibility," *Harvard Business Review* (December 2004).

28. Heidi von Weltzien Hoivik and Deepthi Shankar, "How Can SME's in a Cluster Respond to Global Demands for Corporate Responsibility?," *The Journal of Business Ethics* (2011).

29. Copenhagen Sustainable Meetings Coalition, *Copenhagen Sustainable Meetings Protocol*. Accessed November 11, 2011, from www.csmp.dk.

30. Ibid., p. 8.

31. United Nations, *Our Common Future: Report of the World Commission on Environment and Development*. Retrieved December 5, 2011, from www.un-documents.net/wced-ocf.htm.

32. Barbier, E. (1987). The Concept of Sustainable Economic Development, in Environmental Conservation, Vol. 14, no. 2, pp 101–110.

33. Matt Alderton, "Hilton: Green Operations Saved More Than $74 Million in 2010," *Successful Meetings* (October 31, 2011). Accessed November 22, 2011, from www.successfulmeetings.com/Conference-News/meeting-facilities-/Articles/Hilton--Green-Operations-Saved-More-Than-$74-Million-in-2010/.

The Doubletree Hotel has partnered
with Herb Girl, a sustainable local business to
design these centerpieces which feature local
herbs, Cedar Grove compost, and Oregon moss

*Following GMIC, herbs will be used by the culinary
team or planted in Doubletree's rooftop garden*

At the Green Meeting Industry Council's 2011 Conference, the Doubletree Hotel, Portland partnered with Herb Girl, a local business to create centerpieces from fresh herbs that were later planted on the hotel grounds.
Photo courtesy of Elizabeth Henderson

CHAPTER 7

Communication, Marketing, and Public Relations

"People don't want to buy a quarter-inch drill. They want a quarter-inch hole!"
—*Theodore Levitt, Harvard Business School*
Marketing Professor (1925–2006)

Learning Objectives

After reading this chapter, you will be able to:

- Explain the differences between communication, marketing, and public relations and how these three relate to each other.

- Explain how effective communication with your stakeholders helps to achieve CSR goals, including engaging participants and partners in sustainable behaviors.

- Identify and avoid greenwashing in your purchasing and marketing practices.

- Provide consistent information about your CSR initiatives through your communication, marketing, and public relations channels.

- Demonstrate best practices in communication, marketing, and public relations related to CSR for meetings and events.

Overview of Communications, Public Relations, and Marketing

Key Terminology and Distinctions

This chapter will focus on issues related to three interrelated concepts: communications, marketing, and public relations. As we start this chapter, we would like to clarify the distinction between each of these.

Let's begin by examining definitions for public relations and marketing from trade associations:

- The Chartered Institute of Public Relations (CIPR), the United Kingdom's trade association for public relations professionals, provides the following definition: "**Public relations** is about reputation—the result of what you do, what you say and what others say about you. Public relations is the discipline which looks after reputation, with the aim of earning understanding and support and influencing opinion and behavior. It is the planned and sustained effort to establish and maintain goodwill and mutual understanding between an organisation and its publics."[1]
- The American Marketing Association (AMA) provides the following definition: "**Marketing** is the activity, set of institutions, and processes for creating, communicating, delivering, and exchanging offerings that have value for customers, clients, partners, and society at large."[2]

To summarize, public relations includes *actions* and *messaging* to the public for reputation management purposes. Marketing, by contrast, is focused on *activities related to exchanges with customers.*

Both public relations and marketing will include aspects of **communications**: *relaying of information to and from others.* Communications can take various forms, including face-to-face, written, electronic, social media, and signage. Communications can be internal (within an organization) and external with partners, clients, stakeholders, and the public.

For the context of supporting a meeting or event's sustainability and corporate social responsibility goals, we will be examining the following issues within each of the three areas shown in Figure 7.1.

Communications	Public Relations	Marketing
• Communication with event participants, partners, and other stakeholders to encourage sustainable behavior. • Reporting about sustainable and socially responsible practices.	• Communication with media and the public (stakeholders) about CSR and sustainability-related initiatives. • Actions that support communities and foster goodwill for the organization.	• Promoting products and services (including meeting and events) in a more sustainable fashion. • Effective promotion of sustainable and socially responsible products and services.

Figure 7.1 Communications, Public Relations, and Marketing

Communications

The first area that we'll examine is communications. In the context of this book, we are going to focus on two specific aspects:

1. Communication with event participants, partners, and other stakeholders to encourage sustainable behavior (see Chapters 8, 9, and 10 for more discussion on stakeholders and sustainable practices).
2. Reporting about sustainable and socially responsible practices (see Chapter 10 for a detailed discussion on reporting).

Before looking at these two areas in depth, it is valuable to consider how to communicate in a more sustainable manner. There are a number of ways that you can help make your communications more sustainable, including being strategic about the use of printed materials, and, when you are printing, using post-consumer recycled paper. Jill Taub Drury, CEO of Drury Design Dynamics, a full-service strategic communications company, offers further recommendations:

- Opt for electronic communication when effective and possible. Drury Design Dynamics recently converted from using printed showbooks for all core team members (executive producer, line producers, office managers, and production accountant) and client contacts that are on-site for an event by providing iPads with the showbook information included. This has significantly reduced paper use and allows them to send real-time updates to team members if changes are needed.
- Look at ways of repurposing materials produced for an event, including banners and signs. Drury Design Dynamics works with an organization called Repurpose America to donate leftover event products to community organizations.

■ Encouraging Sustainable Behavior

Meeting and event professionals can only directly control some aspects of the sustainability of their events. In the case of event planners, direct control aspects include choice of venue, destination, products, and suppliers. In the case of event suppliers, direct control aspects include equipment provided and labor practices. Other aspects are outside of the direct control of event professionals, but within the scope of their influence. As such, effective communication is needed to encourage sustainable behavior. Examples of these areas of influence include the following:

- Transportation methods used by participants, and carbon offsetting
- Utilization of more sustainable waste management practices, including recycling and composting
- Actions of exhibitors and vendors

The communication plan to achieve sustainable behavior in others involves three stages, as shown in Figure 7.2.

Figure 7.2 Communication Plan Stages for Encouraging Sustainable Behavior

Case Study: Common Thread

Common Thread is a Vancouver-based cooperative whose members include organizations that have a primary social purpose; for example, creating work for a specific group such as newcomers to Canada or Aboriginal communities. They also provide flexible employment options for people recovering from mental illness. Members include organizations and companies that support the cooperative's goals. Common Thread reclaims street banners from events, such as the Vancouver 2010 Olympic Games, and turns them into new products, like tote bags. This arrangement repurposes products that would otherwise be disposed of, and creates job opportunities. As Melanie Conn, manag-

Production of conference bags using 2010 Olympic banners by Common Thread.
Photo Courtesy of Melanie Conn

ing director of Common Thread, explains, the organization was formed in 2007 when five separate organizations came together to form the cooperative. The cooperative is able to secure higher-volume contracts and more regular and reliable work than any of the organizations would be able to do individually. Some of the members work from home, while others work from one of the member facilities. One of these, The Kettle Friendship Society's Sewing Room, is designed to be what Conn describes as a more comfortable setting than a usual factory environment. This allows people to "thrive in an accommodating work environment." As Conn explains, this type of flexible production format enables "people who are new immigrants, or have language barriers, or are living with mental illness, or who have not worked in a long time, who are new at sewing find a

way into that work." One important aspect of Common Thread's model is the training element. A teacher is available to support members, and this is funded through grants to the cooperative or to its members. These granting organizations, in addition to providing a critical source of funds, also act as a watchdog of sorts, as they require reporting on working conditions to provide funds.

At the time of the interview, Common Thread was preparing bags to celebrate the United Nations' International Year of Cooperatives in 2012. Purchasing products from cooperatives is an excellent way for meetings and events to support social enterprises. According to United Nations Secretary-General Ban Ki-moon, *"Cooperatives are a reminder to the international community that it is possible to pursue both economic viability and social responsibility."*[3]

The goals of each of these stages are as follows:

1. *Pre-event communications:* Think about who will have to do what, so that they have the education, resources, training, and lead time required to achieve the goal. During this phase, focusing on both the *what* (the behavior that you are hoping to achieve) and the *why* (the benefits of these actions) is essential. This information must be communicated in a timely manner to ensure that it is feasible. For example, exhibitors will need to know well in advance if there will be restrictions on the type or quantity of materials that they can have available at a tradeshow. To be successful, the communication plan may need to include reminder mechanisms, such as including information about bringing refillable water bottles in the event confirmation.
2. *On-site communications:* During the event itself (or when the behavior is required), meeting and event professionals should follow up to verify that the goals are being achieved. This will provide validation to others that you value this behavior and encourage it to happen again. It also gives you an opportunity to make any necessary course corrections before the event concludes, generate data for post-event reporting, and gather information to use in future planning and communications.
3. *Post-event communications:* Following the event, reporting results can help to encourage future sustainable behavior, and recognizes the achievements. More information about this is available in Chapter 10.

■ Reporting Practices

The second aspect of communications related to sustainability is the reporting aspect. During the event itself, meeting and event professionals have an opportunity to communicate the sustainable practices that they have implemented. Some of the methods for doing this include:

- Providing a list of sustainable practices on your event website or in your event materials
- Providing on-site signs highlighting your initiatives, such as information about sustainable food options on buffet tables
- Including announcements about your initiatives during your program

Post-event reports can be in-depth, such as through the use of a sustainable event standard, and they can also be quite simple, such as posting results of initiatives through social media. Event standards related to this topic will be covered in greater detail in the reporting chapter; however, a few best practices to follow include the following:

- Provide post-event information in a timely manner. You are more likely to be able to garner media attention if the information is released while the event is still recent.
- Use sustainability-related reports to set goals for future events.
- Recognize key participants, including volunteers, for their contributions.
- Use your post-event communications to celebrate your achievements and build enthusiasm.
- Allow opportunities for feedback from your participants. Valuable suggestions on how to improve your results can come from your stakeholders, and a formal process of engaging them is often required or suggested by formal sustainable event reporting standards.

Case Study: The Vancouver Folk Music Festival

Dr. Eyal Lebel practices Acupuncture and Traditional Chinese medicine. He has been volunteering with the Vancouver Folk Music Festival for over 20 years with the environment committee of the Festival. For the last seven years he has been acting as the committee's supervisor/coordinator. During this time, they have implemented continuous changes and improvement in waste collection reduction. Lebel is responsible for all waste collection, managing a group of 90 volunteers for the three-day event that attracts between 30,000 and 50,000 people. He is responsible for the maintenance and cleaning of the grounds, and is involved with the implementation of new contracts with both food vendors and art booth vendors. He continues to be instrumental in the planning of the environmental side of the whole event, including connecting and contracting with the waste haulers and ordering of all waste collection infrastructures. In order to achieve their

Image of the A-frame signs at the Vancouver Folk Music Festival.
Photo Courtesy of Louise Schwartz, Recycling Alternative

sustainability goals related to waste management, engaging stakeholders, notably festival-goers and vendors, is critical.

In 2011, the Festival decided to require that all vendors use only compostable service ware. The communication plan to achieve this goal includes the elements shown in Table 7.1.

In addition to promoting composting with the vendors, the environment committee actively worked to improve the environmental behaviors of the festival participants (see Table 7.2). This included encouraging lower carbon transportation and reducing the amount of waste sent to landfills. One of the successful initiatives was to drastically reduce the number of garbage drums on the festival grounds from between 50 and 80 in 2009 to only 10 in 2011. Lebel explains that if you offer garbage bins, many people will use them, even if recycling and composting stations are located adjacent to them. Instead, they replaced the garbage bins with large signs (see photo) that directed people to the recycling stations.

Public Relations

Public relations, at its core, is about shaping and managing public perceptions about your organization. CSR and sustainability initiatives can create positive perceptions and can attract media attention when they are done effectively. The concept of reputation risk, and managing this risk through authentic CSR practices, will be discussed in greater detail in the risk management and legal considerations chapter. Here are some recommendations for attracting media attention:

- *Design your event to be newsworthy.* From a sustainability perspective, look at initiatives that are more likely to attract media attention. For example, are you competing for a

Table 7.1   Vancouver Folk Music Festival Vendor Communication

Pre-Festival	Requirement that all vendors use only compostable service ware was included in the contract.
	A list of compostable service ware suppliers was provided to all vendors.
During the Festival	Environment committee verified compliance with all the vendors.
	For those found to be not in compliance, efforts were made to immediately source appropriate service ware.
Post-Festival	Policy was reviewed and updated so that 2012 contracts will include fines for failure to comply.

Table 7.2   Vancouver Folk Music Festival Attendee Communication

Pre-Festival	The Festival website included information about environmental initiatives, including the ban on bottled water, ride share programs, bike valet services, and the no-smoking policy in the park.
During the Festival	A-frame signs (see photo) were prominently placed around the festival grounds directing participants to the recycling stations.
	As the festival progressed, fewer garbage bins were made available, increasing the use of recycling and composting.
	Volunteers were available at the recycling stations to direct proper waste disposal.
Post-Festival	Environment committee members participated in press interviews after the event, highlighting their sustainability-related accomplishments.

particular honor that might attract attention, or does your program include a famous performer or celebrity that can help convey your message? Try to include a "human element" that will attract interest.

- *Designate a spokesperson for your event.* Ensure that this person has accurate and interesting facts and stories readily available to provide to the media.
- *Identify specific columnists who focus on sustainability issues.* In addition to sending news releases to major media outlets, contact individuals who include sustainability issues in their "beat" (area of coverage). Take the time to personalize story ideas for them.
- *Request that sponsors for any sustainability or CSR-related activities leverage their media connections as well.* Many organizations have public relations departments that have built solid relationships with the media.

ignition's Kia activation team set a Warped Tour record, filling dozens of bags with recyclable bottles and cans as part of the Tour's eco challenge.
Photo courtesy of Mikey Hersom, ignition

Be careful to note that you do not want to attract media attention for the wrong reasons. For example, a lack of attention to sustainability and social responsibility issues as compared to either past performance or to industry peers can generate negative publicity.

■ Actions to Promote Goodwill

Meetings and events can be an excellent tool for promoting goodwill with the community. They can also be public relations nightmares. An example that attracted considerable attention was a weeklong executive retreat at a resort by a subsidiary of the insurance company AIG, which was held only a few days after the company received an $85 billion bailout package.[4] The public backlash that occurred had a ripple effect on the entire incentive travel industry: The term *AIG effect* was coined to describe the flood of cancellations that occurred irrespective of cancellation fees by companies looking to save face with the public.[5] The impact of the AIG effect included meetings choosing lesser-known hotels, avoiding waterfront properties and golf resorts, and generally making programs less lavish.[6] The underlying issue with this situation was the public perception that extravagant business events were irresponsible given the economic climate. What made the issue even more complex was balancing public relations issues with promised incentives and contractual obligations.

Meetings and events can also contribute to positive public relations in a number of ways. As examples, cause-related events, such as fundraising concerts or benefit walks, can be excellent opportunities to build brand awareness for the events sponsors. In addition, community service projects that are included as part of an event program can be positive for the organization's reputation.

One note of caution: Community service projects should be designed using ethical principles such as those presented in the MAUDE framework in Chapter 4. Failure to do so can backfire on the organization, as it can be viewed as what we call **photo-op CSR**, one that is done with an imbalance of benefits in favor of the organization performing the community service.

Marketing

In this section, we examine four issues related to marketing:

1. The 8Ps of sustainable event marketing
2. Marketing of products and services (including meeting and events) in a more sustainable fashion
3. Effective promotion of sustainable and socially responsible products and services
4. Sustainable practices for experiential marketing events

■ The 8Ps of Sustainable Event Marketing

According to Joe Goldblatt in his book *Special Events: A New Generation and the Next Frontier*, marketing students traditionally recognize the following 5 Ps of Marketing,[7] with a sixth (promotion), which he adds based on Leonard Hoyle's book *Event Marketing*:[8]

1. Product
2. Promotion
3. Price
4. Public relations
5. Place
6. Positioning

In addition to these six elements, we add two more in order to incorporate sustainability and ethics into the marketing process (see Figure 7.3):

7. Proof
8. Principles

Sustainability and CSR issues and questions arise for each of the 8Ps, not just the two new elements that focus on verifying the accuracy of the sustainable claims and ensuring that the marketing process is conducted ethically and sustainably. Table 7.3 shows questions to ask in relation to sustainability and CSR for each of these areas.

■ Marketing Products and Services in a Sustainable Fashion

In a market environment where vendors compete primarily on price, differentiating based on sustainability may provide a decisive competitive advantage. To determine this, it is helpful to begin by mapping competitors in a perceptual map looking at different criteria. In the following example, we map competitors based on two criteria only: price and corporate social responsibility.

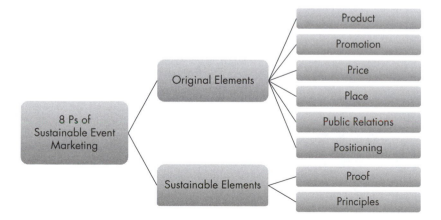

Figure 7.3 The 8 Ps of Sustainable Event Marketing

Table 7.3   CSR, Ethics and Sustainability Questions for the 8Ps of Sustainable Event Marketing

Product	• What are the sustainable attributes of the product? In event marketing, the product is typically the meeting or event itself. • Was the product made, packaged, and distributed in a sustainable and socially responsible manner? • What are the sustainability-related requirements for using the product? • What are the sustainability-related issues related to the disposal of the product?
Promotion	• Are the promotional materials used made from sustainable products, such as recycled materials? • Are there ethical issues with any of the messages in the promotional materials?
Price	• Are the prices that are being charged for sustainable products appropriate? • Are clients able to benefit from cost savings to the supplier from sustainable behavior on the part of the client?
Place	• Does the place (including the destination and the venue) that has been selected for event have a positive track record in relation to environmental and social issues? • Is the place of the event accessible via sustainable travel options for attendees?
Public Relations	• Are the CSR and sustainability initiatives that are being done meaningful in nature, or are they being done for "photo-op" purposes? • Have the CSR and sustainability initiatives that are being done initiated to improve a negative public image without addressing the original underlying issue?
Positioning	• Can the product or event gain new market share by implementing sustainability to position itself as a sustainable option in a competitive environment? • Is the product or event being positioned as a sustainability leader without having merited the distinction?
Proof	• Have the sustainability-related claims been verified by a reliable third party? • Are the claims measurable, or are they subjective?
Principles	• Are the sustainability-related claims true? • Does the organization making the claims consistently demonstrate a commitment to sustainability? • Is the marketing process itself ethical and sustainable? • Is information on how to use the product in the most sustainable manner included? This includes education to event participants on how to make use of sustainability-related initiatives.

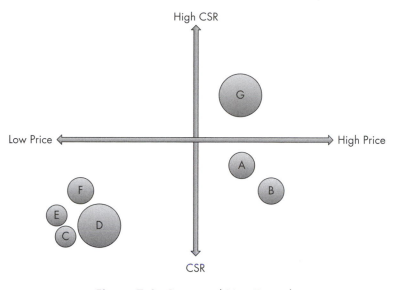

Figure 7.4   Perceptual Map Example

In Figure 7.4, the size of the circles indicates the relative market share of competitors. In this example, it is clear that there are several competitors using a low-price strategy that have a poor track record on CSR. Should one of them increase their CSR qualities without increasing their costs, they would move to an empty area of the perceptual map, where they would have fewer competitors. Perceptual maps can be used to compare competitors according to various sustainability-related attributes, such as a comparison of environmental performance and working conditions (see Figure 7.4).

Greenwashing

Both proof and principles are key aspects of both identifying and preventing the use of greenwashing. **Greenwashing** is a term used to refer to the practice of claiming environmental benefits that are false, superficial, misleading, or unproven. From the proof perspective, claims should be verified and verifiable.

To avoid greenwashing in the meetings and events field, both as a supplier and a consumer, recommendations include those shown in Table 7.4.

Marketing in a More Sustainable Manner

Marketing practices can be made more sustainable through the selection of more environmentally and socially responsible products. The recommendations provided in the communications section of this chapter form a basis for these practices. In addition to these recommendations, a special focus will be made on

Greenwashing concept.
Photo courtesy of iStockphoto/Jakub Jirsák

Table 7.4 Recommendations for Avoiding Greenwashing

Buyer	Supplier
• Be attentive to vague claims or terms including "green" and "environmentally friendly." • Look for reliable third-party certification and scientific backing to claims. • Investigate supply chain practices of your suppliers: Verify that all the elements of the value chain comply with the claim.	• Work with credible third parties to certify and verify your claims. • Ensure that all your business practices align with the sustainable mandate to avoid claims of hypocrisy. • Plan through end of use for your products: for example, if your claim is that your product is compostable, will it be compostable in the region you are selling your products?

promotional products, as these are often given away at events in great volumes and present a great opportunity to make an event more sustainable.

Promotional Products

Promotional products such as custom-branded items that might be given to event participants are an area where there are many issues related to sustainability and corporate social responsibility. Table 7.5 shows these issues.

Heidi Thorne is editor and founder of the Promo with Purpose Today blog. Her promotional products marketing company, Thorne Communications, offers a special collection of greener promotional product alternatives on their online shop site. Her company has implemented

Table 7.5 CSR and Sustainability Issues and Promotional Products

Environmental Issues	Does the item add value? This is the first question to ask when purchasing promotional products. If it is a product that is unlikely to be used, or is of such poor quality that it will not be functional, consider whether it should be purchased in the first place. Tradeshows can generate an enormous amount of waste if the recipients do not value the items being given away.
	How will the product be disposed of? **Extended producer responsibility** is defined as "a policy approach in which a producer's responsibility, physical and/or financial, for a product is extended to the post-consumer stage of a product's life cycle."[9] This is a practice that is gaining ground. This could have financial implications for meeting and event professionals should requirements develop in this field.
Social Issues	Under what types of working conditions were the products made?
	Was child labor or forced labor used in the production?
Business Issues	Is it a quality product that is representative of the organization's image? Consider whether you will want your brand associated with that product.

several measures in selecting sustainable promotional products. These include:

- Working with trusted suppliers to provide accurate information and follow best practices in the green arena
- Knowing why a product we offer is green (i.e., recycled, recyclable, biodegradable, etc.)

In general, Thorne recommends that people steer clear of products whose only green claim is that they are "eco-friendly" or "green." She further adds that the U.S. Federal Trade Commission is stepping up its efforts on green claims. The one caveat that she adds to this is that while she recommends avoiding products with loose green claims, "eco-friendly products" or "green products" can also refer to a category of products, such as a department in a department store. Many shop sites in both the promotional and retail areas will have a page or microsite dedicated to green

Meeting and event professionals should be cautious of eco-labels with vague claims.
Photo courtesy of iStockphoto/Oehoeboeroe

or eco-friendly products, which help direct buyers to a vendor's greener selections. This is not so much a green claim as it is a grouping mechanism. But when shopping in these green "departments," she suggests that event professionals carefully read the product description to verify why the product is green and, if necessary, ask the vendor about questionable claims.

Eco-labels, symbols used to indicate that a product has sustainable qualities, are not all created equal. Some are more robust in their requirements. Others can be very costly for participation. According to Thorne, the third-party certification and eco-labeling situation is complicated, particularly in light of the hundreds of separate eco-friendly certifications and/or labels. She adds, "This is a nightmare for both consumers and commercial buyers. The labels with the greatest recognition include Energy Star, the familiar triangular loop recycling symbol, USDA Organic, and LEED certification. Otherwise, it's all over the map, making it an insufficient tool." More information about eco-labels is provided in Chapter 9.

In respect to selecting products where there are trade-offs, such as balancing between more environmentally or more socially responsible options, Thorne comments, "To select meaningful and effective promotional products, meeting and event professionals really need to look at the values driving the event. For some events and organizations, green is not even on their emotional radar. Respect their values, whether they are green or not, but always encourage them to make baby steps toward more sustainable choices. Maybe this year do a bag that has recycled content or limit automatic distribution of bags. Next event, offer recycling stations for badges and lanyards. Greening promotional products is a process."

■ Effective Promotion of Sustainable Products and Services

This chapter began with a quote by marketing theorist Theodore Levitt: "People don't want to buy a quarter-inch drill. They want a quarter-inch hole!" In an interview for HBR Green, Steve Bishop of IDEO applies this to green marketing: "Consumers—whether they are green or mainstream—don't simply want green products, they want solutions to their day-to-day problems that also make sense for our environment."[10]

ICOMEX 2011, a tradeshow for the meetings and events industry held in Mexico and organized by Grupo Fidalex, provided speaker gifts from the Fondo Nacional para el Fomento de las Artesanias FONART, a federal government program that carries out different activities to support local artisans.
Photo courtesy of M. McIlwraith

This is a key point for marketing and promoting sustainable events and sustainable products and services for meetings and events: *the meetings, events, products, and services need to meet the underlying needs of the attendee or consumer.* It is not sufficient to be sustainable. Green marketing experts Jacquelyn A. Ottman, Edwin R. Stafford, and Cathy L. Hartman describe this issue as, "Green marketing must satisfy two objectives: improved environmental quality and customer satisfaction. Misjudging either or overemphasizing the former at the expense of the latter can be termed **green marketing myopia**."[11]

Critical for avoiding event green marketing myopia is ensuring that the initiatives to make your event more sustainable don't come at the expense of your event or meeting not realizing its objectives successfully. For example:

- Delivering high-quality education or networking opportunities for meetings
- Building brand loyalty for experiential events
- Providing exceptional entertainment for festivals

■ Sustainable Practices for Experiential Marketing Events

Experiential marketing creates opportunities for clients, customers, and the public to interact with a brand, its values, and its products through a face-to-face experience that involves both awareness and education, as well as corporate culture and emotional aspects. Among the benefits of experiential marketing is to develop such a high level of brand loyalty that participants become not only consumers of the brand's products but evangelists for the brand by promoting the brand to their own networks. If a brand is hoping to convey that it is socially and environmentally responsible, then its actions, including sustainability-related aspects of its experiential events, can strengthen this message.

An Interview with Denise Taschereau, Fairware

Denise Taschereau is the co-founder of Fairware, a Vancouver-based purveyor of custom-branded sustainable products. Her previous roles include seven years as the director of sustainability and community for Mountain Equipment Co-op (MEC) and as the director of policy and communications for the Recycling Council of British Columbia.

What is greenwashing, and what steps do you employ to avoid it?

We define greenwashing as the act of misleading consumers on the social or environmental merits of a product. We look to the FTC (U.S. Federal Trade Commission) guidelines on greenwashing to guide our clients in their communications regarding environmental products. E.g., one of the most common requests we get from clients is to print "recyclable" on products. However, while some products are technically recyclable, they are not easily recyclable to an end consumer via a blue box. In those situations, we advise clients that to put such a statement on a product would not meet FTC guidelines (a common product for this issue is the ubiquitous polypropylene shopping tote bags).

How important is third-party certification or eco-labels? Do you recommend them, and if so, which ones?

Although there are still few labels out there in our sector, we look to Bluesign Certification and Oeko-Tex 100 for textiles as well as the range of ASTM standards for biodegradability and compostability. Eco-labels are far and few between for other products in our line.

What are ethically sourced products, and why should meeting and event professionals use them?

We define ethical sourcing as ensuring that worker rights and health and safety concerns are addressed in the supply chain. We believe that how products are made is as important as what products are made from. We encourage folks to take this approach to sourcing by asking their suppliers (ideally in a formal questionnaire) what efforts they've taken to ensure worker rights are respected in their supply chain.

What considerations do you take in selecting products?

We look at the environmental attributes, the usability/durability of products, and the supply-chain efforts of our suppliers. We also keep an eye to emerging trends and new products. We supply marketers, so we need to always be on the edge of what's new and innovative—but where we differ from others is our ability to review new products through a lens of social and environmental responsibility. We want our clients to use products to do one of three things:

1. Educate (on sustainability issues)
2. Change behavior (e.g., lug a mug) or
3. Close the loop (help generate more markets for recycled and reclaimed products).

How has marketing, and event marketing in particular, evolved in recent years to be more ethical?

Our clients now recognize there is potential for brand risk in running events, by where you have them (is the hotel on board on these issues?); to what you hand out (excessive paper); to the products you use (are they environmentally responsible?) to the speakers you choose (reflective of diversity, etc.). I think a lot of our clients realize that running an event can be a showcase for their efforts in this area . . . or can show that they're disconnected from what they say and what they do.

(continued)

What trends are you seeing in sustainable products for meetings and events? Can you tell us more about your lanyard library?

We developed the lanyard library in response to seeing groups spend limited funds on what is often a one-use item. We'd rather folks spend those dollars on more useful items or not at all. So we created a subtlety branded lanyard and created a library of 1000+ lanyards. We loan them to event planners who pay for shipping and promise to load up pictures of the lanyards in use. We ask the planners to collect them after the event and ship them back to be cleaned and used again. They've been a great hit so far, and it's an example of an area we felt we could impact through our business.

How do you balance trade-offs between sustainable attributes? Such as choosing between a fair trade product or a more environmentally sustainable product? How do you avoid "analysis paralysis" in selecting products?

This is a big challenge but the place we start is to find out what is important to our clients. Analyzing trade-offs can drive decision makers crazy. We always determine whether there are key goals or priorities in our client's commitments that can guide the trade-offs. For example, if "Made in U.S." is a key issue, we might trade-off an organic tee-shirt for a made-in-U.S. tee-shirt where their budget can't allow for both, or if we have a client launching a zero-waste lunch program, we'd get them into a recycled poly lunch kit instead of an organic cotton lunch kit—the recycled poly can help tell a story of "closing the loop." It's really a case-by-case situation with the goal being aligning the product with the corporate goal or priorities.

What recommendations do you have for meeting and event professionals related to sustainable products?

Be mindful of what products you really need. We've seen a lot of products that have questionable value to the end user get handed out at events only to end up in a hotel room after check-out. If the product doesn't serve a purpose, don't bother.

Fairware's Supplier Code of Conduct is modeled after the Fair Labor Association's Workplace Code of Conduct, reprinted below:

2011 FLA Workplace Code of Conduct
Preamble

The FLA Workplace Code of Conduct defines labor standards that aim to achieve decent and humane working conditions. The Code's standards are based on International Labor Organization standards and internationally accepted good labor practices.

Companies affiliated with the FLA are expected to comply with all relevant and applicable laws and regulations of the country in which workers are employed and to implement the Workplace Code in their applicable facilities. When differences or conflicts in standards arise, affiliated companies are expected to apply the highest standard.

The FLA monitors compliance with the Workplace Code by carefully examining adherence to the Compliance Benchmarks and the Principles of Monitoring. The Compliance Benchmarks identify specific requirements for meeting each Code standard, while the Principles of Monitoring guide the assessment of compliance. The FLA expects affiliated companies to make improvements when Code standards are not met and to develop sustainable mechanisms to ensure ongoing compliance.

The FLA provides a model of collaboration, accountability, and transparency and serves as a catalyst for positive change in workplace conditions. As an organization that promotes continuous improvement, the FLA strives to be a global leader in establishing best practices for respectful and ethical treatment of workers, and in promoting sustainable conditions through which workers earn fair wages in safe and healthy workplaces.

Employment Relationship

Employers shall adopt and adhere to rules and conditions of employment that respect workers and, at a minimum, safeguard their rights under national and international labor and social security laws and regulations.

Nondiscrimination

No person shall be subject to any discrimination in employment, including hiring, compensation, advancement, discipline, termination or retirement, on the basis of gender, race, religion, age, disability, sexual orientation, nationality, political opinion, social group or ethnic origin.

Harassment or Abuse

Every employee shall be treated with respect and dignity. No employee shall be subject to any physical, sexual, psychological or verbal harassment or abuse.

Forced Labor

There shall be no use of forced labor, including prison labor, indentured labor, bonded labor or other forms of forced labor.

Child Labor

No person shall be employed under the age of 15 or under the age for completion of compulsory education, whichever is higher.

Freedom of Association and Collective Bargaining

Employers shall recognize and respect the right of employees to freedom of association and collective bargaining.

Health, Safety and Environment

Employers shall provide a safe and healthy workplace setting to prevent accidents and injury to health arising out of, linked with, or occurring in the course of work or as a result of the operation of employers' facilities. Employers shall adopt responsible measures to mitigate negative impacts that the workplace has on the environment.

Hours of Work

Employers shall not require workers to work more than the regular and overtime hours allowed by the law of the country where the workers are employed. The regular work week shall not exceed 48 hours. Employers shall allow workers at least 24 consecutive hours of rest in every seven-day period. All overtime work shall be consensual. Employers shall not request overtime on a regular basis and shall compensate all overtime work at a premium rate. Other than in exceptional circumstances, the sum of regular and overtime hours in a week shall not exceed 60 hours.

Compensation

Every worker has a right to compensation for a regular work week that is sufficient to meet the worker's basic needs and provide some discretionary income. Employers shall pay at least the minimum wage or the appropriate prevailing wage, whichever is higher, comply with all legal requirements on wages, and provide any fringe benefits required by law or contract. Where compensation does not meet workers' basic needs and provide some discretionary income, each employer shall work with the FLA to take appropriate actions that seek to progressively realize a level of compensation that does.

Coca-Cola celebrated its 125th anniversary with a record-setting concert attended by 16,000 people. It achieved iSES™ Gold, the scorecard's highest ranking. (*ignition's* proprietary Sustainability Execution Scorecard [iSES™] was built on the British Standard 8901™—a globally recognized benchmark for sustainable events. iSES is a practical and customizable tool that helps deliver activations in an environmentally, socially, and fiscally responsible way.) Robust recycling and composting programs diverted landfill waste, stage banners were recycled into reusable bags, and green energy supplemented by carbon offsets was deployed.
Photo courtesy of Mikey Hersom, ignition

One example is *ignition*, an experience-based marketing agency that has been at the forefront of incorporating sustainability into experiential marketing events. At the 2010 Ex Awards given by Event Marketer to celebrate excellence in experiential marketing, *ignition* won both the Best Activation of a Cause Sponsorship/Tie-in and Best Green Event/Trade Show Campaign for their Aquarius Spring! Road Trip for Coca-Cola Co.

Mikey Hersom is the owner and president of *ignition,* and his view is that "sustainability is a journey, not a destination." He recognizes that there are challenges along the journey, but you need to keep trying. As he says, "If you look at the marketing mix, advertising, digital, PR, experiential . . . we are without any doubt the most wasteful, largest footprint . . . marketing discipline if you will, of the major ones, . . . we have massive amounts of stuff, big trucks, big events, lots of people, . . . it's big, and so we have to figure it out." The practices that we have discussed throughout this book and in this chapter related to sustainable events, including designing them to be more socially and environmentally responsible, are important for addressing Hersom's challenge.

Measuring Communications, Public Relations, and Marketing Success from a Sustainability Perspective

In the beginning of this chapter, we introduced several objectives for communications, public relations, and marketing for meetings and events related to sustainability (see Figure 7.1: Communications, Public Relations, and Marketing). In this final section of the chapter, we'll introduce methodologies for measuring success in these fields. The success will involve measuring **key performance indicators (KPIs)**. KPIs are pre-determined, quantifiable measurements of factors that are critical for success. Meeting and event professionals should develop specific KPIs to measure the success of their initiatives. Examples of ones that can be used as a starting point are included in Table 7.6.

These examples illustrate the types of KPIs that can be used to measure the sustainable aspects of communications, public relations, and marketing campaigns. These KPIs should be adapted to specific meetings and events by asking: How can the success of this initiative be measured from a sustainability perspective?

Table 7.6 Key Performance Indicators for Success in Sustainable Communications, Public Relations, and Marketing for Meetings and Events

Field	Objective	Example of a Key Performance Indicator (KPIs)
Communications	Communication with event participants, partners, and other stakeholders to encourage sustainable behavior	Percentage of participants that utilized public transportation or offset their carbon emissions
	Reporting about sustainable and socially responsible practices	Production of post-event reports; could include utilization of GRI reporting guidelines
Public Relations	Communication with media and the public about CSR and sustainability-related initiatives	Number of articles generated for the event that feature sustainability-related initiatives
	Actions that support communities and foster goodwill for the organization	Outcomes of community service project (such as number of trees planted, bikes built, or amount of garbage collected)
Marketing	Promoting products and services (including meeting and events) in a more sustainable fashion	Percentage of printed materials replaced by electronic formats from previous year or percentage printed on recycled paper
	Effective promotion of sustainable and socially products and services	Percentage of increased sales that can be attributed to sustainability initiatives

Chapter Review

This chapter focused on issues related to three interrelated concepts: communication, marketing, and public relations. Best practices for engaging stakeholders in participating in sustainable behavior, attracting media attention, and understanding motivations of green consumers were reviewed. Key takeaways from the chapter include recognizing and avoiding greenwashing, practical tools for communicating and marketing in more sustainable ways, and incorporating proof and principles into the marketing process.

Review Questions

1. What are the differences between communications, public relations, and marketing?
2. What are the 8Ps of sustainable event marketing? What is the significance of proof and principles?
3. What is green marketing myopia, and how is it relevant for meetings and events?
4. What are key performance indicators, and how can they be used to measure the success of communications, public relations, and marketing initiatives?

Group Exercises

Develop a communication plan with pre-event, on-site, and post-event elements for the following initiatives:

1. Increase the number of participants using public transportation from the airport to host hotels for an international conference.
2. Reduce the amount of printed materials offered by exhibitors at a tradeshow.

Key Terms

- public relations
- marketing
- communications
- photo-op CSR
- greenwashing
- promotional products

- extended producer responsibility
- eco-labels
- green marketing myopia
- experiential marketing
- key performance indicators (KPIs)

Recommended Books

Goldblatt, Joe. *Special Events: A New Generation and the Next Frontier*. Hoboken, NJ: John Wiley & Sons, 2011.

Goldblatt, Sam. *Greener Meetings and Events*. Hoboken, NJ: John Wiley & Sons, 2011.

Hoyle, Leonard H. *Event Marketing*. New York: John Wiley & Sons, 2002.

Kotler, Phil, John T. Bowen, and James Makens. *Marketing for Hospitality and Tourism*, 5th ed. Upper Saddle River, NJ: Prentice Hall, 2010.

Ottman, Jacquelyn A. *The New Rules of Green Marketing, Strategies, Tools, and Inspiration for Sustainable Branding*. San Francisco: Berrett-Koehler Publishers, Inc., 2011.

Preston, Chris, and Hoyle, Leonard H. Hoyle. (2012) *Event Marketing: How to Successfully Promote Events, Festivals, Conventions, and Expositions*, 2nd ed. Hoboken, NJ: John Wiley & Sons, Inc., 2012.

Notes

1. The Chartered Institute of Public Relations, "What Is PR?" www.cipr.co.uk/content/careers-cpd/careers-pr/what-pr.
2. American Marketing Association, "Definition of Marketing," www.marketingpower.com/AboutAMA/Pages/DefinitionofMarketing.aspx.
3. United Nations, "International Year of Cooperatives 2012." social.un.org/coopsyear/.

4. Derek Kravitz, "AIG Executive Retreat Irks Lawmakers," *The Washington Post* (October 7, 2008). voices.washingtonpost.com/washingtonpostinvestigations/2008/10/after_bailout_aig_execs_took_4.html.

5. Mark Lewis, "The AIG Effect," Forbes.com (February 2, 2010). www.forbes.com/2010/02/16/aig-business-travel-leadership-meetings-10-corporate-conferences.html.

6. Barbara De Lollis, "'AIG Effect' Tones Down Lavish Business Events," *USA Today* (January 29, 2009). www.usatoday.com/travel/news/2009-01-26-aig-effect_N.htm.

7. Joe Goldblatt, *Special Events: A New Generation and the Next Frontier* (Hoboken, NJ: John Wiley & Sons, 2011).

8. Leonard H. Hoyle, *Event Marketing* (Hoboken, NJ: John Wiley & Sons, 2002).

9. Canadian Council of Ministers of the Environment, "Extended Producer Responsibility" (2009). www.ccme.ca/ourwork/waste.html?category_id=128.

10. Brian Walker, "Don't Bother with the Green Consumer (interview with Steve Bishop, IDEO)," *Harvard Business Review* (January 23, 2008). www.hbrgreen.org/2008/01/dont_bother_with_the_green_con.html.

11. Jacquelyn A. Ottman, Edwin R. Stafford, and Cathy L. Hartmann, "Avoiding Green Marketing Myopia: Ways to Improve Customer Appeal for Environmentally Preferred Products," *Environment*, 48 (5) (June 2006).

Local ingredients make delicious offerings for Green Meeting Industry Council conference attendees.
Photo courtesy of Green Meeting Industry Council, 2011 Annual Conference

CHAPTER 8

Sustainable Supply Chains for Meetings and Events

"The only source of knowledge is experience."

—*Albert Einstein*

Learning Objectives

After studying this chapter, you will be able to:

- Define and use key terms, including sustainable supply chain management.

- Identify advantages of and barriers to sustainable supply chains, so you are in a better position to implement them within the organization.

- Discover how to map your supply chain, using the process demonstrated.

- Follow the seven steps illustrated in this chapter to implement a sustainable supply chain management system for your meetings and events.

- Recognize a vendor code of conduct as a possible tool in the practical implementation of your sustainable supply chain management process.

An Emerging Practice

While **supply chain management** (often abbreviated SCM) has been used in business for many years, the practice of **sustainable supply chain management** (SSCM) is fairly new to business. One study focusing on the evolution of sustainable supply chain management in the business literature found that its focus in the period of 1991–2000 was mainly on the environment, with issues such as safety, human rights, and diversity also being mentioned. However, a change was evident in the period of 2001–2011, as more holistic concepts entered the vocabulary—terms such as corporate social responsibility, stakeholders, and sustainability.[1]

The use of sustainable supply chain management in meetings and events can at best be called *emerging;* the use of supply chain management at this time is likely used primarily in large marquee events, such as the Olympics. However, its use is practical for events of all sizes, and is particularly relevant to those organizations that view meetings and events as an essential part of strategic delivery of their objectives; those that manage their risk profile; organizations that want to embed sustainability, transparency, and accountability throughout their organizational culture; and organizations that forge and maintain strong relationships with their stakeholders.

To illustrate that this concept is emerging into related and overlapping spheres of business, a group has recently been formed called the Hospitality Sustainable Purchasing Consortium, the goal of which is to rank products used in the hotel industry, using standards such as the GRI and ISO as guidelines, based on environmental and corporate social responsibility factors. Marriott International Inc. is a founding member of this initiative.[2] Because this is an emerging area, this chapter will both use existing concepts and build new ones for the use of meeting and event practitioners.

What Is a Supply Chain?

A **supply chain** is the system in place to bring products and services to the market or to the end consumer. The system can include other organizations, raw materials and other resources, goods, services, technology, and people. Although it is often shown as a straight line, in practice it more resembles a web of interactions. We have introduced the concept of a supply chain in Chapter 3, when we discussed sourcing of food items at the Portland Doubletree Hotel. A simplified supply chain for the food and beverages at an event in a hotel might look like Figure 8.1.

What, then, is a sustainable supply chain? The United Nations defines *supply chain sustainability* as "the management of environmental, social and economic impacts, and the encouragement of good governance practices, throughout the lifecycles of goods and services."[3] This brings in the concept of the triple bottom line (people, planet, and profit) to management of goods and services, and the lens through which we look at our supply chain. Researchers from Leeds Metropolitan University in the United Kingdom on sustainable supply chain management in tourism define it as "a philosophy of management that involves the management and integration of a set of selected key

Figure 8.1   Simplified Food and Beverage Supply Chain

business processes from end user through original suppliers, that provides products, services and information that add value for customers and other stakeholders through the collaborative efforts of supply chain members."[4] In essence, an organization's sustainability is only as strong as its supply chain;[5] the purchasing function therefore is essential to the management and application of sustainability in an event and through a strategic meetings management process.

Meegan Jones, technical director for GreenShoot Pacific, based in New Zealand, in an interview on October 5, 2011, defines a sustainable supply chain and sustainable supply chain management like this:

> *The bulk of event production is delivered through the supply chain—be they suppliers of materials and products, of services or workforce. So in having a sustainable supply chain, you are well on your way to sustainable event production. We are currently in a situation where the supply isn't offering us sustainable solutions as a matter of course, and therefore "sustainable supply chain management" is the process through which we push back on our suppliers to present us with the most sustainable options.*

For example, the organizing committee for the 2012 London Olympic Games approaches sustainable sourcing by answering these questions:

1. Where does it come from?
2. Who made it?
3. What is it made of?
4. What is it wrapped in?
5. What will happen to it after the Games?[6]

Mitchell Beer, president of the Conference Publishers and a contributor to CSRWire who has written about sustainable supply chains, says that this is what a sustainable supply chain means to him: "In meetings and events, a sustainable supply chain would be the end result if an organization took a long, informed, courageous look at its inventory of goods and services, made best efforts to procure items that were as sustainable as possible, then made sure customers had access to the whole story, the gaps as well as the successes."

He continues with emphasis on the life cycle of products and services that go into the total event scenario:

> *A focus on the whole supply chain means tracing an item back to its original ingredients, then taking responsibility for all the inputs along the way. That's something our industry rarely if ever does, and the result is that we can never know whether our own sustainability claims are particularly valid—or whether they at least need to be qualified by acknowledging that sustainability is a journey, and we're not yet all the way there.*
>
> *A food product might come from within a 100-mile radius, but if it comes from a factory farm where it was drenched in pesticides, that's a pretty significant limitation. If we point out that virtual and hybrid meetings reduce the costs and carbon built into air travel, but fail to acknowledge the increased demand on IT data centers, we're missing part of the picture. (Hybrid meetings win out in the comparison, but we should still tell the whole story.) If a gift item made of recycled glass is shipped from Europe to North America by airfreight, its carbon footprint in transit has to be a part of the sustainability equation. And if we shift the picture slightly and procure that gift item from a country with poor labor standards or a history of human rights abuses, that's another sustainability impact that is built into the product, which means it's built into the meeting.*

Local and regional food being sold at a street market in Milan, Italy.
Photo courtesy of Elizabeth Henderson

Beer is realistic in his stance on the ability to implement a completely sustainable supply chain in meetings and events:

None of this is to suggest that a 100 percent sustainable supply chain is realistic for any meeting, or for any facility, destination, or organization within the meetings industry. But that's all the more reason to get an accurate assessment of where we actually stand. With better information, suppliers can make knowledgeable decisions that move in a more sustainable direction, planners can make accurate supply choices that favor sustainability, and meeting clients can do the same. None of that is possible until we look at the whole supply chain, rather than the tip of the iceberg at the end of the chain.

Linkages

Sustainable supply chain management of meetings and events has benefits for the organization, such as transparency, accountability, traceability of products, and clarity of products and services acceptable to the enterprise. It also has a positive impact on society as a whole through creating greater demand for sustainable products and services, which stimulates environmental management, the prosperity of local or minority-owned enterprises and more awareness of issues such as human rights and forced labor. The benefits for the event and/or the event owner are multiple, including risk management, transparency brand awareness, and reputation management. If the lens of sustainability is put on the supply chain, the level of complexity in making decisions increases. The chain might therefore start to look something like Figure 8.2.

Farmer	Distributor	Hotel	Event
• Environmental management • Labor rights • Human rights	• Fair trade • Local • Ethics • Labor rights • Human rights • Environmental management • Sustainable sourcing	• Fair trade • Local purchasing • Labor rights • Ethics • Human rights • Environmental management • Supplier management • Community development • Sustainable sourcing	• Policy • Sustainable sourcing • Risk management • Reputation management • Environmental management • Economic impact • Stakeholder engagement • Measurement • Auditing • Reporting

Figure 8.2 Complexities of a Sustainable Food and Beverage Supply Chain

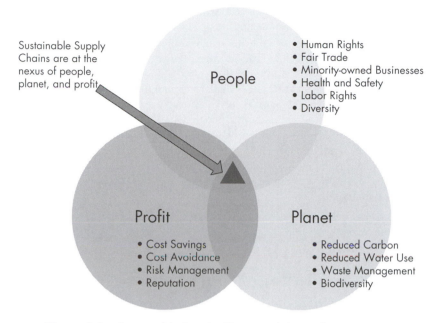

Figure 8.3   Sustainable Supply Chains and the Triple Bottom Line

As we move up the supply chain, from the farmer to the end user (the event), the level of complexity starts to increase. A sustainable supply chain sits at the middle of the conjunction of the triple bottom line, as seen in Figure 8.3.

Sustainable Supply Chains and Meetings/Events

If an event, or the organizational owner of a meeting/event, aims to be *sustainable*, it must manage its supply chain or the impacts will be relatively superficial. In other words, it is not enough to compost leftover food; to more effectively manage your impact, you must look at where that food comes from, how it is grown, who grows it and how they are treated, how it is packaged, how much it costs, and how it is transported to you. This may sound daunting, but once a system is in place within your organization, it becomes much easier to manage. It also promotes streamlining of the system for greater efficiencies of time and cost in the long run.

Implementing a sustainable supply chain management system complements existing measurement and reporting standards and practices such as British Standard 8901, ISO 20121, APEX/ASTM green meeting standards, and the Global Reporting Initiative event organizer sector supplement. It is also a practice advocated by the United Nations Global Compact for use by signatories to the compact; it has created a site dedicated to sustainable supply chain management tools and resources.

Relationship Management

Relationships are often viewed as essential in the meeting and events industry, and they can be employed productively when creating a sustainable supply chain. By creating an environment that is open and collaborative, it is much easier to transform your supply chain into a sustainable one. Researchers delving into creating sustainable supply chains in the construction industry suggest, "Relationship management is a sustainable approach to the industry in terms of social, environmental and economic sustainability and can provide a positive contribution to sustainability and help to satisfy client and stakeholder interests."[7]

Meegan Jones of GreenShoot Pacific says that she would prefer to work "with my trusted and familiar suppliers who have offered me great service thus far, and to get them to look back at their own business and clean up their act, and in so doing, help clean up mine."

NH Hoteles, based in Spain but with properties worldwide, incorporates relationship management into their sustainable supply chain management system: "The suppliers of NH Hoteles are not only components of the value we offer in our products and services, but also collaborators in the continuous enhancement of our work, adding their effort to ours in innovating and developing our lines of business."[8]

As you can see, creating a sustainable supply chain does not necessarily mean abandoning all of your current suppliers. It can mean working with your existing suppliers to make everyone more sustainable.

Influencing Factors

You may not be able to manage your entire supply chain, particularly if you are just beginning the process. There are factors that might be more influential than others and should be taken into account; this will vary based on your organization and the objectives of your event and your sustainable supply chain management policy. Factors that should be taken into consideration include:

- *Organizational strategy.* The strategy, goals, objectives, and existing programs of your organization will be key factors influencing your area of focus.
- *Expectations.* Your expectations about environmental, economic, and community objectives will help determine what areas of the supply chain you focus on.
- *Money.* The total amount of money spent in any one area. If the spending is small, the area might not be critical. The other side of money is any cost savings you expect.
- *Location.* Countries differ in their environmental and social justice policies. Countries at risk include those that do not have a good record of human rights, do not support the rights of labor, or discriminate based on sex, sexual orientation, or religion. The location of the event itself should be taken into account, as well as the location of goods and services sourced from these areas.
- *Severity.* If an area is experiencing severe conditions, such as the discovery of child or forced labor in the supply chain, or an environmental crisis, more focus should be given to this area.
- *Business critical.* Is the area critical to the success of the event? For example, critical areas for a convention might be location, transportation, venues, food and beverage, and accommodation.
- *Direct or indirect.* Is the supplier direct, or is it a sub-supplier? Whenever possible, sub-tier suppliers (suppliers to your suppliers) should be taken into account, but if this is your first implementation, it might complicate the process.
- *Risk.* What is the risk that the event supplier incurs or alleviates in supplying goods and services? For example, technology providers that allow the event to be recorded or simultaneously broadcast in a hybrid format may help to alleviate risk associated with travel interruptions.

Start with those suppliers that are deemed business critical, have a high risk factor, where you spend most of your money, and that are direct rather than indirect. As your management plan gets implemented, it will be easier to expand to other areas. Meegan Jones of GreenShoot Pacific echoes this: "Look at your line items and work out where your big spends are in physical materials. Catering, printing, branded merchandise, décor, signage. These all stand out for most events. Buying less stuff means budget savings. When looking at services, waste contracting, catering, and venue choice are also big ticket items with lots of potential for great sustainable options."

Mitchell Beer of the Conference Publishers has this to say about where meeting and event professionals should focus their efforts: "Different sustainability practitioners will answer the question about what key areas to focus on in different ways. My preference is to start with energy, water, waste, and carbon, because if those problems were solved, a lot of the other issues would fall into place. For example, there's a growing body of evidence pointing to climate change and competition for nonrenewable energy resources as background causes contributing to armed conflict, human rights abuses, and poverty."

Beer recognizes that meetings and events are beginning to get noticed by influential world bodies that may one day advise regulation:

Meetings and events consume an inordinate amount of fossil energy—directly, through facilities, freight, and ground transportation, and indirectly as a catalyst for air travel. At one point, the World Tourism Organization was considering whether meetings were integral enough to air travel that the airlines couldn't survive without meetings, and while WTO eventually concluded that the connection wasn't quite that important, it was quite revealing that they asked the question. This is a footprint for which we have to take responsibility—but to take responsibility, we first have to understand the breadth and complexity of our reach.

His conclusion on why meeting and event professionals should focus on a holistic view of the supply chain? "Sustainable meeting practitioners often tend to focus on more obvious fixes, like green food and beverage. Those inputs are very important, too, which is why an understanding of how supply chains work and why they matter is ultimately more important than any single improvement."

Issues in Sustainable Supply Chain Management

Barriers to Implementation

In implementing a sustainable supply chain management program for your meeting or event, you may encounter barriers at different levels or points of contact within the supply chain:

- *Supplier resistance.* Change can be difficult for people as well as enterprises. Changing focus from practices that focus entirely on providing desired goods and services at the lowest possible price to factoring in environmental and social considerations can be challenging. It can also be tempting to charge a price premium for these changes, even when the impact on cost may be neutral or positive.
- *Lack of expertise.* Even when suppliers are willing or supportive of the change, they may lack expertise in providing the goods, services, or information that you are asking for.

- *Apathy.* Some people simply won't care. Apathy will be found in suppliers and even within your own organizations. This may be because of a perceived low market interest in sustainability, nonfamiliarity with the issues, or unwillingness to learn.
- *Difficulty in evaluating suppliers.* It may be difficult to evaluate suppliers based on the information they are currently able to provide in a logical and systematic way.

Advantages of Sustainable Supply Chain Management

Advantages of implementing a sustainable supply chain for meetings and events are many:

- *Collaboration.* Implementing a sustainable supply chain means working closely with your suppliers. Collaboration can mean greater innovation, economic and environmental savings, and other efficiencies.
- *Cost reduction.* By identifying areas in the supply chain where improved processes might be implemented, duplication removed, or partnerships formed, there is the opportunity to reduce the costs of your operation.
- *Risk reduction.* Familiarity with the supply chain allows you to identify and manage any associated risks with suppliers, from their financial viability to the conditions under which their products are sourced, made, or transported.
- *Environmental management.* A sustainable supply chain management system allows you to identify environmental impacts and mitigate or manage them, from those products and services that may be carbon intensive to those that generate the most waste or use the most water and energy.
- *Brand management.* The reputation of your organization is important to preserve and improve. Events animate your organization—they serve as avatars representing mission, vision, and values.
- *Community engagement.* Strengthening your organization's ability to engage stakeholders and achieve a social license to operate in the communities where it does business improves the long-term economic viability of the enterprise. This was discussed in the "Public Relations" section of Chapter 7.

An example of the benefits of sustainable supply change management within the supply chain of the meetings and events industry can be found at Marriott Hotels. In 2009, Marriott challenged its suppliers to innovate and source or create price-neutral products that reduced energy and waste and incorporated more sustainable raw materials. The results of this challenge include card keys made out of 50 percent recycled materials, eliminating an estimated 66 tons of plastic from landfills; bio-degradable laundry bags for guest use; and the purchase of recycled material pens.[9]

An additional example can be found at Scandic hotels, which operates 125 hotels in Europe and is a leader in the Scandinavian hotel industry. Originally founded by Exxon as a business hotel, it adopted the Natural Step as part of an effort to align with sustainable principles; its marketplace indicated it preferred to do business with companies with positive reputations. Innovations resulting from involving its supply chains in its sustainability quest include using a bulk shampoo and soap dispenser that not only reduces the waste of one-use bottles but is fully recyclable itself at end-of-use; working with Ecolab to reduce packaging, chemicals, and the transportation of housekeeping chemicals; and creating the "recyclable room," which replaces metals, plastics, and carpet with wood, and acrylics with wool and cottons.[10]

Meegan Jones of GreenShoot Pacific sees this advantage to sustainable supply chain management: "Unless you ask, or unless there are other external or market pressures on the supply chain, they are going to keep doing what they have always done. By working with, demanding from, and encouraging engagement by the supply chain, we can fast track sustainable solutions. By having a sustainable supply chain, you will be working towards improved sustainability performance an credentials for your organization and your events."

Mitchell Beer of the Conference Publishers sees other advantages:

Aquaponics system, California Academy of Sciences.
Photo courtesy of Laura T. Gonzalez

> *The other important point the industry is missing is that sustainable supply chains, like other aspects of sustainability, are about saving money and cutting inefficiencies. Some items will cost more, others will cost less, but once the transition is complete, a sustainable supply chain should bring savings right back to a company's bottom line.*
>
> *Installing compact fluorescent (or, soon, LED) lighting involves an initial capital cost, but the units use much less energy over a longer operating life. Reglazing a convention centre with low-emissivity glass, or adding passive solar features, reduces energy costs and delivers a more comfortable, productive working environment for participants and staff. Facilities can minimize the cost of these and other sustainability improvements by building them into their routine maintenance schedules. On the operations side, hotels can learn from the example of the Portland Doubletree hotel, which switched its supply chain from frozen Atlantic to fresh Pacific salmon and saw costs plummet from $21 to $6 per pound.*

Set up for Event Camp Pow Wow at the Vancouver Convention Centre.
Photo courtesy of Three Sixty Photography

Working Knowledge: MeetGreen

Shawna McKinley, in the Canadian office of Portland, Oregon-based MeetGreen, has worked increasingly with her clients on creating sustainable supply chains. To her, a sustainable supply chain means deeply considering how any purchased items contribute to the long-term success of an organization, and broader society. She believes "that how an organization defines success may differ—maybe a company is interested in profits, or an association wants to grow membership. Ultimately, all organizations need to look at the myriad of goods and services they buy and make sure they contribute to sustainability by considering issues like: financial cost, environmental impacts, stakeholder relations, risk, legal obligations, ethics, waste, and/or health and safety."

MeetGreen has a sustainable supply chain policy, although most of its meetings and events clients do not. McKinley says:

For those that have a policy it is usually fairly simple, often ensuring accountability in the RFP process. The policies I've seen don't often include a requirement for reporting, mainly because the non-budgetary impact of meetings and events are still floating under the radar for many organizations. There are a few that do, however. It will often include a statement about the company's general priorities and vision for sustainability and any specific objectives that have been adopted. The most common issues addressed in the policies I've seen include energy and water conservation and carbon and waste reduction.

The role of policy in the process can't be emphasized too strongly. McKinley comments: "Policies express preference for vendors who align with these objectives and can provide evidence of performance during the tendering process. One company I've worked with uses a scoring system to select vendors. Their system allocates up to 5 percent of points to sustainability aspects. Some policies take a general approach that ask a handful of universal sustainability questions, leaving it more open for vendors to offer their own practices, such as:

- Do you have a sustainability policy?
- Do you train your staff in sustainable practices?
- Please list your best practices in the area of sustainability.
- Do you measure and report on sustainable practices?
- Have you ever been cited or fined for environmental, social, or ethical infractions?"

McKinley continues on the topic of frequently used products and services:

Other policies may get more specific for certain services they purchase a lot of, frequently, such as guest rooms, catering and meeting space. The policy may or may not include actual contracting for these practices. One organization I work with is accountable for the policy by including in vendor agreements the right to audit the service for sustainability performance and issue a "vendor sustainability scorecard." This is used during renewal negotiations and in some instances specific targets for improvement may be set.

MeetGreen usually works with the supply chain for its clients on an event-by-event basis. McKinley elaborates on this:

Mainly that is because sustainable event initiatives often begin in the planning department, so event teams just start doing what they can, where they can on projects they are responsible for. It's a bit like a grassroots effort. Often these efforts eventually encounter a roadblock and start to realize procurement can help to make things easier, more systematic and less ad-hoc. Maybe managing the "green" event checklist gets too difficult, or the team realizes it's easier to measure if procurement uses its buying power across events rather than planners making attempts on isolated events. Once event departments build a bridge to procurement, it becomes longer-term and typically easier.

The impact of a sustainable supply chain on the success of an event is multi-sided, including alignment with an organization's priorities and corporate social responsibility program, if it exists. There are also measurable effects. McKinley says:

It also greatly helps with successful measurement across events where you're using the same supplier, especially if those events are small, given small events may be challenged to measure on their own. In all honesty though, it's about making the process easier, and saving time and therefore money. If you can embed sustainable event requests in supplier RFPs, preferred vendor agreements and contracts universally it becomes a consistent expectation. Procurement then also becomes a central point for receiving and automating data about impacts. So, for example, if you have a preferred relationship with a hotel supplier, having a universal requirement to submit a footprint report for every event held at one of their properties can be embedded into a standard agreement. This is really a win-win for everyone. The planners don't have worry about unique requests and tracking down the data for each event. They can focus on making sure things are in place and a great event is had. Procurement is able to add value to their role because now they don't only centrally manage supplier relationships and agreements, but can offer additional, reportable information to corporate responsibility departments and shareholders about how buying power is being used. And suppliers win because they can maximize the value of creating sustainability programs where they fill a customer need.

Mapping Your Supply Chain

A **supply chain map** gives a visual representation of how everything from products and services to money, energy, carbon, waste, and time flow in the event-planning process, depending on the level of detail and the focus of the map. A supply chain map provides a way to analyze your supplier relationships and see if there are possibilities for simplification; it can also help identify barriers or bottlenecks in the process.

A supply chain map is relatively easy to use, highlights efficiencies and inefficiencies (depending on what you decide to map), supports your goals and objectives of a sustainable supply chain, and might even help you rethink how to do things more effectively.

Step 1: Identify Categories to Map

For example, the organizer of a convention of 1000 people might map categories for services like transportation, convention centers, food and beverage, and hotels. Using the nine APEX categories is a possible option:

Destination selection	Venues	Audiovisual
Transportation	Communication	Exhibitions
Accommodation	Food and beverage	On-site office

For more complex events, such as mega-events that might build their own facilities, categories will need to be revised and added to, such as raw construction materials, energy, infrastructure, services, and manufacturing.

Step 2: Flow Chart

For each category, trace the flow of materials, resources, goods, and services through users and suppliers. For example, maps for transportation and food and beverage might look something like the maps in Figures 8.4 and 8.5.

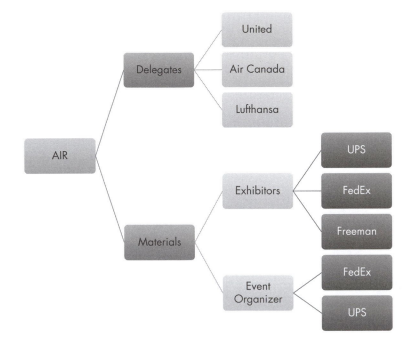

Figure 8.4 Possible Air Transportation Supply Chain Map

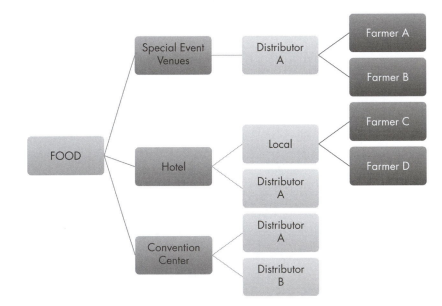

Figure 8.5 Possible Food Supply Chain Map

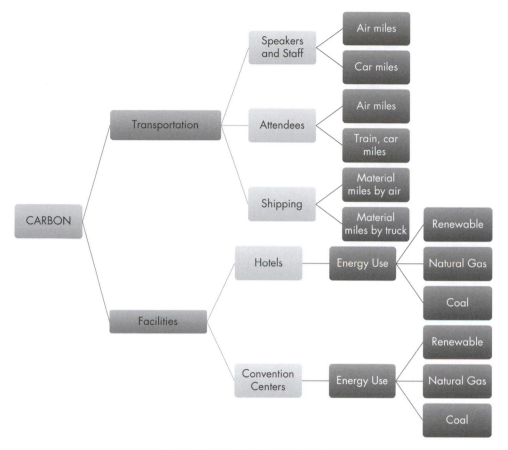

Figure 8.6 Possible Carbon Map

This kind of a supply chain map allows meeting and event professionals to map their supply chains and collect information from suppliers. It also allows them to see possible synergies. For example, if you notice that one supplier is common to many branches of the supply chain, there might be an opportunity for efficiencies in price or for status as a key supplier, pending the objectives of your sustainable supply chain policy. It might be found that a specific common supplier does not meet your standards.

Used in a slightly different way, it helps map out and track the flow of waste, energy, and resources. For example, a carbon map for an event might look like Figure 8.6.

Seven Steps to Create and Manage a Sustainable Supply Chain

Here are seven basic steps to creating and implementing a sustainable supply chain for your meetings and events. These steps are illustrated in Figure 8.7.

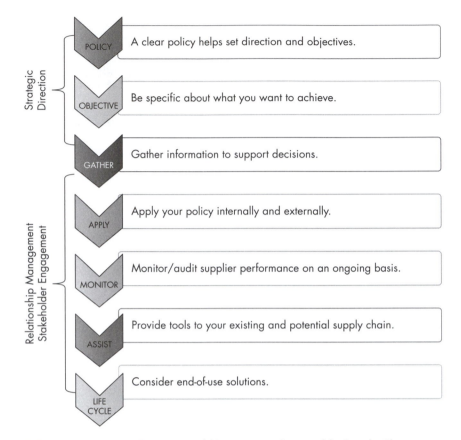

Figure 8.7 Seven Steps to Creating and Managing a Sustainable Supply Chain

Step 1: Create a Policy

As with many other CSR-related activities, the first step is to formulate a supply chain policy. This should reflect your objectives as an organization and the objectives of the event, and take into consideration issues (environmental, social, and economic), risk, and the resources of the organization to effectively manage the policy. Risk management considerations related to supply chains are also discussed in Chapter 11. A policy might include:

- Desire to form strong relationships with suppliers
- Need to demonstrate integrity and transparency through actions
- A goal of reducing harm to the environment
- Commitment to human rights and fair labor practices
- Need to factor in economic considerations

It is important to get buy-in for the policy from senior-level management. In some cases, purchases for meetings and events are controlled by a procurement department. This makes it desirable to create a strong relationship with this area so the department understands your needs and the objectives of the policy.

For example, NH Hoteles has a sustainable supply chain policy that focuses on strategic purchasing, including service, quality, and compliance with accepted standards (including social and environmental standards). It strives for transparency, audits its suppliers, and reports through the Global Reporting Initiative.[11]

Step 2: Set Your Objectives

What do you want to achieve with your sustainable supply chain? As seen in the MeetGreen example, certain meetings and event organizers insert objectives about reducing waste, water, carbon, and energy use. Environmental objectives are not the only consideration, however. Your objectives may also want to consider social and economic goals. Here are some examples:

▮ Vancouver 2010

The Winter Olympic Games in Vancouver created a sustainable purchasing program called Buy Smart, which had several objectives:[12]

- Improved triple bottom line performance
- Growth of Aboriginal, minority-owned, and sustainability-focused enterprises
- Creation of jobs for the disadvantaged
- Creation of venues that performed better than anticipated
- Economic support locally and regionally

▮ Olympic Delivery Authority (ODA), London 2012

The ODA, in charge of the facilities for the London 2012 Games, has two key controlling factors: it must deliver venues and other infrastructure on time and on budget. In addition, these must be technically safe, and able to be used for the purpose they were designed for. The objectives ODA has set in addition to these controlling objectives include:

- Recognition of London as a sustainable event destination
- Long-term diversity and growth in the community
- Environmental improvement
- Regeneration and development of the local community
- Safety
- Maximization of economic benefits[13]

▮ Le Meridien Mina Seyahi, Dubai

This hotel, part of the Starwood chain, has identified the following objectives as part of its sustainable purchasing policy:[14]

- Sourcing the most environmentally sustainable products available
- Identifying possible alternatives
- Working with suppliers on how they choose their sub-suppliers to create a more accountable supply chain
- Emphasizing local sourcing
- Banning illegally traded and endangered species

You will need to balance people, planet, and profit when setting your objectives.
Photo courtesy of iStockphoto/ Murat Giray Kaya

■ Edinburgh International Conference Centre

This conference centre gives preference to environmentally sustainable/ beneficial products that meet these objectives:[15]

- They meet client needs with 100 percent satisfaction.
- They are equal or superior in quality, cost, and safety.
- They are certified by specific organizations.

Step 3: Gather Information

You have a sustainable supply chain policy, and you have set specific objective that you want to achieve using this policy. The next step is to collect information from existing and potential suppliers. This could include:

- Mapping your supply chain
- Supplier policies
- Names of sub-suppliers
- Information on specific goods, such as composition and recyclability
- Employee retention rate and diversity of employment
- Environmental or corporate social responsibility reports
- Any infractions of existing regulations or voluntary standards and certifications that have occurred within a specific time frame
- Geographic areas from which your suppliers source
- Any certifications or compliance with standards

This is an opportunity to engage your supplier stakeholders as you consult with your existing supply chain. This engages them in the process, educates them about expectations, and allows feedback about possible issues you might not have considered. Good relationship management in this stage of the process is critical, especially since "sustainable" can mean different things to different people or organizations.

For example, the Olympic Delivery Authority for the London 2012 Games uses a *balanced scorecard* approach, where in addition to information about cost and quality, ODA also collects from potential suppliers information about equality and diversity, community engagement, fair employment and wages, and ethical sourcing. This is done in a pre-qualification questionnaire.[16]

Documenting this information will help you analyze the information you have gathered. A possible template might look like Table 8.1; it should be customized to reflect your policy and objectives.

Step 4: Apply Your Policy

Ensure that your policy is embedded into both internal and external operations. Internally, it is important to educate staff on the policy and train them in its implementation in the event procurement process. Posting it on any organizational intranets and in any printed or online resource materials will allow access on demand; it should also be a part of the on-boarding process for new employees or contractors. If the events team works through a purchasing or

Table 8.1 Simplified Sustainable Supply Chain Tracking Form

Product or Service	Supplier	Country of Origin	Method of Transport	Cost	Human Rights Issues	Labor Rights Issues	Environmental Issues
Registration bags	Supplier A	China	Ship	$2.00/unit	Possible forced labor	No min. wage	Material is non-recycled poly
	Supplier B	China	Ship	$2.40/unit	None	None	Material is recycled bottles; eco-labeled
	Supplier C	Canada	Ground	$2.50/unit	None	None	Material is non-recycled poly

procurement department internally, facilitating communication between the two functional areas is important.

Externally, the policy should be applied through:

- Posting on your website
- Including it in requests for proposal
- Ensuring expectations are outlined in contracts
- Including it in newsletters or other communications media

Step 5: Monitor/Audit Your Supply Chain

The point of this is twofold. First, it is to ensure that your suppliers are doing what they said they would. The second is to establish a baseline from which you can measure improvements. Third parties can be useful at this point, either to directly check with suppliers or as certification or reporting bodies such as ISO, the Global Reporting Initiative, Green Key Global, Occupational Health and Safety, or other organizations.

Because the "product" is the meeting or event, meeting professionals are in an excellent spot to employ on-site monitoring or auditing during an event. This assists with meeting requirements for standards such as British Standard 8901 or ISO 20121, allows you to report specifically back to your supply chain, and gives you a basis to make decisions on your future use of these suppliers.

For example, while on-site for a typical convention or smaller event, meeting professionals could potentially monitor/audit any of these suppliers:

- Hotels
- Meeting or event venues
- Audiovisual providers
- Decorators
- Food and beverage suppliers

Meegan Jones of GreenShoot Pacific offers this advice to evaluate sustainable suppliers:

The first thing I do is ensure I am fully informed on what the sustainability issues are regarding a particular product, material, or service. Then I look at that sector of the industry and see if there is an existing independent program that certifies, accredits, endorses, or audits sustainability credentials and performance. If there is no formal program in place (like an eco-label or industry benchmark best practice program), I will then assess a supplier's offerings based on my knowledge of the issues in the sector. I want to know that the supplier has a sustainability policy for their business as well as for the product/material they supply. Depending on the event, I prioritize various elements of sustainability—local, organic, or "has a sustainability policy" or is eco-labeled, or meets ISO 14001 or other barometers of sustainability performance.

Step 6: Assist Your Supply Chain to Meet Your Needs

Providing information about your expectations to your potential supply chain will help them meet your policy needs and objectives. This could be as simple as posting guidelines for submissions in an easily accessible spot, to providing examples of existing suppliers that meet your guidelines and contacts of organizations or information that can help organizations get up to speed. It is also a good idea to provide the weighting each objective has in the final decision so that providers can focus on the areas most important to your organization.

Step 7: Lifecycle Planning

Meetings and events have many suppliers. Some, like destinations, do not necessarily fit the concept of lifecycle planning, as they are not typically "single-use." However, many meeting and event elements, such as food, supplies, or building materials, can contribute to end-of-event waste unless the entire life cycle of the materials are taken into account.

Reverse logistics is the term that is typically used to describe planning for the acquisition, use during the event, and eventual reuse of materials after the event is over. For example, a conference might decide to source registration bags with the intent of donating them to a school after the event is over. Therefore, a logo is not printed on the bag and the design of the bag purchased is appropriate to carry books in—for example, a briefcase style. A school that is interested in the bags is contacted well in advance, and the pickup of the bags occurs when the event is over. Communications to attendees should go out well in advance so they know that there is an option to donate this item when the event is over.

An excellent example of reverse logistics is found in the World Skills Competition. The event, which has been likened to the Olympics for trades, was held in Calgary, Canada, in 2009; an essential part of the planning was integrating final use for the products created in the competition. For example, the offset printing competition had competitors produce posters. Instead of trashing them at the end, the product competition was to specifically create posters for War Child Canada, ensuring the final products had a home and a use. The cooking competition, which tested new recipe preparation and menu planning, donated all food created to a local homeless shelter. The cabinet-making competition donated its final products to Habitat for Humanity.[17] By ensuring that all products made from raw materials from the competition had a planned reuse, World Skills successfully turned its supply chain into a closed-loop system, reducing waste and increasing the value of what would otherwise be waste products from the event.

Supplier Code of Conduct

As stated in Chapter 1, a **code of conduct** provides direction to individuals within an organization about expected behaviors and communicates these expectations to the broader community. It is not sufficient to expect that everyone will act according to an organization's standards if they are not clearly stated.

Many important elements of supply chains may not be immediately evident. A useful analogy is that of an iceberg, where you only see the smallest part above the surface of the water, while the majority of it is submerged. Above the waterline, we see goods and services, like registration bags, food, wine, venues, ribbons, badges, airlines, and raw materials. But below the surface, where they are not easily seen, are issues like human rights, pollution, underage or forced labor, health and safety, unsafe working conditions, and environmental degradation.

In implementing a sustainable supply chain management system, a useful tool might be the creation and use of a supplier code of conduct. Many industries, such as the pharmaceutical industry, have codes that are regulated and that must be followed.

The Future of Sustainable Supply Chain Management

The meetings and events industry is tipping toward more sustainable practices and a greater understanding of the holistic view of sustainability, which encompasses economic, environmental, and social aspects. Some meetings industry organizations are innovating and adopting best supply chain practices from other industries to ensure their competitiveness into the future.

Global drivers like oil prices, globalization, and increasing awareness of environmental, social, and economic inter-relationships in business and the public at large will eventually drive the meetings and events industry from reactive to proactive. Mitchell Beer of the Conference Publishers says, "If they're not sustainable, they'll eventually be untenable. And if we aren't paying attention, we won't see the problems on the horizon until they're too big to miss. By far the best outcome would be for destinations, facilities, and other meetings organizations to embrace sustainable supply chains as a matter of deliberate strategy, based on their own (reasonably quick) timelines. If that doesn't happen, a number of outside influences could force the issue: the expectations might come from customers or from government regulation, but if all else fails, market forces will be the catalyst."

He continues: "For example, we already know that meetings and travel (along with the rest of the economy) take a hit whenever oil prices go above US$90 or $100 per barrel. They peaked at US$147 before the economic crash of 2008, and economists like Jeff Rubin foresee an era of $200 per barrel oil. That possibility, alone, should be enough to motivate drastic energy efficiency improvements, right across the industry. If we don't do it with foresight and planning, we'll still have to react when energy prices become an industry crisis."

Case Study: Sample Code of Conduct

An example from the meetings and events industry of a partner/supplier code of conduct is found at the Green Meeting Industry Council (GMIC). In it, GMIC outlines what it expects from its partners in terms of their environmental and social practices. It is based on the 10 principles of the United Nations Global Compact. A second code of conduct example is provided in Chapter 7 from the Fair Labor Association.

GMIC Partner Code of Conduct

The GMIC is the leading global community for sustainability education, research, policy, and standards for the meetings and event industry. Our mission is to transform the global meetings industry through sustainability. As signatories of the United Nations Global Compact, the GMIC is committed to promoting sustainable practices in the meetings industry. This Partner Code of Conduct sets the minimum performance standards for the purchases our suppliers make on behalf of our company or our clients. The GMIC shall apply this code of conduct as one of the criteria used in the selection of business partners and suppliers and strongly encourage that suppliers and their subcontractors/suppliers follow and support this code.

1. Legal and Ethical Requirements

GMIC encourages our partners and suppliers, as well as their sub-contractors, to comply with national and other applicable law of the country of manufacture of products including those laws relating to labor, worker health and safety, and the environment.

2. Child Labor

GMIC is committed to the promotion of human rights and has a special focus on promoting the welfare of children. GMIC relies on suppliers and their sub-contractors to be able to show that they purchase no products, or support in any way, business that harms children or benefits from child labor. GMIC defines a child as any person less than 15 years of age.

3. Forced Labor

GMIC suppliers and their sub-contractors may not use forced, illegal, or prison labor, including indentured or bonded labor, or any form of compulsory labor to manufacture products or to provide services.

4. Disciplinary Practices

GMIC suppliers and their sub-contractors will treat workers with respect and dignity and ensure workers are not subjected to any form of physical, sexual, psychological, or verbal harassment or abuse.

5. Freedom of Association

GMIC suppliers and their sub-contractors will recognize and respect that workers have the right to form or join trade unions of their own choosing and to bargain collectively.

6. Wages and Benefits

GMIC suppliers and their sub-contractors will recognize that wages are essential to meeting employees' basic needs and will make every effort to ensure that workers receive wages that meet basic needs by local standards.

7. Discrimination

GMIC suppliers and their sub-contractors will consider employees for positions on the basis of their qualifications and abilities. GMIC will not work with suppliers who discriminate on the basis of race, gender, political or religious beliefs, social, ethnic or national origin, marital status, age, union affiliation, sexual orientation, or disability.

8. Health and Safety

GMIC suppliers and their sub-contractors will:

Provide their workers with safe and healthy work environments, which, as a minimum standard, is in compliance with country and local health and safety laws and regulations.

Take adequate steps to prevent accidents or injuries to health arising out of, associated with, or occurring in the course of work.

9. Environmental Commitment

GMIC is taking action and making investments as an effort to begin to take responsibility for environmental impacts in areas under its control. We expect a strong environmental commitment and aggressive efforts to protect and restore the natural environment. We will favor partners who:

Have a management system demonstrating environmental commitment; publicly disclose environmental impacts and activities through regular reporting;

Eliminate toxic and hazardous substances from products and operations;

Increase efficiency and thereby minimize pollution and waste;

Reduce use of natural resources including raw materials, energy and water;

Take responsibility for proper waste management and any environmental problems associated with disposal of wastes;

Promote the use of renewable energy through support of innovation and integration in operations.

GMIC seeks to work with business partners who have published commitments to environmental responsibility and encourages all suppliers to seek industry specific third party environmental certification as a way to express their commitment. With proven scientific integrity, triple bottom line focus and ability to build stronger business.

10. Partnership

GMIC understands that sustainability requires collaboration and engagement with all its suppliers. GMIC invites suppliers who respect its partner code of conduct to join the effort to promote more responsible business practices and to actively do their utmost to achieve the standards outlined here.

Chapter Review

In this chapter, we introduced the concept of a sustainable supply chain management process for meetings and events. An emerging process in this industry, there are some examples of pioneering organizations that are implementing these concepts in their meetings and events. Once you have determined your sustainable supply chain policy and specific objectives supporting the triple bottom line concepts of economy, environment, and community, mapping your supply chain is a good place to start, as this gives a visual representation of the chain and allows it to be easily understood and assessed for efficiencies, overlap, and impacts. A seven-step process of creating and implementing a sustainable supply chain management process within your meetings and events provides a guideline for introducing the process into your meeting and event management activities. Using a supplier code of conduct helps you to integrate desired activities and reporting into the supply chain through clarity of expectations.

Review Questions

1. What is a supply chain?
2. Compare your answer from above with the definition of a sustainable supply chain.
3. What is sustainable supply chain management?
4. Why is sustainable supply chain management considered an emerging practice in meetings and events?
5. What are possible benefits to society gained through implementing a sustainable supply chain management process? What are possible benefits for your organization?
6. What barriers to implementing a sustainable supply chain management process exist? Suggest ways to overcome these barriers.

Project

1. Choose an event or create a fictional event for which you map out its supply chain. List all possible areas that could be mapped, suggest ones that may be critical, and choose two to map in full.
2. For the above map, choose one product or service and, using a process similar to the one suggested in Table 8.1, identify the supplier(s), possible issues in the country of origin related to human rights, labor rights, and environmental issues that might occur during production of the product or service. Be as specific as possible.

Key Terms

- supply chain management
- sustainable supply chain management
- supply chain
- supply chain map
- reverse logistics
- code of conduct

Resources

Related to the Resources listed below, please visit the Book Companion Site (located at www.wiley.com/college/henderson) for a complete list of websites. Additional referential websites related to this chapter's content can also be found on the BCS.

Buy Smart

The sustainable procurement program used at the Vancouver 2010 Olympic Games provides a leading example of sustainable supply chain management, which integrates social, economic, and environmental aspects. It provides a legacy to the meetings and events industry.

London Organizing Committee of the Olympic Games (LOCOG) Sourcing Code

The London 2012 Games are the first Olympic Games to explicitly base their bid to host on sustainability. They have released a sourcing code, "Source," which details these objectives.

Olympic Delivery Authority (ODA) Procurement Policy

This is the London organization responsible for building the venues and other infrastructure for the London 2012 Games. ODA also has a procurement code that reflects its overall mission.

United Nations Global Compact Sustainable Supply Chain Resources and Practices

This website was created by the UN Global Compact to help organizations find information and resource on supply chain sustainability. It includes case examples, resources, and tools and articles.

NH Hoteles Promoting Responsibility in the Value Chain

This is a section of the NH Hoteles Corporate Responsibility Report addressing the supply chain.

IMEX/Green Meeting Industry Council Green Supplier Awards

These awards are given annually at IMEX in Frankfurt. There are case studies of the various winners since 2008.

Eco Label Index

This is a list of eco-labels around the world, for assistance in finding suppliers that meet certain qualifications.

Green Meeting Industry Council

This is a meetings and events industry association based in North America but with membership worldwide. Its mission is to promote sustainability in meetings and events.

Notes

1. Craig Carter and P. Liane Easton. "Sustainable Supply Chain Management: Evolution and Future Direction," *International Journal of Physical Distribution and Logistics Management*, 41 (1) (2011).
2. Hospitality Sustainable Purchasing Consortium. Founding and Contributing Members. Retrieved February 8, 2012, from www.hspiconsortium.com/founding-members/.
3. The United Nations Global Compact and Business for Social Responsibility. *Supply Chain Sustainability: A Practical Guide for Continuous Improvement* (2010). www.unglobalcompact .org/docs/news_events/8.1/Supply_Chain_Sustainability.pdf.
4. Xavier Font, Richard Tapper, Karen Schwartz, and Mairanna Kornilaki, "Sustainable Supply Chain Management in Tourism, in Business, Strategy and the Environment," *Journal of Sustainable Tourism* (2006): 260–271. See onlinelibrary.wiley.com/doi/10.1111/ j.1745-493X.2009.03173.x/abstract.
5. Daniel Krause, Sephan Vachon, and Robert Klassen, "Special Topic Forum on Sustainable Supply Chain Management: Introduction and Reflections on the Role of Purchasing Management," *Journal of Supply Chain Management* (October 2009). www.london2012 .com/publications/locog-sustainable-sourcing-code.php
6. London Organizing Committee of the Olympic Games and Paralympic Games, *LOCOG Sustainable Sourcing Guide Third Edition* (July 2011). www.london2012.com/publications/ locog-sustainable-sourcing-code.php
7. Yan Ki Fiona Cheung and Steve Rowlinson, "Supply Chain Sustainability: A Relationship Management Approach," *The International Journal of Managing Projects in Business*, 4 (3) (2011).
8. NH Hoteles. *Promoting Responsibility in the Value Chain*. Accessed October 5, 2011, from corporate-information.nh-hotels.com/wda/eng/informes_anuales/2006/archivos/ 2006_3-4_2.htm.
9. Marriott Sustainability Report 2008–2009. Accessed September 24, 2011, from www .marriott.com/Multimedia/PDF/CorporateResponsibility/Marriott_Sustainability_ Report.pdf.
10. The Natural Step. "Sandic Hotels: A Natural Step Network Case Study." Accessed October 4, 2011, from thenaturalstep.org/en/usa/scandic-hotels.
11. NH Hoteles. *Promoting Responsibility in the Value Chain*. Accessed October 5, 2011, from corporate-information.nh-hotels.com/wda/eng/informes_anuales/2006/archivos/ 2006_3-4_2.htm.
12. Vancouver Organizing Committee for the 2010 Olympic and Paralympic Winter Games, *Buy Smart Case Study on Sustainable Sourcing*, March 2010.

13. Olympic Delivery Authority Procurement Policy (2007). Accessed September 24, 2001, from www.london2012.com/documents/business/oda-procurement-policy.pdf.

14. Starwood Hotels and Resorts Worldwide, "Environmental Purchasing for Policy Le Meridien Mina Seyahi Beach Resort and Marina." Accessed September 24, 2001, at: www .lemeridien-minaseyahi.com/en/purchasing.

15. Edinburgh International Conference Centre, "Our Commitment." Accessed September 24, 2011, at www.eicc.co.uk/organising_an_event/plan_it_green/our_commitment/.

16. Olympic Delivery Authority Procurement Policy Executive Summary, available at www .london2012.com/documents/business/oda-procurement-policy-executive-summary.pdf and A Suppliers Guide to Using the eTenders System available at etenders.london2012.com/ web/eTender%20guide.pdf.

17. Calgary Herald, "WorldSkills Goes Green to Benefit Charities" (September 3, 2009). Accessed at www2.canada.com/calgaryherald/news/story.html?id=d1c51940-8955-4cb4-9e79-fd30bbea4259&p=1.

Cardboard to be recycled at an event, baled, and waiting to be weighed.
Photo courtesy of Elizabeth Henderson

CHAPTER 9

Sustainability Measurement and Evaluation

"If you cannot measure it, you cannot improve it."

—*Lord Kelvin (1824–1907)*

Learning Objectives

After studying this chapter, you will be able to:

- Explain why measurement and evaluation is an important part of an event-based corporate social responsibility (CSR) program.

- Distinguish between qualitative and quantitative measurements in general.

- Identify various qualitative and quantitative measures that can be used to measure and evaluate an event-based CSR program in key areas.

- Decide what scale of measurement and evaluation most likely applies to certain sizes of events.

- Implement the integrated sustainable event management framework in assessing competency.

Introduction

Measurement is something that is often out of the comfort zone of meeting and event professionals, and yet it can greatly improve their ability to show relevance, track success, and plan for the future. In this chapter, we will introduce the concepts of measurement, explore key qualitative and quantitative areas that can be measured, and help you decide what scale of measurement may be appropriate for specific events.

Linkages

Measurement and evaluation are important in order to ensure that we take the information we have about our meetings and events and use it to make better decisions in the future. Measurement and evaluation help ensure that information is both valid and reliable. In terms of the organization holding the meeting or event and the meeting or event itself, it is important for these reasons:

- *Accountability.* Measurement and evaluation of our actions allow us to see the trail of accountability and responsibility. This is important for most organizations and is a key part of any employee evaluation. It also allows us to see any possible gaps in accountability that can be improved upon.
- *Transparency.* A key element of a CSR program is transparency of actions. Measurement and evaluation are agents in proving transparency, especially when coupled with reporting and other forms of internal and external communications. Transparency helps build trust within the supply chain and among stakeholders.
- *Awareness and insight.* Measurement and evaluation allow us to have insights about our actions, and help us model the future more effectively; that is, help us decide what our next event or series of events will look like as we learn from the past.
- *Responsiveness.* Events happen in the context of a wider social, environmental, and economic reality, and conditions tend to change, either slowly over time (e.g., new technologies are introduced and adopted) or suddenly, as in the case of an economic recession, earthquake, or volcanic eruption. For example, the Icelandic volcano that erupted in April 2010 changed the conditions dramatically for meetings and events that had participants flying to or from northern Europe. Measurement and evaluation can help event professionals respond to uncertain conditions in the future, as they are better able to know their own issues and stakeholders and respond to risk in the form of changing conditions.
- *Consistency.* Measurement and evaluation also help to ensure that everyone is on the same page, that knowledge of past actions and trends is consistent among a team and throughout the decision-making system.
- *Link to strategy and objectives.* As with any business activity, meetings and events should have a link to organizational strategy and objectives. Measurement and evaluation help organizations to see and to strengthen those linkages and be able to see the relative effectiveness of their actions and decisions.
- *Understanding impacts.* Impacts for an organization can be financial and nonfinancial, tangible and intangible. Measurement and evaluation help to identify and quantify those impacts.

- *Influence.* Measurement and evaluation, through identifying and quantifying impacts and providing links to organizational strategy and objectives, help give meeting and event professionals influence within the organization, sometimes known as getting a "seat at the table."
- *Benchmarking.* The purpose of **benchmarking** is to identify and adopt known best practices that help identify gaps and lead to better performance and greater alignment with strategy and objectives. Benchmarking can be done internally or externally, but can only be achieved if measurement and evaluation are present.

Dual Measurement: Qualitative and Quantitative

In any organization and any meeting or event, measurement can take two broad forms, **qualitative** and **quantitative**. Although quantitative measurement is often presumed to be the most valid (people like to see numbers!), both have importance in the measurement and evaluation of meetings and events. The triple bottom line of environment, economy, and community can be used to structure these measures.

Qualitative measurement uses descriptive words and feedback. By its nature it is more subjective than quantitative measurement, and may rely on things such as interviews or surveys to gather data.

Quantitative measurement, by contrast, is objective. It uses numbers to describe data collected and to measure progress.

Qualitative Measurement

Often, qualitative impacts focus on community factors as well as intangible economic factors. Some qualitative measurements related to social responsibility at meetings and events are:

- Community
  - Delegate behavior change
  - Stakeholder satisfaction
  - Attendee education
  - Community impact
- Economy
  - Brand enhancement
  - Product or service loyalty
  - Goodwill

■ Delegate Behavior Change

If your meeting/event has a goal of changing the behavior of delegates—for example, increasing the number of people who implement what they have learned about sustainable events or the transportation choices they make locally (such as public transit vs. taxis)—then measuring that change will be important. This measurement is "quasi-quantitative" in that numbers of people or actions can be measured, but the underlying qualitative measurement is behavior change.

Case Study: International AIDS Society

The XVII International AIDS Conference, organized by the International AIDS Society, was held in August 2008 in Mexico City. Over 20,000 delegates attended from all over the world, including the major regions of Sub-Saharan Africa, Middle East, North Africa, Eastern Europe, Western Europe, Asia, Oceania, Latin America, Caribbean, and North America. Organizers attempted to measure the performance of the conference and its longer-term influence on delegates' behavior in the medium-to-long term after the conference.

To do this, they first sent a survey to all attendees three weeks post-conference. They also conducted other surveys and individual face-to-face interviews to supplement the survey. They asked all delegates responding to the survey to complete action plans detailing one objective to be achieved within one year, including outcomes, specific activities, and resources that would be required to complete the objective.

Ten months later, in June 2009, all delegates who had submitted an action plan were e-mailed to assess whether the plans had turned into concrete action. Ninety-seven percent of those who responded to this step indicated that they had started implementing their plans and that they were useful or very useful.

Eighteen months later, in January 2010, the conference evaluation coordinator e-mailed all original delegates of the 2008 conference to collect feedback on the long-range impact of the conference.

Influences of the conference measured in the medium-to-long term:

1. Changes in delegates' HIV work (79 percent of surveyed delegates)
2. Direct influence on delegates' organization HIV work (49 percent of surveyed delegates)
3. Influence on HIV work, policy, and advocacy in delegates' countries (39 percent of surveyed delegates)
4. Increase in delegate collaborative capacity through an increase in network size (75 percent of delegates stayed in contact with people they met at the conference; 50 percent stayed in touch with five or more people)

Now that the organization has this information, it can better understand its impact on communication and behavior change, monitor its influence geographically, and benchmark future conferences against this **baseline**. A baseline refers to a starting point for future calculations. For example, the first year you measure the impact of an event will then become the baseline from which you can measure improvements or changes in future years. A baseline gives a standard of comparison. The results also provide awareness and insight as to the types of benefits delegates experience, so organizers can enhance the effectiveness of specific program elements.[1]

■ Stakeholder Satisfaction

Once again, a number may be assigned (such as 5 out of 6) to this qualitative measure. Stakeholder satisfaction should be measured in relation specifically to CSR efforts as well as to the meeting or event as a whole. This is often the first step of a return on investment (ROI) measurement strategy for events.

■ Attendee Education

This doesn't need to be formal education, as in an education session on CSR specifically. It could include signage or other notifications that attempt to educate people on what you are trying to achieve, from greater recycling to greater awareness of organizational efforts relating to the business, such as outreach into communities where you do business.

■ Brand Enhancement

This qualitative measure is very difficult to quantify at a meeting or event, or even after one has taken place. However, tracking such things as sales levels, positive press mentions, or customer loyalty as reflected in repeat sales of products and services can all reflect enhancement of the brand.

■ Community Impact

Community impact can be considered in several ways. First, there is the economic impact of the event on the community. This can be quantified (see "Quantitative Measurement," next). The same is true (in many respects) for environmental impact. The impact that is difficult to quantify is social impact, the positive or negative impact on the people and human networks within the community of the event. These are sometimes referred to as "soft" or intangible impacts, and include factors such as the health benefits of hosting large sporting events on the host community, civic pride, and an increased skill level in volunteers leading to a more skilled workforce post-event.

Quantitative Measurement

Quantitative measures relating to events are numerous, and can be measured in all triple bottom line areas of environment, economy, and community. Quantitative measures typically relate to resource consumption and outputs. There are a number of event sector standards that outline the major elements, including the Global Reporting Initiative Event Organizers Sector Supplement and the APEX Green Meeting Standard, which was developed in conjunction with ASTM. The GRI standard was released in January 2012. Due to timing, this discussion will refer to the APEX Green Meetings Task Force Report, published in 2004 and available on the Convention Industry Council website, which was the catalyst from which the standard began, as well as available online literature about the process and standard.

The **Global Reporting Initiative** (GRI) is a network-based organization that developed a sustainability reporting framework, the G3 Guidelines, in 2006. It allows organizations to report on the economic, environmental, social, and governance aspects of sustainability. This has become the most-used reporting framework in the world, used by hundreds of corporations and organizations.

The **GRI Event Organizers Sector Supplement** (EOSS) is a reporting framework specifically for the meetings and events sector. In addition to the G3 Guidelines, it covers event-sector specific issues such as knowledge transfer, sourcing, legacy, commissions, gifting, site selection, and participant and attendee management. It was created by a multinational and multi-stakeholder group consisting of event organizers and nongovernmental organizations (NGOs). This approach lends credibility to the supplement. The group included Olympic organizing committees from the London 2012 Summer Games and the Vancouver 2010 Winter Games, as well as REED Exhibitions, IMEX, MCI Group, MeetGreen, Meeting Change, Live Earth, the Swiss and Austrian governments, Julie's Bicycle, CSO International, and Transparency International.

Table 9.1 Select areas of Quantitative Measurement for Meetings and Events

Environment	Economy	Community
• Water (conserved, quality and used)	• Direct costs	• Procurement
• Energy (conserved and used)	• Cost savings	• Discrimination
• Emissions	• Cost avoidance	• Labor rights
• Air quality	• Direct economic impacts	• Security
• Noise	• Indirect economic impacts	• Employment
• Waste	• Partners	• Training and education
• Transportation emissions	• Sponsors	• Diversity
• Diversion from landfill		• Health and safety
		• Marketing and communications
		• Privacy

APEX (Accepted Practices Exchange) is an initiative of the Convention Industry Council (CIC) and ASTM, a U.S.-based standards-setting body. It also used a multi-stakeholder approach to creating green meetings standards.

A sample of such measures includes those in Table 9.1.

Measuring Environmental Factors

Measuring environmental impact at meetings and events is easy in concept but may involve some legwork on the part of the event organizer to compile. According to APEX, green meeting activities where event organizers will incur environmental impacts are organized into nine main areas:[2]

1. Audiovisual
2. Accommodation
3. Communications
4. Destinations
5. Exhibits
6. Food and beverage
7. Meeting venue
8. On-site office
9. Transportation

To this list might reasonably be added supply chain impacts not related to any of the above areas, such as sourcing of registration bags, giveaways, or other material inputs that result in waste, energy use, or emissions. For the purposes of this discussion, we will discuss these areas without the intention of replicating existing information.

Audiovisual

Measurable environmental issues associated with the selection and use of audiovisual and related technology may include energy use and efficiency, sourcing and transportation, certification, and waste management. See the interview with AVW TELAV on Page 211.

▓ Energy Use and Efficiency

It might not be possible for AV suppliers to measure exact energy usage; indeed, this may be tracked in a general way only if the facility has room-specific energy meters in the meeting rooms. What is possible to measure is the percentage usage of energy-efficient technology:

- Percentage of ENERGY STAR certified (or equivalent ratings system) equipment used
- Percentage and type of energy-efficient lighting used, such as LED (light-emitting diode), CLF (compact fluorescent lamps) or CCFL (cold-cathode fluorescent lamps) sources as compared to traditional, more energy-intense lighting
- Lumen output for projectors
- Percentage of alternative energy sourced
- Practical application of 50 percent lighting/AC for setup and tear-down times

▓ Sourcing and Transportation

Sourcing of equipment can also be measured. Using local suppliers that do not have to ship their equipment for long distances is preferable. This can be measured using the concept of event miles. **Event miles** refer to the total number of miles (or kilometers) that all components of an event travel to get to the event destination. This may include staff, food and beverage, audiovisual, or other equipment and materials, speakers, performers, athletes, attendees, exhibitors, participants, volunteers, or any other significant component. Distance should be measured return for two-way travel; for consumables such as food, one-way is acceptable. Event miles should be considered when selecting the most appropriate destination for a meeting or event. This can save the organization money in travel and shipping.

For example, Walmart does something similar with what it calls *food miles*. All its buyers have a food miles calculator that allows them to enter the source and the destination to help them make buying decisions.[3]

Sourcing and transportation also has an impact on the local economic impact of your meeting and event. Possible metrics include:

- Percentage of equipment locally sourced
- Percentage equipment shipped by ground versus air

▓ Certification or Eco-labels

It is possible for meeting professionals to ask for, and measure, the certifications and eco-labels that providers of audiovisual equipment have. These may include:

- British Standard 8901
- ISO 140001
- ENERGY STAR
- Audiovisual Systems Energy Management Performance Standard (in development)

■ Waste Management

Waste in regard to audiovisual and set design may include hazardous materials, leftover materials, packaging, and miscellaneous waste such as tape. Measurements include the following:

- Volume or weight of waste that is traceable specifically to the audiovisual function
- Change in baseline measurements of the volume or percentage of waste directly attributable to the audiovisual function
- Volume or weight of material repurposed
- Volume or weight of donated materials
- Volume or weight of materials recycled
- Amount of e-waste and how it is disposed of

Accommodation

The environmental impact of your hotel and other accommodation choices can be measured in many different ways. Usually, you will need to involve more departments than those meeting professionals typically deal with (the sales and event management departments):

- Water management
- Energy management
- Waste and recycling management
- Delegate/attendee participation
- Procurement policies
- Certifications and eco-labels

The Vancouver Convention Centre's sophisticated black water treatment plant provides toilet flushing water as well as rooftop irrigation during warmer weather. The facility also runs a desalination plant that purifies seawater for additional nonpotable uses. This system combined with the Black Water Treatment Plant allows the facility to save a great deal of municipal potable water.
Photograph courtesy of the Vancouver Convention Centre

■ Water Management

Information can be garnered from the housekeeping and operations departments of hotels/other accommodations. Reporting water use and sources are part of the Global Reporting Initiative (GRI) event sector supplement guidelines, and also form a part of the APEX green meeting report. Metrics for water management include:

- *Does the accommodation have a towel/linen reuse program?* When assessing possible accommodation, the existence of such programs may indicate that properties are concerned with the water and energy footprints of their properties and are taking steps to manage it. If meeting professionals want to select properties with viable sustainability programs, this is an initiative that is extremely common globally, including in North America, Australia, and Europe.
- *Percentage of fixtures that are low-flow, including faucets, toilets, and urinals.*

The presence of a high percentage of these fixtures indicates a well-established water management program.

- *Average water consumption per guestroom*. This metric can be obtained by using average occupancy monthly and the monthly water bill. To get an estimate of water use by a specific group in-house, the ratio of group occupancy to this number can be used.
- *Percent of greywater used in facility*. This is likely to be an estimate. Use of greywater includes watering of plants.
- *Percentage of grounds with xeriscaping*. This technique reduces the amount of water used in landscaping, and may help planners identify properties with good water management programs.

■ Energy Management

Much of this information is available from the operations department of the hotel. The sales or event manager can ensure that this department is brought into the loop from the beginning of the RFP process, right through to the pre-event meeting typically held before the start of the event. Metrics for energy management include:

- *Percentage of fixtures with high-efficiency lighting*. If the meeting professional is interested in selecting a property with a lower average energy footprint, this measure may help identify properties that have taken steps to reduce that footprint.
- *Percentage of energy from alternative sources*. **Alternative energy** usually refers to renewable energy such as geothermal, hydro, solar, or wind; it can also refer to biofuels. These sources of energy are assumed to have less polluting effects than convention fuels such as oil, gas, coal, or other fossil fuels, which emit carbon and can contribute to climate change when burned. This could include energy offsets or purchase of renewable energy from wind or solar projects. It is an important measure to consider when selecting accommodation if interested in properties with a lower footprint. Please see Chapter 5 for more information about alternative energy.
- *Percentage of guestrooms with motion sensors*. Motion sensors control the time that lights are on to when the room is occupied. Rooms that control access to lighting and power with card keys are common in Europe and China but less so in North America, but represent a good best practice. It is estimated that 50 percent of energy use in hotels comes from guestrooms; 20 to 25 percent of the time from 11:00 A.M. to 5:00 P.M., when most guests are not in the rooms, lights are still on. Studies show that the bathroom light is most frequently left on when rooms are occupied, consuming unnecessary (and expensive!) energy.[4]
- *Percentage of windows that open*. This measurement is more important when assessing possible accommodations, and is possibly geographically and seasonally dependent; for example, it is more common in Europe. It is important when evaluating the natural cooling possibilities of the venue without resorting to air conditioning.
- *In certain cases, hotels will be able to measure the actual energy use with the use of meters*. This is more typical of meeting rooms rather than guestrooms. Otherwise, energy use by specific in-house groups can be estimated on a per-guestroom basis using average occupancy and monthly energy bills.

For example, in 2010 Autodesk estimated that their six largest events were responsible for 14 percent of the total organizational carbon footprint, generating 7,063 metric tons of carbon.[5] The meeting department has selected six areas on which to focus their measurement efforts:

1. Sustainable practices of destinations
2. Choosing a destination that minimizes travel

3. Using technology to maximize remote participation
4. Reusing materials and purchasing sustainable materials
5. Reducing waste
6. Working with suppliers to measure and reduce their event footprint

▨ Waste and Recycling Management

This information is typically available from the operations department of the hotel, although certain hotels have specific waste management departments that should be contacted. In other cases, event managers may need volunteers to help sort and weigh waste during the event. In certain cases, the kitchen staff is better able to track this information. Metrics for waste management include:

- *Total diversion rate.* The diversion rate is the amount of waste diverted through recycling, compost or re-purposing, divided by total waste generated and multiplied by 100 to get a percentage.
- *Percentage of waste allocated to group from overall facility.* This is difficult to do for specific in-house groups, but can be estimated as a ratio between percent occupancy and total waste removal by weight or volume.
- *Percentage of waste recycled.* Divide the amount of total waste recycled by the amount of total waste (for groups using part of a facility, use the number as calculated above). Multiply this by 100 to get a percent.
- *Percentage of waste composted.* This can be calculated as a ratio of total weight or volume of composting compared to total weight of waste similar to the calculation above.
- *Amount of leftover food donated.* This is more typical when the meeting/event is being held in the primary guestroom venue and can be measured by number of meals or weight of food.

▨ Delegate/Attendee Participation

Meeting professionals can measure participation in environmental programs by:

- *Percentage of event participants selecting the linen/towel reuse program.* Ask housekeeping to use daily checklist to track participating rooms in the block.
- *Percentage of delegates/attendees/other participants who self-declare participation on surveys.*

▨ Procurement

Procurement policies of prospective hotels are an important part of assessing and measuring their sustainability. This may be information that several departments need to collaborate on, including purchasing, housekeeping, and operations, depending on where the function lies internally. More detailed information on sustainable procurement practices is found in Chapter 8 on sustainable supply chains.

Metrics to help meeting professionals determine the environmental sustainability of purchasing and procurement policies might include:

- *Percentage of paper products with recycled content.* The minimum percentage of recycled content desirable is usually 20 percent recycled/post consumer content.
- *Percentage of products purchased in bulk to reduce packaging.* Items may include foodstuffs such as sugar and condiments.
- *Percentage of cleaning products that is nontoxic and certified "green."* Look for labels such as Green Seal or Ecologo.

■ Certifications, Eco-labels, and Green Ratings

Eco-labels are voluntary recognition programs, sometimes—not always, so buyer beware—awarded by third-party organizations. They indicate a minimum compliance with a specific set of criteria. They can be industry-specific, such as the Marine Stewardship Council (MSC) or Forest Stewardship Council (FSC), or can be production-oriented, like Fairtrade or ENERGY STAR. Eco-labels were started by NGOs to promote sustainable purchasing and consumer awareness. Recently governments have gotten into the game; for example, Canada has EcoLogo, the European Union has EcoLabel and the United States has ENERGY STAR. There has been a large influx of eco-labels in the last number of years, which may dilute their effectiveness in the marketplace. According to the Ecolabel Index website, there are almost 400 eco-labels globally.

Hotels have a variety of certifications and eco-labels that they may have achieved, or be in the process of achieving. Typically, the process of getting a certification makes it more likely that the venue has in place solid and reputable sustainability processes and programs. Such certifications and eco-labels could include:

- *ISO 14001 or the 14001-derived 9001.* This is the International Standards Organization Environmental Management System and is globally applicable.
- *LEED.* The Leadership in Energy and Environmental Design certification is for building systems and is awarded by the U.S. Green Building Council (USGBC) as Platinum, Gold, or Silver. It is most recognized in North America, but has eighteen international affiliates.
- *Green Key Global.* This program is a self-certified green rating system administered by the Hotel Association of Canada. Over 1100 hotels in North America (Canada and the United States) participate and can show the Green Key Eco-label once they have undergone the self-assessment.
- *Audubon Green Leaf.* This program rates properties in four areas: energy efficiency, environmental management, pollution prevention, and resource conservation. Although this is self-assessed, the program will send someone to certify that assessment within one year of completion. It is best known in the United States and Canada.
- *Green Globe.* This organization offers certification for travel and tourism-related products and services (including their supply chains). It uses 337 indicators in 41 sustainability criteria and is based on several international agreements, including Sustainable Tourism Criteria and ISO 14001, 9001, and 19011.
- *Nordic Swan.* The official eco-label for the Nordic countries, including Finland, Sweden, Denmark, Norway, and Iceland. It is a rigorous certification with specific limits defined for the use of energy, water, and chemicals and the production of waste, with limits defined by occupied room night and/or square feet of space. The assessment covers the areas of operations and maintenance; facility and purchasing; guestrooms; food and beverage; cleaning; waste; conference facilities; and environmental management.

A generic eco-label.
Photo courtesy of iStock/Arkadi Bojarsinov

- *Green Tourism.* This is the national green tourism certification for the United Kingdom and Ireland. Certification is independently assessed on 145 criteria, including energy and water efficiency, waste management, purchasing, use of local produce, recycling, and support of public transit. Members may be any sort of accommodation, from hotels to bed-and-breakfasts and hostels. They must recertify every two years.

Communications

Communications are an important part of a corporate responsibility program and have an added dimension when applied to sustainable meetings. Measurement can be related to both waste and behavior change. This is discussed in greater detail in Chapter 7.

■ Waste Reduction

- *Percent of processes that are electronic, such as registration, exhibitor packages, handouts and speaker presentations, surveys, networking tools, invoices, and receipts.* This reduces the need for printing and provides resources to stakeholders on an on-demand, just-in-time basis, being online when stakeholders need them.
- *Percentage of marketing materials that are electronic, such as online or on electronic storage devices.* Eliminating the need for printed materials is a cost-saving measure.
- *Percentage of materials that are printed, double-sided, on recycled paper.* This is a cost-reducing strategy as well as one that decreases waste, as it reduces overall consumption of paper.
- *Percentage of materials that are reused, such as name badges and signage.* The reuse of name badges involves engaging the participation of attendees to increase the success of this initiative; it may also generate new strategies, such as the production of permanent name badges for long-term attendees. Strategies like this reduce waste and potentially increase attendee loyalty, an important strategy if the meeting generates money for the organizer.
- *Percentage change in name badges and signage that is reused from baseline.*
- *Percentage decrease of use of registration bags and materials used to stuff them from sponsors and partners.*
- *Percentage reduction in volume of giveaways that are not consumable.* Consumables do not create waste, assuming that they are in fact consumed!
- *Percentage of attendees bringing their own conference bags or lanyards.*

■ Energy

Communications also involves shipping in certain circumstances, such as the shipping of printed materials. Measurements in this area could include:

- *Percentage of goods purchased locally.* This eliminates the need to ship long distances, and has the added benefit of increasing local economic impact.
- *Percentage of goods shipped by ground versus air.* Although impractical if goods are being sent from overseas unless you have several months' advance time, goods shipped by ground or sea are normally considered to have a lower carbon footprint than shipment by air.

■ Sustainable Sourcing

With the advent of the Internet in the 1990s and more recently the rise of social networking and mobile applications, much conference-and-event-related communications is done electronically. However, some is not, and the origins of these products can be an important metric for environmental, community, and economic reasons.

- *Percentage of paper purchased from sustainable-forestry initiatives, preferably FSC (Forest Stewardship Council).* This is the gold-standard eco-logo for the paper industry.
- *Percentage of recycled content of paper.*
- *Percentage of plastic materials that are of recycled or biodegradable materials.*

■ Information

An important part of communication is to communicate with your stakeholders about your sustainability-related initiatives, whether this takes the form of sustainable education sessions or if it is simply making the community aware of the actions your organization has taken to make the meeting or event sustainable. Measurement may take these forms:

- *Number of sessions at your educational event about sustainability.* Sessions can be in your field of expertise or industry sector.
- *Percentage of responses to stakeholder outreach on sustainability issues specific to your meeting or event.* Outreach to stakeholders is an essential component of industry standards such as British Standard 8901 or ISO 20121.
- *Percentage of suppliers, partners, and delegates who received your sustainability policy.* Having a sustainability policy and ensuring that your stakeholders are familiar with it will be an essential part of APEX green meeting standards and is part of British Standard 8901 and ISO 20121.

Destinations

There are few decisions that will affect the sustainability of a meeting or event as much as the choice of destination. The infrastructure of the destination controls many factors. For example, you will not be able to manage or measure recycled materials if the destination does not have a recycling facility or access to one. It can also be a matter of degree; the destination may have a recycling facility for some materials and not others, or the ability to compost some food products but not others. Other elements important to selecting a sustainable destination may include the availability of public transit between the airport and the event venue and the **walkability** of the area where the meeting or event will be held. Walkability is a descriptive term for the area where a meeting or event is to be held. It usually implies that the main event venue is within walking distance of half or more of the accommodation options booked for delegates and other participants. Although distance is a main criterion, other factors, especially safety, must be taken into account.

Additionally, an important criterion is the availability of sustainably managed facilities such as convention or conference centers and hotels or other accommodations within the budget range of your meeting or event. Of course, the willingness of the destination's convention and visitor's bureau or equivalent organization to support your sustainability objectives is very important, and something that can't be measured.

Management of destination factors starts with the request for proposal or bid guidelines for major events. This document should outline policy and expectations for all major areas, including venues and infrastructure, whether already in place (as is the case for most meetings and conventions) or needing to be built (as may be the case for mega-events).

Destination selection affects the sustainability of meetings and events.
Photo courtesy of Elizabeth Henderson

Some things can be measured and can assist in selecting a destination:

- Number of renewable energy options available to purchase for the event (Renewable energy includes wind, solar, hydro, and geothermal)
- Number of hotels or percentage of hotels available that have sustainability programs
- Percentage of key items—paper, cardboard, aluminum, glass, food and plastic, for example—that can be recycled, repurposed, or composted in existing facilities
- Number or percentage of hotels within walking distance of the main meeting facility

Exhibits

Exhibitions typically generate masses of waste products unless carefully managed. Management comes through policy, contracts, pre-event communications, and on-site management.

■ Policy and Contracts

Policy and contracts are critical in managing exhibition-related waste, since third parties will be responsible for much of the materials brought on-site. Ensure that contracts have clauses that limit or control the amount and type of materials brought on-site. Measurement might include:

- Percentage of exhibitors that have signed the contract with explicit environmental sustainability guidelines

■ Communications

Communications can be managed to reduce waste specifically related to exhibitions. Measurements include:

- Percentage of contracts sent electronically
- Percentage of contracts returned electronically
- Number of exhibitor prospectuses printed

■ On-site Materials

The amount and type of materials brought on-site is where "the rubber meets the road" for exhibitions. Measurement in this area includes:

- Total waste generated by weight
- Total change in amount of waste generated compared to baseline

- Amount of waste by type
- Amount of waste diverted from landfill (recycled, repurposed, donated)
- Amount of materials brought by each exhibitor, by weight
- Percentage of exhibitors meeting the standards required by sustainability clauses in their contracts
- Number of exhibitors that are "waste-free" at the end of the show

A tradeshow floor awaits cleanup after move-out.
Photo courtesy of Elizabeth Henderson

A tradeshow floor awaits cleanup after move-out.
Photo courtesy of Elizabeth Henderson

Carpet underlay from a tradeshow is removed for disposal.
Photo courtesy of Elizabeth Henderson

Signage from a convention awaits disposal or recycling.
Photo courtesy of Elizabeth Henderson

Case Study: The Copenhagen Conference of Parties Sustainability Report

In December 2009, one of the most famous international meetings of the last decade took place in Copenhagen, Denmark—the COP 15, otherwise known as the Climate Conference. The *Event Sustainability Report* is one of two key documents that resulted from this. The *Event Sustainability Report* provides numerical measurements of specific areas of importance to the conference (see Table 9.2).

Table 9.2   COP 15 Summary of Quantitative Measurements[6]

Category	Indicator	Value
ECONOMIC		
Direct investment	Estimated direct cost	58,400,000 euro
Direct income	Amount of in-kind sponsorship	15,300,00 euro
Sustainability	Direct investment in event sustainability	932,000 euro
	Savings as a result of sustainable initiatives	562,000 euro
SOCIAL		
Participation	Number of delegates	33,536
Local labor	Number of technical staff hired locally	8,000
Stakeholder engagement	Suppliers and sponsors with sustainability clauses in contract	100%
	Number of hotel beds with independent sustainability certification	7,264
	Percentage of total in greater Copenhagen area	53%
Health	Space designated smoke free in venue	99.87%
Community investment	Donations to charitable causes	537,000 euro

Food and Beverage

Food and beverage can be a major waste—and cost—driver at meetings and events, and can have significant social impacts. Measurements used to guide the environmental, social, and economic impacts of food and beverage choices include:

- Percentage procured that is fair trade
- Percentage procured that is local

Category	Indicator	Value
	ENVIRONMENTAL	
Greenhouse gas emissions (GHG)	Total carbon footprint (tons)	72,374
	Emissions from air travel (carbon equivalent)	66,374
	Local emissions	6,000
	Local emission reductions through sustainability initiatives	22%
	Emissions per participant (tons)	2.16
	Emissions offset	100%
Energy	Total energy consumed (kilowatt-hours)	954,204
	Energy produced by on-site wind turbine	38,168
	Energy produced by conversion of food scraps to biofuel	26,726
Transport	Delegates using public transport	93%
Paper usage	Sheets of FSC paper used for printing	8 million
	Percentage from 50% or more recycled paper	0%
Waste management	Total waste in tons	103,720
	Total per participant in tons	3.09
	Food waste (tons)	23
Water	Total amount used at venue in liters	3,083,000
	Percentage of nonpolluting cleaning supplies	100%
Food	Percentage organic/local food and beverage	75% organic, 40% local

- Percentage procured that is organic
- Percentage or weight of food that is composted
- Percentage or weight of food that is donated
- Amount of condiments served in bulk containers
- Percentage of food served on china or re-usable service ware
- Percentage of food served in disposable containers
- Percentage of disposable containers that are compostable using available facilities
- Percentage of seafood sourced sustainable from Marine Stewardship Council (MSC) or equivalent sources

Compost bins are lined up outside a convention center.
Photo courtesy of Elizabeth Henderson

Recycling bins and food waiting for disposal on a convention center loading dock.
Photo courtesy of Elizabeth Henderson

Meeting Venues

The choice of venue is also a controlling factor in the ability to measure sustainability. In addition, it needs to align with your organizations' CSR policy in the areas of human rights and labor practices, specifically with regard to unions, diversity initiatives, and recent record of labor disputes. Things to measure include:

- Percent of venues with CSR, sustainability or ethics policies
- Percent of waste diversion facility-wide
- Percent of energy from renewable sources
- Certifications received, such as LEED or ISO

For specific areas of water, waste, and energy management, see the indicators in the Accommodations section.

On-Site Office and Operations

In other areas such as accommodation, venue, or destination selection, meeting professionals need to make choices based on others' sustainability infrastructure. The on-site office and operations is an area where your choices directly impact the outcome. Use your organizations' guidelines for sustainable procurement to help guide choices. Things to measure include:

- Percent recycled paper used
- Percent of FSC paper
- Percent of ENERGY STAR or equivalent-rated equipment
- Percent of printing double-sided

- Percentage of planning documents printed as opposed to electronic
- Percentage of packaging reused for return shipments
- Percent of local labor hired if needed

Transportation

Transportation can be considered either locally (at the destination) and/or from point of departure for delegates/materials. In order to successfully report and meet expectations for emerging standards such as APEX and the GRI event sector supplement, meeting professionals should consider measuring:

- Average miles [kilometers] traveled per attendee/staff/participant
- Method of transportation by percentage
- Carbon emissions per attendee/staff/participant
- Percent of materials shipped by ground versus air
- Percentage of attendees using public transit on-site
- Percentage of carbon emissions offset by delegates

Community and Economy

When meeting professionals think of corporate social responsibility, they often equate this with *green (or greener) meetings*. The previous section looked at environmental measurements that can be made at meetings and events. However, corporate social responsibility is much broader than simply green meetings. In the triple bottom line approach, community and economy should be considered as well.

How can these things be measured? Specifically with regard to community, some of the measurements already cited are applicable, such as percentage of items procured from fair trade, or local sources. Fair trade purchases promote social equity, often in developing countries. Buying locally has a social impact in the community where the event takes place, by increasing its prosperity. These considerations related directly to the concept of Social Return on Investment (SROI) that was discussed in Chapter 6.

Other aspects of community in the triple bottom line approach that are measurable include:

- Percentage of suppliers with diversity programs that support minority employment, such as women or indigenous peoples
- Percentage of suppliers with health and safety programs and no infractions
- Percentage of suppliers with no records of human rights abuses, such as child labor
- Percentage of suppliers with fair wages
- Percent of event workforce hired locally
- Destinations supporting laws and international agreements around labor and human rights; this can also apply to the source of goods purchased. For example, you might buy registration bags from a North American distributor, but they sourced them cheaply from a factory where there is known child labor.

Economic impact can be easier to estimate and measure. Specific metrics include:

- Amount of direct spending in the community on the event (e.g., rent of facilities, purchases of food and beverage).
- Amount of estimated indirect spending in the community by event participants. Work with the local convention and visitors bureau on this, as they often have specific estimates that they use to estimate the impact on the local economy.
- Amount spent on sustainability initiatives, such as carbon offsets, water coolers, transit passes.
- Amount saved by implementing sustainability initiatives, such as savings from eliminating bottled water and reduced printing.

Community Outreach

A common inclusion in conferences, meetings, and events is a community outreach program. This can be especially powerful if it is aligned with the corporate social responsibility priorities of the organization. Typically, a community outreach program will be a transactional type of program, where participants donate time, money, or skills to a specific on-site project (for more information on "transactional" programs, please see Chapter 6). These are easy to measure. Some metrics for this type of program would include:

- Number of volunteer hours
- Number of volunteers
- Amount of money donated
- Amount of goods collected (e.g., pounds of food collected for the local food bank)
- Number of houses built
- Number of people assisted (e.g., 100 pounds of food fed 25 families of four)
- Numbers of trees planted
- Number of bikes built for local children
- Number of scholarships endowed

Creating a community outreach project that is strategically aligned with organizational priorities, including the mission, vision, and CSR objectives, is more difficult. This type of alignment is what could be called strategic CSR or transformational community programming. Strategic CSR originated from Harvard Business School authors Michael Porter and Mark Kramer in a paper called "Strategy and Society." The idea is that organizations attempt to find the intersection between their company's skills and core competencies and the needs of the community, then build on that intersection to increase competitiveness and provide a meaningful benefit to the community. Meetings and events, as physical expressions of an organization's mission and vision, are ideal communications vehicles for aligning organizational strategy with the needs of the community. The MAUDE framework, discussed in Chapter 4, is a tool for meeting professionals to use to accomplish this alignment.

In strategic CSR, the goals of the CSR program—in this case, the community outreach program—are aligned with the organizational mission, vision, and values. An example of this would be an organization such as the American Mortgage Association supporting a community project benefiting Habitat for Humanity, because both of them have "affordable housing" as a mandate. A transformational project, by contrast, would create benefits for both organizations. In addition, both parties would have the ability to affect how the project was structured. This can be more difficult to implement during a time-bounded event like a conference, meeting, or event. It is also much more difficult to measure easily.

Legacy

Legacy refers to the outcomes of an event in terms of its lasting impact on physical, economic, social, or environmental areas of the community. The Global Reporting Initiative Event Organizers Sector Supplement defines legacy as "(Legacy) refers to event outputs or outcomes, and includes the enduring physical, economic, social and environmental impacts of an event or events. Legacy also includes new capacities acquired as a consequence of events, such as new knowledge, training, standards, best practices, skills, organizations, systems, relationships, partnerships and innovations."[7] This could be buildings, skills, standards, or partnerships, among others. Mega events are perhaps better suited to provide transformational community projects. For example, VANOC (Vancouver Olympic Organizing Committee) 2010 had a goal for social inclusion and responsibility. It had six areas of focus, including inner-city inclusiveness; employment and training; business development; accessibility; ensuring safe places to live; and providing a good place to work.[8]

The community program from an Olympics is typically called a legacy, emphasizing its transformational nature. VANOC had a third party, PricewaterhouseCoopers, verify its environmental, social, and economic indicators. Key performance indicators were measured for social inclusiveness and responsibility.[9]

VANOC tracked, measured, and reported their key performance indicators (KPIs) for 2007–2008, 2008–2009, and 2009–2010; this allowed it to benchmark progress internally. As described in Chapter 7, a key performance indicator is a measurement of a specific, significant factor that defies organizational success. Indicators are set in advance; they must be quantifiable to measure progress. KPIs are typically long-term indicators that will change only when the strategy and focus on an organization shifts.

Economic Impact

VANOC also had KPIs in place for its economic impact. With an event the size of the Olympics, these measurements had significance for various levels of government and for the tax-paying public. Some of the KPIs included the value of contracts awarded, amount of local spending, and the number of sustainability innovations introduced.[10]

Deciding What to Measure, and When

Most events will not measure all of the above factors. This will depend on several attributes of the event and the host organization:

1. *What is the size of the event?* If the event is small, you may want to select a few specific measurements that address key sustainability issues, such as reduced use of materials. If the event is large, you will likely want to measure more areas.

2. *What is the scope of your event?* Make sure you define the boundaries. If you are measuring one event, is that on-site only, or are you planning on measuring the event life cycle, from destination selection to legacy?

3. *What is the profile of the event?* If the event is high profile, you may want to ensure you measure more factors than if it was a very low-key event.

4. *What have you measured in the past?* Continuation of measurement allows you to benchmark your progress.

5. *What areas are significant to your organization?* If your CSR policy focuses on diversity, then this will likely be a key area to measure. If it focuses on waste reduction, then this will become important.

6. *What areas are important to your stakeholders?* This is especially important for not-for-profits, associations, and corporations with multiple shareholders.

7. *What are key issues for the destination?* If you are having your meeting in a desert, then water may be a key issue.

8. *What standards or certifications are you hoping to achieve?* If you are trying for third-party certification, more rigorous measurements will be required in more areas.

9. *What expertise do you have available?* This is important to determine if you have in-house expertise or need to outsource this activity to others.

10. *What regulations or voluntary codes do you need to meet?* This includes regulations within destinations and countries as well as compliance with industry codes or voluntary reporting standards such as The United Nations Global Compact or the Global Reporting Initiative.

Case Study: Vancouver 2010 Olympic Winter Games

The 2010 Olympic Winter Games in Vancouver, British Columbia, Canada had a comprehensive social responsibility program in place. They measured the social, environmental, and economic impact of the Games. Their Sustainability Scorecard, part of their sustainability report, summarizes the economic benefits, environmental stewardship and impact reduction initiatives, social inclusion and responsibility, and Aboriginal participation and collaboration. A fifth category is Sport for Sustainable Living.

Although they used several indicators and associated aspects from the Global Reporting Initiative G3 Guidelines, such as environmental performance indicate number 11 (EN11), "Location and size of land owned, leased, managed in, or adjacent to, protected areas and areas of high biodiversity value outside protected areas,"[11] they also created key performance indicators that measured specifically what they thought was important environmentally, economically, and socially. Examples of these KPIs are:

- [Number and value of Buy Smart program contracts and percentage of total value of VANOC contracts
- Number and type of initiatives to support sustainable living
- Number of pre-Games and Games-times volunteers
- VANOC contribution to number of affordable beds as a legacy of the Olympic and Paralympic Village][12]

An Interview with AVW-TELAV

What contribution can audiovisual providers make to sustainable events?

Audiovisual providers can keep event waste to a minimum by including providing quotations and floor plans in soft copy format; using LED lighting, which consumes less energy; and digitally audio-recording and video-recording sessions, which eliminates the use of tapes. Providing digital event services, like videoconferencing and webcasting, also decreases a meeting's environmental impact by allowing audience members and presenters to attend remotely, which diminishes potential carbon emissions due to airline flights.

AVW-TELAV has launched a multi-media technology solution, called ImaginAction™, which combines multiple projectors with wide multi-screen displays and fills much of the audience's peripheral vision with rich, extreme-resolution images—this solution eliminates the need for a hard wall set, which would likely be disposed of after the event.

What specific AV items can meeting professionals measure?

There are two main areas in which you can quantify your AV equipment energy savings: lighting and display. LED lighting products are comparable to conventional light fixtures but consume about 50% less energy. Unfortunately, the availability of LED-based lighting solutions has not quite reached that of conventional lights; however, there is collection of conventional lights, called ETC Source Fours, which are about 40% more efficient than traditional cathode-ray tube (CRT) lights with similar output. Flat panel video and computer displays have moved away from CRT technology; LCDs and plasmas are the displays of choice. LCDs are the most energy efficient option and use only about 25% of the energy that CRTs use. Plasma is not quite as power efficient as LCDs but are more efficient than CRTs. It is important to note that more and more flat panels are using LED backlighting over florescent lighting because LEDs consume much less energy—and even more importantly, LEDs do not have the highly toxic chemicals, like mercury and phosphorous, that florescent tubes contain.

What should meeting professionals avoid and what should they request?

Focus on lighting—it is the key to energy savings at an event. Lighting is the single greatest power draw, in terms of AV, because it takes the most energy to produce. Anything that can be done to minimize your lighting's energy consumption will make the biggest impact on your power savings. When possible, request LED lights from your AV vendor or a class of conventional light that is more energy efficient, like ETC Source Four fixtures.

When it comes to displays, the best possible choice is LED-backlit LCDs, which are even more environmentally-friendly than your standard LCDs because they contain lower levels of toxic chemicals. When choosing an AV vendor, it's also important to consider whether or not they have local resources or will have to bring equipment in from other locations, which will contribute to carbon emissions from air or ground shipping. Carefully evaluate the AV provider's approach to sustainable practices in everyday business—from equipment recycling to battery disposal. It's not always simple to quantify your carbon footprint in terms of AV, but rewarding companies that are trying to make a difference is supportive to the green movement and your overall environmental sustainability goals.

The Integrated Sustainable Event Management Model (Measurement)

In Chapter 2, we introduced the Integrated Sustainable Event Management Model. We use it again in this chapter and in Chapter 10 on reporting. For the visual framework, please see Chapter 10.

The model is useful for assessing how an organization currently approaches sustainable event management. It is contingent on five factors:

1. Skill level of the meeting professional
2. Support and focus of top management
3. Size of the event
4. Integration into organizational decision making
5. Purpose of the meeting/event

For this reason, models like this one are typically called *contingency models*.

Chapter Review

Meeting and event professionals can be intimidated by measurement, but it is important to ensure the best decisions are being made. Measurement ensures both reliability and validity of reporting, and increases accountability, transparency, responsibility, and consistency within the event and the event management system. Measurement provides clarity of the relationship between organizational strategy and objectives and the event. This clarity can raise the influence of meeting professionals within their organizations. It also allows benchmarking within the organization or with other organizations.

Both qualitative and quantitative measurements can be important. Specific examples of potential measurements in each of the nine areas of APEX—audiovisual, accommodation, communication, food and beverage, exhibitions, destination selection, meeting venues, on-site offices, and transportation were offered. Measurement does not end with environmental measurement; community and economic measures are also important, and lead into the concept of legacy. All events do not need to measure all aspects. Relevant questions to help decide when specific measures are appropriate include size, scope, profile, what's been measured before, what is important for your organization, what is important for your stakeholders, and what might be event specific in terms of the destination itself. Available expertise and the desire to gain certification may also be drivers.

Review Questions

1. Why is measurement important to meetings and events?
2. What are the differences between qualitative and quantitative measurements?
3. What are the nine areas of APEX?
4. Define an eco-label. What eco-labels might be relevant in the meetings and events industry?
5. What is meant by the terms *walkability* and *event miles*?
6. What is meant by an event legacy?

7. What is strategic CSR?
8. What questions might you ask yourself when trying to decide which measurements may be important?

Group Activities

1. Read the following (fictional) case study and answer the questions.

   Organization: Association of Professional Accountants.

   Mission: We make it count for you.

   About the organization: The Association of Professional Accountants (APA) is a North American association, based in Chicago, Illinois, with members from Canada, Mexico, and the United States. It has roughly 5,000 members who meet twice a year for education sessions. This year, the APA is meeting to discuss the 2011 implementation of the new International Financial Reporting Standards (IFRS). Part of the new standards is increased scrutiny of environmental costs and their inclusion on financial statements such as the balance sheet and annual reports.

   The semiannual events generate approximately $300,000/year, representing 40 percent of the operating revenue for the association and so are an important part of their operations. This year, the events team has been asked to cut costs and increase revenue if possible. Attendees pay a registration fee and all expenses related to their travel, including air and hotel. Typically, each meeting attracts about 1,200 attendees, the vast majority of whom are from Canada, the United States, and Mexico. Attendance at the meeting follows the same distribution as the membership: the majority of these—50 percent—are from eastern cities such as Ottawa, Toronto, Washington, D.C., and Boston. The remainder are from various regions, representing cities such as Mexico City, Atlanta (south), San Francisco (west), Salt Lake City (central), Denver (central), Calgary (west), and Vancouver (west).

   The events team has been asked to reduce the environmental footprint of the event and report back out. The team has also been asked to make recommendations for tracking and reducing the cost of the meeting. Your boss has requested that you make recommendations for specific areas to begin measuring at the next event.

   1. What economic measurements can you make that will help track cost reduction and/or saving?
   2. What environmental aspects will you measure?
   3. Are there areas of intersection where something that will save you money will also decrease your environmental footprint?
   4. Where will you recommend that the meeting be held to create the smallest environmental footprint?
   5. Create a short plan that details the process you will take to decide and your recommendations.

2. With respect to the Integrated Sustainable Event Management model, choose an organization and assess where it is on the model. Explain why.

Key Terms

- benchmarking
- qualitative
- quantitative
- baseline
- Global Reporting Initiative
- Global Reporting Initiative Event Organizers Sector Supplement

- APEX
- event miles
- alternative energy
- eco-labels
- walkability
- legacy

Resources

Related to the Resources listed below, please visit the Book Companion Site (located at www .wiley.com/college/henderson) for a complete list of websites. Additional referential websites related to this chapter's content can also be found on the BCS.

Global Reporting Initiative Event Sector Supplement
This sector supplement will be released in its final form in 2012.

Convention Industry Council
The Convention Industry Council (CIC) is the parent organization to APEX (Accepted Practices Exchange).

APEX Green Meetings Report
This report, authored in 2004, formed the basis for green meeting standards development.

Committee for the 2010 Olympic and Paralympic Winter Games
"Social Inclusion and Responsibility," in *Vancouver 2010: Sustainability Report 2009– 10* (Vancouver: VANOC, 2010).

Notes

1. International AIDS Society, "AIDS 2008 Follow up Survey Report: Overview of Long-term Impact Assessment of the XVII International AIDS Conference."
2. Conventional Industry Council, press release, "APEX/ASTM Green Meetings & Events Standards Final Draft Ready for Comment" (August 12, 2009), www.conventionindustry .org/Newsroom/pressreleases/PressReleases2009/pr08122009.aspx.
3. Walmart, "Walmart Produce: Our Commitment to You." Accessed September 26, 2011, from instoresnow.walmart.com/article.aspx?Center=Food&top=87508&id=44214.

4. Wattstopper, "Hotel Lighting Controls—Reduce Energy Waste While Guests Are Away." Accessed September 26, 2011, from www.wattstopper.com/getdoc/2211/HS_NewProdBroch_08.pdf.

5. Autodesk, "Greening Our Events." Accesses September 26, 2011, from www.south-apac .autodesk.com/adsk/servlet/pc/item?siteID=1157326&id=17454781.

6. The COP 15 United Nations Climate Conference Copenhagen, *Event Sustainability Report*. www.e-pages.dk/visitdenmark/473/.

7. Global Reporting Initiative Event Organizers Sector Supplement. p. 16.

8. Committee for the 2010 Olympic and Paralympic Winter Games, "Social Inclusion and Responsibility," in *Vancouver 2010: Sustainability Report 2009–10* (Vancouver: VANOC, 2010). Accessed September 26, 2011, from www.2010legaciesnow.com/fileadmin/user_ upload/About_Us/VANOC/6_Social_Inclusion_and_Responsibility.pdf

9. Ibid.

10. Ibid.

11. Global Reporting Initiative G3 Guidelines.

12. Committee for the 2010 Olympic and Paralympic Winter Games.

Screen capture of the number of "Acts of Green" that Event Camp Vancouver participants completed over the course of the event.
Photograph courtesy of Three Sixty Photography

CHAPTER 10

Sustainability Reporting for Meetings and Events

"It's not too late at all. You just don't yet know what you are capable of."

—*Mahatma Gandhi*

Learning Objectives

After studying this chapter, you will be able to:

- Explain why reporting is an important part of an event-based corporate social responsibility (CSR) program.

- Align meeting and event reporting within reporting methodologies including a simple post-event report (PER), the business-focused balanced scorecard, the International Standards Organization (ISO) 20121 event sustainability management system, and the Global Reporting Initiative (GRI) Event Organizers Sector Supplement.

- Link key event objectives, processes, and success factors to organizational or client strategies for greater alignment, generation of value, and accountability.

- Identify key stakeholders based on your specific event to better engage them, determine relevant impacts, and manage or mitigate those impacts.

- Implement the integrated sustainable event management framework in assessing existing and potential meeting professional competencies.

Introduction

This chapter will explore reporting as the formalization of the measurement process and as a key tool in stakeholder engagement. Reporting as part of a sustainable event management system demonstrates transparency and accountability both internally and externally. More than this, it explicitly makes a link between sustainable event objectives and corporate strategy. Although event professionals may not be comfortable with reporting, there are existing tools that may be familiar to them that can be adapted for use on smaller events. Other meeting and event professionals may prefer to use reporting tools that business is more familiar with, to increase their profile within the organization and prove that they speak the language of business. Both types will be introduced here.

Linkages

We've learned that measurement is important to ensure we take the information we have about our meetings and events and use it to make better decisions in the future. A report is the formalization of the measurement process; it provides context, scope, and credibility, gives detail on measurements, identifies significant issues and their materiality, creates relevance for event stakeholders, and formalizes the achievement of targets and goals.

A report can be a very simple accounting of quantitative data, but can also illuminate an organization's ethical, legal, and moral actions in the form of policy, activities, organizational structure, or strategies. A CSR report by its very nature is meant to go beyond financial reporting and comment on the social and environmental issues of the organization in terms of ethics and values, in this case, as expressed through its meetings and events. Because this is hard to define, the scope of ethical, social, and environmental issues and values is usually defined through discovering and managing the expectations of stakeholders. The quality of dialogue with stakeholders is therefore very important.

The level of evaluation, analysis, and knowledge exchange derived from a thorough and thoughtful reporting process is a critical part of meeting and event management. Many people view reporting as boring, intimidating, or without value, but that simply means they have not recognized its value to their own future success. Reports are catalysts for continual improvement.

Maaike Fleur is the sector supplement manager helping the global working group (consisting of event professionals, government representatives, and international nongovernmental organizations) to develop the new **Global Reporting Initiative Event Organizers Sector Supplement**. She gives some background on the purpose of the new reporting standard and why it was created.

Why did GRI decide to create an event-sector supplement?

The London Olympic Committee approached GRI in 2008 asking what the conditions for developing a new sector supplement were. Some months later, the Swiss and Austrian Organizers of the European Football championship came to GRI with the same question. We put the two together and decided to collaborate on the design of a new sector supplement.

What kind of organizations do you anticipate will use it?

We anticipate professional event organizing companies to use the supplement, as well as organizations running one-off events. These may be companies, international organizations, or even governments, and all may be organizing different types of events; cultural, conferences, sports events, or trade shows.

When the first set of GRI Guidelines launched in 1999, only ten companies used it to report. Now we see about 1,850 organizations reporting (as of 2010). Do you anticipate that there will be a similar adoption curve for the Event Organizers Sector Supplement?

It would be excellent if in ten years time we see close to 2,000 GRI reports from event organizers. But the sector can really make a difference if the take-up follows a steeper line and reaches this within five years. With the support of the International Olympic Committee, Meeting Professionals International, and the Green Meeting Industry Council this should be possible.

Will the GRI use the event-sector supplement to report on its own conferences and events?

GRI will be using the supplement to reports on the bigger conferences and events. The draft supplement is now used for the design of the next GRI conference planned for 2013, and GRI is aiming to publish a report on the GRI conference based on the supplement.

If you were just starting to use the event-sector supplement, what three things would you focus on?

GRI offers a comprehensive reporting framework with a wide range of sustainability reporting indicators. Everybody starting the GRI reporting process will need to find the topics and indicators that are most important to include in the report. Having worked with the event organizers sector, I would consider the following three things quite important: Measuring attendee travel as distances traveled by transportation means, provision of sustainable food and beverages, and focus on legacy of the event including sustainability topics.

How do you think that the event-sector supplement might be able to work with other industry sustainability standards, such as ISO 20121?

The ISO 20121 works very well with the GRI Event Organizers Sector Supplement: ISO 20121 lays out the management system that helps measure and manage the same topics as those covered in the GRI guidance. The supplement focuses on disclosing the actual performance that follows from the appropriate management system.

Context

The event sustainability report defines the context of the event, and should make it clear how the event and its sustainability achievements relate to other organizational initiatives, such as event objectives, organizational goals and strategy, values, overall corporate social responsibility programs, and other organizational reporting, such as annual CSR and financial reports.

Scope

The scope of the event refers to how you as the event professional have defined its limits. For example, while an event might have satellite events associated with it, you as the event professional may choose not to include those in the scope of your event report. This may be because you don't have direct control over certain aspects, or it may be that you do not believe them to be material. This could also apply to an organization that has several large events a year as well as many smaller events; the event professional could choose to define the scope of the report to include only the large events. However, events and aspects of those events that are material, relevant, and of importance to stakeholders should be included in the scope.

Credibility

Because a report is formal and concrete, it can lend credibility to your sustainable event. Credibility is enhanced if the report acknowledges and involves stakeholders, is third-party audited, admits both limitations and mistakes, and states a clear link to organizational values and strategy. A report that is used primarily as a communications vehicle and does not contain relevant information will be perceived as greenwash.

Significant Issues

Significant issues are significant not just to the organization but also to event stakeholders. Stakeholders might include the community in which the event is taking place, shareholders in a corporation, members in an association, employees, volunteers, or suppliers. The key takeaway is that stakeholders are both internal and external to the organization, and do not need to have a monetary interest in the success of the organization. Significant issues are those that need active management after they have been identified.

Materiality

The concept of **materiality** in a sustainable event report relates to the importance, or significance, of a particular measure in relation to economic, environmental, and/or social impacts. (In a standard financial report, materiality is viewed a little differently, as information that will influence specific financial decisions.) The significance usually relates back to one or more of policy, organizational objectives, event objectives, stakeholder concerns, commitments, financial concerns, and societal expectations. For example, you can have a policy on outside noise levels so as to not unduly impact the surrounding community, but if you do not have any events planned outside, this is not material to your reporting.

The Global Reporting Initiative defines materiality in this way: "The information in a report should cover topics and Indicators that reflect the organization's significant economic, environmental, and social impacts, or which would substantively influence the assessments and decisions of stakeholders."[1]

Measurement Detail

The report gives detail on the factors you decided to measure. The detail usually comes in clusters. For example, here are four possible clusters:

1. **APEX cluster:** The information will be organized into the nine APEX (Accepted Practices Exchange) areas of destination selection, venue and accommodation, transportation, communication, food and beverage, on-site office, exhibits, and audiovisual.
2. **Triple-bottom-line cluster:** The information will be presented in the three areas of people, planet, and profit.

3. **The GRI cluster:** The information will be organized into the standard GRI G3 guidelines of economy, environment, social (including human rights, labor, society, and product responsibility), as well as legacy. Note that G3 indicates that it is the third generation of the guidelines.

4. **Customized cluster:** There is nothing wrong with customizing the reporting cluster to your needs. For example, a small event might focus exclusively on waste; a large event might have identified its impact on the community as the most important aspect that it needs to report on.

How to Report

There are many different ways you can create an event sustainability report. Some reporting formats are private; that is, they are created using a template or process from a sustainability reporting company or sustainable event consultant. However, there are some ways of creating a report that use either industry sustainability standards or integrate the information into reporting templates commonly used in business. We will look at:

1. APEX Post-Event Report (simple)
2. Balanced scorecard (business-oriented)
3. ISO 20121
4. Global Reporting Initiative event organizers sector supplement

APEX Post-Event Report (PER)

APEX, the Accepted Practices Exchange, overseen by the Convention Industry Council (CIC), created the first template for a post-event report in the early 2000s. If this is what you use already, if this is a relatively simple or small meeting/event, or if you want a simple template just starting out, this is a good tool, to which sustainability can be added quite easily. First we will give a brief outline of the existing sections of the **APEX post-event report (PER)** and then we will suggest how this can be adapted to include sustainability factors in these same areas.

The Existing PER

The APEX Post Event Report template has nine sections:[2]

1. *Event information:* This includes the name and type of the event, the host city, the start and finish dates, and the event owner, as well as the organizational mission and vision.
2. *Contact information:* This is essentially contact information for the primary event organizer(s), including staff, volunteers, event professional, or other contacts.
3. *Hotel room/housing information:* This includes the number of hotels, block of rooms in each hotel, and the number of rooms on peak night.
4. *Room block information:* This is a detailed form specific to each hotel being used. It includes the pickup from 90 days out, so an event professional can see the pickup trend. It also includes the number of double and single rooms occupied.

5. *Food and beverage:* This section tracks what kind of meals were served (breakfast, lunch, reception, or dinner), the day of the event it was served, the guaranteed number, and the actual number of people fed.
6. *Function space information:* This section details how many people attended each session, what kind of a setup it was (theater, hollow-square, conference, rounds, etc.), the audio-visual setup, number of breakout sessions, utilities used (Internet, electricity), and other function room-related information.
7. *Exhibit space information:* This tracks the square footage used, what kind of displays (e.g., table top or 10 × 10), the number of days the show runs, and the utilities used (Internet, electricity).
8. *Future event dates information:* Are they confirmed? If not, what are the open dates and preferred locations?
9. *Report distribution tracking:* This section tracks reporting responsibility, such as who put the report together and who it was distributed to.

Adapting the PER to Include Sustainability

The PER is easily adaptable to include sustainability elements. What follows is a discussion of some of the areas that can be easily added; the list is not exhaustive. You might find that there are areas specific to your meeting and event that are not included here. Environmental, economic, and social factors have been included for a more complete picture of sustainability.

■ Event Information

This section is a good location to add information about the sustainability elements tied to destination selection. The sustainability policy can be added here, as well as sustainable event goals. It is also logical to include specific information about public transportation and citywide recycling and waste management facilities. This section of the PER also collects and reports information on the origin of attendees, making this a natural place to also collect information on the number of miles [kilometers] traveled by attendees, speakers, and staff for possible carbon offsetting, as well as the amount of the eventual offset (if used). It also helps to track and reduce overall event miles over time.

■ Contact Information

This section collects contact information, and so is the natural place to include stakeholder information. This includes contacts at community organizations in the host location that are willing to take donated materials, such as that generated by tradeshows or excess giveaways and registration bags, leftover meals, or other food. Also, if the event has a community service aspect, this is the place to include information about the organization, including on-site contact information.

■ Hotel Room and Housing Information

This section is normally used to collect basic information, such as what housing bureau was used and what hotel. To customize this section to also collect sustainability factors, it can also track what hotels have a linen-towel reuse program, recycling programs, and other sustainability policies and programs specific to each hotel, as well as the hotel sustainability contact (many major hotel chains have these). It is a good place to list out the specific sustainability clauses that each hotel has agreed to in its contract.

Room Block Information

This section already collects data that support economic sustainability, such as the percentage of the room block that was picked up. This is helpful when reporting on the economic impact of the event. Sections that can be added include tracking of how many rooms utilized the towel-line reuse program by day, and how many pounds of recycled goods were collected from the block (this is trickier to track and will depend on how the hotel sorts recyclables and waste).

Choice of water stations at Event Camp Vancouver as supplied by Vancouver Convention and Exhibition Centre. *Photograph courtesy of Three Sixty Photography*

Food and Beverage

This section traditionally collects information about the type and number of meals served on what days. It can be adjusted to collect information about the food itself, including percentages of fair trade; local, seasonal, and organic food served; pounds of food donated to local community organizations; money saved by substituting one product for another (such as replacing bottled water with filtered water); and pounds of food waste generated and/or composted.

Function Space

Typically used simply to track number of rooms used, their setup, and the audiovisual required, this section can be adapted to include tracking the percentage of function rooms with natural lighting; number or percentage of rooms with motion-sensitive lighting to save energy; square footage of rooms used to help track energy use calculations; and number of tables available that do not require linens to be used (saves the washing of table linens, reducing the amount of energy and water used). It can also be used to note the environmentally sustainable audiovisual equipment used, such as equipment with Energy Star or other ratings.

Exhibit Space

To customize the exhibit space section of the PER to include sustainability information, include information on the number or percentage of exhibitors who signed sustainability clauses; the number of exhibitors who did not bring printed materials and who gave out consumable giveaways; the amount of recyclable material and waste collected from the tradeshow floor post-show; and any policies the event organizer has on amount of material that can be brought in per exhibitor and what is to be done with the remainder.

Future Dates

This section can easily include the desirable sustainability factors for future destinations, meeting venues, and hotels, such as recycling infrastructure, walkability factors, and public transit.

■ Report Distribution Tracking

This section already does essentially what we want it to. However, it should be made explicit that the people and organizations it is going to are key stakeholders, both internal and external. It should also specify the method by which it was communicated. For example, it should indicate that it was sent electronically and printed copies were not distributed. If the event had a third-party auditor for sustainability purposes (for British Standard 8901, for example), that information should be included here.

These suggestions are summarized in Table 10.1.

Table 10.1   Potential Sustainability Elements in a Post-Event Report

PER Section	Potential Sustainability Elements				
Event Information	Public transit from airport	Recycling facilities	Sustainability policy	Sustainable event goals	Transportation options (train, plane, automobile)
	Event miles (attendees)	Event miles (speakers)	Event miles (staff)	Carbon offsets	
Contact Information	Stakeholders' contact information	Emergency contacts	Local recyclers if not included in facility services	Community organizations for donation of food/goods	Community organization partner for service activity
Hotel Room & Housing Information	Linen/towel reuse program	In-room or back of house recycling	Hotel sustainability policy and programs	Hotel sustainability contact	Contracted sustainability clauses specific to the property
	Hotels with green certifications (e.g., LEED)	Any sustainability awards won by hotels			
Room Block	Number of guests using linen/towel recycling	Number of pounds of waste and recycling from guest room block	Percentage of pickup over or under contract	Percentage of profit over or under expectations (hotel perspective)	
Food and Beverage	Percentage of free trade food procured and served	Percentage of local and seasonal food procured and served	Percentage of organic food procured and served	Pounds of food donated to local organizations	Pounds of waste generated and/or composted
	Money saved by offering filtered vs. bottled water	Money saved by portion control			

PER Section	Potential Sustainability Elements				
Function Space	Percentage of space with natural lighting	Percentage rooms with motion sensors for lighting	Energy-efficient audiovisual equipment	Clothless tables available	Square footage, to help track energy use prorated by space
Exhibit Space	Exhibitor policy on amount of material	Number of exhibitors with green booths	Number of exhibitors with consumable giveaways	Pounds of recycled material by type	Pounds of waste generated
	Number of exhibitors who signed sustainable clauses in contracts	Amount of money charged for waste disposal	Amount of money saved on waste disposal through recycling		
Future Dates	Desirable sustainability factors of future destinations	Desirable sustainability factors for future venues	Desirable sustainability factors for future hotels		
Report Distribution	Key internal stakeholders	Key external stakeholders	Method of distribution (electronic vs. print)	Third-party auditor contact information	

Lawrence Leonard stewards APEX for the Convention Industry Council (CIC). He had this to say about the current post-event report and about plans for future adjustments.

When did APEX create the post-event report, and why?

   The APEX post-event report was created in the early 2000s. The first version was released in 2003, with an update in 2005. The post-event report was developed as a solution to recognized inconsistencies or deficiencies in the way key pieces of event data were collected and reported. The data in the PER help both suppliers (hoteliers and other venues) and planners understand and communicate the event's logistical parameters and business value (to suppliers) of an event and to have accurate data when planning and budgeting for future iterations of the event. The design of the PER was coordinated with DMAI (Destination Marketing Association International) to keep the PER aligned with DMAI's MINT (Meeting Information Network) project.

   (Note: To read more about MINT, please visit the Book Companion Site [located at www.wiley.com/college/henderson] for a list of additional reference websites.)

I have heard that APEX is considering adjusting the PER to include sustainability factors explicitly. Is this being done?

   The APEX Leadership Council's (ALC) position is that the APEX/ASTM Environmentally Sustainable Event Standards are APEX products and that all APEX documents/best practices should work together. This means that all of the APEX documents/best practices should be reviewed to ensure that they embrace and support the APEX/ASTM standards.

The APEX Standards Review Council (SRC) is tasked with ongoing review and maintenance of the APEX materials. The SRC's reviews look at all aspects of the materials, but they are particularly focused on accessibility, usability, and in keeping the documents relevant and up to date with current practices. The SRC is currently starting work on the APEX Event Specification Guide and then will move on to the PER sometime in early to mid-2012. Past revision projects, notably the APEX Industry Glossary, have involved direct work by the SRC supplemented by small volunteer subgroups. I would anticipate this is the approach that will be taken on the PER, particularly as it relates to sustainability elements where SRC will want to make sure it has input from a selection of SMEs.

How would you suggest that people use the existing PER and include sustainability?

The work schedule the SRC has put into place probably won't produce a revised PER until 2012. Until then, we certainly want planners to use the PER. I think there's still quite a bit of healthy discussion taking place around the topics of data and reporting. The area will certainly continue to mature, and organizations like GMIC will likely guide the way forward in terms of fostering that conversation, and offering education and resources.

Balanced Scorecard

The **balanced scorecard** is used extensively in corporations, not-for-profits, and government to align activities to strategy. For event professionals wanting to talk the language of business, using the principles of a balanced scorecard in your event report will give you some needed fluency. This type of a meeting/event report is most appropriate when the reporting is for internal purposes.

■ What Is the Balanced Scorecard?

The balanced scorecard (BSC) was created in the 1990's by Robert Kaplan and David Norton and published in the Harvard Business Review. It was intended to broaden the scope of management from traditional financial measures to encompass nontraditional measures such as employee engagement, customer viewpoints, and other internal perspectives. The *balance* refers to the fact that the financial perspective is being balanced out by nonfinancial measures that are critical to organizational success, such as employee training and motivation[3]. In recent years, some organizations have added another level, that of sustainability. The levels are:

1. Financial perspective
2. Customer perspective
3. Internal business perspective
4. Learning and growth perspective
5. Sustainability (newer perspective)

■ Financial Perspective

Financial metrics are the traditional measure of business success, so people can usually readily identify with this perspective. From an events focus, financial metrics depend on the nature of both the organization and the purpose of the event.

Associations

Often for associations, the annual meeting or other events are revenue generators, a major contributor to the annual operating budget. In this case, a financial metric would include profitability. Profitability is, of course, a mix of two other measures, cost and revenue, which might also have financial targets.

Corporations

Corporations often use meetings and events not as revenue generators but to accomplish other purposes such as training, sales, or customer appreciation. In these cases, revenue is not the appropriate metric. The cost of the event is likely the key metric, so working within the event budget is important. In the case of something like training, not controlling the budget, but spending the budget in its entirety might also be appropriate.

Government

Government meetings or events may be revenue generators (rare) or public consultation, mega events, elections, or training. In these cases, cost control may be a primary driver.

Other financial metrics associated with meetings and events might include the following:

- Increased registration
- Increased sponsorship
- Reduced costs of materials
- Reduced cost of shipping
- Reduced overall event cost
- Increased exhibitor revenue
- Increased sales, tracked post-event
- Decreased employee turnover (reduces costs of hiring, training, etc.)

■ Customer Perspective

This is called the *customer* perspective, but in terms of meetings and events should actually be viewed as the *stakeholder* perspective because the "customers" are not necessarily buying a product or service, such as when the event is targeted internally to employees. Customers of all types drive the focus of the event; they should, at a basic level, be telling event professionals what to do. Four measures are important to this level specific to meetings and events:

1. Member, employee or customer satisfaction
2. Member, employee or customer retention
3. Repeat attendance (loyalty)
4. Referrals

■ Internal Business Perspective

This is the level of internal business processes. The event should reflect organizational objectives, goals, mission, and vision, as well as those specific to the event. These metrics should allow the meeting professional to gauge how well they are operating in the event context. Measures and targets important to this level might include these questions:

- Is the event process on time?
- Have 90 percent of speakers been confirmed?
- Is the general session within 5 minutes of schedule?
- Have we reviewed sustainability policy and goals?
- Are the sustainable event objectives set?
- Is our event management system (e.g., British Standard 8901) operating?
- How many incidents have there been?

■ Learning and Growth Perspective

This is the level of organizational and event team culture. Areas of importance include training, the appropriate use of technology, and internal communications. It is about self-improvement, with the realization that people are valuable resources to an events team. Experienced events people provide a wealth of opportunities to train those without as much experience and to ensure that meetings and events are operationally excellent. This has great value to an organization in filling its mission and meeting its objectives. Five measures and targets are appropriate to the learning and growth perspective:

1. Percentage of team trained on sustainability and CSR policy
2. Event team satisfaction and retention
3. Development of competencies related to meetings and events
4. Competitive reward and compensation system
5. Opportunities for career growth

Tim Sunderland of Sustainable Event Certification (SEC), based in the United Kingdom, is an experienced auditor who has audited and then certified several events to British Standard 8901. He also has some experience with use of the BSC in corporations. Here are some of his ideas about the connection between reporting, the balanced scorecard, and event sustainability.

How can the balanced scorecard be used to report sustainability?
    A balanced scorecard is simply a tool that could be used to track the performance of an event, or an organization in the events industry. The scorecard includes the key performance indicators (KPIs), which relate to the strategic success of the event (or the organization in the event industry). These KPIs are then monitored pre-, during, and post-event to ensure the event has been successful in achieving its objectives. The trick is to focus on a few key indicators and review performance on a regular basis, and be able to take corrective action if the KPIs indicate that the goals are unlikely to be met. The term *balanced* means that the focus is not just on money and revenue but also on a mix of indicators—preferably lead indicators. The Global Reporting Initiative (GRI) is developing KPIs for the events industry, and this could be a good start when constructing a scorecard.

Specifically with regard to events, how can this concept be used effectively?

A balanced scorecard can be set up for each event. This would be based on understanding the key issues and objectives of the event (as per BS 8901) and constructing a scorecard based on the specific performance objectives that have been set—this could include, for example, number of delegate registrations, whether learning objectives were achieved, delegate satisfaction, electricity consumed, even the length of the registration line (which could be a good lead indicator of delegate satisfaction).

Do you have any suggestions for events practitioners wanting to implement this reporting tool?

The trick is to keep it simple and visual. Focus on the five to six KPIs for the event, decide what the metrics are going to be, and implement systems to track performance on a regular basis.

Will using the balanced scorecard as an event reporting tool increase the relevance of events in corporations?

Balanced scorecards are well-established concepts in corporations—by event organizers using this approach, they will be talking the same language as the corporations.

■ Sustainability Perspective

Each sustainability category may have multiple performance measures, which are linked to specific targets and initiatives. A balanced scorecard for a fictional event might look like Table 10.2.

Table 10.2   Sample Balanced Scorecard for Sustainable Meetings and Events

Perspective	Performance Measure	Target	Initiative
Financial	Increased event registration Increased community outreach participation	20% increase in registration 10% increase in profit	Promoting CSR program and partnerships
Customer	Improved event brand image	Increased market share Increased customer satisfaction	Expand into new markets
Internal	Create community partnerships	2 new partners	CSR community outreach program development and implementation
Learning and Growth	CSR training for event staff	90% trained by next event	Information to exhibitors, partners, and sponsors on event goals, CSR policy, and how they can help
Sustainability	Reduced environmental footprint Increase positive social footprint	25% less waste 50% increase in outreach participation	Policy on amount and type of materials brought on-site Tie mission to outreach opportunities

The meeting and event sustainability balanced scorecard is a good way of linking environmental, or green meeting, initiatives to organizational benefits, including financial benefits. It works from the bottom up; that is, you build it starting with sustainable initiatives and then link them logically to the level above. In this way, they work as a cause-and-effect chart.

Think of the scorecard as telling your event sustainability story in a way that links it to organizational and event objectives. There are three keys to making it work:

1. Start at the bottom with sustainability, not at the top with financial.
2. Don't skip a level, work through them all.
3. Tell a reasonable story through the linkages you make.

The benefit of this balanced scorecard is that it works with both financial and nonfinancial measures. Financial measures are known as "lag" measures; that is, you don't know how they turn out until after the event. Nonfinancial measures, like staff training and registration, are known before financial outcomes, and are called *leading* measures. Because it illustrates cause and effect, it makes it easier for people to link your sustainable event initiatives to expected outcomes. Strategy, therefore, becomes more transparent, actions more obvious, and outcomes more easily tracked and revised.

International Organization for Standardization (ISO) 20121

The International Organization for Standardization is the world's largest developer and publisher of international standards. It comprises a network of national standards organizations from 162 countries, including Canada, the United States, United Kingdom, Australia, and much of the European Union. Because the acronym for International Organization for Standardization would be different in each language (IOS in English, for example), the organization uses a standard acronym of ISO to designate itself. This is from the Greek word *iso*, which means "equal."[4]

ISO is a nongovernmental organization, or NGO. It bridges the private (business) sector with the public sector, and works to attain consensus in standards that meet both the needs of business and the needs of society. Standards in general serve to ensure quality, environmental friendliness, safety, reliability, and efficiency, among other benefits. Most standards are voluntary and are not enforced by law.

ISO develops standards when practitioners from the sector request they do.[5] In 2009, the events sector requested that ISO develop a standard for sustainable event management. In 2007, the British Standards Institution (BSI) published a national standard, BSI 8901 for sustainable event management. It is this standard that formed the basis of the new ISO standard. Still in development, **ISO 20121** is on track to be approved by June 2012 in time for use at the London 2012 Olympic Games.

The purpose of ISO 20121 is to provide an event management system from which a framework to consider sustainability in relation to the specific organization's issues is created. ***Although ISO 20121 is not strictly a reporting system but a management system***, it does include the need to report and so is included here. It also works in conjunction with other reporting frameworks, such as APEX and the Global Reporting Initiative (GRI).

ISO 20121 can be certified on one of three different levels:

1. *First-party certification.* This means that the organization itself declares it has met the requirements of the standard. This has a low level of credibility and transparency.

2. *Second-party certification*. This means that compliance can be claimed if it has been attested to by parties having an interest in the organization, such as a supplier or client.
3. *Third-party certification*. This means that an independent third party, such as a certification organization, has audited the system and has attested to its completeness. This level of certification has the most credibility and transparency.[6]

ISO 20121 uses a common business cycle of Plan-Do-Check-Act (the PDCA cycle, also known as the Deming Cycle)[7] to implement the management system. It is *iterative*, meaning that the cycle doesn't end; you keep doing it throughout the process. This ensures that event professionals learn from actions taken in the past and are able to apply this knowledge to future actions.[8]

■ Planning

The planning phase is where event professionals and senior management within their organizations are expected to align strategy to the sustainable event management system. This ensures that the sustainable objectives of the event management system support the economic, environmental, and social development of the organization, and also ensures the support of top management. Top management is expected to be committed to the sustainable event management system and to support it as necessary through internal and external communications and the development and support of policy.

The actions included in the planning part of the cycle include determining the scope of the management system (what aspects of operations does it manage?); defining its primary purpose; ensuring that there is a policy in place; identifying and evaluating issues; and aligning event objectives with policy, issues, and organizational objectives. The planning part of the cycle also requires the identification and engagement with relevant stakeholders.

The identification of both risk factors and opportunities is a key activity. This allows event professionals to identify and evaluate specific risks in the context of their sustainable event objectives and their ability to mitigate them. This is explored in greater detail in the risk management section of Chapter 11.

■ Doing

This is the part of the cycle that event professionals are often best at because they are logistically competent. This section involves not only the event itself but also the management system as a whole, including allocation of resources, competence of human resources, communication and documentation, and operational planning and control—the guts of the event. It also includes supply chain management. Although many event professionals create strong relationships with their supply chains, the sustainable event management system requires them to include sustainability explicitly as a condition of doing business. Remember that sustainability includes not just environmental aspects but also economic and social aspects.

Management and deployment of resources include direct items such as people and money, and also indirect items that influence the success of the management system, such as training. Those in charge of the management system must be able to prove that they are competent to do so. Training will help make this case. Competence in this case is not defined, but could potentially include university or college degrees in related disciplines, training sessions on sustainable events, or equivalent experience in a sustainability function.

This part of the cycle includes documentation, which leads directly into reporting. It is helpful, for example, if event professionals create a consistent information architecture for each event. Do this by creating (electronic) folders for each event that are consistent in name and content.

For example, folders for contracts, stakeholder communications, policy, or event objectives would likely be common to all events. By ensuring consistency, not only will event professionals be able to find information more quickly but also they will be able to prove documentation under the management system. This is especially important if your organization decides to become certified under the ISO standard.

◼ Checking

This part of the cycle is where event professionals must ensure that they are meeting their performance objectives by measuring, monitoring, and auditing their actions. The results of these measurements then go into an event report to ensure that whatever was learned can be implemented next time. It is important to ensure that challenges as well as successes are measured and reported.

◼ Acting

Measuring and reporting have no utility unless the results are then acted upon. In this part of the cycle, reports are reviewed by the events team and by management. Corrective action can then be taken to create continual improvement over time. The results of this stage flow directly back into the planning stage of the PDCA cycle.

Fiona Pelham is the managing director of Sustainable Events Limited and the international co-chair of ISO's 20121 technical committee. To help illustrate how useful the new ISO 20121 will be for the meetings and events community, and how it plays with other emerging standards, she answered the following questions.

What is the purpose of ISO 20121, and how is it useful for meetings and events?

ISO 20121 provides a framework for your way of working so you can consider sustainability at every decision point. ISO 20121 is a management system standard. This means it is not a checklist that must be followed but steps that help you identify your specific issues and set an action plan to deal with these issues. ISO 20121 makes good business sense as it supports a way of working that considers your economic, social, and environmental impacts.

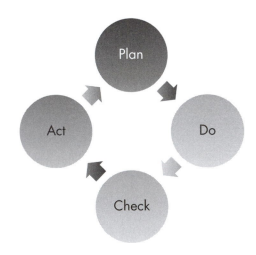

Figure 10.1 The Plan-Do-Check-Act Cycle

ISO 20121 has been created by an international committee of people from the event, standards, and sustainability sectors and has been specifically created for the event sector. It is rare for an ISO to be created for one sector, and ISO 20121 will give the event sector the opportunity to lead in the consideration of sustainability, which all companies will be addressing over the next few years.

If you were using ISO 20121 for the first time, what would you focus on accomplishing?

One of the most immediate benefits people see from the implementation of ISO 20121 is the identification of and understanding of their unique sustainability issues. As soon as you are aware of your economic, environmental, and social challenges, you can take steps to address them and turn challenges into opportunities.

Once you have a process for identifying your issues, you can engage your stakeholders with this (including your staff, supply chain, and the communities that you operate within). By sharing your issues and plans to address them with your stakeholder you are sharing the fact that you are on a journey to sustainability and you are giving them the opportunity to get involved.

How do you think ISO 20121 might be able to work with other emerging standards and sustainability reporting for events such as the GRI Event Organizers Sector Supplement and APEX green meeting standards?

ISO 20121 is a framework for your way of working. GRI is a framework for reporting on this way of working and key measurements. The APEX ASTM standard is a checklist approach for meetings and events. Depending on your event type, location, and experience, you might be able to use all of these standards together. Or you may decide to start with a way of working (ISO 20121) or a checklist approach (APEX ASTM) and over time build up to using all standards together.

There is significant synchronicity between ISO 20121 and GRI. For example, within the GRI framework you are asked to report on a number of areas related to *ways of working* (e.g., how you engage with your stakeholders). These ways of working are ISO 20121 requirements, so when you are implementing ISO 20121 you will have the material to report on required by the GRI framework.

If you wanted people to remember three things about what ISO 20121 can help event professionals attain, what would those three things be?

The three things that ISO 20121 can help event professionals attain are: (1) Creating a path for your sustainability journey: understanding your issues, creating an action plan with roles and responsibilities, and sharing this with your stakeholders are all parts of the steps in ISO 20121, which will create positive business benefits; (2) Supporting the identification of the issues unique to your situation will allow you to have ownership and understanding of your issues, as opposed to following a list of issues created by someone else, which may have limited relevance for you; and (3) Engaging with your stakeholders on your sustainability journey will build your relationships with groups including your supply chain, staff, and local communities.

What specific elements of your sustainability report are you most proud of?

Sustainable Events Ltd.'s first sustainability report was created in Autumn 2010, and we wrote the report as a guide for others to be able to understand how to write a GRI report. Leadership is one of our business values, and the entire team has been proud of the number of people who have told us our report has helped them understand how to write a GRI report.

Global Reporting Initiative (GRI)

The **Global Reporting Initiative (GRI)** is the world's largest voluntary sustainability reporting framework. In 2010, almost 1,850 organizations globally used it to structure their sustainability reporting, and this number increases annually. When the GRI began in 1999, only ten companies reported. Many sectors (distinct branches of industry) are represented, as shown in Table 10.3.

Using this reporting template for meetings and events will add value to the organization-wide CSR program and reporting. This enhances the value of the meetings and events function and makes a strong tie to organizational strategy.

This is a reporting standard for intermediate to advanced practitioners, although the standard does encourage all organizations (nonprofit or for profit, small or large) and all levels, from beginner to experienced, to use this to report. Although it can be used for any size of meeting, it is more likely to be applicable to somewhat larger events, from conferences to major sporting events. Smaller meetings and events are unlikely to need to report on many of the indicators. Reporters do not need to report on all indicators, especially if they are not relevant, and are encouraged to expand the scope of the report over time.

■ The GRI G3 Framework

The framework of the report has five main sections:

1. Strategy and analysis
2. Organizational profile
3. Report parameters
4. Governance, commitments, and engagement
5. Management approach and performance indicators

For meetings and events, it might be useful to look at the framework as shown in Figure 10.2.

Table 10.3 Sectors Represented in the Global Reporting Initiative

Construction	Food and beverage	Computers
Tourism	Forest/paper products	Chemicals
Energy	Finance	Health care
Construction	Public agencies	Agriculture
Nonprofit	Logistics	Automotive
Aviation	Mining	Retail
Textiles	Personal care products	Technology
Universities	Telecommunication	

Figure 10.2   Framework for Viewing Meetings and Events within the G3 Guidelines

■ Strategy and Analysis

This is a top-level look at your organization's relationship to sustainability, and provides context for the report. It has two major areas. The first is a statement from the organization's senior decision maker (the CEO or president) about the relevance of sustainability to the organization in a triple-bottom-line context. The statement should outline key challenges faced in an economic, environmental, and social context, their priority to the organization, trends, and key achievement of performance to date, all within the context of organizational strategic priorities.

Here are sample statements from senior decision makers at various organizations, excerpted from longer statements in featured Global Reporting Initiative reports:

> . . . *the WyndhamGreen program fits (our) strategic commitment to corporate social responsibility and the environment. It is not just a program but a way of . . . working based on our vision and values, . . . by improving the environment, supporting our local and global communities and developing sustainable programs that deliver economic benefits.*[9] *(Steve Holmes, President and Chief Executive Officer, Wyndham Hotels)*
>
> *Without a doubt, the tourism market is changing . . . which forces us to review our business models. In 2010, we have progressed in our goal to position ourselves as a leading responsible company in our sector, thanks to our sustainable innovation*[10] *(Mariano Perez Claver, Chairman, NH Hotels)*

The second major area in this section is an outline of the key risks, effects, and opportunities around sustainability and how the organization has prioritized them. For example, the issue might be a significant risk (i.e., the price of oil affecting cost of delegate travel and shipment of goods) but the organization has no control over it, so the priority given to this issue is very low. It should also outline the process by which they are addressed in performance management of the event.

An important part of this section is addressing the economic impacts of sustainability trends. For example, if the price of oil increases, it could have the following effects on your event:

1. Cost of travel for attendees and staff increases.
2. Cost of goods, such as food or ribbons shipped from elsewhere, increases.
3. Venue costs for heating and cooling increase, meaning an increase in facility rental charges or ancillary fees.
4. Fewer people will be able to pay to attend, meaning lower registration revenues.

■ Organizational Profile

This section covers the basics, such as the legal name of the organization, what products and services it offers, the operational structure, location of the headquarters facility, geographic markets served, and the scope of the organization—for example, number of employees and net sales. This is also the section where you can address things like awards your organization has won.

■ Report Parameters

This section asks for the reporting period, the date of the most recent report, the reporting cycle (e.g., annually, or by event), and the main contact for the report. It also asks to define the scope and boundary of the report, as well as the material issues it addresses. *Materiality* is defined as those issues both relevant and significant to an organization's stakeholders.

For example, the London 2012 Organizing Committee defines the scope of their report in the following statement:

> *Scope: It is an annual report which relates to the programme-wide activities of the official London 2012 stakeholders. However, the programme-wide format presents a challenge for GRI reporting which is normally predicated on a single reporting organisation. To address this we are treating LOCOG as the principal reporting organisation.*[11]

The scope therefore tells you what organizations are involved in the reporting directly. For example, it may be simply your organization, or you could decide to report on behalf of your organization and select stakeholders.

The boundary of the report is what specific events you are reporting on. For example, an organization might choose to report on all its events in a reporting period (say annually) or on only specific individual events. The boundary of the report should be chosen with consideration for activities that the organization both controls or that can be significantly influenced.

■ Governance, Commitments, and Engagement

This is where you describe the governance of the organization, including the executive and any committees that determine activities and mission. Also include those people who have control over major event-related decisions. Any direct triple-bottom-line responsibility (for economic, environmental, and social factors) should be indicated.

Mechanisms that are used to engage stakeholders should be outlined here (e.g., surveys, focus groups, or other mechanisms). Issues that are identified through these mechanisms should be identified throughout the report.

Sustainability commitments to external organizations (e.g., the United Nations Global Compact) should be identified in this section. This includes organizational membership in relevant associations.

■ Management Approach and Performance Indicators

This section is organized according to the triple bottom line: economic, environmental, and social. There are core indicators for each section; this means that organizations should report on at least the core indicators unless they have been determined not to be relevant. Other noncore indicators may be relevant and material for some events and not for others. If they are not relevant or material, do not report on them, but indicate why you chose not to.

Mike Wallace, the director of the Global Reporting Initiative's Focal Point USA, had this to say about sustainability reporting in general and specifically for the event sector.

Why is sustainability reporting important for businesses?

Sustainability reporting puts a more comprehensive frame around an organization's overall performance. This is useful as companies and other types of organizations begin to understand their sustainability performance, not just their financial performance. Formalizing understanding of their footprint through reporting increases an organization's understanding of total impact. It also provides a benchmark useful on two levels: externally to compare the organization to their peer group, and internally to track progress from one reporting period to the next.

In a business context, what is the importance of reporting for the event sector?

For businesses promoting their own commitment to sustainability, the importance of reporting on the sustainability of their events is to demonstrate how they are "walking the talk." This holds true especially if the event is billed as a sustainable event, or if the content is focused on sustainability. Ultimately, the event is a living, breathing organism with its own footprint. It is important that attendees, organizers, and destinations (i.e., host cities) understand that an event does have a footprint. Destinations specifically need to understand that their green city initiatives need to extend to the events that they try to attract to their cities.

Reporting is a way to establish credibility, transparency, and trust. Companies are sometimes seen as not being trustworthy by the general public. We are at a unique moment in the marketplace where the majority of large companies are producing sustainability reports and the majority of those reports are done in accordance with GRI. Companies that use the GRI framework often see sustainability permeate the fabric of the organization. Cross-functional teams evolve with participants from all parts of the organizations, and because employees typically become passionate about these issues, companies begin to even look at events through a sustainability lens.

It's like accounting across any large organizations. Divisions and functions report up to the headquarters, and all the information is then rolled up into one report. Events are another function within many organizations and therefore become part of the overall operational reporting for a company.

Do you think the event organizers sector supplement will increase reporting in the sector?

It will raise awareness about the importance of sustainability even within events. The sector supplement will also stimulate awareness of formal reporting. For example, the London 2012 Olympic Games will raise the bar for sustainable events. Currently, possibly only 2 to 3 percent of events report because often there is a lack of awareness about the impact of events, as well as dedicated resources to report on the performance of events. As more large corporations expand their own scrutiny of supply chains and suppliers, however, even the suppliers to the events industry will be asked to report on the sustainability of the goods and services they provide for an event. In the future, I believe suppliers in certain sectors like events will differentiate their services by providing clients with an independent product/service sustainability report along with your invoice.

Reporting using the GRI Event Organizers Sector Supplement is less likely to be used in the near term for smaller events—those with fewer staff and financial resources to integrate reporting. As we have typically seen over the past decade of GRI's work, the majority of reporters are larger entities that have more human and financial resources available for these types of activities. We will see a ripple effect, much like what we are seeing in global supply chains. The Olympics are very likely to generate such a ripple effect. Large corporate sponsors, construction firms involved building the venues, food and accommodation providers are all part of the supply chain of any Olympics, including the host city and country. What might the IOC start to ask in the future about the sustainability of any of these suppliers? In addition, what about the prequalifying events leading up to the Olympics? Are these too not likely to start to implement similar sustainability requirements? If so, then what about the massive professional and athletic associations that represent each sport? What might their role be in sustainability as they train, transport, feed, house, and clothe their respective athletes?

In an ideal world, what would sustainable event reporting look like?

If organizations are ready to take the responsibility to host events, they should also be willing to take responsibility for managing that event's footprint. This is especially true for CSR-focused events. Transparency is important. Events may need to do a cost-benefit analysis to help them focus on what they can measure, manage, and report; they won't be able to tackle everything all at once. But doing an analysis of the true impacts, or true performance of an event helps us all make better decisions, from attendees to corporate sponsors, local governments, destinations, and event organizers.

Linking Key Objectives to Organizational Strategies

Whether you choose to implement basic reporting or more advanced reporting, being able to link your sustainable event goals to organizational objectives is a key consideration. As was discussed in Chapter 6 regarding strategic CSR, events that promote the achievement of organizational strategy will be considered as more successful and important by the organization than if no link can be made.

Organizational strategy, mission, and objectives can be found in annual reports, departmental strategic planning documents, or sometimes even on the organizational website. Event professionals should treat these as a roadmap to ensure the event lives and breathes the corporate objectives.

Using a sustainable management framework, such as ISO 20121, can help planners define the issues and link them to organizational strategy. This is a very tangible way to use both ISO 20121 and the GRI event organizers sector supplement. For example, ISO 20121 requires planners to identify environmental, social, and economic issues, including those identified by stakeholders. They then need to prioritize the issues, based on importance and ability to control or influence. Issues that relate directly to organizational strategy will be prioritized as long as they are controllable by the event professional.

Identifying Key Stakeholders

The idea of stakeholders was introduced in Chapter 9. These may vary based on the type of event, its location, and its purpose.

For example, a corporate sales rally is focused on the internal sales team, and therefore, the sales team automatically becomes a key stakeholder. It is not client-focused, and so clients might not be stakeholders for this particular event. To identify stakeholders, ask the questions in Table 10.4.

Once stakeholders have been identified, then you can decide what media are best to engage them. Stakeholders will also expand or contract based on the scope of your reporting. For example, if you are reporting on one large event, you will identify only the stakeholders relevant to that event. If you decide to report on all the events you hold in one year, your list of stakeholders may increase accordingly.

The organizing committee for the England 2018 bid to host the World Cup used the GRI guidelines to report the results of its bid. The following graphic illustrates the stakeholders that they identified and the means used to communicate with them:

Table 10.4   Ten Key Questions for Identifying Meeting and Event CSR Stakeholders

Questions
1. Who is the event for?
2. Are there location-specific issues?
3. Who will attend?
4. What communities or sectors will be affected, if any?
5. Who will benefit?
6. What suppliers are being used?
7. Who may be negatively impacted?
8. Do the products and services I use have an impact, and on whom?
9. Where is the event being held?
10. Who are the opinion leaders in this sector?

OUR BID STAKEHOLDERS

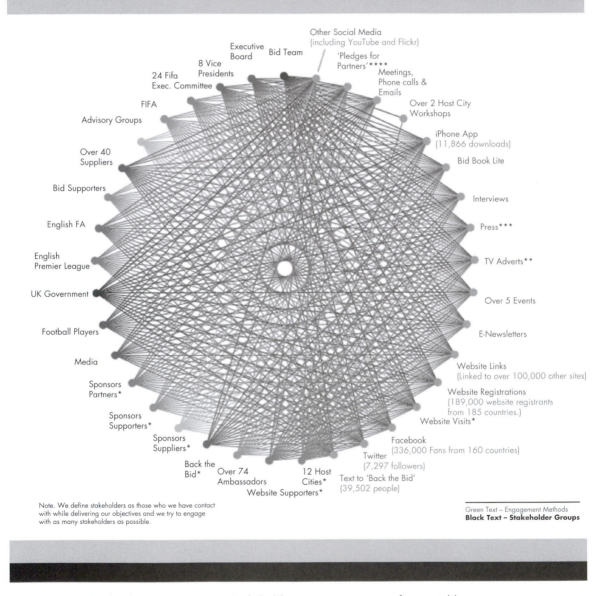

Other Social Media
(including YouTube and Flickr)

Executive
Board   Bid Team

8 Vice
Presidents

'Pledges for
Partners'****

24 Fifa
Exec. Committee

Meetings,
Phone calls &
Emails

FIFA

Over 2 Host City
Workshops

Advisory Groups

iPhone App
(11,866 downloads)

Over 40
Suppliers

Bid Book Lite

Bid Supporters

Interviews

English FA

Press***

English
Premier League

TV Adverts**

UK Government

Over 5 Events

Football Players

E-Newsletters

Media

Website Links
(Linked to over 100,000 other sites)

Sponsors
Partners*

Website Registrations
(189,000 website registrants
from 185 countries.)

Sponsors
Supporters*

Website Visits*

Sponsors
Suppliers*

Facebook
(336,000 Fans from 160 countries)

Twitter
(7,297 followers)

Back the
Bid*   Over 74
Ambassadors   12 Host
Cities*   Text to 'Back the Bid'
(39,502 people)

Website Supporters*

Note. We define stakeholders as those who we have contact
with while delivering our objectives and we try to engage
with as many stakeholders as possible.

Green Text – Engagement Methods
Black Text – Stakeholder Groups

England 2018 GRI report. Stakeholder engagement map of sustainable events.
Design by Typocom. Used with permission from Sustainable Events Limited

Although this stakeholder web is fairly complex, simpler ones are also helpful. For example, here is a stakeholder web from a GRI report submitted by Sustainable Events Limited out of the United Kingdom. Notice the difference in scope from the England 2018 stakeholder web.

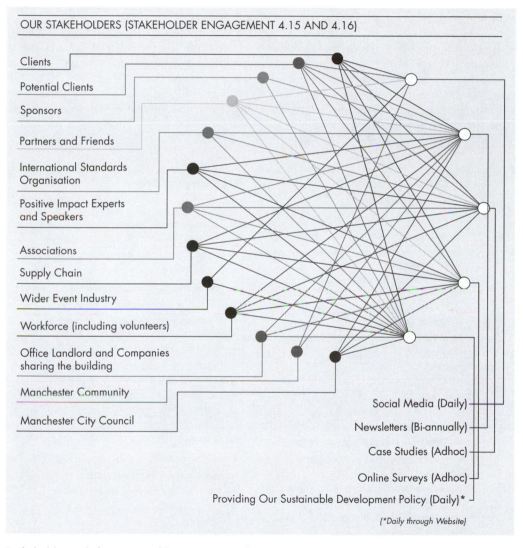

OUR STAKEHOLDERS (STAKEHOLDER ENGAGEMENT 4.15 AND 4.16)

Clients

Potential Clients

Sponsors

Partners and Friends

International Standards Organisation

Positive Impact Experts and Speakers

Associations

Supply Chain

Wider Event Industry

Workforce (including volunteers)

Office Landlord and Companies sharing the building

Manchester Community

Manchester City Council

Social Media (Daily)

Newsletters (Bi-annually)

Case Studies (Adhoc)

Online Surveys (Adhoc)

Providing Our Sustainable Development Policy (Daily)*

(*Daily through Website)

Stakeholder web for Sustainable Events Limited.
Used with permission from Sustainable Events Limited

Integrated Sustainable Event Management Model (Measurement and Reporting)

The Integrated Sustainable Event Management Model can be used to assess both measurement and reporting. In each of the four quadrants, you will find typical characteristics of meeting/event professionals related to the level of sustainable implementation.

The model shown in Figure 10.3 is useful for assessing how an organization currently approaches sustainable event management. It is contingent on a number of factors, including the skill level of the meeting professional, support of top management, strategic relevance, stakeholder engagement and strategic versus logistic competence.

It is important to realize the model is not making a value judgment; one quadrant of the model is not necessarily better than another. It does, however, plot a progression in skill levels, communication, and organizational support.

<table>
<tr>
<td>

High CSR/Ethics Focus

- Lacks external reporting
- Reliable and/or integrated supply chain
- Management support
- Competent in identifying and addressing green meeting issues
- Aware of economic and social issues but does not always link them to events
- May not link organizational strategy and objectives to events
- May identify but does not usually engage stakeholders

</td>
<td>

High Integrated Focus

- integrates logistics, environmental sustainability, social equity and economic profitability with objectives, communication, measurement and reporting
- Accountable, responsible, transparent
- Code of conduct
- Selects, manages and integrates supply chain
- Support of senior decision maker
- Identifies material and relevant issues in relation to organizational objectives
- Integrates standards
- Uses reports to show strategic relevance and benchmark progress (internal/external)
- Evaluates reporting needs based on event profile

</td>
</tr>
<tr>
<td>

Low CSR/Ethics and Strategy Focus

- May not have support of management or other colleagues
- May be aware of green meeting issues but needs to acquire logistic proficiency
- Does not identify or engage stakeholders
- Little or no reporting beyond budget compliance

</td>
<td>

High Strategy Focus

- Low level of competency in sustainable logistics
- Has support of top management
- Adept at creating reports
- Links organizational strategy with event reporting
- Identifies stakeholders but does not thoroughly engage them
- Limited expertise coupled with high communication skills may result in real or perceived greenwashing

</td>
</tr>
</table>

Increasing CSR and Ethics Competency ↑

Increasing Strategic Competency →

Figure 10.3 Integrated Sustainable Event Management (Measurement and Reporting)

Chapter Review

This chapter explored sustainability reporting specifically in the meetings and events industry. Reporting methodologies included those currently used in meetings, such as the APEX post-event report (PER), for which adaptations to include sustainability factors were suggested. The balanced scorecard, a tool commonly used in other business sectors, was presented and adapted for use in sustainable meetings and events. Other common business reporting frameworks, the Global Reporting Initiative (GRI) and the International Organization for Standardization (ISO), have recently produced sustainable event-sector-specific management and reporting frameworks.

Linking sustainable event objectives to organizational strategy can raise the profile and importance of events within the organization. Sustainable event management frameworks provide a useful tool to create this alignment. Identifying stakeholders is a key step that facilitates communication and reporting; stakeholder webs provide a visual representation of stakeholders for simple communication and review.

Review Questions

1. What does reporting accomplish?
2. In what circumstances would you use a post-event report (PER)?
3. How can the PER be adjusted to include sustainability?
4. Why is the balanced scorecard a good tool for meeting professionals to consider using?
5. What are the five levels of the balanced scorecard (four traditional and one newer)?
6. What is the purpose of ISO 20121?
7. When is it appropriate to use the GRI Event Organizers Sector Supplement?

Group Activities

1. Choose a company. Locate its annual report and strategic objectives. For that company:
   a. Write three sustainable event objectives for an internal product/service education session. How have you linked the event objectives to both corporate objectives and to sustainability?
   b. Write three sustainable event objectives for a customer appreciation event. How have you linked the event objectives to both corporate objectives and to sustainability?
2. Using the objectives you created in Learning Activity 1, create a balanced scorecard for your sustainable event objectives.
3. Explain how ISO 20121 can work together with the Global Reporting Initiative Event Organizers Sector Event Organizers Sector Supplement. How do they complement each other?

Key Terms

- Global Reporting Initiative Event Organizers Sector Supplement
- materiality
- APEX cluster
- triple-bottom line cluster
- GRI cluster
- APEX post-event report (PER)
- balanced scorecard
- ISO 20121
- Global Reporting Initiative (GRI)

Resources

Related to the Resources listed below, please visit the Book Companion Site (located at www.wiley.com/college/henderson) for a complete list of websites. Additional referential websites related to this chapter's content can also be found on the BCS.

The Global Reporting Initiative (GRI)

The GRI is a highly respected voluntary reporting system that is becoming common in business. Recently it developed the Event Organizers Sector Supplement, which will be released in 2012.

The International Organization for Standardization (ISO)

ISO systems are commonly used in business to create standardized products and services. ISO is currently developing standard 20121, a sustainable event management system, to be used at the 2012 Olympics in London.

APEX Post Event Report

The Convention Industry Council (CIC) is the parent organization of APEX. More information on the CIC and a template for the post-event report (PER) can be found at the Convention Industry Council website.

The Balanced Scorecard

More information on the balanced scorecard can be found at the Balanced Scorecard website.

London 2012

This is the official site for the 2012 Olympic Games. Here you will find sustainability policies and reports.

Green Meeting Industry Council

This association for event professionals is focused on sustainability.

Meeting Professionals International CSR Resources

    This industry organization offers some tools and educational resources on sustainability for event professionals.

Sustainable Events Limited

    This is the company interviewed that supplied the stakeholder maps. The president, Fiona Pelham, chaired the ISO 20121 process.

Notes

1. Global Reporting Initiative, "Materiality." Accessed September 25, 2011, from www.globalreporting.org/ReportingFramework/G3Online/DefiningReportContent/LowerBlock/Materiality.htm.
2. Convention Industry Council Post Event Reporting, retrieved from http://www.conventionindustry.org/StandardsPractices/APEX/PostEventReporting.aspx
3. "Kaplan, Robert S. and David Norton. The Balanced Scorecard: Measures that Drive Performance, In Harvard Business Review, August 2005.
4. International Organisation for Standardization (2012). Discover ISO. Retrieved February 13, 2012, from www.iso.org/iso/about/discover-iso_isos-name.htm.
5. International Standards Organisation (2012). Discover ISO. Retrieved February 13, 2012, from www.iso.org/iso/about/discover-iso_the-iso-brand.htm.
6. International Organization for Standardization, "ISO Frequently Asked Questions." www.mpiweb.org/Libraries/Magazine/Frequently_Asked_Questions.pdf.
7. Balanced Scorecard Institute. The Deming Cycle. Retrieved February 17, 2012, from www.balancedscorecard.org/TheDemingCycle/tabid/112/Default.aspx.
8. International Organization for Standardization, "Understand the Basics." www.iso.org/iso/iso_catalogue/management_standards/management_system_basics.
9. Wyndham Green, "Global Best Practices." Accessed September 25, 2011, from www.wyndhamgreen.com/pdf/Global-Best-Practices-2010Final.pdf.
10. NH Hoteles, "Corporate Sustainability Report 2010. Wake Up to a Better World." Accessed September 25, 2011, from: corporate-information.nh-hotels.com/wda/eng/pdfs/NH%20Corporate%20Responsibility%202010.pdf.
11. London Organising Committee of the Olympic Games, "London 2012 Sustainability Report, April 2011, A Blueprint for Change." Accessed September 25, 2011, from: www.london2012.com/documents/sustainability/london-2012-sustainability-report-a-blueprint-for-change.pdf.

Volunteer workers digging a trench for a housing project in the Jordanian desert.
Photo courtesy of iStockphoto/kandelfire

CHAPTER 11

Risk Management and Legal Considerations

"I detest life-insurance agents: they always argue that I shall some day die, which is not so."
—Stephen Leacock, Canadian humorist,
political scientist (1869–1944)

Learning Objectives

After studying this chapter, you will be able to:

- Learn key steps for risk management related to sustainable meetings and events.

- Recognize that there are differences between jurisdictions and how to find information relevant to your event.

- Learn how to ensure the successful implementation of sustainability goals through contracts.

- Understand the types of insurance available for sustainability-related issues for meetings and events.

Overview of Event Risk Management and Legal Considerations

The information provided in this chapter, including information and quotes provided by practicing lawyers and risk management professionals, is general in nature and intended for educational purposes only and should not be considered to be legal advice in any respect. The chapter broadly addresses issues related to event risk management and legal issues and is not a substitute for professional legal or risk management advice. It should also be noted that laws and regulations are not universal: They will vary by jurisdiction and can change over time.

This chapter complements more extensive works on event risk management that form part of the Wiley Event Management Series. For more information on these works, see the resources section at the end of the chapter.

Proper risk management and legal compliance is a key aspect of corporate social responsibility: the best intentions, if undertaken with little or no regard for risk and regulations, can be damaging to an event, its stakeholders, and its participants. Meeting and event professionals can benefit from an understanding of risk management and legal considerations related to corporate social responsibility (CSR). In many ways, CSR practices are an effective tool for risk management. There are, however, times when new risks and potential liability will result from CSR-related activities.

Meeting and event professionals can apply their expertise in planning to risk management. Gene Takagi, San Francisco–based nonprofit attorney from the NEO Law Group and publisher of the Nonprofit Law Blog, recommends that risk management be undertaken throughout the entire planning process. It is not to be seen as reactive or addressed through last-minute corrections. This chapter will focus on this proactive approach to risk management by providing processes for identifying, assessing, and managing risk, and provide general guidelines for identifying legal issues and resources applicable to meetings and events.

Key Concepts and Terms

In examining risk management and legal considerations for meetings and events, a few key concepts and terms need to be understood.

■ Risk Management

The Convention Industry Council defines **risk management** as "Recognizing the possibility of injury, damage, or loss, and having a means to prevent it or provide insurance."[1] Note that this definition of risk differs from that used in other disciplines, notably project risk management, where risk is defined as uncertainty and can be either a threat or an opportunity.[2] Meeting and event professionals need to manage various types of risks including health and safety issues, environmental damage, and failure to achieve objectives or financial targets.

■ Jurisdiction

Jurisdiction refers to the entity with the authority to make decisions on legal matters based on a particular subject and/or geographic area. From a meetings and events perspective, many jurisdictions might oversee a single event, and these will vary in different communities. For example, the municipal government may have jurisdiction to determine gaming licenses, while the local police may have jurisdiction to regulate alcohol sales at an event. In another community, other entities may have the authority over these same issues. Meeting and event professionals need to understand which entities have jurisdiction over their programs.

■ Liability

In the context of this chapter, **liability** refers to being responsible for damages or loss. A person or organization found to be liable for actions or inactions may be required to compensate for the damage or loss resulting therefrom and there may be both criminal and civil applications of this. An example for meetings and events is to be liable for damages to a venue by an event attendee. The event organizer may be found liable for the damage, regardless of whether or not the organizer personally is directly at fault for the damage. This is distinct from the financial accounting term, where a liability refers to an obligation to settle a debt.

Pediment sculpture of the Old Supreme Court, City Hall, Singapore. The central figure in the tympanum is that of Justice, with a figure immediately to its left representing the lost soul begging for protection from it.
Photo courtesy of iStockphoto/Aneurysm

3 Ps of a CSR-Focused Event Risk Management Strategy

The goals of a CSR-focused event risk management strategy can be categorized under three themes: *protect*, *prepare*, and *process*.

■ Protect

- Protect the health, safety, and security of event attendees, workers, organizers, and stakeholders.
- Protect the health, safety, and security of the communities and environments in which we conduct our events.
- Protect against threats to the organization's mission, financial objectives, legal standing, and public image.

■ Prepare

- Prepare for possible incidents and emergencies related to the event, destination, and venue.

■ Process

- Develop a process for risk identification, assessment, and management.
- Develop a process for evaluating and continuously improving your event risk management strategy and execution.

Figure 11.1 Continuum of Systemic Event Risk and Specific Event Risk

Systemic and Specific Risks

Investors will often use the terms *systemic* and *specific* to refer to risk. In the financial system, systemic risk refers to the risk of the entire financial system collapsing, while specific risk refers to the risk associated with a specific investment. One of the most popular strategies for addressing specific risk is through **diversification**—investing across various types of asset classes (such as stocks and bonds), as well as in different regions and industries. A popular analogy would be the expression, "Don't put all your eggs in one basket." This way, if one investment performs poorly, not all of an investor's assets will be lost.

As shown in Figure 11.1, these categories form a continuum, and not all types of risks will fall neatly into one of the two categories. Examples of risks closer to the systemic end of the spectrum would be a downturn in the economy or a major airline strike. Examples closer to the specific event risk end of the spectrum include audiovisual equipment not functioning or your program materials not arriving at your event. Diversification strategies, such as having program materials available in multiple formats, having multiple sources for local food products, or using technology to create a hybrid meeting, might help to manage these risks, as you would have more options available to you. Applying this concept to meetings and events, the following terms have been developed and are shown in Figure 11.1.

The Meeting and Event Risk Management Team

Many people may be involved in the formal or informal event risk management team. Depending on the event type, complexity, size, and risk factors, those that may be involved in developing, implementing, and reviewing the event risk management team include:

- Meeting or event planner
- Senior management of the host organization
- Suppliers (e.g., representatives from the venue, food service providers, and performers)
- Local, state, or provincial government, police, or security personnel
- Health authority and/or emergency medical services
- Legal counsel
- Insurance representative
- Information technology (IT) personnel
- On-site staff representatives (may be represented by a union)
- Other stakeholders (including event sponsors and community members)

Table 11.1 provides a discussion framework for the event risk management team to assess and manage potential risks. Stage 1 of the table considers issues related to risk assessment. According to Joan Eisenstodt, chief strategist of Eisenstodt Associates, LLC, and inductee of the Convention Industry Council's Hall of Leaders, during the risk assessment stage, think through what the risks are and what is the worst that can happen to help make appropriate risk management plans. In the risk management plan, she adds, it is critical to understand not only what you will do if a crisis

Table 11.1   Risk Management Team Discussion Questions

	Stage 1: Risk Assessment	**Stage 2: Risk Management**
Who	• Who is at risk (attendees, host organization, venue, environment, community, other)?	• Who is responsible for managing the risk? • Who would be liable if the risk occurred? • Who else is accountable, or needed? • Who should be consulted? • Who is the spokesperson for the organization if the risk occurs? • Who will have authority to make decisions if the risk occurs?
What	• What is (are) the risk(s)? • What is the potential impact? • What is the worst that can happen?	• What actions will you take to manage the risk?
Where	• Where is the risk likely to occur? • Can a change in location help to reduce the risk?	• Where will you manage the risk? • Where will you communicate your risk management strategy?
When	• When is the risk likely to occur (*prior to, during, or after* the event)?	• What actions need to be done *prior to, during, and after* the event to manage the risk?
Why	• Why does the risk exist? How can these factors be eliminated or managed?	• Why would you be willing to or not willing to accept the risk?
How	• How will you identify and assess risks? • How likely is it that the risk will occur?	• How will you manage the risk (avoid, mitigate, transfer, or accept)? • How will you review and improve your risk management strategy? • How will you ensure effective communication of your risk management strategies? • How will you implement a recovery plan? • How will you fund a contingency fund, and do you need one?

happens but also who will have specific responsibilities. This includes measures such as appointing a media spokesperson for the organization and determining who has the authority to make decisions such as evacuating a venue or destination, or returning to a building after a disaster. Note that although identification of risks is a specific stage in the risk management process, risks can—and should—be identified, managed, and documented as they arise throughout the event cycle. In addition, stakeholders should be communicated with regularly.

The Event Risk Management Process

Each individual and organization will have a different risk tolerance: some might be more comfortable with risks than others. As an example, a recent Deloitte report found that Canadian business leaders are 18 percent more risk averse than their American counterparts.[3] How an individual risk is managed might also depend on both the likelihood of it occurring and the potential impact if it does occur. Although there may be differences in risk tolerance, risk management should not be disregarded by meeting and event professionals.

A process for risk assessment and management is depicted in Figure 11.2, and explained in greater detail next.

The risk management process begins with *identifying possible risks* that your meeting or event may face. From there, you need to *assess both the potential impact (including multiple scenarios of outcomes) and the probability* that these outcomes will occur. Risk can be assessed both qualitatively and quantitatively. It might be valuable to consult experts at this point, particularly those with event expertise. Once you've identified and assessed the risks, you can begin to *develop and implement your risk management strategy*. Figure 11.3 illustrates a matrix of risk impact and

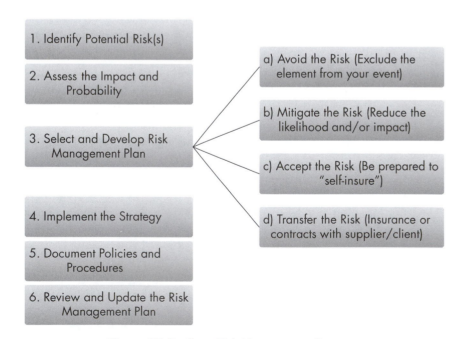

Figure 11.2 Event Risk Management Process

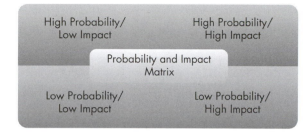

Figure 11.3 Probability and Impact Matrix

probability. The approach for a low likelihood/low impact risk will be very different from the approach for a high likelihood/high impact risk.

Four approaches to managing risk are introduced in Figure 11.2:

1. *Avoid the risk.* You may determine that the potential benefits do not outweigh the risk, and/or that the severity or likelihood of the risk occurring is so great that you decide to avoid it altogether. For example, you might opt to not have an event in a remote area where access by emergency medical services would be difficult and instead opt for a more accessible (though possibly less attractive) alternative.
2. *Mitigate the risk.* You might choose to lessen the impact or likelihood of the risk occurring, such as by providing safety equipment and training to participants, or by sharing it with other key stakeholders.
3. *Accept the risk.* In some cases, you may be willing to accept a risk, particularly if it is unlikely to occur, and if it does, the results would not be severe. This can be considered "self-insuring."
4. *Transfer the risk.* In cases where the likelihood is low, but the impact would be severe, you might choose to transfer the risk through insurance. In this way, you would pay a premium to an insurance agency that would then be responsible if the risk occurs. Not all risk can be transferred, and meeting and event professionals should gain a clear understanding of what is covered by their insurance and what is not. Furthermore, although the risk may be transferred to an insurance company, meeting professionals continue to have an ethical obligation to implement risk mitigation strategies and may still be sued if something goes wrong.

Risk Management Strategies in Action

These strategies can be illustrated by looking at four different approaches for addressing the same risk related to an event-related activity: the possibility of injury while participating in a volunteer activity that involves hiking to the event location. The four approaches are shown in Table 11.2.

Once the risk management strategy is selected and developed, it needs to be implemented. Critical elements in this stage are communication with stakeholders—particularly those that are tasked with implementing the strategy and providing any necessary training. *Policies and procedures related to risk management need to be documented.* Finally, your *risk management plans need to be reviewed regularly* to ensure that they continue to be relevant and are updated as new factors emerge.

Table 11.2 Example of Risk Management Approaches: Volunteer Activity with Hiking

Avoid the risk	Choose an alternate activity or location that does not require hiking.
Mitigate the risk	Provide clear instructions to participants about appropriate footwear and provide on-site training on proper stretching and warm-ups to reduce the likelihood of injury. Have first aid kits and individuals trained in first aid available.
Accept the risk	You may determine that the risks associated with the event are minimal in terms of likelihood and severity should they occur. In this case, you would opt to accept the risk.
Transfer the risk	Secure insurance for the event. If you are working on behalf of another organization, have them add you as an additional insured on their insurance policy if possible and appropriate.

Risk Reduction and Corporate Social Responsibility (CSR)

In respect to risk reduction, corporate social responsibility (CSR) practices can be valuable for addressing various forms of risk.

■ Reputation Risk

Reputation risk arises when an organization's actions (or inactions) result in damage to its reputation. From a meetings and events perspective, examples include the following:

- A company's reputation could be damaged for failing to implement basic sustainable meeting practices, especially if this is in contrast with their CSR statement or plan. Companies whose products or services are known for being sustainable might be particularly vulnerable to this risk, as it would contrast with the brand's reputation.
- Organizations with a social mandate, or a specific mandate to support labor organizations, would face a reputation risk for booking a non-unionized venue or vendor, crossing a picket line, failing to honor a boycott, or hosting an event in a destination with a record of human rights violations. Some potential attendees might choose not to attend an event or meeting or stay off-site, resulting in an added financial risk to the host organization.

Reputation risk is also related to the concept of **social risk**: "When an empowered stakeholder takes up a social issue area and applies pressure on a corporation (exploiting a vulnerability in the earnings drivers—e.g., reputation, corporate image), so that the company will change policies or approaches in the marketplace."[4] An example from the meetings and events field is pressure from either event planners or attendees on suppliers to offer fair trade products. (Fair trade issues are discussed in greater detail in Chapter 3.)

■ Regulatory Risk

Around the world, sustainability is becoming increasingly regulated. **Regulatory risk** will have direct and indirect implications for meetings and events. Some of these regulations cover issues related to global warming, corporate reporting, and carbon taxes. Examples include California's Assembly Bill 32: Global Warming Solutions Act, which regulates the implementation of greenhouse gas emission reduction goals; Article 116 of France's Nouvelles Regulations Economiques, which requires the disclosure of environmental and social data in corporate annual reports; and Finland's carbon tax. Integrating sustainability into the business operations of meeting and event professionals helps to ensure compliance with existing requirements and helps to prepare for new regulations that might be introduced in the future.

■ Financial Risk

From a financial perspective, sustainable practices can provide significant cost savings. These savings, from initiatives such as reduced printing and energy consumption, can reduce the risk that an event will not meet financial targets. Furthermore, with organizations such as the U.S. government implementing purchasing policies that place a higher preference on environmental products, sustainable practices can become a competitive advantage. Finally, as more jurisdictions implement or consider environmentally related taxes and fines, proactively implementing sustainable practices may help organizations adapt more rapidly to these changes. As an example, California's Assembly Bill 32, passed in 2006, set specific emissions reduction requirements. Hotels that had already implemented environmental practices were better able to respond to the new requirements.

■ Health and Safety Risk

Sustainable practices, such as the elimination of harsh chemicals in cleaning products and improved air quality in venues, can help protect the health and safety of meeting and event workers and attendees. Many event planners are now starting to incorporate healthier menu choices and fitness into their schedules for participants' well being. This is in addition to traditional risk management practices related to food, such as ensuring that the food service providers practice proper food safety measures and avoid cross-contamination risks. As an example, Fairmont Hotels and Resorts has introduced its Lifestyle Cuisine *Plus* menu with alternatives to meet various caloric and dietary restrictions designed for guests with health conditions, including diabetes and heart conditions.[5]

Legal Considerations

Contracts and Vendors

Effective contracts play a key role in ensuring that sustainability objectives are met. Not only do they clarify expectations and allocate risks on all sides, they also set out how to address any conflicts that might arise. Consider this: If you've set objectives for waste management for an event that you are planning, do you have an agreement in place with your key venues to ensure that they are following through with the objectives? What remedies will you have in place if the commitments are not met?

Figure 11.4 Process for Implementing Sustainability Initiatives into Contracts

According to Tyra W. Hilliard, Ph.D., JD, CMP, associate professor, restaurant, hospitality, and meetings management at the University of Alabama, contract language should be specific about what the planner expects the venue or vendor to do in terms of sustainability. Hilliard says that the key to any good contract clause is that it must have a *hammer*. She offers the example of an agreement by a hotel to have a towel reuse program in place by the time of the meeting. If the hotel fails to do so, it would be a breach of contract, but a meeting planner may not be able to prove that it was damaged by the lack of the program. Lawyer 2 recommends including "what if" language in the contract—IF the hotel does not have this program in place, THEN the hotel will offer . . . (concessions, discounts, or other predetermined arrangement). The "what if" gives the hotel an incentive to meet the contract requirements.

The process in Figure 11.4 outlines steps for implementing sustainability initiatives into contracts.

1. *Set clear objectives.* These objectives should be specific, relevant, and achievable. The chapter on sustainable event practices provides examples of clear objectives.
2. *Discuss your objectives with the vendor.* During the discussion, be open to flexible ways of achieving the objectives, rather than prescriptive. For example, if the objective is to provide recycling options, planners should be flexible to alternatives such as in-room recycling or back-of-house recycling, as long as the basic objective is met that the recycling program is both visible (or communicated) *and* effective.
3. *Determine measurable objectives.* When negotiating contract requirements related to sustainability, it may be important to determine in advance the data that will be collected to measure the results. It may be most practical to determine this as part of the selection process for the venue or vendor. The data requirements need to be both specific to the goal, but also practical to deliver. According to Kelly Bagnall, an attorney with Dykema Gossett PLLC's Dallas office who specializes in hospitality, commercial litigation, and general business counseling matters, meeting professionals need to determine "reasonable expectations of the type of data that can be reported." Determining the exact amount of materials recycled for a specific event might be almost impossible in a venue that is holding multiple concurrent events. The chapter on measurement provides practical alternatives, including strategies such as applying the ratio of the venue occupied by the group to estimate this information.
4. *Include sustainability initiatives in your contract.* Once you have determined the specific actions and services that are needed, document them in your contract. Be as specific as possible, and include the "what-if" language if the measures are not done or provided. Review the contract carefully to ensure that your intentions and discussions have been accurately captured in the contract and not misunderstood.
5. *Verify the implementation of your initiatives.* It is important to verify compliance with the contract. Doing so at various milestones prior to the event will help you to make alternate arrangements if needed. This could be done through progress reports from the venue or vendor at predetermined times.

Event-Related CSR Initiatives and Risk Management

As has previously been discussed in this chapter, CSR initiatives can be an important tool for risk management. There are times, however, when some initiatives will introduce new elements of risk, and meeting and event planners need a risk management plan to address this and need to consider the trade-offs of these initiatives. To illustrate, two examples are listed:

- Example 1: A planner asks for air conditioning to be turned off in meeting rooms on equipment move-in days as a way of conserving energy and simultaneously reducing costs. This may result in health and safety concerns for workers if heat levels rise too high.
- Example 2: A conference offers a carpooling option for delegates to reduce travel-related carbon emissions. This introduces new risks if volunteer drivers are inexperienced, have a poor driving history, or are uninsured, and may expose the conference organizers to liability.

Charitable Fundraising and Gaming

Many events raise money for a cause or charitable organization by holding fundraising events, raffles, auctions, or contests. Most jurisdictions have regulations about this, and some even prohibit these types of activities. Event planners need to research these as early as possible to ensure that they are not exposing themselves to unnecessary legal or regulatory risks, or potential reputation risks if concerns are raised about gambling. It is advisable to determine this before contracting in a location in case the fundraising activities you have in mind will not be permitted. If in doubt, seek legal advice before proceeding. Gene Takagi recommends also researching if and when tax receipts may be issued, and the value of the receipt that can be given. For example, it is possible in some jurisdictions to issue tax receipts for charitable fundraising event tickets, provided that the fair market value for the event is deducted from the value of the tax receipt.

Local charitable fundraising regulations should be sought out by event planners before undertaking a program. This information is commonly available from local authorities (municipalities) or convention and visitor bureaus. In many cases, an organization needs a special permit or status (such as being a registered charity) to hold fundraising or gaming activities, including raffles, bingo games, and auctions. This will vary according to the jurisdiction. Obtaining a permit might take a significant amount of time, so ensure that you research the requirements well in advance. While each jurisdiction will be different, some of the frequent considerations for being able to obtain a permit to hold a fundraising event include being a registered charitable organization, whether or not alcohol will be served at the event, and the age of the participants. As well, the regulations vary, depending on the expected revenue that will be generated from the event and if you are raising funds for a third party (e.g., ABC Corporation hosts an event to raise funds for a children's charity).

Food Donations

Reducing the amount of food waste is an important step in making an event more socially responsible and sustainable. Reducing the amount of food provided at events is a good start, and organizations including the U.S. Department of Justice are implementing policies to this effect (see the USDOJ's *Audit of Department of Justice Conference Planning and Food and Beverage Costs*).[6] Although reducing the amount of food provided can be an important step, attendance unpredictability, quality standards, and traditional practices might make this impractical. As an alternative, many event planners arrange for leftover food to be donated. In doing so, event planners must consider their legal liability. Once again, regulations on this issue vary according to the jurisdiction. In some jurisdictions, protection may be available for food donors, provided that they acted in good faith, without the intention to cause harm, and were not grossly negligent. In other jurisdictions, food donations may be prohibited. In addition to researching local regulations, meeting and event professionals should discuss food donation considerations with their insurance provider. Examples of legislation addressing food donations include:

- In the United States, the 1996 Federal Bill Emerson Good Samaritan Food Donation Act helps make it easier for organizations to donate food by bringing standardization on this issue in the United States and providing some protection to donors.
- In the Philippines, RA 9803 (An Act to Encourage the Donation of Food for Charitable Purposes) was passed in 2009.

If you are planning to make food donations, consider the following steps:

Photo courtesy of iStockphoto/mangostock

- Discuss with the venue how it currently manages food waste. Some sustainable practices include using the food internally for an employee cafeteria, donating to charitable organizations, donating to farms for animal consumption, or organic composting.
- Practice safe food handling and ensure that the venue and any community partner also does this, including during the transportation stage.
- Identify and work with a reputable organization that regularly handles food donations.
- Understand your legal liabilities. In some jurisdictions, addition to direct liability (for your own actions) you may also run the risk of vicarious liability (for the actions of others, such as your employees) from food and beverage issues

such as contaminated or spoiled food that result in injury to the food recipients. Consult a lawyer for advice based on the jurisdiction of your event and the event's insurance provider.

Responsible Alcohol Management

The serving of alcohol at events introduces several risks: participant risks from intoxication, liability risks for the event hosts, and community risks related to activities such as driving while intoxicated. An excellent resource for managing alcohol-related risks can be found in *Event Risk Management and Safety,* by Peter E. Tarlow, Ph.D.[7] From a CSR perspective, in addition to the strategies outlined by Tarlow such as utilizing only servers who have been trained to serve alcohol, ensuring that there are designated drivers, and not providing free alcohol, some events are adding elements such as 12-step program meetings (such as Alcoholics Anonymous) during conferences or arranging with community programs (such as Operation Red Nose in several Canadian cities that operates during the month of December) to safely drive attendees and their vehicles home.

Community Service Projects

Many meetings and events are incorporating **community service projects** into their programs. Community service projects involve having the group or part of the group perform volunteer activities, usually to help address a social or environmental need. These programs have sometimes involved activities with a certain degree of risk, such as hiking to remote areas, working with children or animals, and construction work. In these cases, planners, in addition to implementing safety measures, should have volunteers sign release forms. Release forms may provide a degree of liability protection but are not a substitute for risk mitigation strategies, including professional management of the volunteers and volunteer education on safety measures that they should take, such as appropriate protective clothing and footwear. Your insurance provider and/or legal counsel may be able to provide forms for you to use and must review your release forms in advance of issuing them. In developing your risk management plan for a community service project, consider the following areas depicted in Figure 11.5.

- *Health and safety of participants:* Issues might include access to food, water, shade, heating, and cooling offered and medical services. Safety training might also be needed, particularly when manual labor will be performed. A good best practice is locating the nearest hospital or emergency service providers and ensuring organizers and participants have this information. It is also a best practice to do a site visit in advance to discover any issues about the site that might impact health and safety. Advise participants regarding what to wear and any safety equipment needed; ensure access to first aid kits.
- *Experience of community partners:* Issues may include the community partner's supervision and training skills and their safety record.
- *Community service objectives:* From this perspective, it is valuable to consider if the objective is best met through the initiative that you have selected.

Figure 11.5   Community Service Project Risk Management Areas

- *Insurance and liability:* Meeting and event professionals should determine if their insurance will cover potential issues that might arise from their community service project, and if they or the event sponsor could be potentially liable if something goes wrong.
- *Reputation risk:* When deciding to initiate a community service project, organizations should consider the potential for damage to their reputation if an accident occurs, or if the project does not align with the mission, vision, or values of the organization.
- *Logistics:* In this respect, community service projects face the same types of risks as other meetings and events, from achieving optimal attendance levels, to venue, transportation, and equipment issues.
- *Volunteer management:* Consideration for proper volunteer management is needed when undertaking a community service project. This includes supervising volunteers, assigning them to appropriate tasks, and arranging for sufficient numbers of volunteers with the appropriate skills.

Marketing

The term *greenwashing* was coined in 1986 by Jay Westerfeld in reference to the practice of hotels promoting a towel reuse program but then not following through with other green initiatives that were not cost-cutting.[8] TerraChoice Group, Inc., an environmental marketing firm and author of *The Sins of Greenwashing,* defines greenwashing as "the act of misleading consumers regarding the environmental practices of a company or the environmental benefits of a product or service."[9] Meeting and event professionals who falsify or exaggerate claims run the risk of consumer backlash and potential lawsuits. Kelly Bagnall, an attorney with Dykema Gossett PLLC's Dallas office who specializes in hospitality, commercial litigation, and general business counseling matters, gives the example that people have different interpretations of what it means to be a *green meeting*: "Groups should avoid misrepresentations to their attendees related to the scope of sustainable initiatives in connection with the meeting and, for example, why there might be additional costs." She adds that in the United States, in addition to a number of potentially applicable laws, many states have enacted laws governing deceptive trade practices that impose liability if misrepresentations are made. Greenwashing is discussed in greater detail in Chapter 7.

In-Depth Example: Hybrid Meetings

Hybrid meetings have live and virtual elements. They combine both a face-to-face event, such as a conference, with simultaneous online or virtual features. They have two distinct and often overlapping audiences: those that are participating in person at the main venue and those participating virtually. Each of these audiences will have distinct needs, and planners should develop engagement plans for each of these two groups. Virtual elements may include:

- Live video and/or audio streaming of meeting sessions and presentations to virtual attendees
- Speakers in off-site locations presenting to the live audience via streaming video
- A hub-and-spokes model, where a main conference location is live-streamed to other gathered groups that might be referred to as *pods,* in other locations
- Opportunities for virtual attendees to participate through an online chat or discussion forum, which might include the integration of social media tools, such as Twitter or Facebook

Hybrid meetings offer an option for reducing the carbon footprint of an event by making it possible for prospective attendees to participate without needing to travel. It may also make it possible for those who would not be able to participate due to financial or time restrictions to be able to do so.

From a risk management perspective, hybrid meetings can help reduce some types of location-related risks as they act as a diversification strategy. For example, by having smaller groups located in different locations, if one location experiences adverse weather conditions, other locations will likely not be affected and your event will be able to proceed. While reducing some types of risks, hybrid events introduce new risks—for example, Internet access failure. As well, not all potential audiences will respond well to a hybrid event format. Factors to consider include access to technology infrastructure at the live site and for attendees, time zone differences for attendees, receptiveness of the audience to a virtual format, and response of prospective sponsors and/or exhibitors. Recommendations for managing hybrid event–related risks include the following:

- Technology-related risks:
  - Work with experienced suppliers familiar with hybrid meetings.
  - Include sufficient funds in your budget to cover the costs for the most appropriate technology to meet your needs.
  - Test and retest the technology before the event and assess the capabilities of the venue and service providers in advance of the event.
  - Research your prospective audience's access, familiarity, and comfort with technology.
- Stakeholder engagement
  - Consider adding a hybrid-meeting moderator that will be responsible for monitoring virtual attendees, engaging with them and facilitating their participation in the live discussion.
  - Engage with stakeholders, including sponsors and prospective attendees, prior to the event to ensure that their needs will be met with the hybrid-meeting format.

Insurance

As previously discussed, one option for managing risk is to transfer it through the use of insurance in exchange for a payment (referred to as an **insurance premium**). When you purchase event liability insurance or event cancellation insurance, the insurance company then becomes responsible for paying for the losses, up to the amount of the insurance coverage.

Selecting and Working with an Insurance Agent or Broker

Some insurance professionals specialize in event liability and/or cancellation insurance and will have a deeper understanding of event-related risks. While an insurance agent represents a particular insurer, a broker will offer products from various companies that it contracts with. When working with your insurance professional, it is critical that you provide detailed information

Photo courtesy of iStockphoto/alexsl

about your program, including sustainability-related initiatives such as food donations and community service projects. A checklist for selecting an insurance broker is provided here:

- Review quotes from at least three different brokers or agents.
- Evaluate the quotes based on:
  - Cost
  - What is included and what is excluded
  - Experience of the agent/broker with your type of event
  - Reputation, including references from other event planners and relevant certifications
  - Help and support available if a claim is made
  - Their ability to provide additional services to help you manage risk, such as waiver forms and on-site inspections
- Interview the agent/broker to assess their specific knowledge about event-related risks and their ability to answer your questions.
- Keep in mind that your insurance agent/broker is one of your event partners: You should feel comfortable working and communicating with them.

General Liability Insurance and Sustainability-related Initiatives

Meeting and event planners need to have a clear understanding of what is covered through their general liability insurance policy and if sustainability-related initiatives, such as having carpooling options, volunteers involved in community service projects, or food donations are covered. According to Michelle A. Leigh-Evans, assistant vice-president of Aon Association Services, a division of Affinity Insurance Services, Inc., a key issue in planning community service projects is knowing who is responsible for the event. For example, if you are an event organizer and you are planning a volunteer project with a charitable organization, you should determine in advance who is considered to be sponsoring the event. Depending on the contracted arrangements, it could be the charitable organization or the event organizers that are considered responsible. When working with a charitable organization in this capacity, it is important to check their insurance coverage. It might be possible for either the event organizers or the charitable organization to name the other as an additional insured on the insurance policy.

Sustainability Issues and Event Cancellation Insurance

Seth J. Fleischer, account executive with Aon Association Services, a division of Affinity Insurance Services, Inc., advises that meeting and event planners should obtain cancellation insurance early in the planning process. "Once you start signing contracts with venues and incurring expenses, that's the time when you start looking at putting the event cancellation policy in place." Major disasters, such as earthquakes and hurricanes, can result in event cancellations for months after they occur. Cancellation insurance for these types of occurrences cannot be purchased after the fact. For example, if a hurricane that happens in August results in the cancellation of an event scheduled to take place the following May, the insurance would only cover the cancellation if it specifically covers this type of disaster and if it had been purchased prior to the hurricane. Preexisting conditions (such as earthquakes and hurricanes that have already occurred) would be excluded from the policy. However, this does not mean that future occurrences of earthquakes and hurricanes would also be excluded from the policy. The exclusion would be for disasters that caused damage prior to binding the policy.

When purchasing event cancellation insurance, it is important to discuss with your provider the specific coverage and exclusions that will exist related to environmental or social issues such as an oil spill, or an airline or hotel labor strikes. If it is not typically covered, you may be able to purchase additional insurance for these issues. As discussed earlier in the chapter, a thorough examination of possible event risks, including those that may result from environmental or social issues, will be valuable for securing the appropriate type of insurance coverage.

Photo courtesy of iStockphoto/alexsl

Green Insurance

More and more venues are introducing sustainable features or obtaining Leadership in Energy and Environmental Design (LEED) certification. Typical building insurance might not fully cover these features, and so in recent years, a new form of insurance has been developed: green insurance. Stephen G. Bushnell, senior director of Product Development, Commercial Insurance with Fireman's Fund Insurance Company, offers the examples of a vegetative roof, underground cistern, or alternative energy systems as types of environmental feature that could be covered through green insurance. Typical property insurance may only cover a small proportion of the costs of these building features. According to Bushnell, in its research, Fireman's Fund Insurance Company concluded that the process that LEED-certified buildings go through addresses many of the areas where the company normally pays for losses, and therefore it can afford to offer such coverage. As well, green insurance can be purchased for buildings that do not currently have environmental materials, so that in the case of a loss, the facility could be rebuilt using environmentally preferred products.

Ethics, Policies, and Regulations

What happens when ethics, policies, and regulations are in conflict? Ideally, this wouldn't occur, but there may be times when meeting and event professionals find that their personal ethics are in conflict with corporate policies or local regulations. As one example, a corporate purchasing policy may be to always select the lowest bid, with no consideration of sustainability issues.

When facing issues like this, meeting and event professionals need to understand their legal obligations. Failing to follow a corporate policy might negatively impact their employment or performance reviews. Failing to comply with a law could result in further legal repercussions.

In some cases, it might be possible to have a policy changed. In the example already given about the corporate purchasing policy addressing only financial considerations, there might be greater chances of success in changing the policy if you are able to effectively argue the business case for adding nonfinancial criteria to the supplier selection process. This might include examining the long-term cost savings from purchasing a more energy-efficient product, surveying potential meeting and event attendees about their sustainability priorities and the impact on the organization's reputation.

Regulations and ethical views about some issues vary significantly across different jurisdictions and regions, resulting in times when meeting and event professionals might have an ethical conflict with local regulations. In these circumstances, issues to take into consideration include health and safety of participants and workers, the impact on the event, and the organization's reputation and legal risks.

Chapter Review

This chapter has focused on key risk management and legal considerations related to the implementation of corporate social responsibility initiatives for meeting and event professionals, with the recognition that these considerations will vary across jurisdictions, and the importance of seeking specific legal advice that is relevant to your particular circumstances. From a risk perspective, sustainable practices can both reduce risk and introduce new ones. The chapter examined a number of risk management techniques, including contract considerations, risk mitigation, and risk transferring through the use of insurance. In concluding this chapter, we reviewed how conflicts might arise between ethics and policies and regulations, and key factors that meeting and event professionals should consider under those circumstances.

Review Questions

1. Describe the differences between event-specific risks and systemic risks. Determine if the following risks are closer to an event-specific risk or a systemic risk:
   - Keynote speaker fails to arrive.
   - The price of oil increases by 30 percent.
   - A protest occurs against your event or conference or another in the same venue.
   - There is a downturn in the global economy.
2. Review the four approaches to risk management and determine which is most likely to be used for each category of the probability and impact matrix.
3. Compare and contrast the process for obtaining permission to hold a raffle as a charitable fundraiser in the following locations (Please research this information using government websites):
   - State of California
   - Toronto, Canada
   - United Kingdom
   - Your own community

Group Exercises

For each of the following scenarios:
1. Identify the potential risks.
2. Assess the impact and probability of these risks.
3. Develop a risk management strategy for the scenario.

Scenario Discussion #1

You have been asked to develop a risk management strategy for a fundraising event for a not-for-profit organization. The board of directors describes the elements of the event as follows:

○ The event will be an outdoor fair, with live concerts, food concession stands, and children's activities. Some of the food stands will also sell alcoholic beverages.

○ The organization has several of its own volunteers that will be responsible for selling raffle tickets at the event and monitoring access to the event.

○ The event will take place in a community park in the middle of summer, and hot weather is expected. Limited parking is available, and access to the area of the park where the event will take place involves a 10- to 15-minute walk.

Scenario Discussion #2

You have been asked to develop a risk management strategy for a community service project for a scientific conference. The meeting planner describes the event as follows:

○ The event will involve taking a group of delegates to conduct a shoreline cleanup.

○ Volunteers from the conference will be responsible for collecting garbage from a local beach.

○ The conference attracts international attendance, and it is expected that there will be several languages spoken by the delegates.

○ The beach itself has an uneven terrain, with rocks, sand, and shells.

○ A bus has been arranged to transport the delegates to the beach, and it will return three hours later to take the delegates back to the conference venue.

Key Terms

- risk management
- jurisdiction
- liability
- diversification
- reputation risk
- social risk
- regulatory risk
- community service projects
- hybrid meetings
- insurance premium

Resources

Related to the Resources listed below, please visit the Book Companion Site (located at www.wiley.com/college/henderson) for a complete list of websites. Additional referential websites related to this chapter's content can also be found on the BCS.

Association of Fundraising Professionals
> This site provides information on ethical and effective fundraising practices. The website includes a section on public policy issues in Canada and the United States related to fundraising.

Nonprofit Risk Management Center
> This site includes resources for nonprofit organizations in the areas of volunteer risk management, financial risk management, employment practices, and youth protection.

Recommended Books

Berlonghi, Alexander. *Special Events Risk Management Manual*. Self-published, 1990.

Goldblatt, Joe.*Special Events: A New Generation and the Next Frontier, 6th ed*. Hoboken, NJ: John Wiley & Sons, 2011.

Goldblatt, Samuel deBlanc.*The Complete Guide to Greener Meetings and Events*. Hoboken, NJ: John Wiley & Sons, 2011.

Project Management Institute. *Practice Standard for Project Risk Management*. Newtown Square, PA: Project Management Institute, 2009.

Silvers, Julia Rutherford. *Event Risk Management*. Oxford: Elsevier Butterworth/Heinemann, 2008.

Silvers, Julia Rutherford. *Professional Event Coordination, 2nd ed*. Hoboken, NJ: John Wiley & Sons, 2012.

Tarlow, Peter. *Event Risk Management and Safety*. New York: John Wiley & Sons, 2002.

Notes

1. Convention Industry Council,*APEX Industry Glossary—2011 Edition*.www.conventionindustry.org/StandardsPractices/APEX/glossary.aspx.
2. Project Management Institute (2009), *Practice Standard for Project Risk Management* (Newtown Square, PA: Project Management Institute, 2009), p. 9.
3. Barrie McKenna, "Canadians Score Lower on Risk Tolerance," *The Globe and Mail*, June 15, 2011 (Updated September 12, 2011), www.theglobeandmail.com/report-on-business/economy/canadians-score-lower-on-risk-tolerance/article2060767/

4. Beth Kytle and John Gerard Ruggie, "Corporate Social Responsibility as Risk Management: A Model for Multinationals," *Corporate Social Responsibility Working Paper No. 10* (Cambridge, MA: John F. Kennedy School of Government, Harvard University, 2005).

5. Fairmont Hotels and Resorts, "Fairmont Shows Healthy Doesn't Have to Mean Flavor Free" (June 1, 2011). www.fairmont.com/EN_FA/Articles/RecentNews/lifestylecuisineplus.htm.

6. U.S. Department of Justice, *Audit of Department of Justice Conference Planning and Food and Beverage Costs*, available online at: www.justice.gov/oig/reports/plus/a1143.pdf.

7. Peter Tarlow, *Event Risk Management and Safety* (New York: John Wiley & Sons, 2002).

8. Jim Motavalli, *A History of Greenwashing: How Dirty Towels Impacted the Green Movement* Accessed February 15, 2012 from: www.dailyfinance.com/2011/02/12/the-history-of-greenwashing-how-dirty-towels-impacted-the-green/.

9. TerraChoice Group Inc., sinsofgreenwashing.org/.

Sustainability is a journey.
Photo courtesy of Elizabeth Henderson

CHAPTER 12

Backcasting and Scenario Planning for a Sustainable Meetings and Events Industry

"'Men's courses will foreshadow certain ends, to which, if persevered in, they must lead,' said Scrooge. 'But if the courses be departed from, the ends will change. Say it is thus with what you show me!'"

—*A Christmas Carol, Charles Dickens, English novelist (1812–1870)*

Learning Objectives

After studying this chapter, you will be able to:

- Learn how to apply principles of backcasting for sustainability.
- Review key concepts from the book.
- Become familiar with the basic principles of scenario planning for use on an industry-wide level.
- Recognize how scenario planning can help the industry move to a sustainable future.

Introduction

This chapter provides both a review of concepts we have introduced in previous chapters and a call to action. We offer tools to help you remember, use, and share the knowledge you have gained. It is not enough to acquire existing knowledge; knowledge needs to be applied to be useful, and the quest for new knowledge and better applications must be undertaken. Therefore, we suggest a tool to explore possible alternative futures at an industry level. Use of such creative, collaborative processes will help us envision and attain a more sustainable future for the meetings and events industry within the context of a world that changes at an increasing rate—a global community whose complexities of culture, economy, and environment are only starting to be recognized and recombined in a kaleidoscope of colors, expressed in challenges, opportunities, and alternatives. The future starts here, and it starts with you.

Meetings and Events: Ghosts of Past, Present, and Future

In Charles Dickens's classic novel *A Christmas Carol,* the protagonist, the miserly (and legendary) Ebenezer Scrooge is visited by four ghosts. The first ghost is his deceased business partner, Jacob Marley, who cautions Scrooge to change his ways or be condemned to a terrible future. Marley foretells that Scrooge will be visited by three spirits, and that Scrooge should take heed of their warnings. Scrooge, terrified, reluctantly agrees to the visits. The first of these spirits delves into Scrooge's past, when he chose greed over happiness, love, and possibly even his own inclinations as a young man. The second spirit explores Scrooge's present life, illuminating his negative impact on those he interacts with. Here he sees the family of his clerk, Bob Cratchit, creating much joy with very little despite great financial and physical hardship. Finally, the third spirit shows Scrooge a possible future: one where he visits his own grave, and sees that despite his great riches, he has died, unloved and unlamented by anyone. Seeing this dark and dismal future, he changes his ways. The novella ends with Scrooge sharing his wealth and living a happier life with friends and family.[1]

Imagine the meetings and events industry as Ebenezer Scrooge: What would the spirits show us for our past, present, and future? Perhaps history would show us that there was a moment in our past when we lost track of the goal to create meaningful and valuable human connections, and somewhere turned our attention to profit at the expense of others, including that of our communities and the environment. Perhaps the present would show us that while we as an industry are focused on profit at any costs, that there are also many Cratchit families in our world—those highlighted in the case studies in this book are doing great things with fewer resources and are creating the types of connections that are at the heart of meetings and events. Finally, perhaps the future would show us that greed will be our demise. But, like Scrooge, we have an opportunity to undertake a course correction: by incorporating responsible practices, we can still have a successful and sustainable industry.

Backcasting—The Natural Step

A key concept in the Natural Step, and an approach to sustainability that was introduced at the beginning of this book, is **backcasting**. As explained on the Natural Step's website, "The concept of 'backcasting' is central to a strategic approach for sustainable development. It is a way of planning in which a successful outcome is imagined in the future, followed by the question: 'what do we need to do today to reach that successful outcome?'"[2]

Jan Peter Bergkvist has been active in the field of sustainable business at an executive level in the hospitality industry since the early 1990s. He spent 15 years with Scandic hotels and 4 years with Hilton International as director of environmental sustainability. In January 2009, he moved to the role of senior advisor, sustainable business, within his own business, SleepWell AB, based in Stockholm, Sweden. Bergkvist is an expert in the application of the Natural Step in the meetings and events industry. He comments that "one of the things that very often are in common when you look at . . . really successful companies for sustainability, it really has become part of the strategy, it is very often that they in some way have been in contact with or inspired by the Natural Step or for that matter any other systems thinking framework." He adds that the Natural Step "has turned out to be an extremely powerful tool for me as a hotelier when I tried to implement sustainability."

Bergkvist says backcasting is a valuable methodology, because "it's an excellent idea to have a goal when you start a journey." However, Bergkvist says:

> *Unfortunately, there are so many great organizations today if you ask the leader if sustainability is important he or she would answer "Yes, sustainability is important," and then if you ask him or her "and what is sustainability?" unfortunately you would get the same answer: "Sustainability is important," and so there is a need of a clear, robust definition of sustainability, and I think that is one of the things that TNS gave us with the sustainability principles and then secondly with the method of backcasting.*

This concluding chapter will apply backcasting methodology to envision a sustainable future for our industry, and then identify the necessary steps to achieve this future. These steps will be drawn from the concepts previously introduced in this book.

The Vision: A Sustainable Future for Meetings and Events

We began this book with our vision for a sustainable future for the meetings and events industry, modeled on the concept of the triple bottom line. This vision addresses three facets, presented in Figure 12.1.

Achievement of this vision will require changes in the way the business of meetings and events is conducted. It is a new journey that we will begin, and to guide us on this journey is our roadmap for sustainability in meetings and events.

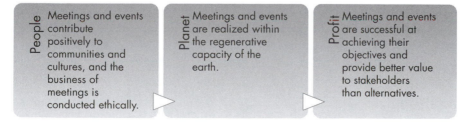

Figure 12.1 Our Vision for a Sustainable Meetings Industry

The Roadmap for Sustainability in Meetings and Events

The remainder of this chapter will focus on the steps that we recommend be implemented to secure a sustainable future for our industry. These steps will be drawn from the key concepts presented that will help us to reach our vision, which you will remember from the opening chapter of this book: *An industry where meetings and events contribute positively to communities and cultures, and the business of meetings is conducted ethically; a future where meetings and events are realized within the regenerative capacity of the Earth, and where meetings and events are successful at achieving their objectives and providing better value to stakeholders than alternatives.*

This roadmap has been developed so that each of the components can be sent via Twitter; each one is less than 140 characters. Please feel free to use them as micro-educational and micro-motivational clips of ethical and responsible triple-bottom-line best practices—and in some cases, next practices—in the meetings and events industry for any of your friends and followers in your various social networks. For example, a suggested hashtag (#) is #eventprofs. Other industry organizations have their own hashtags that might also be applicable. The hashtag for this book is suggested as #eventCSR.

Introduction to Corporate Social Responsibility and Ethics

Within this chapter, we defined the context of sustainability and introduced common frameworks for assessing sustainability. This led into the concept of corporate social responsibility (CSR) and the various ways of examining and applying it. We suggest using the hashtag #eventCSR to promote discussion.

- It is important to use the language of CSR and ethics to promote common understanding. #eventCSR
- Meetings and events can positively contribute to communities and culture through CSR & ethical business practices.
- It is possible to create meetings & events with footprints within the regenerative capacity of the Earth.
- CSR in meetings and events can help achieve organizational objectives effectively.
- Meetings and events have an obligation to operate in an economically, environmentally and socially responsible way.
- CSR and ethics will help move the industry & its businesses from reactive to proactive in the face of change.
- Culture and geography influence the perception of CSR & sustainability as applied in meetings and events.
- Sustainability is the sweet spot where environmental protection, economic prosperity, and social justice MEET.
- Meeting and event organizations can build a social license to operate by acting as good global citizens.
- Meetings and events are organizational missions, visions, & values in action. Act responsibly!

Business Ethics and the Meetings and Events Industry

If you remember (and hopefully you do!), this chapter provided a framework for addressing ethical dilemmas. It examined ethical situations that meeting and event professionals might face during their careers. The chapter explored rationalizations that might be used to justify potentially unethical behavior, as well as possible repercussions. We offer the following micro-bytes to reinforce what you have learned. We suggest using the hashtag #eventCSR to promote discussion.

- Meetings industry organizations will develop & implement a code of conduct/ethics policy. #eventCSR
- Codes of conduct will address business operations, environmental, & social issues.
- Human resource practices will be aligned with ethics policies to encourage ethical behavior.
- An infrastructure for anonymous feedback on ethics is developed within organizations.
- Ethical behavior is demonstrated from the top down & from the bottom up in organizations.
- Ethics policies will clearly state organizational priorities for addressing trade-offs in ethical dilemmas.
- Leading industry associations will model ethical behavior & help to champion and promote ethics in the industry.
- Ethics will be found not only in policy manuals but also in the daily actions of organizations and individuals.
- Ethical behavior & related policies are practiced throughout the supply chain for meetings & events.
- Ethical behavior & policies are demonstrated in the communities where meetings & events are held.

Strategies for Sustainable Meetings

In this chapter, we used a systems view to demonstrate linkages between the elements of sustainable meetings and events. We then introduced a decision model to guide basic sustainability and CSR decisions in a meetings and events context. This included recognizing that impacts of sustainability-related decisions have an impact on more than just you and your organization. We provided guidance on assessing service providers based on sustainable criteria. Areas included consumption, waste, renewable energy, destination and material selection, positive impacts and legacy, and the use of technology to enhance inclusiveness and mitigate risk. We suggest using the hashtag #eventCSR to promote discussion.

- Our industry will recognize a broad view of sustainability, including social, environmental, and economic aspects. #eventCSR
- We will be conscious of our choices & continually ask if our consumption choices advance our objectives.
- Meeting & event professionals will apply a systems view of sustainability in designing their programs.
- Waste reduction will be a primary focus for sustainability initiatives for meetings & events.
- Renewable energy sources will be utilized by venues, suppliers and meeting & event organizers.
- Destinations & products used for meetings & events will be selected in consideration of carbon footprint implications.
- Material selection criteria will include a product's origins, transportation, purpose, production, & waste created.
- Increasing the positive impact & reducing the negative impact of our industry on communities will be a key focus.
- Meetings & events will create positive legacies in communities where they are held.
- Our industry will leverage technology to enhance programs, promote inclusivity, & reduce environmental damage.

Social Responsibility and Culture

This chapter focused on the ways that meetings and events can promote social responsibility through strategies and activities, including through community service. We introduced the MAUDE framework to help industry professionals develop community service projects that are meaningful, aligned with organizational objectives, which apply the organization's unique skills, and are both destination-specific and engaging for stakeholders. The authenticity of the experience is important in a cultural context. The ability of meeting and event professionals to leverage their activities and networks to create increased social well-being was explored. We suggest using the hashtag #eventCSR to promote discussion.

- Meetings & events will support the social, environmental & economic well-being of their host communities. #eventCSR
- Authentic cultural experiences & education will be a part of events to showcase, celebrate, & sustain local cultures.
- Meeting & event professionals will promote and support fair labor practices in our industry.
- Meetings & events will be socially responsible for participants by promoting health, wellness, & diversity.
- Community service projects will be meaningful, aligned, unique-skills based, destination specific, & engaging.
- Close attention will be paid to social issues affecting event participation, such as access to child care and travel costs.
- Meeting & event professionals will source fair trade products for their programs and menus.
- Meeting & event professionals will help support secure employment and reduction of precarious employment.
- Local cultural authorities will be consulted in the development of cultural experiences for meetings & events.
- Meeting & event professionals will leverage their economic influence to create positive social change.

Meetings, Events, and Environmental Science

Most meeting and event professionals do not have core competencies in science, and so this chapter introduced some of the invisible environmental effects generated by meetings and events, and their potential effects on the ecosystem. We outlined strategies to measure, reduce, eliminate, or mitigate that impact of meeting and event activities, including reduction in consumption; controlling those factors under our direct control by choosing products and services that have less of an environmental impact; and choosing to influence the sustainable practices of those we do business with but do not have direct control over. We suggest using the hashtag #eventCSR to promote discussion.

- Meetings & events will apply carbon reduction strategies first, followed by carbon offsetting strategies. #eventCSR
- Our industry will reduce its dependence on nonrenewable energy sources, including fossil fuels.
- Our industry will promote more sustainable transportation practices, including public transportation.
- Meeting & event professionals will choose sustainable options for decisions within their direct control.
- Meeting & event professionals will leverage their influence to promote sustainable decisions outside their direct control.
- Natural capital will be valued alongside financial or real capital in our industry.

- Our industry will focus on increasing positive externalities and reducing negative externalities from our actions.
- We will develop and implement technologies to easily measure and monitor our environmental impact.
- We will consciously focus on reducing event miles for our events, and maximizing the benefits from the miles incurred.
- Our industry will avoid the *ostrich effect* and acknowledge and address our impact on the environment.

Shared Value and Strategic Corporate Responsibility

There is a solid business case for corporate social responsibility. This chapter outlined that business case. Different types of CSR (transactional, transitional, and transformational) were introduced, as well as the concepts of strategic CSR and shared value. We introduced the concept of cluster CSR, where several entities act together to increase the effectiveness of CSR applications as a concept that might have applicability to the meetings and events industry. The Copenhagen Sustainable Events Protocol can be considered a type of cluster CSR. We suggest using the hashtag #eventCSR to promote discussion.

- Shared value will be at the heart of the new business model for our industry. #eventCSR
- Long-term economic, social, and environmental health will be considered in our meeting and event design.
- CSR initiatives will be designed to maximize the intended benefits and increase engagement of stakeholders.
- Meeting & event professionals will leverage the skills and resources of partners to make initiatives more effective.
- Cluster CSR principles will be applied to encourage greater industry participation toward sustainability goals.
- Industry professionals will align business, social, and environmental goals to develop strategic CSR initiatives.
- The impact of social and environmental issues on business operations will be examined to identify strategic initiatives.
- Industry partners will act as cluster CSR facilitators, helping to coordinate efforts of multiple events in destinations.
- Industry professionals will learn to articulate the business case for CSR, sustainability, and ethics.
- CSR practices will be leveraged to foster healthy, supportive, and motivating work places for our industry professionals.

Communications, Marketing, and Public Relations

This chapter discussed how to promote our events in a more sustainable way, how we communicate with our stakeholders to promote sustainable behaviors, and how we can leverage CSR to create authentic experiences that generate goodwill among our stakeholders and in the communities we are active in. Greenwashing in marketing messages is discouraged in the quest to be transparent and ethical. We also offer suggestions on how to evaluate eco-labels for validity, reliability, and credibility. We suggest using the hashtag #eventCSR to promote discussion.

- Effective pre-event, on-site, and post-event communication is used to encourage sustainable behavior by participants. #eventCSR

- Greenwashing will be avoided in marketing practices for meetings & events and our industry's supply chain.
- Proof of claims and principled messaging about sustainability will be practiced in marketing.
- Sustainability and supply chain issues will be considered when purchasing and designing promotional products.
- CSR and sustainability will be performed in a meaningful way, not simply as a PR photo-op.
- Meeting & event professionals will be transparent in their reporting on sustainability-related issues.
- Promotion of products and services (including events) will be done in a sustainable manner.
- Eco-labels will be examined cautiously to ensure that they are valid, reliable, and independent.
- A focus on sustainability will not detract from a focus on ensuring high-quality meetings and events.
- Key performance indicators will be developed to ensure that sustainable marketing objectives are realized.

Sustainable Supply Chains for Meetings and Events

Sustainable supply chains are a core element of producing sustainable meetings and events. This chapter introduced key terminology and demonstrated how to map your supply chain. We discuss seven steps as a tool to implement a sustainable supply chain in your organization, and give examples of supplier codes of conduct that you may want to use to create your own, to help reinforce your expectations, sustainability objectives, and values with partners and suppliers. We suggest using the hashtag #eventCSR to promote discussion.

- Sourcing from sustainable supply chain practices will become standard operations for industry professionals. #eventCSR
- Procurement criteria will include transparency, accountability, and traceability of products.
- Industry professionals will investigate downstream elements of the supply chain of their purchases.
- Industry suppliers will monitor the activities of their supply chains to encourage sustainable behavior and reduce risk.
- Industry professionals will work toward addressing barriers to sustainable supply chain management.
- Our industry will develop metrics for evaluating supply chains across multiple facets of sustainability.
- Increased communication and collaboration between buyers and suppliers will result in innovation toward sustainability.
- Industry professionals will use tools including supply chain maps and flow charts to identify supply chain risks.
- Industry professionals will develop, implement, and regularly evaluate sustainable supply chain policies.
- Life-cycle planning and reverse logistics practices will become a focus for meeting and event professionals.

Sustainability Measurement and Evaluation

Measurement is an essential component of sustainable meetings and events, helping not only to prove actual performance but to track performance over time. This increases accountability and responsibility as well as making benchmarking (both internal and external) possible. Measurement is essential to the next logical step, which is reporting. In this chapter we identified measurements that can be used within the context of sustainable meetings and events, and how to determine what should be measured based on the scope and scale of the event. We introduced new sustainable event standards in more detail, including APEX green meeting standards, the Global Reporting Initiative Event Organizer Sector Supplement, and ISO 20121. We suggest using the hashtag #eventCSR to promote discussion.

- Meeting & event professionals will increase accountability and responsibility by measuring and evaluating actions. #eventCSR
- Measurement & evaluation will increase transparency, building trust within the supply chain and with stakeholders.
- Sustainability-focused innovation will result from measuring our industry's social, environmental, and economic impact.
- Consistent measurement and evaluation will make benchmarking across our industry possible and practiced.
- Industry professionals will measure qualitative and quantitative sustainability aspects of meetings and events.
- Industry benchmarks and historical event performance will instill a culture of continuous sustainable improvements.
- Industry standards, including APEX, GRI EOSS, and ISO 20121, will be used to develop key performance indicators (KPIs).
- We will measure for the purpose of management of triple-bottom-line success factors.
- We will measure the long-term impact of our events, not only the time-bound aspects of the on-site experience.
- Industry professionals will develop consistent measurement practices to allow for comparison of events.

Sustainability Reporting for Meetings and Events

Reporting allows you to share successes and challenges encountered in the planning and execution process with key stakeholders. It also allows meeting professionals to integrate what they have learned into the next iteration of planning and strategy, to improve performance. In this chapter, we explored several reporting methodologies that can be used by meeting professionals, including the APEX-sponsored green meeting report, the Global Reporting Initiative Event Organizer Sector Supplement, and ISO 20121, all of which were introduced in earlier chapters. We provided guidance on linking event objectives with broader organizational strategies and the identification and engagement of key stakeholders. We suggest using the hashtag #eventCSR to promote discussion.

- Sustainability reporting will become integrated into event reports. #eventCSR
- Increasingly, events will use established reporting guidelines, such as APEX, GRI EOSS, and ISO 20121.
- Increased sustainability reporting will allow our industry to better respond to questions about corporate responsibility.
- Cross-functional teams within organizations will allow for more integrated reporting outcomes.
- Event reports will increasingly link sustainable event goals with organizational objectives.
- Industry professionals will utilize stakeholder webs to identify event stakeholders and key reporting areas.
- Industry professionals will utilize organizational strategic and sustainability objectives as a reporting roadmap.

- Industry professionals will become increasingly adept in sustainability reporting.
- Increased training and standardization of reporting practices will result in reporting becoming common practice.
- Event sustainability reports will be used as tools for strategy development.

Risk Management and Legal Considerations

This chapter delved into the key issues related to risk management and legal considerations as they relate to ethics and CSR. It explored ways that CSR and ethics can be used proactively as a risk management tool as well as how to effectively manage the risk—including liability, safety, and insurance—that CSR activities might expose you and your organization to through activities such as food donation, community service projects, or charitable gaming. We suggest using the hashtag #eventCSR to promote discussion.

- Risk management will become a proactive, not reactive, activity for industry professionals. #eventCSR
- CSR, sustainability, and ethics will be used as tools for risk reduction for meetings and events.
- Industry professionals will gain an increased knowledge of legal and liability considerations related to CSR initiatives.
- Industry professionals will become more proficient in developing sustainability-related enforceable contracts.
- Sustainability initiatives will be incorporated into contracts, policies, and procedures.
- Industry professionals will monitor the implementation of sustainability-related aspects of contracts.
- Responsible risk management will be practiced for CSR initiatives such as food donations and charitable gaming.
- Community service projects will be designed with safety, experience, training, and volunteer management in mind.
- Industry professionals will consult with insurance and legal experts to improve risk management and liability protection.
- Sustainability considerations will be included in event insurance policies.

Future Forecast: 2020 Sustainable Meeting or Event Award Winner

In imagining our sustainable future, we present what we hope could be a successful case study for a bid to win a sustainable event award in the year 2020.

Award Recipient: The International Association of Something or Other's (IASOO) 100th Annual Meeting

IASOO held its 100th annual meeting in May 2020 at the newly opened Sustainability Center for Meetings and Events in Imagine, Nation. The municipality of Imagine was a key partner in the provision of essential infrastructure that made this event so successful. Imagine, Nation, has focused on making itself a truly sustainable community, and IASOO benefited from this focus as well as from its own actions, which emphasize environmental protection, economic prosperity, social justice, and the consumption of eco-efficient and fair-trade goods and services.

■ Business Ethics

In this section, please outline strategies and activities taken to demonstrate your commitment to operating an ethical meeting or event, and how those commitments are reflected in the operating policies and processes of your organization. Include measurements, if applicable. Be specific.

- IASOO developed an ethics policy that was consulted regularly as part of their event planning and design process, which was adopted by the organization for continual use in its business operations generally.
- Team members from IASOO were trained in ethical dilemma problem solving.
- IASOO team members had access to an anonymous reporting mechanism for any ethical issues that they observed or were confronted with.
- Human resource practices, including hiring and performance evaluations at IASOO, were aligned with IASOO's ethics policy. This ensured that the organization "walked the talk" in respect to ethics.
- IASOO has an ethics committee that meets regularly to evaluate potential ethical issues related to the organization. The committee is an available and highly utilized resource for the event management team, and includes a broad range of IASOO's stakeholders.
- IASOO's ethics policy addressed a broad range of meeting and event issues including gift giving, supplier selection, behavior of team members, and environmental and social issues.
- Ethical behavior was demonstrated throughout the organization from senior leadership to frontline staff members.
- Regular reference to the ethics policy and how it was incorporated into decision making was made in team meetings during the planning of IASOO's annual meeting.

Presented to: IASOO

Our vision for a 2020 Sustainable Event Award winner.
Photo courtesy of iStockphoto/ andreaastes, adapted by M. McIlwraith

■ Strategies for Sustainable Meetings

In this section of the award application, please detail strategies, policies, processes, and measurements implemented to ensure your meeting or event was environmentally sustainable. Be specific with regard to the rationale for holding the meeting or event, where the meeting or event takes place, and the materials and services procured and how they are provided in a service context.

- IASOO decided to hold the meeting, as it is part of its mandate as an association.
- IASOO chose Imagine, Nation, due to its environmentally superior technology and central location, making travel shorter for most attendees.
- IASOO's event was carbon-positive. It implemented a significant number of carbon-reduction strategies, including use of electric-powered public transportation, site selection that reduced the number of long-haul flights and indirect flights, and the sourcing of local, in-season and naturally low-carbon food for their menus.
- Imagine, Nation's existing waste management infrastructure facilitated the IASOO event becoming zero-waste. Several close-loop initiatives, such as donating compost from the event to local farms where food was sourced, were introduced.
- IASOO proactively reduced the amount of waste generated by working with vendors and exhibitors to reduce the amount of materials brought and distributed at the event that

were likely to generate waste. It approached this aspect of the planning with an extended producer responsibility mentality.

- The event venue, Imagine, Nation's Center for Sustainable Meetings and Events, is a living building. It contributes energy to the local grid from its solar panels and water from its rain collection to neighboring farms, and it acts as a carbon sink thanks to its green roof.

- Accommodation selected for event participants also met leading sustainability standards. IASOO selected a wide range of accommodation types, allowing for participants from any economic background to participate. Accommodation options were also selected to be within walking or cycling distance of the main venue. Hotels that were located outside of a three-block radius of the hotel all offered complimentary bicycles for participant use.

- All of the hotels used for the event implemented sustainable practices, including waste recycling, composting, towel reuse, and amenity recycling, achieving a 98 percent waste stream diversion rate.

- All suppliers were required to sign a code of conduct ensuring that they supported IASOO's human and labor rights policies.

- IASOO leveraged hybrid-meeting technology to engage participants that could not participate in the face-to-face experience. This allowed them to offer an option with reduced carbon and financial implications for attendees. Conscientious efforts to make the virtual experience engaging and beneficial for live and virtual audiences resulted in increased participant satisfaction with the event.

■ Social Responsibility and Culture

In this section of the application, tell us how you implemented strategies, policies, and processes to enhance the positive social and cultural impact of the event, ensured the well-being of attendees, and guaranteed the event was accessible. Be specific.

- IASOO selected its dates to consider and avoided faith-based celebrations and holidays.
- Menu options based on faith-based, medically based, and values-based considerations were offered to participants.
- IASOO set as a goal that participants would leave the event healthier than they arrived. This goal was achieved through healthy menus and the incorporation of physical and mental wellness activities.
- Venues for the event were selected to ensure that they were accessible for all participants.
- Materials produced for the event were available in several languages. Braille materials and sign language interpretation were available.
- Authentic cultural experiences were offered to participants to celebrate Imagine, Nation's rich cultural diversity and heritage. Educational aspects were included as part of these experiences to provide participants with a richer understanding of local cultures.
- The event registration pricing included special incentives to encourage diversity and accessibility for a broad range of economic backgrounds.
- The program included daily community service projects. These were developed using the MAUDE framework. This ensured that events were meaningful, aligned with IASOO's organizational objectives, applied IASOO's unique skills, were destination specific contributing to Imagine, Nation's sustainability, and were engaging to IASOO's diverse group of participants.

■ Meetings, Events, and Environmental Science

In this section, please outline strategies, activities, policies, and processes implemented to reduce the carbon footprint of your meeting or event. Please pay specific attention to transportation, waste streams, the use of alternative energy, and communication of your objectives and strategies to stakeholders.

- IASOO applied carbon-reduction strategies throughout its planning process. Thanks to these efforts and the infrastructure available in the venues that it selected, the event was carbon-positive.
- IASOO sourced all of its energy from renewable resources. No fossil fuels were burned for the event. This involved coordination with a number of suppliers, including airlines, to provide non–fossil-fuel-based energy sources.
- IASOO coordinated sustainable transportation options at key locations, including the airport and train stations. Volunteers were on-site to help participants to use public transportation and ride-share programs to their hotels. All hotels and the main conference venue were located on direct public transportation routes from the airport and train stations.
- IASOO event planners worked actively to reduce negative externalities and increase positive externalities from the event. Examples of this included reduction of energy and water consumption and supporting the development of local infrastructure for recycling and composting.
- Prior to the event, IASOO worked closely with the Imagine, Nation's local government to identify and implement the necessary infrastructure to deliver a sustainable meeting. This buyer involvement helped Imagine, Nation's local government to allocate sufficient funds for these infrastructure investments.
- Reduction of event miles for the implementation of the event was a major focus for IASOO. This was communicated in advance to all the event partners to ensure that this was a priority that was implemented and reported throughout the supply chain for the event.

◼ Shared Value and Strategic Corporate Responsibility

In this section of the application, tell us about how your meeting or event generated shared value within the community and the long-term impact it generated (legacy).

- IASOO incorporated concepts of shared value throughout the event design process: program elements included aspects of benefits to the local community as well as for IASOO. For example, community service projects were beneficial to Imagine, Nation's local organizations and were effective team builders for IASOO.
- Long-term relationships with community-based organizations were created, involving exchanges between Imagine, Nation, and future destinations to help build capacity in other destinations and improve the sustainability performance of the event in the future.
- Community service projects were designed to be sustainable in the long term. To this effect, capacity building was a key focus of IASOO's community service programs. Not only was there an immediate benefit to the local community, but through collaboration with local destination management companies (DMCs), they were able to ensure that the legacy continued beyond the time-bound event.
- IASOO designed its program to maximize the intended benefits and increase engagement of stakeholders. This was done through a robust communication plan to inform participants of their actions, as well as initiatives that appealed to a variety of motivations for event stakeholders.
- IASOO event planners worked with their partners to extend the impact of their sustainability-related initiatives. As an example, IASOO gave the venue's food and beverage department authority to develop the most sustainable menu possible within the constraints of local seasonal availability and the group budget.

- IASOO applied cluster CSR principles by engaging with other events that were scheduled to take place at the same time as their annual conference. This allowed them to coordinate menus, reducing potential waste, and, in certain cases, share subject matter experts.
- Cluster CSR principles were also applied to engage vendors, exhibitors, and event participants in social and environmental initiatives.
- IASOO also applied cluster CSR principles by encouraging partners to participate in community service projects.

■ Communications, Marketing, and Public Relations

In this section, please detail both the method of communication and the message with specific reference to sustainable elements. As a simple example, include both the type of paper, what was written on it, and how it was distributed to communicate sustainable initiatives effectively and without greenwashing.

- IASOO used sustainable marketing practices, including almost zero use of paper made from wood pulp, use of sustainable materials, and increased use of e-communications. For the 2 percent of communications requiring paper, paper made from easily renewable straw pulp was used.
- IASOO's participants were informed of sustainable actions that they could practice during the event, including recycling, composting, and smart water and energy use. These actions were encouraged through a communication plan that included pre-event, on-site, and post-event communications and reinforced through an on-site incentive program.
- Media attention was garnered for local community needs by leveraging IASOO's media connections to draw attention to the social initiatives that IASOO was practicing. This led to sustained and increased local support for these community groups.
- IASOO's event spokesperson was trained in the sustainability-related aspects of the event.
- IASOO monitored all sustainability claims from suppliers to ensure that they were verified and accurate.
- All promotional products used by vendors at the event and by IASOO for the event followed strict sustainability guidelines.
- A focus on sustainability, while a key consideration for IASOO, did not come at the expense of a focus on delivering a high-quality event. IASOO recognized the mission-critical need to ensure that the investment of financial, environmental, and social resources have a positive return. This was ensured by producing a high-quality event that delivered on objectives.
- IASOO carefully monitored all of its own sustainability-related claims in marketing campaigns to ensure that they were truthful, accurate, verified, and measurable.

■ Sustainable Supply Chains for Meetings and Events

In this section, please detail how you managed your supply chain. Include policies, processes, and implementation strategies to ensure the procurement of products and services that helped you achieve your sustainability goals and objectives.

- IASOO's supplier campaign "Step it up for sustainability: Don't just rest on your organic laurels" was included in all of its vendor-selection processes. This campaign required that all the event suppliers go further with their sustainability initiatives, implementing permanent business improvements, and that they not rely exclusively on their existing high standards. IASOO monitored compliance with this campaign and provided expert consultants for these businesses to help them to achieve the goals.

- IASOO monitored closely its supply chain with attention to sustainability considerations.
- Environmental issues, including the production, use, and disposal of products sourced for events, was a top priority for vendor and product selection.
- IASOO monitored social issues of its purchasing, excluding products made under forced or child labor conditions.
- Fair-trade products were used extensively for the event.
- IASOO examined not only its direct vendors but also the supply chain of its vendors to ensure that sustainability was considered throughout all levels of the supply chain.
- IASOO actively sourced products from social enterprises.
- IASOO coordinated with other events that were to be held in Imagine, Nation, to promote sustainable practices with local suppliers. Leveraging the buying power of multiple events helped to strengthen the business case for these suppliers to offer more sustainable options to IASOO and all future events to be held in Imagine, Nation.

■ Sustainability Measurement and Evaluation

Tell us about how you measured your success. Outline specific measurements taken, tools used, and strategies implemented to ensure both accuracy and future improvements.

- IASOO produced a post-event report that included extensive sustainability-related aspects. This report conformed to the guidelines from APEX, ISO 20121, and GRI EOSS.
- Suppliers for the event, including the Sustainability Center for Meetings and Events in Imagine, Nation, and all of the hotels for the event participated in providing post-event reporting information related to energy use, waste management, and water conservation.
- All measurements were third-party certified and benchmarked against previous events to measure improvement. Results were sent electronically to an industry-wide benchmarking database, so other organizations could benefit from benchmarking against IASOO.
- A minimum 5 percent improvement over previous years was logged in all resource efficiency areas.
- IASOO utilized sustainability reports from previous years, as well as benchmarks from industry-leader sustainability results to develop its sustainability goals and objectives. By doing so, it was able to exceed industry expectations and achievements and develop an industry-leading event.
- IASOO measured not only the sustainability-related aspects of on-site event activities, but also the legacy effects of the annual meeting. Post-event surveys were sent to event participants after the event at predetermined intervals (one month, three months, six months, and one year after the event) to track the impact of the event according to strategic and sustainability-related objectives. Based on previous event results, the expectation is that legacy effects will continue to have a strong impact in the community for the next five to ten years.

■ Sustainability Reporting for Meetings and Events

In this section, please outline how (and with whom) you communicated your successes and challenges to stakeholders. Be specific with reference to tools used, strategies implemented, and processes that ensure the integrity and accuracy of the reporting process.

- A final outcome of IASOO's event was an integrated post-event report that included success metrics for economic, environmental, and social aspects.
- The sustainability aspects of the event were broadly communicated to event participants and stakeholders, including the local community.

- IASOO utilized APEX, GRI EOSS, and ISO 20121 standards in the development of its post-event reports.
- IASOO's commitment to transparency and sustainability reporting helped it avoid criticism about its commitment to corporate responsibility.
- All of IASOO's annual meeting stakeholders were identified using a stakeholder web tool. This enabled IASOO to consult with a broad range of stakeholders during the planning stages for the annual meeting and to ensure that the social and environmental needs of each of those stakeholders were considered as part of the planning process.
- Training for IASOO team members and key suppliers on reporting practices was held prior to the event. This had the double benefit of encouraging sustainable behavior during the event and accurate reporting after the event.
- IASOO's final event report included contributions from several departments within the suppliers for the event. Consultation prior to the event with departments, including engineering, housekeeping, food and beverage, and hotel and venue operations, helped to ensure that goals were identified and communicated in advance of the event and accurately reported after the event.

■ Risk Management and Legal Considerations

In this section, tell us:

1. How you incorporated risk management principles to ensure your sustainable meeting or event activities reduced your risk; and
2. How you implemented risk management and legal principles to reduce the risk that sustainability activities might create for your organization.
   - IASOO incorporated sustainability-related initiatives into its contracts with vendors. These were closely monitored prior to and during the event to ensure that the objectives would be met.
   - Contracts incorporated specific noncompliance consequences for failure to meet sustainability objectives.
   - IASOO's event insurance policy incorporated social and environmental considerations.
   - IASOO worked closely with reputable local service organizations to donate leftover food and materials from the event. Strict guidelines were followed to ensure the safety of food and material donations. This included monitoring of food handling and transportation to donation facilities.
   - Community service projects included several risk management aspects. For the off-site events, access to emergency medical services, proper hydration, shade, and nutrition services were secured. Safety training and equipment were also provided.
   - Liability waivers were developed with legal and insurance professional expertise. This did not prevent a conscientious approach to risk management and mitigation, with care and concern for participants and communities as a primary focus.

Exploring the Possible: Scenario Planning for Sustainability

Everything depends on everything else; this is what the *systems view* that we have used in this book tells us. Looking back from the future, or *backcasting,* is a useful exercise. While most people are familiar with the concept of forecasting, in most cases specifically with regard to budgeting, forecasting possible future realities, or scenario planning, is also useful. **Scenario planning** is a tool pioneered by the multinational oil company Royal Dutch Shell, which assumes not only that everything depends on everything else, but also that the future will not look like the present.[3] This kind of planning is useful not only at the enterprise level but also at the industry level. We suggest it here as a call to action for industry leaders and industry leaders of the future.

Scenario planning helps us to plan for "what if" situations.
Photo courtesy of iStockphoto/marekuliasz

We can expect rapid change to be the hallmark of the future. Planning in this kind of an environment needs to be both flexible and creative; any kind of calendar or fiscal year–driven strategic planning may be obsolete in this kind of an environment.[4] Calendar-based strategic planning seems to be endemic to the meetings industry and to the organizations within it, as it seems to be in many organizations and industries. Research, however, illuminates a paradox; actual business strategy is often not the result of strategic planning. Strategic planning instead takes the role of coordination and driving performance improvement. Actual decision making was more likely to take place outside of the formal strategic planning process.[5] Scenario planning does not attempt to predict the future; it envisions alternative futures.[6] The Global Business Network describes this as creating "a map of uncertainty."[7] By doing this, it creates options and makes it possible to be more flexible in responding to actual events. This is a move away from the reactive stance we described to the AIG effect and the Troubled Asset Relief Program (TARP) in the introductory chapter.

Scenario planning identifies the main players, tries to predict their motivations, identifies potentially significant events, and using knowledge of how systems tend to operate, generates alternatives.[8] **Scenarios** are used to "think about the uncertain aspects of the future . . . and to explore ways in which these might unfold. (They) address the same important questions and all include those aspects of the future that are likely to persist, but each one describes a different way in which the uncertain aspects could play out."[9] Scenarios challenge assumptions that are the result of experience, familiar ideas, and trends. They act as an inoculation of new ideas to prevent blind spots.

The Process of Scenario Planning

Scenario planning is a collaborative, multidisciplinary process. For the meetings and events industry, this suggests a number of different players, including industry associations, meeting professionals, airlines, hotels, destinations, and other suppliers. The need is to define alternative future scenarios, not to come to consensus on them. Both qualitative and quantitative information can be used. The goal is to create a guide to unknown territory, written as a story of a possible future.[10]

Planning a scenario exercise should include answers to five questions:[11]

1. Why are we doing this?
2. Who will use them, once they have been created?
3. What are your expectations?
4. What time period will the scenarios include?
5. Who are the key stakeholders we need to involve?

The scenarios themselves address questions such as:

1. What could happen?
2. If it did happen what would be the impact on our organization?
3. How would we respond?[12]

Assumptions

We all hold assumptions, whether we are aware of this or not. We also don't usually hold the same assumptions as others around us. For example, some assumptions held by various players with regard to sustainable meetings and events might be:

1. "Sustainable events will define the future of our industry" versus "Sustainable events are too expensive and will never catch on in a big way."
2. "The airlines will collapse if oil reaches $150/barrel" versus "Governments will never allow airlines to collapse."
3. "Climate change will greatly impact many destinations globally" versus "Climate change is a nonissue."
4. "When oil reaches $150/barrel, the meetings industry will contract as fewer people can afford to travel on the few remaining airlines" versus "People will always find a way to meet face-to-face."

Sample Scenarios: Industry-wide

What does a possible scenario look like? A scenario should have a **focal question**, or a broad definition of the possible future change that has been suggested as an alternative—and the possibility of **branches**, or different possible outcomes resulting from your exploration of the question.[13] For example, we offer the following possible themes that might need to be explored through a scenario planning exercise at an industry-wide level.

▇ Energy and Technology Scenario Question

How will the meetings and events industry continue to thrive in an energy-constrained world where technology increasingly mimics face-to-face interactions and becomes less expensive to implement?

▇ Energy and Major Supplier Scenario Question

How will major suppliers to the meetings and events industry, such as hoteliers and airlines, meet the challenges of an energy-constrained future?

▇ Regulation and Social Factors Scenario Question

How will the meetings and events industry respond to a more highly regulated future in the face of market and energy uncertainty, changing public attitudes to sustainable business, and a more socially, environmentally, and technologically aware workforce?

Sample Scenarios: Enterprisewide

Scenario planning can also be used for specific organizations. Members of the team could include representatives from various departments, who use a centralized meetings and events department or who plan meetings and events independently, as well as management and suppliers. On an enterprise rather than an industry level, scenarios might include the following.

▇ Constrained Resources Scenario Question

How will our organization respond to constrained resources, consistently high oil prices, new regulations, and sustainability standards for meetings and events while meeting our organizational objectives?

■ Technology Scenario Question

Technology is increasingly becoming less expensive to implement and more effective. How will this change the role and the resources required by the meetings and events department?

■ Building Capacity Scenario Question

How does the meeting and event function within our organization build skills capacity to deal with new regulations, new technologies, and constrained resources within the overall context of the enterprise?

We present scenario planning as a tool to be used to move the industry from a reactive stance to a future where, because creative, collaborative alternative futures have been visualized and addressed, responses are flexible, measured, and thoughtful. This helps to ensure the sustainability of the industry in the long term through more efficient use of resources; the achievement of a social license to operate; and the recognition of the overall importance of the industry to both the global economy and to thought-leadership, idea generation, and positive impact.

Ending at the Beginning

We began this book by introducing a conceptual framework for sustainable meetings and events, showing the global and industry-specific drivers that are making CSR critical for meetings and events. From global issues, including consumer and economic trends, to industry drivers including new standards and negative public perception of our industry, there is an increasing need for meeting and event professionals to demonstrate ethics and corporate responsibility.

The various chapters in this book have shown how there are also many opportunities for industry professionals, communities, and natural environments to thrive from the implementation of sustainability, responsibility, and ethics. Figure 12.2., originally seen in Chapter 1, summarizes

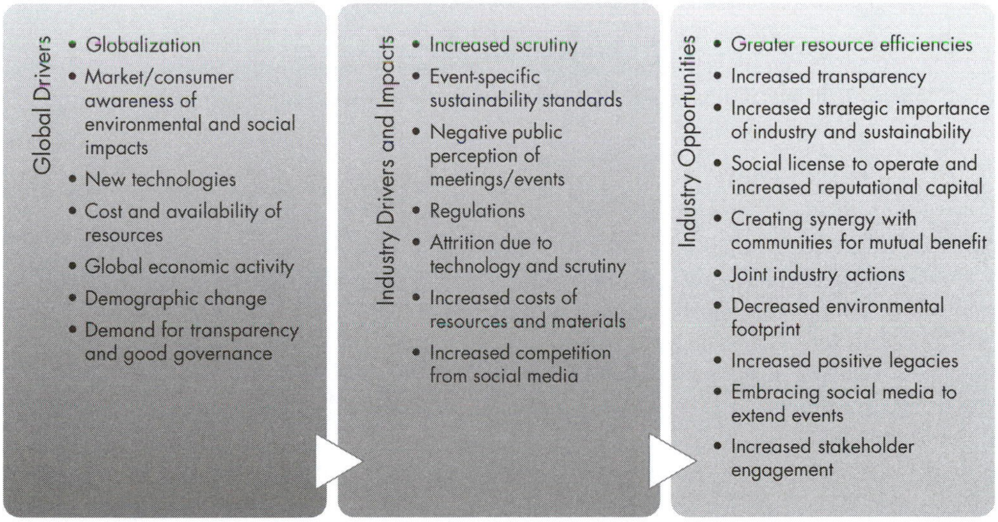

Global Drivers
- Globalization
- Market/consumer awareness of environmental and social impacts
- New technologies
- Cost and availability of resources
- Global economic activity
- Demographic change
- Demand for transparency and good governance

Industry Drivers and Impacts
- Increased scrutiny
- Event-specific sustainability standards
- Negative public perception of meetings/events
- Regulations
- Attrition due to technology and scrutiny
- Increased costs of resources and materials
- Increased competition from social media

Industry Opportunities
- Greater resource efficiencies
- Increased transparency
- Increased strategic importance of industry and sustainability
- Social license to operate and increased reputational capital
- Creating synergy with communities for mutual benefit
- Joint industry actions
- Decreased environmental footprint
- Increased positive legacies
- Embracing social media to extend events
- Increased stakeholder engagement

Figure 12.2 Our Sustainable Meetings/Events Conceptual Framework

the global and industry drivers towards sustainability as well as impacts and opportunities at the industry level for sustainability. Throughout this book, we have referenced several circular concepts, including cradle-to-cradle and a circular economy. It seems fitting, then, that we end where we began: with the call to action that started our journey:

"Great power involves great responsibility."
—*U.S. President Franklin D. Roosevelt (1882–1945),*
in his undelivered Jefferson Day address

Chapter Review

This chapter began with a vision: *an industry where meetings and events contribute positively to communities and cultures, and the business of meetings is conducted ethically; a future where meetings and events are realized within the regenerative capacity of the Earth and where meetings and events are successful at achieving their objectives and provide better value to stakeholders than alternatives.*

This chapter has not only reviewed these concepts but also provided tools to help you remember, apply, and share these ideas through your networks. We provide a view of a possible sustainable future for the meetings industry through the lens of an award-winning sustainable events submission.

Because the industry has both the need and the responsibility to address sustainability over the long term, we present the idea of scenario planning on an industry-wide scale as a tool to create a more sustainable future and an industry that is better prepared to address possible alternative futures.

Review Questions

1. What is backcasting?
2. What is a sustainable future for the meetings and events industry?
3. How can scenario planning be used to address sustainability into the future?

Group Activities

1. Create your own award-winning sustainable event award submission modeled after the IASOO bid in this chapter, this time for 2050. Include the new technologies and standards for sustainable events that you imagine will exist by that time.
2. Develop a social media campaign to promote sustainable meeting and event practices. The roadmap for sustainability at the beginning of this chapter can be used as a starting point.
3. Conduct a mock scenario planning exercise. Appoint a chief storyteller to direct the exercise and generate two possible scenarios for exploration. Outline your purpose, who will use the completed scenarios, over what time horizon the scenario encompasses, and specific stakeholders that should be involved.

Key Terms

- backcasting
- scenario planning
- scenarios
- focal question
- branches

Recommended Books

Bergkvist, Jan Peter. *Sustainability in Practice*. Stockholm, Sweden: SleepWell AB, January 2010. This short book is a guide to implementing sustainability in your business.

Goldblatt, Samuel deBlanc. *The Complete Guide to Greener Meetings and Events*. Hoboken, NJ: John Wiley & Sons, 2011. www.wiley.com/college/goldblatt.

Shell International, Scenarios: An Explorer's Guide. This guide introduces the concept of scenario planning as pioneered by Shell, and walks readers through the process.

Notes

1. Charles Dickens, *A Christmas Carol* (1843; repr. New York: Bantam Books, 1986).
2. The Natural Step, *Backcasting*, www.naturalstep.org/backcasting.
3. Robert M. Grant, "Strategic Planning in a Turbulent Environment: Evidence from the Oil Majors," *Strategic Management Journal* (2003). Published online in Wiley InterScience, www.interscience.wiley.com.
4. Ibid.
5. Ibid., p. 512.
6. Shell International. *What Are Scenarios?* Retrieved November 29, 2011, from www.shell.com/home/content/aboutshell/our_strategy/shell_global_scenarios/what_are_scenarios/.
7. Global Business Network, "Why Scenarios?" Retrieved February 17, 2012, from www.gbn.com/about/scenario_planning.php
8. Shell International. *What Are Scenarios?* Retrieved November 29, 2011, from www.shell.com/home/content/aboutshell/our_strategy/shell_global_scenarios/what_are_scenarios/
9. Ibid.
10. Shell Global, *Scenarios: An Explorer's Guide* (2008). www-static.shell.com/.../scenarios/explorers_guide.pdf.
11. Ibid.
12. David A. J. Axson, "Scenario Planning: Navigating Through Today's Uncertain World," *Journal of Accountancy* (2011). Retrieved February 17, 2012, from www.journalofaccountancy.com/Issues/2011/Mar/20103483.htm.
13. Shell Global, Scenarios: An Explorer's Guide (2008). www-static.shell.com/.../scenarios/explorers_guide.pdf.

GLOSSARY

Additionality: The concept that money raised for and spent on a project would not otherwise be spent in the normal course of business operations; often used in evaluating carbon offsets.

Alternative energy: A general term for energy that is generated without the use of fossil fuels, such as solar, wind, or small-scale hydro.

APEX: An acronym representing the Accepted Practices Exchange, APEX is an initiative of the Convention Industry Council.

APEX/ASTM Green Meeting Standards: These standards focus on the *product aspect* of sustainable events. They include nine standards: exhibits, food and beverage, onsite office, transportation, audiovisual and production, communication, meeting venue, destinations, and accommodations. Each of these nine standards is measured according to eight categories: energy, water, waste, air quality, procurement, community, staff management, and communication.

APEX Post Event Report (PER): A form to be used after the event to report the results of the event; provided by the Convention Industry Council as part of the Accepted Practices Exchange.

Backcasting: The process of defining the future and then working backward to generate processes, policy, and actions to realize that future.

Balanced scorecard: A structured management tool used in business and industry encompassing nontraditional measures and viewpoints from customers and employees, as well as financial measurements.

Baseline: A measurement or calculation used as a basis for comparison.

Benchmarking: Comparison against a standard or with similar organizations to help identify best practices and performance gaps to improve performance and create greater alignment with strategy and objectives

Biofuels: "Fuel produced from renewable biomass material, commonly used as an alternative, cleaner fuel source."[1] Examples of biofuels include biobutanol, biodiesel, bioethanol, biogas, and vegetable oil.

Biogas: Biogas is derived from the breakdown of organic material without the presence of oxygen and can be a substitute for natural gas. It consists primarily of methane and carbon dioxide, and is considered a relatively clean fuel.[2]

Biomass: "Biological material derived from living, or recently living organisms. In the context of biomass for energy this is often used to mean plant-based material, but can equally apply to both animal and vegetable derived material."[3]

Branch: A possible alternative as generated through scenario planning.

British Standard 8901: A sustainable event management standard

Brundtland Commission: 1983 United Nations Commission headed by Gro Harlem Brundtland, which coined the famous definition of sustainable development.

Carbon credits: A permit allowing the owner to emit a certain amount of carbon dioxide equivalent.

Carbon cycle: The series of processes by which carbon is circulated within the environment, primarily between the earth, water, and air.

Carbon dioxide equivalent: A measure used to compare the impact from various greenhouse gases, based on their atmospheric warming potential, through converting the measures into what the impact would be in units of carbon dioxide.

Carbon footprint: The amount of carbon dioxide emitted by a person or organization.

Carbon offsets: A financial tool intended to reduce emissions of carbon dioxide in one place to counteract the effects of emissions in another place.

Carbon philanthropy: A monetary value conversion for carbon (instead of weight, the method used by carbon off-sets) to provide a fixed number for use in budgeting, a method of assessing risk, and the ability to influence corporate philanthropy or CSR programs to mitigate climate change. http://www.thecarbonconsultancy.co.uk/pdfs/Carbon-Philanthropy.pdf

Circular economy: Emphasizes strategies where the use of resources in the production of products and services mimics natural systems and are continually reused and recycled in a feedback loop.

Cluster CSR: A network approach to implementing corporate social responsibility characterized by geographic proximity and sector-specificity.[4]

Community service: In the context of this book, community service is volunteer work that provides a social benefit to the community.

Community service project: A volunteer activity undertaken to benefit a community or community-based organization and to address its environmental or social needs, usually through the donation of time, money, and/or goods.

Code of conduct: A formalized document that provides direction to individuals within an organization about expected behaviors and communicates these expectations to the broader community.

Communications: The relaying of information between parties for the purpose of increasing understanding. Communications can take various forms, including face-to-face, written, electronic, social media, and signage.

Context: The circumstances that define the setting of the event in which it can be understood and assessed.

Copenhagen Sustainable Meetings Protocol: Generated by organizers of the Conference of Parties 15 in Copenhagen (December 2009), it is a framework that can be used to organize meetings and events in a more sustainable way.

Corporate Social Responsibility: Taking accountability for the affect of organizational decisions and actions on the environment, society and the economy, and striving to create a positive impact on all stakeholders.

Cradle-to-cradle design: A holistic framework considering economics, environment, and social systems throughout the life cycle of a product or service, which creates a system that is both efficient and waste-free.[5]

Culture: Although many definitions of culture exist, we will be relying on the United Nations Educational, Scientific and Cultural Organization (UNESCO)'s definition that states, ". . . culture should be regarded as the set of distinctive spiritual, material, intellectual and emotional features of society or a social group, and that it encompasses, in addition to art and literature, lifestyles, ways of living together, value systems, traditions and beliefs."[6]

Cumulative impact: Accumulation of a series of impacts over time. Although insignificant in themselves, together they may have a large impact.

Decision model: A framework that presents information and logical steps to assist you in making relevant decisions, resulting in an action.

Decision point: A specific point in time when a course of action needs to be decided on through evaluating alternatives and choosing a solution.

Diversification: Investing across different classes of stocks, assets, and/or sectors to reduce risk. Diversification strategies can also apply to event decisions to reduce risk.

Eco-efficiency: The creation of goods and services using the least amount of resources.

Eco-labels: A labeling system for products and services that indicates that the product or service meets specific sustainable practices; these practices differ within each eco-label system. Consumer-targeted.

Ecological footprint: A measure of human demand on the ability of the supporting ecosystem (natural capital); it measures the amount of land and water needed to supply the resources consumed.

Ecosystem: A group of living and non-living things interacting with each other.[7]

Emissions scope: The Greenhouse Gas Protocol defines three levels of emissions (scope 1, 2, and 3). Scope 1 emissions are direct emissions from sources owned by the organization, such as a power plant, furnaces, boilers, or owned vehicles. Scope 2 emissions derive from the use of purchased electricity. Scope 3 emissions are caused by organizational activities, but from sources not owned or controlled by the company, such as air travel.

Environmental justice: The intersection of environmental protection and social justice. It involves the "fair treatment and meaningful involvement of all people regardless of race, color, sex, national origin, or income with respect to the development implementation and enforcement of environmental laws, regulations and policies."[8] This concept is viewed differently based on culture and geography.

Ethical dilemma: An ethical dilemma is a situation where a choice needs to be made between two ethical values, where choosing one option comes at the expense of the other. An example for this book would be choosing between an environmental or a socially responsible supplier.

Event miles/Event kilometers: The total distance traveled by components of meetings and events, including participants, speakers, food and beverage, materials, and staff. Event miles/event kilometers can then be converted to carbon dioxide equivalents.

Experiential marketing: Creating opportunities for stakeholders to interact with a brand, its values, and its products through a face-to-face experience that involves both awareness and education, as well as corporate culture and emotional aspects.

Extended producer responsibility: A policy approach in which a producer's responsibility, physical and/or financial, for a product is extended to the post-consumer stage of a product's life cycle.

Externality: A cost or benefit of an activity that is not passed on through pricing mechanisms and therefore does not reflect the full cost of the activity. It can be positive or negative.

Fair trade: The sale of goods and services where the producers are paid fair market price; typically used in developing nations. It can involve a partnership between producers and consumers.

Fairtrade: An eco-labeling system to allow the consumer to recognize products that meet specific environmental, economic, and social criteria. There are currently 19 Fairtrade initiatives in 23 countries.

Familiarization trip: Events where a destination, supplier, or group of suppliers will host prospective clients as a way of introducing them to their destination or venue. The suppliers will cover the costs for the trip and experiences.

Financial capital: Money and monetary instruments.

Focal question: A specific query regarding a possible alternative future and the organizational or industry response to it.

Fossil fuel: A hydrocarbon such as oil, gas, or coal, which was created over geological time from organic matter.

Geographic context: Qualities or conditions of the physical location that influence activities, culture, economy, and environment. Used frequently with specific reference to environmental factors.

Geothermal energy: Renewable energy derived from the heat in the Earth's crust close to the surface; this varies by location, which is known as the geothermal gradient.

Global Reporting Initiative (GRI): The world's largest voluntary sustainability reporting framework.

Global Reporting Initiative Event Organizer Sector Supplement (GRI EOSS): An event-specific supplement to the world's largest voluntary sustainability reporting framework, which identifies specific sustainability reporting for events.

Gold Standard: A standard certification for carbon offset mitigation projects. It was established by the World Wildlife Fund in 2003 and is support by nongovernmental organizations worldwide.

The Goldilocks effect: Describes something that isn't too hot or too cold, such as the Earth's atmosphere.

Greenhouse effect: The process by which a portion of the sun's rays enter the atmosphere as shortwave radiation but do not radiated back out into space; the warmth this creates, similar to how the glass of a greenhouse traps warmth and allows plants to thrive, makes all life on Earth possible.

Greenhouse gas: A gas in the atmosphere that absorbs and emits energy in a specific wavelength, so that it can pass into the atmosphere as heat from the sun but does not get reflected back out to space, creating a heating effect on the atmosphere. Primary greenhouse gases include carbon dioxide, water vapor, methane, and ozone.

Greenhouse Gas Protocol: An accounting tool to understand, quantify and manage greenhouse gases provided by the not-for-profit Greenhouse Gas Protocol, a partnership between the World Resource Council and the World Business Council for Sustainable Development.

Green marketing myopia: Misjudging or overemphasizing improvements in environmental quality and customer satisfaction.

Green (or greener) meeting: Meetings or events planned with the intent of minimizing their environmental impact. Although often referred to as green meetings, *greener meetings* is more accurate, as most, if not all, events will have some degree of negative environmental impact.

Greenwashing: The practice of claiming environmental benefits that are either false, superficial, misleading, or unproven.

The Hamlet decision: After the famous Shakespearean soliloquy in *Hamlet*, "To be or not to be: that is the question," when deciding whether having a meeting will meet specific goals and should therefore be undertaken.

How dimension: Activities of service providers within the context of the meeting/event decision model.

Human capital: The knowledge, skills, and competencies that workers bring to organizations to produce economic value.

Hybrid meeting: An event that mixes face-to-face elements with virtual components through technological solutions.

Hydropower: Renewable energy derived from flowing water such as rivers and dams.

Impact: The outcome of an investment (input) or action, minus what would have happened anyhow in the absence of this investment or action. See Additionality[9].

Input: Resources applied to projects, such as a financial investment, that are a cost to the organization.[10]

Insurance premium: Payment made for insurance coverage.

International Organization for Standardization (ISO): The world's largest developer and publisher of standards, encompassing a network of 162 countries. A not-for-profit organization, it bridges the public and private sectors.

ISO 20121: An international event sustainability management system standard currently in development through the auspices of the International Organization for Standardization; it was based on British Standard 8901 for sustainable event management.

Jurisdiction: The entity with the authority to make decisions on legal matters based on a particular subject and/or geographic area.

Key performance indicator (KPI): A performance measurement regarded to be a significant indicator of success for the organization involved.

Knowledge capital: The intrinsic value of ideas and applied knowledge within organizations.

Legacy: Anything left or handed on by an event, including enduring physical, economic, social, and environmental impacts and new capacities acquired such as new knowledge, standards, best practices, skills, organizations, systems, relationships, partnerships, and innovations.[11]

Liability: Being responsible for damage or losses. A person or organization found to be liable for actions or inactions may be required to pay for restitution for the damage or loss. There may be both criminal and civil applications.

License to operate: Earning the support of the community to operate there through activities associated with being a good corporate citizen, including environmental stewardship and community support. Also called a social license to operate.

Macro level: A large scale, such as that of government and industry.

Marketing: "The activity, set of institutions, and processes for creating, communicating, delivering, and exchanging offerings that have value for customers, clients, partners, and society at large."[12]

Materiality: Relates to the importance, or significance, of a particular measure in relation to economic, environmental, and/or social impacts. Something is material if it is important or significant.

Micro level: A small scale, such as within an organization.

Natural capital: The value of ecosystems and the environment to produce economic value, such as trees, water purification, clean air, and other natural services.

Net present value: The present value of a series of cash flows into the future, recognizing that money has the ability to generate financial returns through the function of interest paid.

Organizational culture: "The pattern of shared values, beliefs, and assumptions considered the appropriate way to think and act within an organization."[13]

Ostrich effect: Dealing with potentially risky situations by pretending they don't exist.

Outboarding: The practice of soliciting business by nonexhibitors or nonsponsors in the area immediately surrounding a convention. Outboarders set up their booth or materials at off-site locations to take advantage of the proximity of exhibit or convention participants.

Outcomes: The change that occurs in the long-term as a result of the original investment of resources (inputs) and the outputs (results).[14]

Outputs: The results of the program, or what is caused by the initial investment of resources (inputs).[15]

Payback period: The amount of time it takes to generate a return on an investment equal to the initial outlay of funds; a simplistic model that does not take into account the present value of future cash flow.

PDCA management cycle: Refers to the management approach utilized in ISO20121—*plan* (align, strategy, purpose, and policy), *do* (allocate resources, communicate, control, and record), *check* (performance measurement, reports), *act* (review, correct, and feedback).

Peak oil: The point in time when oil production will have reached its global maximum point (as a nonrenewable resource) and then declines.

Photo-op CSR: A project where the majority of benefits accrue to the organization performing the community service rather than to the community or community-based organization, to create positive perception among its stakeholders.

Precarious employment: This term refers to employment "with a short time horizon, or for which the risk of job loss is high."[16]

Promotional products: Branded merchandise intended to promote the organization.

Public relations: Actions and messaging to the public for reputational management purposes.

Qualitative: Description based on qualities other than those that can be described numerically, such as color or personal importance.

Quantitative: Measurements based on quantity or number of items.

Rationalization: Rationalizations can be viewed as providing *reasons* and not *excuses* for unethical behavior. Individuals may apply rationalizations in an attempt to excuse unethical actions or avoid ethical dilemmas.

Real capital: Equipment and machinery used to produce goods and services.

Regulatory risk: The risk that a change in existing regulations or the creation of new ones will materially impact current processes and activities of an organization.

Renewable energy: Energy from sources that replenish quickly, such as from the sun, water, earth, or wind. This does not include fossil fuels such as oil or gas.

Renewable energy certificates: Tradable commodities that certify that a specific unit of energy is generated from renewable sources.

Report: A document formalizing the measurement process or an accounting of a process or decision taken.

Reputation risk: When the actions of an organization negatively impact its reputation.

Reverse logistics: The process of planning for the acquisition, use during the event, and eventual reuse of materials after the event is over.

Risk: An uncertain event; a possibility that something will occur.

Risk management: Recognizing the possibility of injury, damage, or loss, and creating the ability to prevent or mitigate it.

Sarbanes-Oxley Act: This U.S. federal act, commonly known as SOX, was enacted in 2002 and set enhanced standards for U.S. public company boards and accounting firms. The act focuses on corporate and auditing accountability and responsibility with a strong focus on good governance.

Sequestration: The capture and storage of carbon in order to remove it from the atmosphere and limit its impact on climate change.

Scenarios: A specific situation envisioned through a future-focused planning process, defined by a focal question and the ability to generate more than one response.

Scenario planning: A flexible, creative, and collaborative process to generate responses to possible alternative futures pioneered by energy company Shell.

Scope: How the event professional has defined the limits of the event. The scope defines what is to be measured, managed, and reported on within the context of the meeting or event.

Shadow cost of carbon: An estimated price based on damages caused by one extra unit of carbon.

Shared value: Creating economic value in a way that also creates value for society by addressing its needs and challenges.[17]

Significant issue: Issues that are significant not only to the organization but also to other stakeholders in the community.

Social capital: The value of connections within and between human communities and networks.

Social risk: The extension of social policy to social protection, typically as pressure applied by stakeholders onto organizations to elevate social issues and their solutions.

Solar energy: A renewable energy using sunlight to create electricity through collection in solar panels, or to passively warm objects.

Stakeholder: A person or organization with an interest in your product or service and its impacts.

Strategic CSR: Identifying and using the intersection of the skills and competencies your organization offers with the need of society to generate opportunity, innovation, and competitive advantage while solving social problems.[18]

Suitcasing: The practice of nonexhibitors and nonsponsors soliciting business at a convention or exhibit. These individuals take advantage of business opportunities created by the convention without paying exhibitor or sponsor fees, often promoting their products or services from their briefcases or suitcases on the exhibit floor.

Supply chain: The system in place to bring products and services to the market or to the end consumer.

Supply chain management: Management of the suppliers and other businesses in the supply chain to produce a product or service and bring it to the end consumer.

Supply chain map: A visual representation of how everything from products and services to money, energy, carbon, waste, and time flow in the process of producing a good or service.

Supply chain sustainability: The United Nations defines this as "the management of environmental, social, and economic impacts, and the encouragement of good governance practices, throughout the lifecycles of goods and services."[19]

Sustainability: The intersection of environmental protection, economic prosperity and social justice. There are many other definitions, including "the capacity to endure."

Sustainable development: Development that meets the needs of the present without compromising the ability of future generations to meet their own needs.

Sustainable Event Measurement Tool (SEMT): An online tool for meeting and event professionals to enter, track, and report their event sustainability data. It is designed to be compatible with all three standards.

Sustainable supply chain management: Management of the suppliers and other businesses in the value chain to produce a product or service with specific consideration of related social, economic, and environmental factors.

Systems view: The process of understanding how elements of the whole relate to each other.

The Natural Step: A not-for-profit organization working to create an environmentally and economically sustainable society, founded in Sweden by Karl-Henrik Robert.

Tidal power: This is a type of hydropower that converts kinetic energy from large tidal ranges into usable electrical energy.

Trade-offs: Situations where being able to take advantage of one quality or aspect in relation to goods and services means not being able to take advantage of another.

Transactional CSR: The provision of information, time, or money in a one-way relationship between the donating organization and the receiving organization based on the concept of giving back to the community.[20]

Transformational CSR: Moves beyond transactional CSR to joint learning and management of projects that are of mutual benefit to both organizations involved. Characterized by achieving outcomes that would not have been possible without the involvement of the community, and by the supporting role taken on by the community.[21]

Transitional CSR: The intermediate form when transactional CSR strategies segue into transformational CSR strategies.

Triple bottom line: A term coined by John Elkington; it refers to the environment, communities, and the economy, and is often referred to as "people, planet, and profit," or "people, planet, and prosperity."

Troubled Asset Relief Program (TARP): A U.S. program designed to strengthen its financial sector after the global recession began in 2008 with the subprime mortgage meltdown. Included in TARP was a clause that prevented some meetings being held if they were excessive or luxury expenditures.

Values: The beliefs, principles, and convictions held by an individual.

Walkability: A descriptive term for the area where a meeting or event is to be held. It usually means that the main event venue is within walking distance of half or more of the accommodation options booked for delegates and other participants.

What dimension: The goods and materials needed for the meeting or event.

Where dimension: The destination decision; where a meeting or event will take place. This involves both the virtual decision (hybrid meeting or virtual meeting) and the physical destination decision.

Why dimension: The goals and objectives of the organization that drive the need to have a meeting or event.

Wind power: A renewable energy that uses the force of the wind to turn turbines and create usable electricity.

Notes

1. Clean Energy Ideas, "Biofuel Definition." Accessed February 7, 2012, from http://www.clean-energy-ideas.com/energy_definitions/definition_of_biofuel.html.
2. Pollution Probe, *A Primer on the Technologies of Renewable Energy* (2003). Accessed February 7, 2012, at www.pollutionprobe.org/report/renewableenergyprimer.pdf.
3. Biomass Energy Centre, "What is BIOMASS?" Accessed February 5, 2012, from http://www.biomassenergycentre.org.uk/portal/page?_pageid=76,15049&_dad=portal.
4. Heidi von Weltzien Hoivik and Deepthi Shankar, "How Can SMEs in a Cluster Respond to Global Demands for Corporate Responsibility?" *The Journal of Business Ethics* (2010).
5. Wikipedia. "Cradle-to-cradle design." Retrieved from http://en.wikipedia.org/wiki/radle-to-cradle_design.
6. UNESCO, "UNESCO Universal Declaration on Cultural Diversity," http://www.unesco.org/education/imld_2002/unversal_decla.shtml#2.
7. The Franklin Institute: Resources for Science Learning, "Neighborhoods." Retrieved from http://www.fi.edu/tfi/units/life/habitat/habitat.html.
8. David Schlosberg, *Defining Environmental Justice: Theories, Movements, and Nature* (London: Oxford University Press, 2007).
9. London Business School. The SROI Primer. Retrieved from http://sroi.london.edu.
10. Ibid.
11. Global Reporting Initiative Event Organizers Sector Supplement, p. 16.
12. American Marketing Association, "Definition of Marketing," www.marketingpower.com/Community/ARC/Pages/Additional/Definition/default.aspx.
13. Stephen P. Robbins and Nancy Langton, *Fundamentals of Organizational Behaviour, 2nd Canadian Edition* (Pearson: Toronto, ON, 2004).
14. London Business School. *The SROI Primer*. Retrieved from http://sroi.london.edu.
15. Ibid.
16. Gerry Rodgers, "Gerry, (1989) Precarious Work in Western Europe: The State of the Debate," in Gerry and Janine Rodgers, ed., *Precarious Jobs in Labour Market Regulation: The Growth of Atypical Employment in Western Europe*. Rodgers, Gerry and Janine, eds. International Labour Organization (Brussels: International Institute for Labour Studies), Free University of Brussels,1989).
17. Michael Porter and Mark Kramer, "Creating Shared Value," *Harvard Business Review* (January/February 2011).
18. Michael Porter and Mark Kramer, "Strategy and Society: The Link Between Competitive Advantage and Corporate Social Responsibility," *Harvard Business Review* (December 2006).
19. The United Nations Global Compact and Business for Social Responsibility, *Supply Chain Sustainability: A Practical Guide for Continuous Improvement* (2010). www.unglobalcompact.org/docs/news_events/8.1/Supply_Chain_Sustainability.pdf.
20. Francis Bowen, Aloysius Newenham-Kahini, and Irene Herremans, "When Suits Meet Roots: The Antecedents and Consequences of Community Engagement," *Journal of Business Ethics* (2010).
21. Ibid.

INDEX